Lecture Notes in Computer Science 2648
Edited by G. Goos, J. Hartmanis, and J. van Leeuwen

Springer-Verlag Berlin Heidelberg GmbH

Thomas Ball Sriram K. Rajamani (Eds.)

Model Checking Software

10th International SPIN Workshop
Portland, OR, USA, May 9-10, 2003
Proceedings

Series Editors

Gerhard Goos, Karlsruhe University, Germany
Juris Hartmanis, Cornell University, NY, USA
Jan van Leeuwen, Utrecht University, The Netherlands

Volume Editors

Thomas Ball
Sriram K. Rajamani
Microsoft Research
One Microsoft Way, Redmond, WA 98052, USA
E-mail: {tball, sriram}@microsoft.com

Cataloging-in-Publication Data applied for

A catalog record for this book is available from the Library of Congress

Bibliographic information published by Die Deutsche Bibliothek
Die Deutsche Bibliothek lists this publication in the Deutsche Nationalbibliographie; detailed bibliographic data is available in the Internet at <http://dnb.ddb.de>.

CR Subject Classification (1998): F.3, D.2.4, D.3.1, D.2

ISSN 0302-9743
DOI 10.1007/978-3-540-44829-7

http://www.springer.de

Originally published by Springer-Verlag Berlin Heidelberg New York in 2003
MyCopy version of the original edition 2003

Typesetting: Camera-ready by author, data conversion by DA-TeX Gerd Blumenstein
Printed on acid-free paper SPIN: 10929896 06/3142 5 4 3 2 1 0
www.springer.com/mycopy

Preface

This volume contains the proceedings of SPIN 2003, the 10th International SPIN Workshop on Model Checking of Software. The workshop was held during May 9–10, 2003, in Portland, Oregon. The program committee of the workshop had the following members:

Thomas Ball (Microsoft Research)
Matthew Dwyer (Kansas State University)
Javier Esparza (University of Stuttgart)
Kousha Etessami (University of Edinburgh)
Patrice Godefroid (Bell Laboratories)
Susanne Graf (VERIMAG)
Somesh Jha (University of Wisconsin)
Peter O'Hearn (University of London)
Andreas Podelski (Max Planck Institute)
Sriram K. Rajamani (Microsoft Research)
Mooly Sagiv (Tel Aviv University)
Scott Stoller (State University of New York at Stony Brook)

The advisory committee for the SPIN workshops consisted of Gerard Holzmann (Chair) and Amir Pnueli. The steering committee for the SPIN workshops consisted of Matthew Dwyer, Stefan Leue, Moshe Vardi (Chair) and Pierre Wolper.

There is a renewed interest in building tools to improve the reliability of software by detecting errors early in the software development process. The SPIN model checker has played a leading role in this new research direction: it has been used in a new tool FeaVer for model checking concurrent software written in ANSI-C. Additionally, there are a variety of techniques for specifying descriptions of intended behavior (such as temporal logics and state machines) as well as techniques to perform the checking (such as model checking, compiler-style static analysis, type systems, theorem proving and run-time analysis). In view of these developments, SPIN 2003 took a broader view and addressed the general problem of specifying and checking properties of software systems. We organized a diverse workshop where people with backgrounds in different analysis areas met and presented different approaches and viewpoints about the general problem of specifying and checking properties of software.

Papers went through a rigorous reviewing process. Each paper was reviewed by three program committee members. Of 39 papers submitted, 14 regular papers and 3 tool papers were accepted.

In addition to the refereed papers, invited talks were given by Gerard Holzmann (Bell Laboratories) on *History of the SPIN Model Checker* and George Necula (University of California at Berkeley) on *Randomized Algorithms for Program Analysis and Verification.*

The program committee is grateful to the following reviewers for their help in evaluating the paper submissions: Luca de Alfaro, Josh Berdine, Dragan

Bošnački, Ahmed Bouajjani, Marius Bozga, Lubos Brim, Cristiano Calcagno, Tom Chothia, Craig A. Damon, Giorgio Delzanno, Juergen Dingel, Nurit Dor, Radu Grosu, Victor Khomenko, Sarfraz Khurshid, Barbara Koenig, Raghavan Komondoor, Gerard Holzmann, Michael Huth, Markus Lohrey, Alexey Loginov, Monika Maidl, Patrick Maier, Roman Manevich, Kedar Namjoshi, Stefan Schwoon, Ran Shaham, Perdita Stevens, Thomas Wilke, Farn Wang, Eran Yahav, and Marc Zeitoun.

We are grateful to the program committee, the reviewers, the invited speakers, the sponsors, the authors of the papers, and the attendees for making the workshop a success.

Redmond, May 2003

Thomas Ball
Sriram K. Rajamani

Table of Contents

Optimal Scheduling Using Branch and Bound with SPIN 4.0

Theo C. Ruys*

Department of Computer Science, University of Twente
P.O. Box 217, 7500 AE Enschede, The Netherlands.
ruys@cs.utwente.nl
http://www.cs.utwente.nl/~ruys/

Abstract. The use of model checkers to solve discrete optimisation problems is appealing. A model checker can first be used to verify that the model of the problem is correct. Subsequently, the same model can be used to find an optimal solution for the problem. This paper describes how to apply the new PROMELA primitives of SPIN 4.0 to search effectively for the optimal solution. We show how Branch-and-Bound techniques can be added to the LTL property that is used to find the solution. The LTL property is dynamically changed during the verification. We also show how the syntactical reordering of statements and/or processes in the PROMELA model can improve the search even further. The techniques are illustrated using two running examples: the Travelling Salesman Problem and a job-shop scheduling problem.

1 Introduction

SPIN [10, 11, 12] is a model checker for the verification of distributed systems software. SPIN is freely distributed, and often described as one of the most widely used verification systems. During the last decade, SPIN has been successfully applied to trace logical design errors in distributed systems, such as operating systems, data communications protocols, switching systems, concurrent algorithms, railway signaling protocols, etc. [13]. This paper discusses how SPIN can be applied effectively to solve discrete optimisation problems.

Discrete optimisation problems are problems in which the decision variables assume discrete values from a specified set; when this set is set of integers, we have an integer programming problem. Combinatorial optimisation problems are problems of choosing the best combination out of all possible combinations. Most combinatorial problems can be formulated as integer programs.

In recent years, model checkers have been used to solve a number of non-trivial optimisation problems (esp. scheduling problems), reformulated in terms of reachability, i.e. as the (im)possibility to reach a state that improves on a given optimality criterion [2, 5, 7, 8, 15, 20]. Techniques from the field of operations

* This work is partially supported by the European Community IST-2001-35304 Project AMETIST (Advanced Methods for Timed Systems).

T. Ball and S.K. Rajamani (Eds.): SPIN 2003, LNCS 2648, pp. 1–17, 2003.

research [22] – e.g. Branch-and-Bound [3] techniques – are being applied to prune parts of the search tree that are guaranteed not to contain optimal solutions. Model checking algorithms have been extended with optimality criteria which provided a basis for the guided exploration of state spaces [2, 15].

Though SPIN has been used to solve optimisation problems (i.e. scheduling problems [5, 20]), the procedures used were not very efficient and the state space was not pruned in any way. This paper shows how the new version of SPIN can be used to effectively solve discrete optimisation problems, especially integer program problems. We show how Branch-and-Bound techniques can be added to both the PROMELA model and – even more effectively – to the property ϕ that is being verified with SPIN. To improve efficiency we let the property ϕ dynamically change during the verification. We also show how the PROMELA model can be reordered syntactically to guide the exploration of the state space. The paper does not compare existing techniques to solve optimisation problems to the one presented here; we only show how one might use *vanilla* SPIN to solve (small) optimisation problems.

The paper tries to retain the tutorial style of presentation of [18, 19] to make the techniques easy to adopt by intermediate SPIN users. The techniques are explained by means of running examples of two classes of optimisation problems. The effectiveness of the techniques is illustrated by some experiments.

The paper is structured as follows. In Section 2 we introduce the Travelling Salesman Problem (TSP) and show how SPIN can be used to find the optimal solution for this problem. Section 3 briefly describes the new primitives of SPIN 4.0. In section 4 we show how the new primitives can be used to solve a TSP more effectively. In section 5 we apply the same techniques to a job-shop scheduling problem and show how Branch-and-Bound techniques can elegantly be isolated in the property which is being verified. The paper is concluded in Section 6.

Experiments. All verification experiments for this paper were run on a Dell Inspiron 4100 Laptop computer driven by a Pentium III Mobile/1Ghz with 384Mb of main memory. All `pan` verification runs were limited to 256Mb though. The experiments were carried out under Windows 2000 Professional and Cygwin 1.3.6; the `pan` verifiers were compiled using `gcc` version 2.95.3-5. For our experiments we used SPIN version 4.0.1 (7 Jan 2003). To compile the `pan` verifiers, we used the following options for `gcc`:

```
GCC_OPTIONS="-w -D_POSIX_SOURCE -DMEMLIM=256 -DSAFETY -DXUSAFE -DNOFAIR"
```

For PROMELA models without a `never`-claim, we added the `-DNOCLAIM` option. We executed the `pan` verifiers using the following directives:

```
PAN_OPTIONS="-m1000 -w20 -c1"
```

2 TSP with Plain Spin

The Traveling Salesman Problem (TSP) [16, 17] is a well known optimisation problem from the area of operations research [22]. In a TSP, n points (*cities*) are

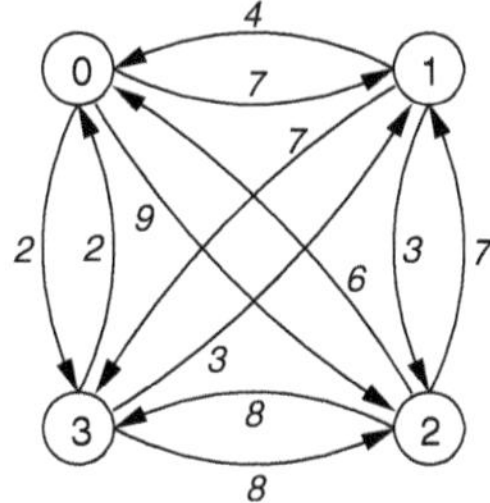

	0	**1**	**2**	**3**
0	-	7	9	2
1	4	-	3	7
2	6	7	-	8
3	2	3	8	-

Fig. 1. Graph and matrix representation of the 4×4 example TSP

given, and every pair of cities i and j is separated by a distance (or cost) c_{ij}. The problem is to connect the cities with the shortest closed *tour*, passing through each city exactly once. A specific TSP can be specified by a distance (or cost) matrix. An entry c_{ij} in row i and column j specifies the cost of travelling from city i to city j. The entries could be the Euclidean distances between cities in a plane, or simply costs – making the problem non-Euclidean. Extensive research has been devoted to heuristics for the Euclidean TSP (see e.g. [17]). Construction heuristics for the non-Euclidean TSP are much less investigated. This paper considers non-Euclidean TSPs only. The TSP is NP-complete.

Modelling a TSP in PROMELA is straightforward. To illustrate the idea we develop a PROMELA model for the sample TSP of Fig. 1. Fig. 1 shows both a graph- and matrix-representation of a 4×4 TSP. Fig. 2 shows the PROMELA model of the TSP of Fig. 1. The salesman itself is modelled by a single process `TSP`. For each place i that the man has to visit, there is a label `P`i in the process `TSP`. The salesman starts at label `P0`. From each label `P`i the salesman can (non-deterministically) go to any label `P`j that has not been visited yet. A `bit`-array `visited` is used to keep track of the places that have already been visited.[1] If, after reaching place `P`i, it turns out that all places have been visited, the salesman has to go back to place `P0`. To keep track of the travelling costs, a variable `cost` is used. This variable is initialised on `0`. When we move from place `P`i to `P`j, this variable is updated with the cost c_{ij} from the cost-matrix of Fig. 1.

Now that we have a PROMELA model of the TSP, we want to use SPIN to find the optimal route of the TSP. Fig. 3 shows a general algorithm for finding an optimal solution for an optimisation problem using a model checker. The procedure has been used in [5, 20]. The algorithm iteratively verifies whether 'the `cost` will *eventually* be greater than `min`'. Each time this property is violated, SPIN has found a path leading to a final state for which the cost is less than `min`. For each error, SPIN generates an error trail which corresponds with the better route. As the number of possible routes is finite, at a certain point SPIN will not find a route for which the `cost` is less than the `min` found so far. Consequently,

[1] In this example we use PROMELA's built-in support for `bit`-arrays. In our experiments, however, we used the `bit`-vector library as discussed in [18], which are more efficient.

```
bit  visited[3];
int  cost;

active proctype TSP()
{
P0: atomic {
        if
        ::  !visited[1] -> cost = cost + 7 ; goto P1
        ::  !visited[2] -> cost = cost + 9 ; goto P2
        ::  !visited[3] -> cost = cost + 2 ; goto P3
        fi ;
    }
P1: atomic {
        visited[1] = 1;
        if
        ::  !visited[2] -> cost = cost + 3 ; goto P2
        ::  !visited[3] -> cost = cost + 7 ; goto P3
        ::  else        -> cost = cost + 4 ; goto end
        fi ;
    }
P2: atomic {
        visited[2] = 1;
        if
        ::  !visited[1] -> cost = cost + 7 ; goto P1
        ::  !visited[3] -> cost = cost + 8 ; goto P3
        ::  else        -> cost = cost + 6 ; goto end
        fi ;
    }
P3: atomic {
        visited[3] = 1;
        if
        ::  !visited[1] -> cost = cost + 3 ; goto P1
        ::  !visited[2] -> cost = cost + 8 ; goto P2
        ::  else        -> cost = cost + 2 ; goto end
        fi ;
    }
end:
}
```

Fig. 2. PROMELA model of the sample TSP of Fig. 1

the error trace which was generated last (corresponding with this optimal `min`) is the optimal route.

This approach works, but is (highly) inefficient: the complete state space already contains the most optimal solution. After a single run over the state space one should be able to report on the optimal solution. The problem, however, is that we cannot compare information (e.g. the `cost`) obtained via different execution paths in standard SPIN. This is inherent to the application of model checkers as a black box for solving optimisation problems.

3 Spin Version 4.0

SPIN version 4.0 [10] – available from [11] – supports the inclusion of embedded C code into PROMELA models through five new primitives:

- `c_decl`: to introduce C types that can be used in the PROMELA model;
- `c_state`: to add new C variables to the PROMELA model. Such new variables can have three possible scopes:

input: PROMELA model M with `cost` added to the states.
output: the optimal solution `min` for the optimisation problem of M.

```
min ← (worst case) maximum cost
do
   use SPIN to check M ⊨ ◇(cost > min)
   if (error found)
   then min ← cost
while (error found)
```

Fig. 3. Algorithm to find the optimal solution for an optimisation problem using SPIN

- *global* to the PROMELA model;
- *local* to one of the processes in the model; or
- *hidden*, which means that the variable will not end up in the state vector, but can be accessed in `c_expr` or `c_code` fragments.

– `c_expr`: to evaluate a C expression whose return value can be used in the PROMELA model (e.g. as a guard);
– `c_code`: to add arbitrary C code fragments as an atomic statement to the PROMELA model. For example, the `c_code` primitive enables to include useful `printf`-statements in the verifier for debugging purposes.
– `c_track`: to include (external) memory into the state vector.

The purpose of the new primitives is to provide support for automatic model extraction from C code. And although "it is not the intent of these extensions to be used in manually constructed models" [10], the extensions are helpful for storing and accessing global information of the verification process.

Within `c_expr` of `c_code` fragments one can access the global and local variables of the currrent state through the global C variable `now` of type `State`. The global variables of the PROMELA model are fields in a `State`. For example, if the PROMELA model has a global variable `cost`, the value of this variable in the current state can be accessed using `now.cost`.

As of version 4.0, the pan-verifier generated by SPIN also contains a guided simulation mode. It is no longer needed to replay error trails with SPIN.

For more details on the new features of SPIN 4.0 the reader is deferred to [10]. The rest of this paper only uses the primitives `c_state`, `c_expr` and `c_code`.

4 TSP with Branch-and-Bound

In this section, we will discuss how the new C primitives of SPIN 4.0 can be used to compute the optimal solution of a TSP more efficiently. We show how SPIN can be used to obtain the optimal solution in a single verification run. Branch-

and-Bound techniques can be used to prune the search tree. We also show how heuristics can be used to further improve the search.[2]

SPIN 4.0 allows us to add *hidden* `c_state` variables to the `pan` verifier within the PROMELA model. Consequently, while exploring the state space, each time SPIN finds a better solution it can save this solution in such a *hidden* variable. To get the best route for our TSP problem with SPIN 4.0, the TSP model needs to be altered as follows:

- Add a hidden, global variable `best_cost` to the PROMELA model and consequently to the `pan` verifier. Initialise this variable `best_cost` on a worst-case estimate of the cost of a schedule, e.g.,
  ```
  c_state "int best_cost = 1000" "Hidden"
  ```
  Due to the scope `"Hidden"`, the variable `best_cost` will *not* be stored in the state vector and will be global to all execution runs. The declaration and initialisation of `best_cost` is copied verbatim to the `pan.c` file.
- Whenever a new solution is found (i.e. when the label `end` is reached), the `cost` for that new route is compared with the `best_cost` sofar. If `cost` is smaller, we have found a better solution, so the variable `best_cost` is updated and the trace is saved:
  ```
  ...
  end:
      c_code {
          if (now.cost < best_cost) {
              best_cost = now.cost;
              printf("\n> best cost sofar: %d ", best_cost);
              putrail();
              Nr_Trails--;
          }
      }
  ```
  The function `putrail` saves the trace to the current state (i.e. it writes the states in the current depth-first search stack to a `trail`-file). The statement `Nr_Trails--` makes sure that a subsequent call of `putrail` will overwrite a previous (less optimal) trail. Both `putrail` and `Nr_Trails` are defined in the generated `pan.c` file.

Branch-and-Bound in the model. Branch-and-Bound (B&B) [3, 22] is an approach developed for solving discrete and combinatorial optimisation problems. The essence of the B&B-approach is the following:

- Enumerate all possible solutions and represent these solutions in an *enumeration tree*. The leaves are end-points of possible solutions and a path from the start node to a leaf represents a solution.
- While building the tree (i.e. the state space), we can stop considering descendents of an interior node, if it is certain that all paths via this node will (i) either lead to an *invalid solution* or (ii) will have *higher costs* than the best path found so far.

[2] This paper only applies heuristics on the PROMELA level. Edelkamp et. al. [6] use a more powerful approach in HSF-SPIN, where heuristics are applied in the internals of SPIN.

The B&B-approach is not a heuristic or approximating procedure, but it is an exact, optimising procedure that finds an optimal solution.

In our PROMELA model of the TSP problem, the B&B-approach can be applied to 'prune' the state space. If in a place Pi the current `cost` is already higher than the best cost so far (i.e. `best_cost`), it is not useful to continue searching. So at the beginning of every place Pi of our model we add the following `if`-statement with `c_expr` expression:

```
if
::  c_expr { now.cost > best_cost } -> goto end
::  else
fi;
```

Branch-and-Bound in the property. Recall the original idea of the algorithm of Fig. 3 which iteratively checks $\Diamond$(`cost` > `min`) to find an optimal solution. Although inefficient, due to SPIN's on-the-fly model checking algorithm, for each subsequent iteration, less of the state space will be checked. For each execution path, SPIN will stop searching as soon as it finds a state for which `cost` > `min` holds. Furthermore, SPIN will exit with an error as soon as it finds an execution path for which the final `cost` is lower than `min`. So, in a way, SPIN's on-the-fly verification algorithm already performs some B&B-functionality by default.

Using the possibilities of SPIN 4.0, we can improve the verification of the $\Diamond$-property by replacing `min` with the *hidden* global variable `best_cost`. We define the following macro using a `c_expr` statement:

```
#define higher_cost (c_expr { now.cost >= best_cost })
```

and we check $\Diamond$`higher_cost`. As the variable `best_cost` is changed during the verification, the property that is being checked is dynamically changed during the verification!

No cycles. SPIN translates the property $\Diamond$`p` to the following `never`-claim:

```
never { /* !<>p */
accept_init:
T0_init:
    if
    ::  (!((p))) -> goto T0_init
    fi;
}
```

Given this `never`-claim, the `pan` verifier will (i) search for states where `!p` does *not* hold (i.e. where `p` does hold, and thus the `if`-statement blocks) or (ii), due to the `accept_init`-label, for each state s where `!p` holds, the verifier will try to find a cycle from s to itself (i.e. an acceptance cycle). For discrete optimisation problems, however, the search space will be a tree without cycles. Consequently, the search for an acceptance cycle will always be in vain and thus unneeded.

```
1  procedure dfs(s: state)
2     if error(s) then report error fi
3     add s to Statespace
4     foreach successor t of s do
5        if t not in Statespace then dfs(t) fi
6     od
7  end dfs
```

Fig. 4. Basic depth-first search algorithm [14]

It is therefore enough to let the `pan` verifier run in safety mode, without the `-a` option to check for acceptance cycles.

Note that due to SPIN's *smart* double-nested depth-first search [14], this optimisation is more effective on the verification time than on the memory needed to store the state space.

Nearest Neighbour Heuristic. When using B&B-methods to solve TSPs with many cities, large amounts of computer time may be required. For this reason, heuristics, which quickly lead to a good (but not necessarily optimal) solution to a TSP, are often used. One of such heuristics is the "Nearest Neighbour Heuristic" (NN-heuristic) [22]. To apply the NN-heuristic, the salesman begins at any city and then visits the nearest city. Then the salesman goes to the unvisited city *closest* to the city it has most recently visited. The salesman continues in this fashion until a tour is obtained.

In order to apply the NN-heuristic to SPIN we must control the order in which neighbour places are selected. In order words, we must control the order of successor states in the state space exploration algorithm of SPIN. The algorithm of Fig. 4 from [14] shows a basic depth-first search algorithm which generates and examines every global state that is reachable from a given initial state. Although SPIN uses a slightly different (nested) depth-first search algorithm, for the discussion here, Fig 4 suffices.

There is only one place in the algorithm where we can influence SPIN's depth-first search: line 4, where the algorithm iterates over the successor states of state `s`. SPIN always uses the same well-defined routine to order the list of successors:

- *Processes.* SPIN arranges the processes in *reverse* order of creation. That is, the process with the highest process id (`pid`) will be selected first.
- *Statements.* Within each process, SPIN considers all possible executable statements. For a statement without guards, there is at most one successor. For an `if` or `do` statement, the list of possible successors is the list of executable guards in the same order as they appear in the PROMELA model.

As the PROMELA processes can be created in any order and we are also free to order the guards within `if` and `do` clauses, we have limited control over SPIN's search algorithm from within the PROMELA model.

Table 1. Verification results (number of states) of verifying PROMELA models of five randomly generated TSP cost matrices using different types of optimisation schemes

	dim=11	*dim=12*	*dim=13*	*dim=14*	*dim=15*
no B&B	572729	1878490	5459480	o.m.	o.m.
unsorted, B&B in model	278753	212984	514332	2478440	2820880
unsorted, B&B in property	111920	72022	173309	1050580	1010080
sorted, B&B in model	132517	54924	140075	1748130	1388100
sorted, B&B in property	49801	16662	43240	737107	480572

Fortunately, the control over the order of the guards within `if`-clauses is enough to apply the NN-heuristic to SPIN. To make sure that in every place Pi, SPIN will first consider the place Pj for which the cost c_{ij} is the lowest, the guards of all `if`-clauses are sorted on the cost c_{ij}, such that the guard with the lowest cost c_{ij} is at the top and the highest cost is at the bottom.

Experimental results. To compare the different approaches w.r.t. the TSP, we have carried out some experiments with some randomly generated TSPs. The original approach which lets SPIN iteratively check $M \models \Diamond(\texttt{cost} > \texttt{min})$ has been left out of the experiments for obvious reasons. Table 1 lists the results of the experiments for randomly generated TSPs of dimension 11–15. We used a script to generate the cost-matrix for these TSPs where each c_{ij} was randomly chosen from the interval 1-100.[3] We used another script to generate the PROMELA models for the particular TSP as described in this section. The entry 'o.m.' stands for 'out of memory'.

From the experiments we can learn that B&B in the property is more advantageous than B&B in the model. This does not come as a suprise as due to the addition of B&B-functionality in the PROMELA model, the number of states of the `TSP` process increases. It is also interesting to see that the NN-heuristic really pays of. As the cost matrices are randomly generated, we cannot compare the results for the different dimensions.

5 Personalisation Machine

In this section, we discuss the application of the B&B-approach to a job-shop scheduling problem. We will extend the 'Branch-and-Bound in the property' technique as discussed in Section 4 by adding more bounding conditions to the property.

Problem description. The problem itself is a simplified version of a case study proposed by Cybernetix (France) within the Advanced Methods for Timed Sys-

[3] If the interval from which the different costs c_{ij} is (much) smaller, e.g. 1–10, the number of states drops significantly due to SPIN's state matching.

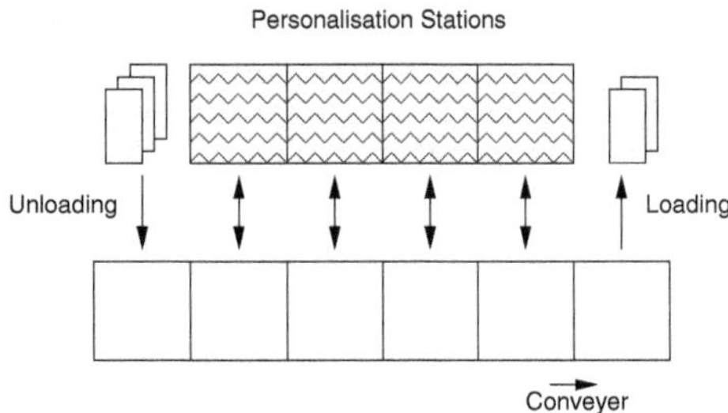

Fig. 5. Schematic overview of the personalisation machine

tems (AMETIST, IST-2001-35304) project [1]. Cybernetix is a company manufacturing machines for the personalisation of smart cards. These machines take piles of blank smart cards as raw material, program them with personalised data, print them and test them.

Fig. 5 shows a schematic overview of the personalisation machine that we discuss in this paper. Cards are transported by a *Conveyer* belt. There are `NPERS` *Personalisation Stations* where cards can be personalised. The conveyer is `NPERS+2` positions long. The *Unloader* puts empty cards on the belt. The *Loader* removes personalised cards from the belt. The order in which the cards are loaded *from* the belt should be same as the order in which they were unloaded *onto* the belt.

The conveyer can only move a step to the right which takes `tRIGHT` time units. If cards are unloaded onto the belt or loaded from the belt, the conveyer cannot move. Unloading and loading can be done in parallel. Unloading and loading takes `tUNLOAD` resp. `tLOAD` time units. If after a conveyer move, an empty card is under a personalisation station, the card might be taken of the belt by the personalisation station and personalisation of the card will start immediately. The personalisation of a card takes `tPERSONALISE` time units. In the original case study description, `tRIGHT` is equal to `1`, `tUNLOAD` and `tLOAD` are both `2`, whereas `tPERSONALISE` lies between `10` and `50`.

Goal. Given `NPERS` personalisation stations, the goal is to find an optimal schedule to personalise `NCARDS` cards.

PROMELA *model.* Modelling the personalisation machine in PROMELA is straightforward. The conveyer belt is modelled by an array of `NCELLS=NPERS+2` cells. A cell is represented by a `short`. If a cell has the value `0` it is empty. If a cell contains a value `n>0` the cell contains an unpersonalised card with number `n`. If `n<0`, the card has been personalised by one of the stations. There is one global variable `time` which is updated by the processes that 'consume time'. So the PROMELA model contains the following global variables:

```
short  belt[NCELLS];
short  time;
```

Apart from the global variables of the model, we also define a *hidden* `c_state` variable `best_time` which holds the time of the best schedule found so far. The behaviour of the model is specified by several parallel processes. The process `Conveyer` just moves the conveyer belt one step to the right. After updating the `belt`, the process increases the variable `time` with `tRIGHT` steps. The `Conveyer` process is modelled as follows.

```
proctype Conveyer() {
    byte i = 0;
    do
    ::  d_step {(belt[NCELLS-1] == EMPTY) && CARD_ON_BELT ->
            i=NCELLS-1;
            do
            ::  (i > 0) -> belt[i] = belt[i-1]; i=i-1
            ::  else    -> break
            od;
            belt[0] = EMPTY;
            time    = time + tRIGHT;
        }
    od
}
```

The macro `CARD_ON_BELT` returns `1` if there is a card on the belt.

The other two *logical* processes that 'consume time' are the *Unloading* and *Loading* process. Because unloading and loading might happen concurrently, the behaviour of both processes is modelled by a single process `UnloaderLoader`. The unloading part just puts cards on the belt. The loading part will remove cards from the belt and will check that the order of the cards is still correct. If not, it sets the `time` to -1.

Below we only include fragments of the loading part of the `UnloaderLoader` process. If the last card has been taken from of the belt, we check whether the schedule found is faster than the best schedule so far. If this is the case, we update the *hidden* `c_state`-variable `best_time`.

```
::  atomic { (belt[LAST] == expectedCard) ->
        belt[LAST]   = EMPTY;
        expectedCard = expectedCard-1;
        time         = time + tLOAD;
        if
        ::  expectedCard <  -(NCARDS+1) -> assert(false)
        ::  expectedCard == -(NCARDS+1) ->
            atomic {
                c_code { if (now.time < best_time) {
                             best_time = now.time;
                             Nr_Trails=0;
                             putrail();
                         }
                };
                break;
            }
        ::  else
        fi
    }
::  atomic { (belt[LAST] !=0 && belt[LAST] != expectedCard) ->
        time = -1;
        break;
    }
```

Each personalisation station is modelled by a process `PersStation(i)`. When an unpersonalised card `n` is in `belt[i]`, a personalisation station might start personalising this card `n`. Unlike the other processes, the process `PersStation` waits for time to pass. After it has taken an card from the belt it sets its `finish_time[i]` to the time that it will have finished the personalisation of `n` (i.e. `time + tPERSONALISE`). Then the process starts waiting till the `time` has reached `finish_time[i]`.

Variable time advance. Because either the conveyer or unloader might have to wait for a personalisation station to finish, we also need a process which consumes 'idle' time. In our initial, naive model we used a process `Tick` which just increases the `time` by 1 time unit. The total number of *ticks* was bounded by a constant. The obvious disadvantage of this method is that the process `Tick` can always do a `time` tick; even when there are no personalisation stations currently 'waiting' for the `time` to reach their finishing time.

Therefore, in our current model we follow Brinksma and Mader [5], who use the well-known *variable time advance* procedure [21]. With a variable time advance procedure, simulated time goes forward to the next moment in time at which some event triggers a state transition, and all intervening time is skipped. With respect to the personalisation machine this means that we let `time` jump to the `finish_time[i] > 0` which is the earliest.

Heuristics. In the discussion on the algorithm of Fig. 4 we noted that we can guide SPIN's depth-first search by changing the order in which SPIN considers successor states of a state `s`. SPIN arranges the processes in *reverse* order of creation. That is, the process that is created last, will be selected first in considering the next successor state.

For optimal schedules for the 'personalisation machine' it is clear that the number of idle time steps by the `TimeAdvance` process should be minimized. So a step of the `TimeAdvance` process should be the last step to be considered by SPIN. Furthermore, as personalisation takes the longest time, starting the personalisation card should be considered first by SPIN.

Branch-and-Bound. Following the conclusions on the TSP, we want to apply the B&B-approach using a dynamic bound in the property. We will check $\Diamond$`too_late_or_wrong_schedule`, where the macro is defined as

```
#define too_late_or_wrong_schedule \
  (c_expr { (now.time >= best_time) || \
            (now.time < 0) || \
            (will_be_too_late()) || \
            (wrong_schedule()) \
  })
```

The macro expands to a `c_expr` expression which apart from the now familiar bound on the `time` and the test on negative `time` due to an incorrect schedule, contains two additional function calls: `will_be_too_late` and `wrong_schedule`. These two functions try to decide at an early stage whether the current schedule leads to an inferior or incorrect schedule. Both C functions only use the current state (i.e. `now`) and the `best_time` found so far.

- The function `will_be_too_late` checks whether the minimum time to finish the cards that are still in the machine already exceeds the `best_time` so far. The function only looks at the last card (i.e. the card with sequence number `NCARDS`) in the machine and computes the minimal time left for this card to reach the *Loader*.
- To signal incorrect schedules, the `UnloaderLoader` sets the `time` to `-1` whenever a card is to be loaded from the belt which is out of order. It will be more advantageous, however, to discover such incorrect schedules (much) earlier. The function `wrong_schedule` returns `1` if either one of the two conditions hold:
  - *Two personalised cards on the `belt` are out-of-order*:
    $\exists 1 \le i, j \le \texttt{NPERS} + 1 :$
    $(i < j) \wedge (\texttt{belt}[\texttt{i}] < 0) \wedge (\texttt{belt}[\texttt{j}] < 0) \wedge (\texttt{belt}[\texttt{i}] < \texttt{belt}[\texttt{j}])$
  - *An personalised card is under a personalisation station containing a card with a lower original sequence number*:
    $\exists 1 \le i \le \texttt{NPERS} : (\texttt{belt}[\texttt{i}] < \texttt{0}) \wedge (-\texttt{belt}[\texttt{i}] > \texttt{card\_in\_pers}[\texttt{i}])$

Both functions together are coded in less than 70 lines of C code.

Get all optimal schedules. Due to the structure of the problem, SPIN will always find just a single (optimal) schedule for a given `time`. The reason for this is that for all schedules with the same end-time, in the last-but-one state, the last card will be under the *Loader*. Due to state matching of SPIN all these states will be regarded to be the same. To obtain *all* optimal schedules, an extra 'magic number' can be added to each state. The magic number ensures that each state will be unique. It is obvious that making the states unique will have a negative impact on the number of states.

Experimental results. To compare the various optimisations on the model of the 'personalisation machine', we have carried out experiments with several combinations of the B&B-optimisations discussed. For these experiments we used the following values for the time-constants: `tRIGHT=1`, `tUNLOAD=tLOAD=2` and `tPERSONALISE=10`. We have verified six different versions of the model. The models can be characterised as follows:

- v1 Model which uses a naive ordering of the creation of processes: `UnloaderLoader`, the `PersStation`-processes, `Conveyer` and finally `TimeAdvance`. The B&B-functionality is isolated in the property, but we only bound on: "`now.time >= best_time || now.time < 0`"
- v2 Model with an improved ordering of the processes: `TimeAdvance`, `UnloaderLoader`, `Conveyer` and finally the `PersStation`-processes. Version v2 uses the same B&B-property as v1
- v3 = v2, but adding "`|| wrong_schedule()`" to the B&B property
- v4 = v2, but adding "`|| will_be_too_late()`" to the B&B property

Table 2. Verification results (number of states, memory consumption in Mb and verification time in seconds) of finding the optimal schedule for PROMELA models of the 'personalisation machine' using several different optimisations

	NPERS=3 NCARDS=4			NPERS=4 NCARDS=4			NPERS=4 NCARDS=5		
	states	mem	time	states	mem	time	states	mem	time
v1	213760	23.2	1.9	1182600	122.6	12.3	o.m	o.m	o.m
v2	161140	18.4	1.4	869594	91.3	8.6	o.m	o.m	o.m
v3	125501	15.4	1.1	677040	72.1	6.4	o.m	o.m	o.m
v4	9709	<5.0	0.1	46600	9.0	0.5	457395	50.1	4.1
v5	6463	<5.0	0.1	33000	7.7	0.3	304731	34.8	2.6
v6	59715	9.8	0.5	477057	54.0	3.6	o.m	o.m	o.m

v5 = v2, but adding "`|| wrong_schedule() || will_be_too_late()`" to the B&B property (so, v5 = v3 + v4)

v6 = v5, but adding a 'magic number' to each state (and thus obtaining all optimal schedules)

Table 2 shows the results of verifying the different versions of the PROMELA model for different values of NPERS and NCARDS. It is clear that the optimisations discussed can be quite effective. The difference between the version with no optimisations at all (v1) and all optimisations enabled (v5) is nearly two orders of magnitude. Note that from Table 2 alone we cannot conclude much on the relative effectiveness of the different optimisations. Only the results between v1 and v2 and between v4 and v5 can be compared directly as apart from the different optimisations nothing has changed in the models. Looking at the results for v4 and v5, it is clear that discarding the schedules that will be too late (v5) is more effective than discarding incorrect schedules beforehand (v4). Also note that changing the creation order of the processes (v1 vs. v2) has a considerable impact on the number of states. As predicted, adding a magic number to states to obtain all optimal schedules (v6) is expensive.

6 Conclusions

The use of model checkers for optimisation problems is appealing. A model checker can first be used to verify that the model of the problem is correct. Subsequently, the same model can be used to find an optimal solution for the problem. Iteratively checking $\Diamond$(`cost` > `best_so_far`) will eventually deliver the optimal solution, but the approach is highly inefficient. We have shown that with the new C primitives of SPIN 4.0, the optimal solution can be found in a single verification run with some minor modifications to the PROMELA model.

The search for an optimal solution can be greatly improved using B&B-techniques in the PROMELA model and/or property. A clear advantage is that the alterations can be done on the level of the PROMELA model. One does not have to alter the source code of SPIN or the verifier pan. We have seen that specifying the B&B-optimisations in the property has several advantages. First of all, all optimising code can nicely be isolated within the property: the PROMELA model does not have to be altered. But more importantly, specifying the B&B-behaviour in the property is more effective (w.r.t. the number of states) than adding it to the PROMELA model. Note that the LTL property that is being verified is dynamically changed during the verification.

The B&B-approach is most effective if SPIN can be guided into finding a good solution as soon as possible. Therefore it is advantageous to apply heuristics to the PROMELA model such that promising successor states are selected first in SPIN's depth-first search algorithm. On the PROMELA level, the user can reorder the guards in `if`- and `do` statements and/or can change the order of process creation (and thus the scheduling of the processes).

Earlier approaches (cite: [2, 7, 15]) have extended existing model checking algorithms with optimality criteria to guide the exploration of states. Behrmann et. al. [2], for example, annotate each state with the estimated minimum cost to reach the goal state and explore the state space by always selecting the state with the smallest minimum cost. Compared to such *local* approaches, this paper applies a more *global* approach in the sense the pruning is isolated in the property that is being checked.

The work might be extended in several ways:

- It would be interesting to see how the *global* approach with SPIN compares to the *local* approaches of [2, 15] and other, more traditional techniques for obtaining optimal solutions for optimisation problems.
- The use of model checkers to solve optimisation problems is limited to the number of states that is needed to find an (optimal) solution. For most classes of discrete optimisation problems, however, there is no need to store the complete state space as the state space is just a tree without loops. The exploration algorithm of SPIN might be changed in such a way that not all states are stored. One might turn off SPIN's state matching functionality all together, or apply a garbage collection algorithm to remove states that are not longer needed, or use a state cache.
- In this paper we used PROMELA to prune the search space of optimisation problems. SYMMSPIN [4] is a symmetry reduction package on top of standard SPIN. The idea is to prune parts of the state space for which there is no need to visit them due to the symmetric nature of the PROMELA model. A drawback of extensions of SPIN like SYMMSPIN is that they are implemented by changing the original source of SPIN or by modifying the source code of the generated `pan` verifier. Consequently, with each new version of SPIN, the extension might cease to work. Now that extensions can be implemented from within the PROMELA model this opens doors to packages on top of SPIN which are easier to maintain.

Acknowledgements

The author wishes to thank Angelika Mader for insightful discussions on the 'personalisation machine' case study. Joost-Pieter Katoen is thanked for valuable comments to improve both the contents and the presentation of the paper. Tomas Krilavičius is thanked for making available UPPAAL-models of the 'personalisation machine' and Kim G. Larsen for showing pointers to related work.

References

[1] Advanced Methods for Timed Systems (AMETIST) Project. IST-2001-35304. Homepage: http://ametist.cs.utwente.nl/. 10

[2] G. Behrmann, A. Fehnker, T. Hune, K. Larsen, P. Pettersson, and J. Romijn. Efficient Guiding Towards Cost-Optimality in UPPAAL. In T. Margaria and W. Yi, editors, *Procs. of the 7th Int. Conf. on Tools and Algorithms for the Construction and Analysis of Systems (TACAS 2001)*, volume 2031 of *LNCS*, pages 174–188, Genova, Italy, April 2001. Springer. 1, 2, 15

[3] O. S. Benli. The Branch-and-Bound Approach. In Anil Mital, editor, *Industrial Engineering Applications and Practice: Users' Encyclopedia*, 1999. CD-ROM edition, chapter available from http://http://www.csulb.edu/~obenli/. 2, 6

[4] D. Bošnački, D. Dams, and L. Holenderski. Symmetric SPIN. In Havelund et al. [9], pages 1–19. 15

[5] E. Brinksma and A. Mader. Verification and Optimization of a PLC Control Schedule. In Havelund et al. [9], pages 73–92. 1, 2, 3, 12

[6] S. Edelkamp, A. L. Lafuente, and S. Leue. Directed Explicit Model Checking with HSF-SPIN. In M. B. Dwyer, editor, *Model Checking Software, Procs. of the 8th Int. SPIN Workshop*, volume 2057 of *LNCS*, pages 57–79, Toronto, Canada, May 2001. Springer. 6

[7] A. Fehnker. Scheduling a Steel Plant with Timed Automata. In *Procs. of the 6th Int. Conf. on Real-Time Computing Systems and Applications (RTCSA 1999)*, pages 280–286. IEEE Computer Society, 1999. 1, 15

[8] A. Fehnker. *Citius Vilius Melius – Guiding and Cost-Optimality in Model Checking of Timed and Hybrid Systems.* PhD thesis, University of Nijmegen, The Netherlands, April 2002. 1

[9] K. Havelund, J. Penix, and W. Visser, editors. *SPIN Model Checking and Software Verification, Procs. of the 7th Int. SPIN Workshop (SPIN'2000)*, volume 1885 of *LNCS*, Stanford, California, USA, August 2000. Springer. 16, 17

[10] G. J. Holzman. *The SPIN Model Checker – Primer and Reference Manual.* Addison-Wesley, Boston, USA, 2003. 1, 4, 5

[11] G. J. Holzmann. SPIN homepage: http://spinroot.com/. 1, 4

[12] G. J. Holzmann. *Design and Validation of Computer Protocols.* Prentice Hall, Englewood Cliffs, New Jersey, USA, 1991. 1

[13] G. J. Holzmann. The Model Checker SPIN. *IEEE Transactions on Software Engineering*, 23(5):279–295, May 1997. 1

[14] G. J. Holzmann, D. Peled, and M. Yannakakis. On Nested Depth First Search. In J.-C. Grégoire, G. J. Holzmann, and D. A. Peled, editors, *The SPIN Verification System, Procs. of the 2nd Int. SPIN Workshop (SPIN'96)*, volume 32 of *DIMACS Series*, Rutgers University, New Jersey, USA, August 1996. AMS. 8

[15] K. Larsen, G. Behrmann, E. Brinksma, A. Fehnker, T. Hune, P. Pettersson, and J. Romijn. As Cheap As Possible: Efficient Cost-Optimal Reachability for Priced Timed Automata. In G. Berry, H. Comon, and A. Finkel, editors, *Procs. of the 13th Int. Conf. on Computer Aided Verification (CAV 2001)*, volume 2102 of *LNCS*, pages 493–505, Paris, France, July 2001. Springer. 1, 2, 15

[16] Princeton University, Mathematics Department. Traveling Salesman Problem – Homepage. http://www.math.princeton.edu/tsp/. 2

[17] G. Reinelt. *The Travelling Salesman – Computational Solutions for TSP Applications*, volume 840 of *LNCS*. Springer, 1994. 2, 3

[18] T. C. Ruys. Low-Fat Recipes for SPIN. In Havelund et al. [9], pages 287–321. 2, 3

[19] T. C. Ruys. *Towards Effective Model Checking*. PhD thesis, University of Twente, Enschede, The Netherlands, March 2001. *Available from the author's homepage.* 2

[20] T. C. Ruys and E. Brinksma. Experience with Literate Programming in the Modelling and Validation of Systems. In B. Steffen, editor, *Procs. of the 4th Int. Conf. on Tools and Algorithms for the Construction and Analysis of Systems (TACAS'98)*, number 1384 in LNCS, pages 393–408, Lisbon, Portugal, April 1998. 1, 2, 3

[21] G. S. Shedler. *Regenerative Stochastic Simulation*. Academic Press, Boston, 1993. 12

[22] W. L. Winston. *Operations Research – Applications and Algorithms*. Duxbury Press, Belmont, California, USA, third edition, 1994. 2, 6, 8

A Requirements Patterns-Driven Approach to Specify Systems and Check Properties*

Sascha Konrad, Laura A. Campbell, Betty H. C. Cheng**, and Min Deng

Software Engineering and Network Systems Laboratory
Department of Computer Science and Engineering
Michigan State University
East Lansing, Michigan 48824 USA
{konradsa,campb222,chengb,dengmin1}@cse.msu.edu

Abstract. We previously developed a framework, *Hydra*, for adding formal semantics to a collection of UML diagrams that enable the automated derivation of formal language specifications for those diagrams. Recently, we have also identified a number of *requirements patterns* for embedded systems that includes sample UML structural and behavioral diagrams for modeling requirements and high-level design for embedded systems. This paper describes a requirements patterns-driven approach for developing UML diagrams for embedded systems, where each pattern has a constraints section to specify safety and other invariant properties. We show how the diagrams for an industrial automotive system, via specifications generated from *Hydra*, can be automatically analyzed for adherence to these formally specified constraints using the SPIN model checker. We developed the *MINERVA* framework to support the graphical construction of UML diagrams and to visualize the results from the SPIN analysis in terms of the original UML diagrams.

1 Introduction

It is well-known that requirements modeling and analysis is one of the most difficult tasks in the software development process [20], but this problem is greatly exacerbated for embedded systems given the hardware constraints and the potentially complex control logic. Previously, we developed modeling/visualization and formalization frameworks and tools to facilitate the rigorous development of embedded systems. Specifically, we have tools to support the graphical modeling of requirements (MINERVA [3]), the translation of these models into formal specifications (Hydra [4, 15]) that can then be analyzed using the appropriate tools, such as the SPIN simulator and model checker [9], and the visualization of errors captured in terms of the original graphical models (MINERVA). Recently,

* This work has been supported in part by NSF grants EIA-0000433, EIA-0130724, CDA-9700732, CC-9984726, and CC-9901017, Department of the Navy, Office of Naval Research under Grant No. N00014-01-1-0744, and in cooperation with Siemens Automotive and Detroit Diesel Corporation.

** Please contact this author for all correspondences.

T. Ball and S.K. Rajamani (Eds.): SPIN 2003, LNCS 2648, pp. 18–33, 2003.

we identified a number of *requirements patterns* for use in the development of requirements and high-level design for embedded systems [14]. We constructed a requirements pattern template, much in the spirit of the template used by Gamma *et al.* [7] for design patterns. This paper describes a three-pronged approach, using Hydra, MINERVA and SPIN, to facilitate the development of *Unified Modeling Language* (UML) diagrams for the requirements of embedded system applications that can be analyzed for the correctness of critical properties. The three components of the approach are the use of requirements patterns, the automatic generation of formal specifications, and the visualization of the analysis results of these specifications. The process is illustrated using an automotive application from industry, an air particulate filter system to reduce the amount of soot emitted from diesel truck exhaust.

Given the safety-critical nature of many embedded systems, methods for modeling and developing embedded systems and rigorously verifying behavior before committing to code are increasingly important. Currently, much of the embedded systems industry uses *ad hoc* development approaches [5]. The embedded systems community appears, however, to be interested in exploring how object-oriented modeling, specifically the UML [2], can be used for embedded systems [5]. Our requirements patterns use the UML to model structural and behavioral information, using class diagrams, and sequence and state diagrams, respectively. This information can be used to guide the construction of UML models for embedded systems. Our modeling tool, MINERVA, and formal specification generation tool, Hydra, enable developers to model their systems and check the models for adherence to critical properties. In addition, our visualization utilities in MINERVA depict errors detected by the analysis tools in terms of the original diagrams, thereby greatly accelerating the development and refinement process. The alternative for evaluating the UML models is to use visual inspection. A few tools that support UML diagrams enable developers to perform high-level syntactic analysis [19], or generate formal specifications, such as SDL [21], animate state diagrams and sequence diagrams [11], or generate code for simulation [8, 18]. But none of these utilities provide the collective capabilities captured by our approach and tools, nor do they attempt to reuse organized information such as that captured by our requirements patterns.

We applied the requirements patterns to several embedded systems to determine their utility. The requirements pattern template includes motivation, consequences, high-level goals, context information, constraints, and diagrams depicting templates for structure and behavior. The **Constraints** field of the template includes formal specifications of properties that should be satisfied in the context of using a given pattern [12]. The constraints are described in prose and specified in LTL (Linear Temporal Logic) according to *specification patterns* developed by Dwyer *et al.* [6]. We found that requirements patterns enable novices, guided by the structure and behavior diagrams in the templates, to quickly construct models of their systems. Also, the requirements patterns prompt developers to consider aspects of a system that might otherwise be overlooked until much later in the development process, such as fault tolerance and safety considerations.

Requirements patterns can provide both guidance to novices of embedded systems development for determining the key elements of many embedded systems, and examples of how to model these elements with a commonly accepted diagramming notation, UML. With the formalization capability, we are able to validate (using simulation) the behavior of the requirements as captured by the state diagrams [3] within the structural context imposed by the class diagrams. Furthermore, constraints from the requirements patterns can guide novices in constructing formal properties to check against their UML models. The result is that developers can accelerate the initial development of requirements models through the use of requirements patterns, and then using our formalization work and tools, they have means to rigorously check the requirements using simulation and model checking techniques.

The remainder of this paper is organized as follows. Section 2 briefly describes our modeling/visualization and formalization frameworks and the tools instantiating them, and overviews requirements patterns. Section 3 illustrates how requirements patterns can be incorporated into our iterative modeling and analysis process for creating, analyzing, and refining UML diagrams. Section 4 contains an overview of the Diesel Filter System (a system of particulate filters to reduce soot in diesel truck exhaust) and describes the preliminary results of developing and analyzing the UML diagrams. Section 5 gives concluding remarks and discusses future investigations.

2 Background

This section overviews several technologies contributing to the project, including MINERVA and Hydra that support UML, and requirements patterns that describe information typically used for describing requirements of embedded systems.

2.1 Modeling/Visualization and Formalization Frameworks

We have developed a general framework [4, 15, 17] based on mappings between *metamodels* (class diagrams depicting abstract syntax) for formalizing a subset of UML diagrams in terms of different formal languages, including Promela and VHDL [15, 16, 17]. The formal (target) language chosen should reflect and support the intended semantics for a given domain (e.g., embedded systems). This formalization framework enables the construction of a set of rules for transforming UML models into specifications in a formal language [4]. The resulting specifications derived from UML diagrams enable either execution through simulation or analysis through model checking, using existing tools. The mapping process from UML to a target language has been automated in a tool called Hydra [15].

To complement Hydra's formalization framework for automatic generation of formal specifications, we developed a modeling and visualization framework [3] to support a number of tasks necessary to model and analyze UML diagrams. These tasks have been automated in a tool called MINERVA [3] that includes the following capabilities: graphical construction of syntactically correct UML diagrams;[1] and visualization of consistency-checking results, simulation traces, and paths of execution that lead to errors, all in terms of UML diagrams. For this paper, we focus on the embedded systems domain, instantiating MINERVA and Hydra with formalization rules for Promela to be used with the SPIN simulator and model checker [9].

2.2 Requirements Patterns

In order to address the needs of requirements engineering, we developed a template to describe requirements patterns [14] by modifying the original design pattern template [7]. Modifications relevant to this paper include extending the original design pattern template with **Constraints** and **Behavior** sections that contain specification-pattern-based [6] representations of properties of interest, and sequence and state diagrams that illustrate sample behavior, respectively. Thus far, our constraints have included representations of two of Dwyer *et al.*'s [6] most commonly used general specification pattern categories, *universality/absence* (to capture invariant properties) and *response* (to capture cause/effect relationships in system behavior). Requirements pattern constraints provide a template for instantiating properties specific to a modeled system in terms of the UML diagrams describing the system. See [14] for further details on the requirements pattern template.

We have identified several patterns to describe requirements for the main elements of an embedded system. Figure 1 gives a list of the requirements patterns that have been identified to date with a brief description of each. The complete set of requirements patterns and their full descriptions are given elsewhere [14].

3 Modeling and Analysis Process

Figure 2 overviews our approach, illustrating how requirements patterns can be combined with the iterative modeling and analysis process supported by MINERVA and Hydra [3, 15] (here instantiated with the model checker SPIN [9]). The user begins by selecting appropriate requirements patterns based on the requirements of the system. Using the structural and behavioral diagrams in the requirements patterns as a guide, the user constructs UML class and state diagrams in MINERVA's graphical editors (Fig. 2, part A). Hydra performs consistency checks (Fig. 2, part B), and MINERVA visualizes structural consistency-checking results (dash-dotted arc in Fig. 2, part F). (We omit discussion of these capabilities in this paper; see [3] for details.) Hydra then generates formal specifications from textual representations of UML diagrams (Fig. 2, part C); these formal specifications can be used to validate the UML diagrams through simulation using

[1] We use Honeywell's domain model editor toolkit, DoME [10], to build the graphical editor for UML diagrams.

Actuator-Sensor:	How to specify various kinds of sensors and actuators and their relationships to a controller in an embedded system.
Controller Decompose:	How to decompose an embedded system into different components according to their responsibilities.
Monitor-Actuator:	How to increase safety and reliability by monitoring actuator behavior for errors.
Fault Handler:	How to integrate a fault handler into an embedded system.
Channel:	How to arrange communication between two components.
Watchdog:	How to monitor a device or system conditions and initiate corrective action(s) if a violation is found.
Examiner:	How to monitor a device and store occurring errors.
User Interface:	How to specify a user interface that is extensible and reusable.
Mask:	How to reduce the burden placed on the computing component when many sensors and actuators are present, whose values need to be sorted or filtered into single values for the computing component.
Moderator:	How to provide an interface to support decoupling of complex subsystems.

Fig. 1. Current list of requirements patterns for embedded systems

SPIN (Fig. 2, part D). In addition, the user may instantiate (as LTL claims) properties from the **Constraints** section of those requirements patterns used to guide the modeling of the system (Fig. 2, part E). These LTL claims, defined in terms of attributes and states of the UML model, can then be checked against the UML diagrams (Fig. 2, part D) through model checking using SPIN. Finally, MINERVA visualizes behavior simulation and counterexample traces (solid arc, Fig. 2, part F) via state diagram animation, generation/animation of *collaboration diagrams* (which depict the paths of communication, or *links*, between objects that exchange messages), and generation of sequence diagrams, thus facilitating the debugging and refinement of the original UML diagrams.

4 Modeling and Analyzing a Diesel Filter System

This section describes how we applied our modeling and analysis process to a high-level description of an automotive application obtained from one of our industrial partners, Detroit Diesel. Specifically, we depict an embedded system controlling a self-cleaning particulate filter that reduces the amount of pollutants emitted from the exhaust of diesel trucks. We illustrate how several requirements patterns interplay to guide the creation of a system model and formal constraints, and how MINERVA and Hydra enable simulation and model checking with SPIN.

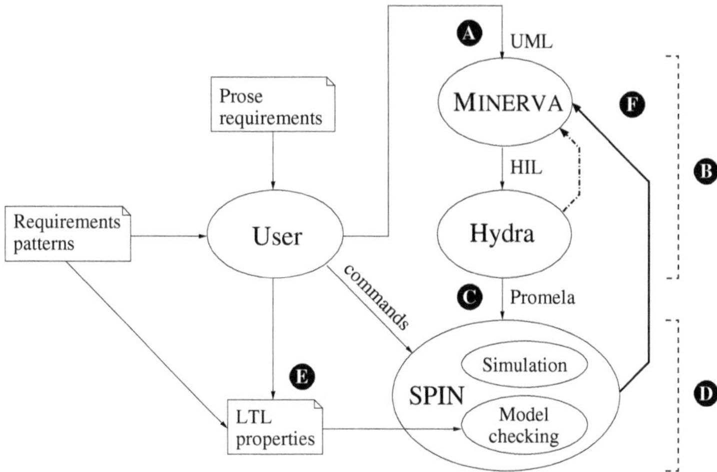

Fig. 2. Overview of our approach

4.1 Application Overview

An effective way to reduce particulate combustion aerosols, or soot, from diesel truck exhaust is to use particulate filters placed in a canister and inserted into the exhaust gas path. A filter comprises several tubes, with each tube consisting of ceramic fibers wound around a metallic cylindrical grid. Exhaust gas flows through the filters, out of the canister, and into the exhaust pipe. To enable the exhaust gas to flow freely through the filters, they must be cleaned periodically. Therefore, the grid wires can be electrified, causing them to heat up and burn off trapped particulates. The Diesel Filter System (DFS) is an embedded system that initiates a cleaning cycle when the differential pressure across the filter canister, as measured in *Pascals* (Pa), is within an acceptable range. The grid heating sequence will not begin if too few engine revolutions have occurred since the last time the cleaning cycle was completed, or the current engine revolutions per minute (RPMs) are too low.

4.2 Requirements Patterns for the Diesel Filter System

We present four requirements patterns that we identified to be appropriate for this system based on the DFS requirements [22]: *Actuator-Sensor*, *Fault Handler*, *Watchdog*, and *User Interface* Patterns. Figure 3 illustrates how the information in the **Structure** section of these patterns can be used to guide the creation of a preliminary UML class diagram for the DFS. The ComputingComponent, shown in bold in Fig. 3, plays a role in all four patterns.

***Actuator-Sensor* Pattern:** The *Actuator-Sensor* Pattern, denoted by dashed boxes and lines, shows how abstract sensor and actuator classes are used to

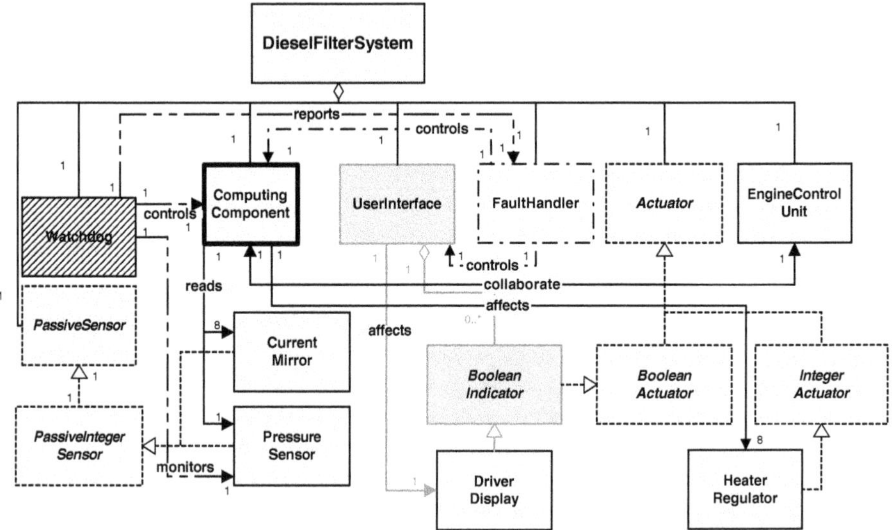

Fig. 3. Requirements-pattern-guided UML class diagram of the Diesel Filter System

give a common interface to the concrete sensors (CurrentMirrors, PressureSensor) and actuators (DriverDisplay, HeaterRegulators) in the DFS.

***Fault Handler* Pattern:** The FaultHandler, illustrated with a dash-dotted box and lines, controls the ComputingComponent to initiate safety actions when errors occur. It also controls the UserInterface, warning the user that errors have occurred.

***Watchdog* Pattern:** The Watchdog, denoted by a striped box and long-short-short dashed lines, monitors the PressureSensor. If it detects a violation of the maximum pressure value, then it notifies the FaultHandler of the error and initiates an emergency shutdown in the ComputingComponent.

***User Interface* Pattern:** The *User Interface* Pattern is represented by the shaded boxes and lines. The UserInterface controls only one boolean indicator, the DriverDisplay, which represents a simple warning device such as an indicator light.

4.3 Abstraction and Equivalence Classes

Abstraction can significantly reduce the state space needed to perform model checking; we use two techniques. First, we model only those portions of the system that are relevant to our focused analysis. In this study, we are interested in specifying and analyzing the DFS cleaning cycle. We model only those components relevant to this analysis. Additionally, we also abstract the number of heater regulators and their corresponding current mirrors from eight in the actual system down to two in our model.

Second, we determine *equivalence classes* for the possible values of system conditions. These equivalence classes are determined according to their impact on the behavior of the system. Generally, the operational status of a component is represented as *non-working* (false) or *working* (true), as shown in Expression (1) in Fig. 4. We model the operational status of the PressureSensor, HeaterRegulator1, and HeaterRegulator2. Ranges for other monitored values (*e.g.*, current system pressure, number of revolutions of the engine since the last cleaning cycle, current engine speed) can be determined from the requirements, as shown in Expressions (2), (3), and (4), respectively in Fig. 4 (∞ represents the target language-dependent upper bound). We also introduce physical abstraction values for modeling purposes (Fig. 4, Expressions (5) and (6)). These values represent the interaction between components due to existing physical relationships (*e.g.*, how much the current pressure decreases after every successful cleaning cycle in the DFS).

4.4 UML Modeling for the Diesel Filter System

Based on Fig. 3 and our abstractions, we created UML object and state diagrams to model the DFS. Figure 5 overviews the UML object diagram for the DFS (attributes and methods have been elided; components attributed to the different patterns retain their shading/line characteristics from Fig. 3). The ComputingComponent, the core of the system, reads values from the sensors PressureSensor, CurrentMirror1, CurrentMirror2, and the EngineControlUnit. It also sets the values of the actuators HeaterRegulator1 and HeaterRegulator2. The PressureSensor senses the current pressure. The EngineControlUnit models an interface to the engine controller to check the current engine speed (RPMs) and the total number of revolutions since the last cleaning cycle. Each CurrentMirror senses the amount of electrical current flowing through its respective HeaterRegulator. The FaultHandler processes error messages received and takes appropriate actions (defined in the FaultHandler state diagram which is not shown due to space constraints). The Watchdog monitors the PressureSensor, notifying the FaultHandler and shutting down the ComputingComponent if the pressure exceeds 10,000 Pa. The UserInterface controls the DriverDisplay, which represents a simple warning light. Additionally, our approach incorporates two special classes, an Environment class that defines the equivalence classes for system conditions of the environment as depicted in Fig. 4, and a _SYSTEMCLASS_ class that represents the aggregation of the main components of the system and non-deterministically selects values for the system and environment conditions according to the determined equivalence classes.

In our approach, each component has its own state diagram; however, due to space constraints, we show only the (elided) state diagram of the ComputingComponent, the central component of the DFS, in Fig. 6. The structure of this state diagram follows that of the state diagram given in the **Behavior** section of the *Fault Handler* pattern [14]. Specifically, it has the state *PowerOff* and the composite states *Initialize* and *NormalBehavior* (elided in Fig. 6). Furthermore, the three states *GetPressure1*, *GetPressure2*, and *Idle* represent the

$$\langle Component \rangle OperationState = \begin{cases} 0 & \text{(non-working)} \\ 1 & \text{(working)} \end{cases} \tag{1}$$

$$CurrentSystemPressure = \begin{cases} [0;\ 8,000] \\ (8,000;\ 10,000] \\ (10,000;\ \infty) \end{cases} \tag{2}$$

Below 8,000 Pa the system remains in an idle phase; between 8,000 and 10,000 Pa the cleaning cycle starts; above 10,000 Pa the system shuts down for safety reasons.

$$TotalRPMValue = \begin{cases} [0;\ 10,000) \\ [10,000;\ \infty) \end{cases} \tag{3}$$

The total number of engine revolutions since the completion of the last cleaning sequence must be at least 10,000; otherwise, the cleaning sequence will not start.

$$CurrentRPMValue = \begin{cases} [0;\ 700) \\ [700;\ \infty) \end{cases} \tag{4}$$

The current engine speed, measured in RPMs, must be at least 700; otherwise, the cleaning sequence will not start.

$$PressureSensorCleanupValue = \begin{cases} -250 \\ 300 \\ 3,000 \end{cases} \tag{5}$$

This value determines how much the pressure decreases each time a heating element is activated. A negative value resembles a defective heating element, letting the pressure rise in every cleaning sequence.

$$HeaterCurrentConversionRatio = \begin{cases} 2 \\ 3 \\ 4 \end{cases} \tag{6}$$

This value determines the amount of increase of the current mirror value per increase of the respective heating element value. The lower the heater current conversion ratio, the faster the current value will increase on a heater value increase.

Fig. 4. Equivalence classes for system conditions

Idle phase of the DFS where the system continuously queries the PressureSensor and initiates a cleaning cycle if the pressure is found to exceed 8,000 Pa. (The dashed and bolded transitions and the italicized elements are added as later refinements based on analysis feedback; they are included in this figure due to space constraints and will be described in the next section as part of the analysis process.)

The DFS performs three main steps. First, on system activation, the DFS enters an *Initialization* phase. If the initialization is performed successfully, then the system enters an *Idle* phase. While in the *Idle* phase, the system continuously

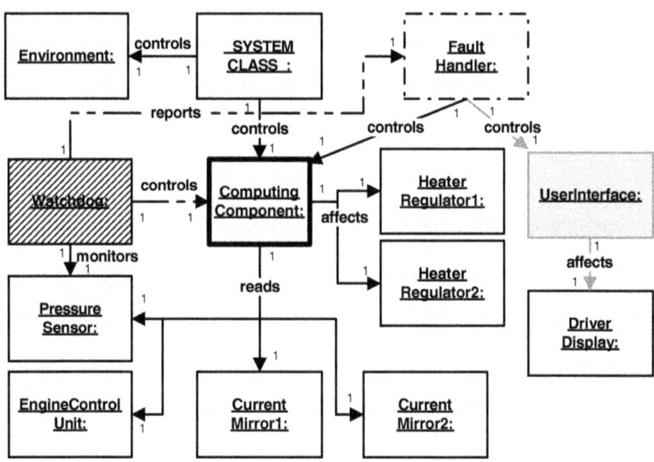

Fig. 5. UML object diagram of the abstracted Diesel Filter System

checks the current system pressure. If a failure occurs during the initialization, then the system shuts down.

Second, if the differential pressure in the filter container exceeds 8,000 Pa, then the cleaning cycle is started. At the beginning of the cleaning cycle, the system waits for the total number of revolutions since the last cleaning cycle and the current RPMs to pass their thresholds of 10,000 and 700, respectively. In a cleaning sequence, each operational heater element is ramped up to burn off trapped particulates and ramped down afterwards. During the ramp-up process of each heater element, the system monitors the current on the corresponding

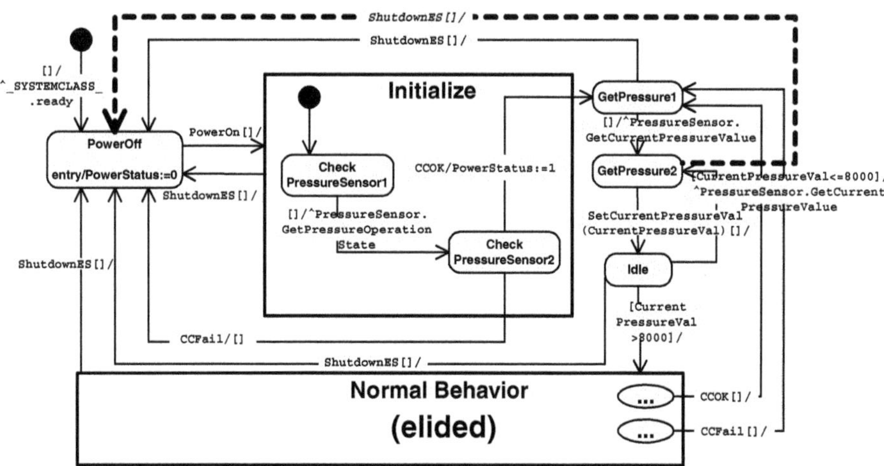

Fig. 6. UML state diagram of the ComputingComponent (elided)

current mirror to detect excess conditions and accordingly ramps down the heating element.

Third, after the completion of the cleaning cycle the DFS returns to the *Idle* phase, waiting for either the pressure to exceed 8,000 Pa again or a system shutdown message to arrive.

4.5 Analysis Using Requirements and Specification Patterns

After we use MINERVA to construct UML diagrams of the system, we use Hydra to generate an executable specification of the system in terms of Promela (not shown due to space constraints; see [13]). Briefly, objects are captured as `proctypes` that communicate via `channels` using queueing semantics [4, 15]. In this section, we examine two requirements for the DFS. In each case, we give the prose requirement, the relevant requirements pattern(s) in bold italics, the relevant specification-pattern-based constraint(s) from the **Constraints** section of each requirements pattern, the instantiated constraints checked against the generated Promela specification, the analysis results (including visualizations), and the corrective actions taken.

Requirement 1:
If the Watchdog detects a violation, then the system should turn off.

Watchdog **Pattern** *Constraint:* If a violation of the system requirements is found, then the Watchdog should start the corresponding *recovery action* appropriate to the system being modeled (*e.g.*, begin error recovery, reset the device, shut down).

```
[] ( ''Violation'' -> <> ''Start recovery action'' )
```

Instantiated Constraint: The attribute `Violation` represents whether or not the Watchdog has detected a violation. Its possible values are *zero* (no violation has been detected) and *one* (a violation has been detected). The attribute `PowerStatus` represents whether or not the Computing Component is on. Its possible values are *zero* (power is off) and *one* (power is on). It is always (`[]`) the case that when a violation occurs, then eventually (<>) the DFS powers off.

```
[] ( ( Watchdog.Violation==1 ) ->
        <> ( ComputingComponent.PowerStatus==0 ) )
```

Analysis Results: SPIN detected a counterexample, from which MINERVA generated the (elided[2]) sequence diagram shown in Fig. 7. In this diagram, the ComputingComponent queries the operational status of the PressureSensor and receives a *CCOK* message, indicating that the PressureSensor is working. It then requests the current system pressure. However, the PressureSensor notifies the

[2] All interactions between the _SYSTEMCLASS_ or Environment classes and the other components of the system have been elided, including the initial *PowerOn* message sent to the ComputingComponent. The lifelines of all objects not participating in the message exchange depicted by the sequence diagram have been elided.

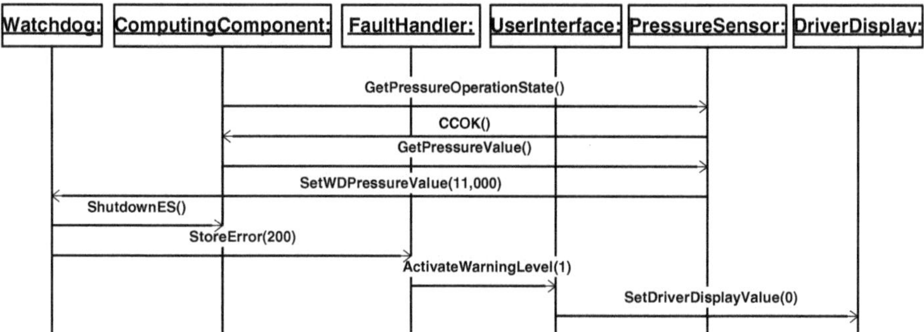

Fig. 7. Elided UML sequence diagram (Requirement 1)

Watchdog that the current system pressure exceeds 10,000 Pa. The Watchdog then sends a *ShutdownES* message to the ComputingComponent and an error code to the FaultHandler, indicating that a violation has been detected. The FaultHandler notifies the UserInterface, which then activates the DriverDisplay. However, the sequence diagram does not provide enough information to determine the cause of the error. (The expected behavior of the ComputingComponent upon receiving a *ShutdownES* message is to power off.) State diagram animation of the entire model, however, reveals that the ComputingComponent becomes deadlocked in state *GetPressure2* rather than returning to state *PowerOff*.

Corrective Actions: We determined that the problem was a missing transition in the ComputingComponent state diagram that unintentionally created a deadlock in the state *GetPressure2*. We added a transition from state *GetPressure2* to state *PowerOff* to handle event *ShutdownES* (depicted by the dashed transition in Fig. 6) and regenerated the specification. SPIN verified the claim after 3,028,470 transitions.

Requirement 2:
If the Watchdog detects a violation, then a warning light turns on. Constraints from several requirements patterns combine to specify this requirement. Upon detecting a violation, the Watchdog interacts with the FaultHandler. Upon receiving an error message, the FaultHandler interacts with the UserInterface. Finally, upon notification from the FaultHandler, the UserInterface takes appropriate action, in this case turning on a warning light. The three constraints are described below:

Watchdog **Pattern** *Constraint:* When a violation is found, a message containing the appropriate error code should be sent to the FaultHandler (indicated by the keyword **sent**).

```
[] ( ''Violation'' ->
     <> ( sent( FaultHandler.StoreError(ErrorMessage) ) ) )
```

Instantiated Constraint: We model only one type of violation, sending the error code "200" to the FaultHandler.

```
[] ( ( Watchdog.Violation==1 ) ->
       <> ( sent( FaultHandler.StoreError(200) ) ) )
```

Analysis Results: SPIN verified this claim after 2,362,780 transitions.

***Fault Handler* Pattern** *Constraint:* When an error message is sent to the FaultHandler, it should activate the appropriate user interface warning level.

```
[] ( sent( FaultHandler.StoreError(Error) ) ->
     <> ''Activate appropriate user interface warning level'' )
```

Instantiated Constraint: We model only one type of error in our system, using the code "200". The possible values of the UserInterface attribute `WarningLevel` are *zero* (no warning) and *one* (warning).

```
[] ( sent( FaultHandler.StoreError(200) ) ->
     <> ( sent( UserInterface.ActivateWarningLevel(1) ) ) )
```

Analysis Results: SPIN verified this claim after 4,283,420 transitions.

***User Interface* Pattern** *Constraint:* Upon receiving a warning, activate the appropriate indicator devices, such as turning on an alarm or a warning light.

```
[] ( ( sent( UserInterface.ActivateWarningLevel(WarningLevel) ) ) ->
       <> ( ''Activate appropriate indicators'' ) )
```

Instantiated Constraint: In the modeled system, a light in the actuator DriverDisplay is represented by the attribute `DriverDisplayValue`. The possible values for this attribute are *zero* (the light is off) and *one* (the light is on).

```
[] ( ( sent( UserInterface.ActivateWarningLevel(1) ) ) ->
       <> ( DriverDisplay.DriverDisplayValue==1 ) )
```

Analysis Results: SPIN detected a counterexample, and MINERVA generated a sequence diagram (not shown). The messages of interest can also be seen as the last two messages in Fig. 7. Although the UserInterface receives the message *ActivateWarningLevel(1)*, indicating a warning, it sends the message *SetDriverDisplayValue(0)* to the DriverDisplay, turning off the light. State diagram animation revealed that the problem was an erroneous guard on a transition in the UserInterface state diagram. The italicized guard on the bold transition in Fig. 8(a) unintentionally creates non-determinism in transitioning from the *Check* to the *Idle* state, which erroneously allows the warning light to be turned off when it should instead indicate a warning to the user. Figure 8(b) shows, in human-readable form generated by MINERVA, only those animation steps pertaining to the UserInterface state diagram. The animation itself highlights in color the transition shown in bold in Fig. 8(a), distinguishing which one of the transitions was taken.

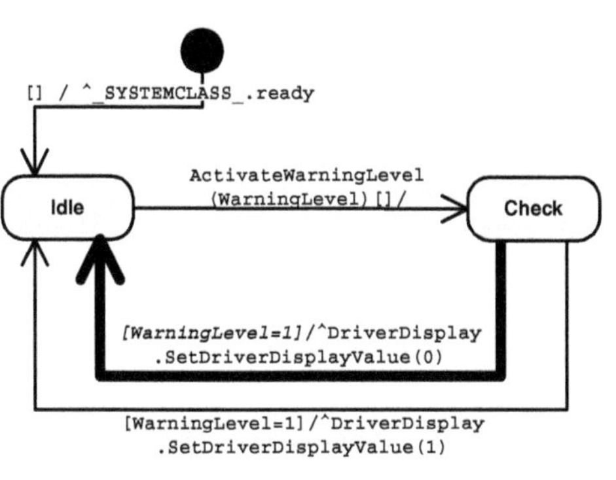

(a) State Diagram

1. Object "UserInterface" transitions from state "Initial" to state "Idle" on event "modelstart"
2. Object "UserInterface" transitions from state "Idle" to state "Check" on event "ActivateWarningLevel(WarningLevel)"
3. Object "UserInterface" transitions from state "Check" to state "Idle" on condition "WarningLevel=1"

(b) Transition Trace

Fig. 8. Animation trace of UserInterface state diagram (Requirement 2)

Corrective Actions: We corrected the guard to compare the warning level to zero and regenerated the specification. SPIN verified the claim after 4,283,420 transitions.

5 Conclusions

Preliminary feedback from industrial collaborators indicates that requirements patterns can be an effective mechanism for describing requirements of embedded systems. Furthermore, by adding specification-pattern-based properties to the **Constraints** field of the requirements pattern template, developers have some guidance as to what kinds of properties can be checked for a given system when a particular pattern is applied. The specification patterns used in conjunction with requirements patterns enable even novice developers to easily formulate claims to check the system for specific constraints. Then using our formalization work and tool suite, developers have a mechanism to rigorously check the requirements using simulation and model checking techniques.

Several major directions for future research are motivated by the validation results obtained thus far. First, we are continuing to identify additional requirements patterns. In particular, we are investigating patterns that address timing issues for embedded systems. Accordingly, our formalization framework is being extended to handle models that contain timing information. Second, additional specification patterns are being sought that capture typical or common constraints applicable to embedded systems. Finally, in order to keep the model checking portion of the analysis tractable, we are exploring numerous abstraction techniques, similar to those used by Heitmeyer *et al.* [1] and others, to reduce the scope of a given analysis scenario.

References

[1] Ramesh Bharadwaj and Constance L. Heitmeyer. Model checking complete requirements specifications using abstraction. *Automated Software Engineering: An International Journal*, 6(1):37–68, January 1999. 31

[2] Grady Booch, James Rumbaugh, and Ivar Jacobson. *The Unified Modeling Language User Guide.* Addision-Wesley, 1999. 19

[3] Laura A. Campbell, Betty H. C. Cheng, William E. McUmber, and R. E. K. Stirewalt. Automatically detecting and visualizing errors in UML diagrams. *Requirements Engineering Journal*, 7(4):264–287, 2002. 18, 20, 21

[4] Betty H. C. Cheng, Laura A. Campbell, Min Deng, and R. E. K. Stirewalt. Enabling validation of UML formalizations. Technical Report MSU-CSE-02-25, Department of Computer Science, Mich State Univ, E Lansing, MI, September 2002. 18, 20, 28

[5] Bruce Powell Douglass. *Doing Hard Time: Developing Real-Time Systems with UML, Objects, Frameworks, and Patterns.* Addison–Wesley, 1999. 19

[6] Matthew B. Dwyer, George S. Avrunin, and James C. Corbett. Property specification patterns for finite-state verification. In *Proceedings 2nd Workshop on Formal Methods in Software Engineering*, pages 7–16, Clearwater Beach, FL, March 1998. 19, 21

[7] Erich Gamma, Richard Helm, Ralph Johnson, and John Vlissides. *Design Patterns: Elements of Reusable Object-Oriented Software.* Addison-Wesley, 1994. 19, 21

[8] Wai Ming Ho, Jean-Marc Jezequel, Alain Le Guennec, and Francois Pennaneac'h. UMLAUT: an extendible UML transformation framework. In *Proc. of IEEE International Conference on Automated Software Engineering*, Cocoa Beach, FL, October 1999. 19

[9] Gerald J. Holzmann. The Model Checker SPIN. *IEEE Transactions on Software Engineering*, 23(5), May 1997. 18, 21

[10] Honeywell. URL: www.htc.honeywell.com/dome. 21

[11] I-logix. Rhapsody. URL: www.ilogix.com. 19

[12] Sascha Konrad, Laura A. Campbell, and Betty H. C. Cheng. Adding formal specifications to requirements patterns. In *Proceedings of the Requirements for High Assurance Systems Workshop (RHAS02) as part of the IEEE Joint International Conference on Requirements Engineering (RE02)*, Essen, Germany, September 2002. 19

[13] Sascha Konrad, Laura A. Campbell, Betty H. C. Cheng, and Min Deng. A requirements pattern-driven approach to specify systems and check properties. Technical Report MSU-CSE-02-28, Computer Science and Engineering, Mich State Univ, E Lansing, MI, December 2002. 28

[14] Sascha Konrad and Betty H. C. Cheng. Requirements patterns for embedded systems. In *Proceedings of the IEEE Joint International Conference on Requirements Engineering (RE02)*, Essen, Germany, September 2002. 19, 21, 25

[15] William E. McUmber and Betty H. C. Cheng. A general framework for formalizing UML with formal languages. In *Proceedings of IEEE International Conference on Software Engineering (ICSE01)*, Toronto, Canada, May 2001. 18, 20, 21, 28

[16] William E. McUmber and Betty H. C. Cheng. UML-based analysis of embedded systems using a mapping to VHDL. In *Proceedings of IEEE High Assurance Software Engineering (HASE99)*, Washington, DC, November 1999. 20

[17] William Eugene McUmber. *A Generic Framework for Formalizing Object-Oriented Modeling Notations for Embedded Systems Development.* PhD thesis, Michigan State University, August 2000. 20

[18] Jorg Niere and Albert Zundorf. Using FUJABA for the development of production control systems. In *Applications of Graph Transformations with Industrial Relevance AGTIVE*, pages 181–191. Springer Verlag, 1999. Volume 1779, Lecture Notes in Computer Science. 19

[19] Rational. Rational Rose. URL: www.rational.com. 19

[20] Ian Sommerville. *Software Engineering.* Addison-Wesley, 1992. 18

[21] Telelogic. ObjectGEODE. URL: www.telelogic.com. 19

[22] Anthony Torre. Project specifications for diesel filter system, 2000. www.cse.msu.edu/~cse470/F2000/cheng/Projects/F00-Cheng/filter /Description/air-filter.html. 23

Formal Modeling and Analysis of an Avionics Triplex Sensor Voter*

Samar Dajani-Brown, Darren Cofer, Gary Hartmann, and Steve Pratt

Honeywell Laboratories, Minneapolis MN
samar.dajani-brown@honeywell.com

Abstract. Digital flight control systems utilize redundant hardware to meet high reliability requirements. In this study we use the SMV model checker to assess the design correctness of a sensor voter algorithm used to manage three redundant sensors. The sensor voter design is captured as a Simulink diagram. The requirements verified include normal operation, transient conditions, and fault handling.

The sensor voter algorithm is a realistic example of flight critical embedded software used to manage redundant air data or inertial reference sensors. We are using it to evaluate different design methods, languages, and tools currently available for formal verification. Key issues are 1) integration of formal verification into existing development processes and tools, and 2) synthesis of the correct environment (world abstraction) needed for analysis of normal and off-normal operating conditions.

1 Redundant Sensors in Flight Control

Early autopilots were allowed a minimum of control authority so they would not cause any serious disturbances if any component failed; they could easily be overpowered by pilot inputs. As the need for aircraft stability and precise flight path following increased, so did flight control authority. This lead to the need for monitoring and the addition of redundant sensors and monitor points to provide the needed information for failure detection (which would then automatically disengage the system). Over time this evolved into a completely redundant channel of sensors and control electronics. At the same time there was a growing demand for increased mission reliability and the need for fail-operative systems arose.

A key part of redundant systems focuses on managing redundant sensors to provide a high integrity measurement for use by down-stream control calculations. Cross-strapping sensors so downstream processing has access to multiple copies of the same variable is an important feature. The advantage of cross-strapping sensors among redundant control channels to improve system availability (or mission success) was recognized in the 1960s but was not exploited due to the limitations of the analog implementations. With the advent of digital

* This work has been supported in part by NASA contract NAS1-00079.

T. Ball and S.K. Rajamani (Eds.): SPIN 2003, LNCS 2648, pp. 34–48, 2003.

flight control it was recognized that fault detection and isolation could be implemented in software. The main advantage of the digital flight control systems which appeared in the mid 1970s compared to earlier analog systems was the ability to handle monitoring, redundancy management, and built-in-test without adding more hardware.

Throughout the 1970s and 1980s many papers appeared describing various algorithms for managing redundant systems and redundant sensors. The NATO Advisory Group for Aerospace Research and Development (AGARD) has sponsored several publications and lecture series dealing with redundancy management in flight control [1],[2],[3]. A recent paper on the subject appears in [4] and textbooks such as [5] now contain chapters on redundancy management in flight control systems.

Many sensors include some internal monitors and provide a logic output to indicate that an internal hardware fault has been identified. These monitors provide on the order of 90 - 95 % failure detection without false alarms. Internal monitors are usually specific to a sensor type. Examples of such internal monitors include checks on power supply voltages, checks on whether ring laser gyros are "lasing", checks on whether vibrating beam accelerometers are at the proper resonant frequency and so forth. If these sensor valid signals are set "false", then the sensor is not used regardless of voter or comparitor algorithm decisions [4]. However, these valid flags are not adequate for detecting all sensor faults; hence the need for real-time software monitors operating at the sampling rate of the sensors.

Sensors exhibit various kinds of deterministic and non-deterministic errors including bias offsets, scale factor errors, and sensitivity to spurious input and environmental factors. The question of what constitutes a "failed" sensor involves certain subtleties. These are reflected in the fact that situations exist, such as when the quantity being measured is zero, in which the behavior of a perfectly functioning instrument is indistinguishable from the behavior of one that is not working. In practice, sensors often fail by small degrees so that the indicated measurement becomes contaminated with nearly unobservable errors. For operational purposes, we can define a sensor as failed when it is contributing measurement errors sufficiently large as to jeopardize the mission. What this imposes on the sensor redundancy management is the requirement that it be able to isolate or tolerate any failure large enough to jeopardize the mission.

Sensor failure detection algorithms ("voters") must detect and isolate a sensor whose output departs by more than a specified amount from the normal error spread. The detailed design of the voter algorithm combined with the downstream control law determines the magnitude of the transient the aircraft may experience as a result of the failed sensor being disconnected. Thus two conflicting requirements emerge:

1. Provide a very low number of nuisance disconnections – if the thresholds are too low a sensor can be disconnected when it is merely at the edge of its tolerances. To further minimize nuisance trips many algorithms may require errors to "persist" for some amount of time before declaring a fault.

2. Provide a minimum transient on disconnecting a failed sensor – if the thresholds are too high when a real failure occurs the magnitude of the resulting transient can be unacceptably large.

The generic voter used in this study is representative of algorithms in use. Many of its features are taken from [4]. This class of algorithm is applicable to a variety of sensors used in modern avionics, including rate gyros, linear accelerometers, stick force sensors, surface position sensors, and air data sensors (e.g. static and dynamic pressures and temperature). Sensor sample rates are based on the bandwidth of the control loops using the measurements; typical values in flight control applications range from 10 - 100 Hz.

Traditionally, the performance of sensor management algorithms are evaluated using simulated sensor failures together with a detailed Failure Modes and Effects Analysis (FMEA) to tune design parameters and establish the correctness of the design. However, this approach cannot guarantee that the worst case combination of sensor inputs and conditions has been identified and that the design meets its performance and safety requirements under these conditions. In this study we will apply formal methods instead of extensive simulations to establish the correctness of the design.

2 Sensor Voter

Simulink [11] is a computer aided design tool widely used in the aerospace industry to design, simulate, and autocode software for avionics equipment. The Simulink diagram representing the sensor management algorithm (Figure 1) incorporates the typical attributes of a sensor management algorithm and is intended to illustrate the characteristics of such algorithms. The design is that of a generic triplex voter utilizing features appearing in the open literature. The voter takes inputs from three redundant sensors and synthesizes a single reliable sensor output. Each of the redundant sensors produces both a measured data value and self-check bit (validity flag) indicating whether or not the sensor considers itself to be operational. The output of a sensor is amplitude limited in hardware by the A/D conversion (+/-20 in the Simulink model). The functionality of the triplex voter is as follows:

1. Sample digitized signals of each sensor measurement at a fixed rate appropriate for the control loop, e.g. 20 Hz. A valid flag supplied by sensor hardware indicating its status is also sampled at the same rate.
2. Use the valid flag and comparison of redundant sensor measurements to detect and isolate failed sensors.
3. Output at a specified sample rate a signal value computed as a composite average of the signals of non-faulty sensors. Also output, at the same specified rate, the status of the composite output by setting an "outputValid" flag.
4. Tolerate "false alarms" due to noise, transients, and small differences in sensor measurements. Sensors are not marked failed if they are operating within acceptable tolerances and noise levels.

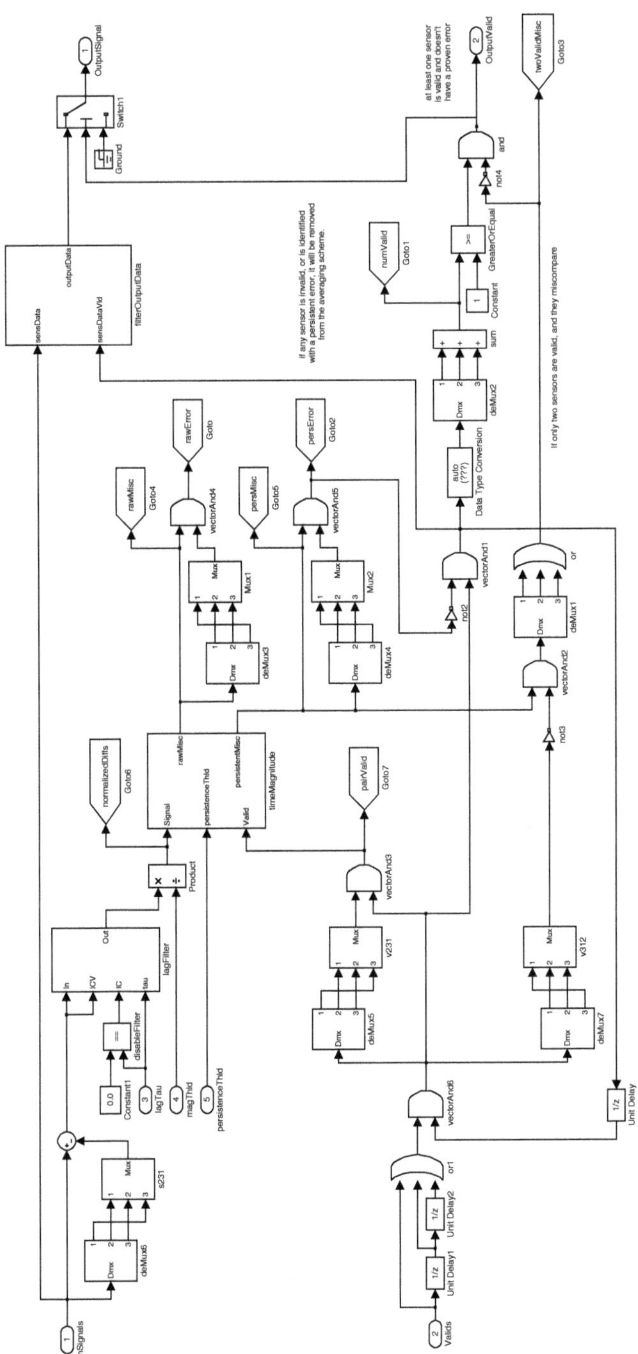

Fig. 1. Simulink diagram of the sensor voter

5. Maximize the availability of valid output by providing an output whenever possible, even with two failed sensors.
6. The algorithm is not required to deal with simultaneous sensor failures since this is a very low probability event.

Sensor faults can be any combination of sudden bias shifts, ramps, or oscillatory faults up to a maximum amplitude of 20. Oscillatory faults are often specifically defined. For this example, oscillatory sensor failures in the frequency range 3 - 7 Hz with amplitudes equal to or greater than 2 unit (zero to peak) should be detected in 1.5 second or less. In general, the "worst case" failure is unknown.

The operation of the sensor voter algorithm is as follows. All valid sensor signals are combined to produce the voter output. If three sensors are available, a weighted average is used in which an outlying sensor value is given less weight than those that are in closer agreement. If only two sensors are available a simple average is used. If only one sensor is available, it becomes the output.

There are two mechanisms whereby a faulty sensor may be detected and eliminated: comparison of the redundant sensor signals and monitoring of the validity flags produced by the sensors themselves.

The differences between each pair of the three input signals are initially computed; i.e., signal one is subtracted from signal two, signal two from signal three and signal three from signal one. These differences then pass through a limiter and a lag filter to remove unwanted noise. In our current version of the model the limiter and lag filter have been disabled since they have no effect given the range of inputs we are considering. Differences that exceed a given magnitude threshold cause a counter in the persistence threshold block to increment by one. Differences below the threshold cause the counter to decrement, but not below zero. When the counter reaches the persistence threshold for two of the pair differences, a persistent miscompare is detected and the sensor that is common to the two pairs is then eliminated from the output average computation.

If the hardware valid signal produced by a sensor is false for three consecutive samples, that sensor is considered to be faulty. The faulty sensor signal is not used in failure comparisons or in the computation of the output signal.

3 Requirements

Behavioral requirements for the sensor voter fall into two categories:

1. Computational, relating to the value of the output signal computed by the voter.
2. Fault handling, relating to the mechanisms for detecting and isolating sensor failures.

Each of these categories includes requirements for reliability (correctness under normal operation) and robustness (rejection of false alarms).

3.1 Computational Requirements

The main purpose of the sensor voter is to synthesize a reliable output that agrees with the "true" value of the environmental data measured by the redundant sensors. Therefore under normal operation, the output signal should agree with this true value within some small error threshold. In the absence of sensor noise or failures the two values should agree exactly. During the interval between the failure of a sensor and the detection of the failure by the voter, it is expected that the output value will deviate from the true value due to the continued inclusion of the failed sensor in the output average. During this reconfiguration interval the transient error in the output signal must remain within specified bounds, regardless of the type or magnitude of the failure.

The acceptable transient error has bounds in both magnitude and time, and is different for the first and second faults detected. The first failure transient must not exceed a magnitude of 0.1 with a duration of less than 0.15 seconds (corresponding to three sample periods at 20Hz). The second fault transient must not exceed 10 units with a duration of less than 0.5 seconds (10 samples). These bounds assume that the sensor inputs are limited to +/- 20 units (based on the A/D scaling).

3.2 Fault Handling Requirements

An important early step in our work was to elicit a precise specification for the fault handling behavior of the voter based on the informal description provided. This resulted in the fault handling state machine shown in Figure 2. Initially, all three sensors are assumed to be valid. One of these sensors may be eliminated due to either a false hardware valid signal from the sensor or a miscomparing sensor value, leading to the "2 valid" state. If one of the two remaining sensors sets its hardware valid signal false, it is eliminated leading to the "1 valid" state. If this sensor subsequently sets its valid flag false it is eliminated and the voter output is set to not valid.

A special situation occurs when there are two valid sensors. If these sensors miscompare, the voter cannot determine which may be faulty. Although there are other possibilities, this voter algorithm continues to keep both sensors in service but it sets its output valid flag false. If the sensors subsequently agree in value, the voter returns to the "2 valid, no miscompare" state and sets its output valid flag to true. Alternatively, if one of the two sensors identifies itself as faulty (via the hardware valid flag) it can be isolated by the voter and the other sensor signal used as the correct output value. If there are only two valid sensors and they have a persistent miscompare, neither sensor is used and the voter output valid flag is set to false. The output valid flag is also set to false if no sensors are valid. In these cases, the output signal is set arbitrarily to zero.

Robustness requirements apply to both the sensor signal comparisons and the hardware valid flags. No sensor is eliminated until it miscompares with others by a magnitude of at least 0.6 units for at least 0.5 seconds. In addition, any valid flags set to false must persist for three consecutive samples before the sensor is eliminated.

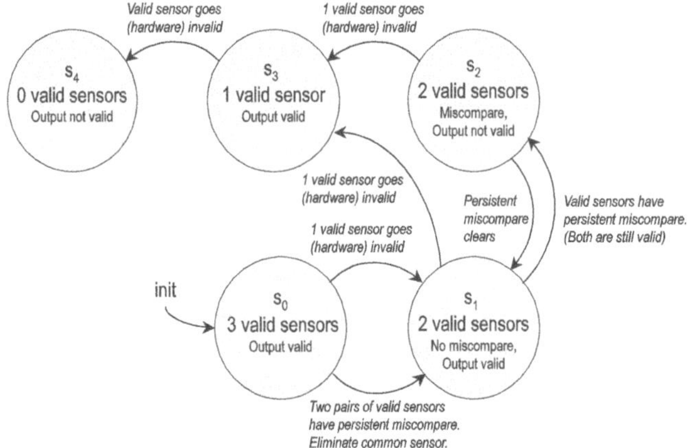

Fig. 2. Fault states of the sensor voter

4 Modeling the Voter and Its Environment

SMV is a symbolic model checker developed by CMU and was primarily developed with hardware verification problems in mind [6], [8]. While Simulink models are generally implemented in software (manually or using automatic code generation tools), the data flow block diagram representation resembles a hardware design. Therefore, it seems reasonable to apply SMV to this problem.

The SMV model we developed captures the design of the sensor voter by directly translating the Simulink diagram into SMV. Each Simulink block corresponds to an SMV module with the same inputs and outputs (Figure 3). As a result, the SMV representation is easy to understand and trace to the original Simulink representation. Furthermore, it should be possible to automate most of the translation process. We are aware of research tools such as sf2smv [9] and Checkmate [10] that have been developed to automatically translate Simulink models into SMV for model checking and representation of counterexamples. However, these tools address only limited portions of the Simulink syntax and were not applicable to our problem. Our concern in this project is not so much

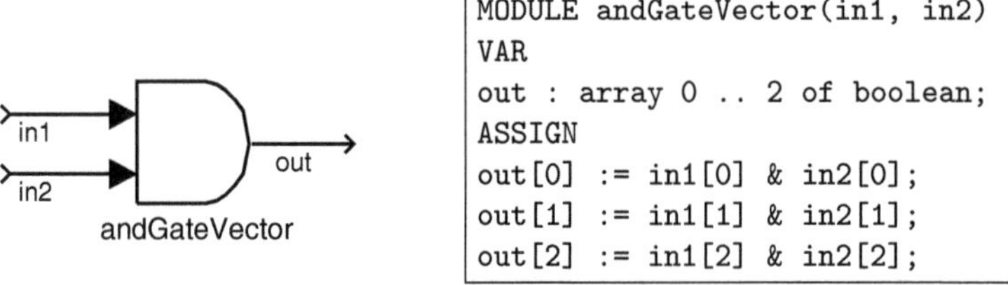


```
MODULE andGateVector(in1, in2)
VAR
out : array 0 .. 2 of boolean;
ASSIGN
out[0] := in1[0] & in2[0];
out[1] := in1[1] & in2[1];
out[2] := in1[2] & in2[2];
```

Fig. 3. Typical Simulink block translated to SMV module

the translation process, but the applicability of model checking to problems of this type.

4.1 Environment

The overall SMV model for verification of the sensor voter is shown in Figure 4. The model includes new modules that represent the environment driving the voter. These modules are the sensor modules and the world module.

The world module generates the data that sensors are to measure. In our current model it produces arbitrary data within the valid range, but it could easily be modified to produce data conforming to some frequency or derivative limitations.

The modules sensor1, sensor2, and sensor3 represent physical sensors that generate the measured signal and valid flags that are provided to the voter. These sensor modules are also used to inject faulty behavior to test the ability of the voter to identify and isolate failed sensors.

The sensorVoter module is the only part of the model corresponding to the real system we wish to analyze. It is implemented as two large modules and a number of small modules, following the hierarchical Simulink representation. Its outputSignal value can be compared to the data produced by the world module to evaluate the performance of the voter.

The distinction between the system under study (the voter) and its environment (the world and sensors) is an important one. To produce a convincing argument in support of certification, the voter should be modeled with the highest possible fidelity. Its structure should be traceable to the original design and it should conform as closely as possible to code generated from the design. It should include a minimal number of abstractions. On the other hand, the level of abstraction used in the environment must be carefully optimized. We must ensure that the environment will exercise all possible behaviors of the voter (including fault conditions) without introducing any unrealistic behaviors.

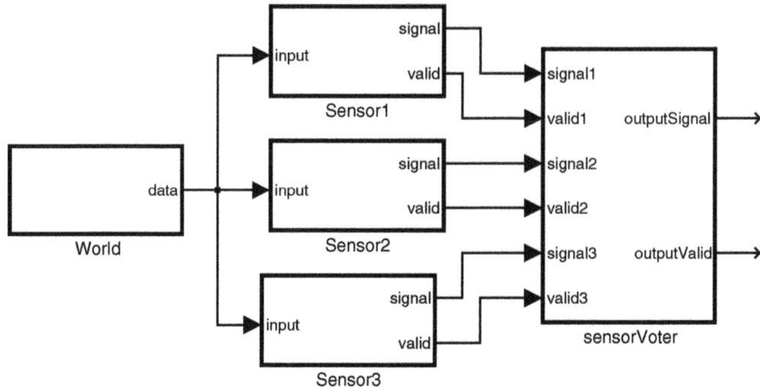

Fig. 4. SMV modules for the voter and environment

4.2 Assumptions and Simplifications

The following assumptions and simplifications have been made in modeling the sensor voter.

No Simultaneous Sensor Failures The algorithm assumes that two sensors cannot fail at the same time. In particular, the first sensor failure must be detected and isolated by the voter before it is able to respond to a second failure. This fault hypothesis is reasonable if sensor failures are independent so that the probability of simultaneous failures is sufficiently low.

We note that under this assumption the number of valid sensors plus the number of sensors declared faulty is more or less constant. That is, when a sensor becomes faulty this sum will temporarily increase by one (the number faulty increments) and when the fault is detected it will decrease by one (the number valid decrements).

This assumption was handled in the SMV model by using the INVAR declaration. The INVAR declaration specifies an invariant that every state in the transition system must satisfy, thus restricting the transition relation to only those states. The invariant used in our model is that the number of valid sensors plus the number of faulty sensors cannot be less than three nor greater than four.

The number of faulty sensors (numFaulty) is computed within the environment as sensors become faulty. However, the number of valid sensors (numValid) is computed within the voter and its correctness must be verified independently.

As we will see in the Analysis section, it turns out that the single fault hypothesis is not entirely valid when there are only two remaining sensors. An indefinitely long time period can elapse between the detection of a fault by miscomparing sensors and a subsequent isolation of the fault based on a hardware invalid flag.

Time Model The SMV model does not explicitly model time. Each execution step in the model corresponds to one sample in the Simulink design, independent of the actual sample rate. The only place where time enters into the model is a gain constant used in the "Time Magnitude" module. This constant serves to convert the number of time steps that a sensor miscompare persists into a time for comparison with the persistenceThreshold time. We have let this value be 1 and adjusted the persistenceThreshold accordingly so that all values will be integers.

Sensor Signals The sensor signals used in the voter design are floating point numbers in the range from -20 .. 20. The sensor signals in our initial SMV model are restricted to be integers. We have also limited the range to reduce the state space of the model during implementation and debugging.

4.3 Translation of Simulink to SMV

The SMV model contains three main modules: realWorld(), sensor(), and voting3Signals().

Module realWorld() This module takes no arguments and non-deterministically generates integer values in a fixed range $\{a..b\}$, currently $\{1, 2, 3\}$. We have selected comparison threshold parameters in the model so that this range is sufficient to trigger the fault detection functions in the voter. We have evaluated larger ranges of input values but with significant increase in verification time and no impact on the verification results.

Module sensor(world) This module takes the output of realWorld() for an argument and contains three internal variables, signal, valid, and fault. The variable fault is initialized to zero and thereafter is assigned nondeterministically any value between zero and two. A fault value of one means that the sensor's signal is faulty, at which point the sensor broadcasts an arbitrary value as signal. A fault value of two means that the hardware flag for the sensor became invalid, at which point the hardware flag takes an arbitrary value. Our model requires that once a sensor is faulty, whether in its signal or hardware flag, then it remains faulty. A non-faulty sensor passes the signal received from the world as well as a hardware flag of true. We do not currently permit a simultaneous hardware and signal failure.

Module voting3Signals() This module takes four arguments as input: an array of signals of all three sensors, array of hardware flags for all three sensors, and two constants defining fault thresholds. This module has several variables, most of which are instances of other modules. The variables' names preserve the name of the logic blocks in the Simulink Diagram, Figure 1.

5 Analysis

The requirements for the sensor voter have been translated to computation tree logic (CTL) specifications and analyzed using SMV. CTL is a temporal logic having connectives that refer to the future [7]. An initial set of specifications derived mostly from the fault handling requirements are discussed in this section, along with the analysis results. These specifications have been derived from the fault handling state machine in Figure 2 and specify what conditions can and cannot occur at any time. We also consider some specifications dealing with the validity of the computed output. Note that the variable names in the detailed specifications match the variable names in the Simulink diagram in Figure 1.

5.1 Fault Handling

We need to verify that faulty sensor detection and elimination is final. The following SMV SPECS verify this desired property.

Three Valid Sensors Given three valid sensors, once a sensor is detected and isolated based either on a hardware fault or persistent miscompare then this isolation is final.

SPEC
`AG(sensorVoter.numValid` $= 2 \rightarrow \neg$ `EFsensorVoter.numValid` $= 3$`)`

This SPEC is true. It states that it is globally true that if the number of valid sensors is two then there is no execution path in which that number may become three again, i.e. once a sensor is eliminated, then it stays eliminated.

Two Valid Sensors A similar SPEC portrays that the same argument holds when only two sensors are valid.

SPEC
`AG(sensorVoter.numValid` $= 1 \rightarrow \neg$ `EFsensorVoter.numValid` ≥ 2`)`

This SPEC is true and states that it is globally true that there is no execution path where the number of valid sensors changes from one to two or more valid sensors.

One Valid Sensor Given only one valid sensor, we need to verify that should this sensor fail then it cannot recover.

SPEC
`AG(sensorVoter.numValid` $= 0 \rightarrow \neg$ `EF sensorVoter.numValid` ≥ 1`)`

This specification is true and states that it is globally true that there is no execution path where the number of valid sensors changes from zero to a number larger than zero. The above set of specifications for the fault handling behavior of the voter was verified to be true using SMV. However, all the specifications described so far do not take into consideration the specific error conditions that trigger the particular fault states. A general specification pattern that would cover each of the state transitions in Figure 2 could be of the form:

SPEC
`AG((state`$_i$ $\wedge$ `errorCondition)` $\rightarrow$ `AF(state`$_j$ `))`

That is, in state$_i$ the occurrence of errorCondition must eventually lead to state$_j$. For example, when there are three valid sensors the occurrence of an invalid sensor flag must cause the voter to eliminate the sensor and go to the two valid sensors state.

Let $\mathcal{V} = (\mathcal{S}, \delta, \mathcal{F})$ be the sensor voter model, where $\mathcal{S}$ is the set of states the sensor voter can be in as shown in the fault-handling FSM in Figure 2, δ is a transition relation, and $\mathcal{F} = \{f_0, f_1, f_2, f_3, f_4, f_5\}$ is the set of possible error conditions. f_0 is no sensor failure, f_1 is the first sensor failure, f_2 is the second sensor failure, f_3 is three sensor failures, f_4 is two miscomparing sensors that return to agreement, and f_5 is a subsequent sensor failure after two remaining sensors miscompare. The transition relation $\delta : \mathcal{S} \times \mathcal{F} \rightarrow \mathcal{S}$ follows Figure 2.

To be more specific, we would like to able to show that

1. AG(($s_0 \wedge f_1$) $\rightarrow$ AF s_1),where $s_0, s_1 \in \mathcal{S}$,and $f_1 \in \mathcal{F}$
2. AG(($s_1 \wedge f_2$) $\rightarrow$ AF ($s_2 \vee s_3$)),where $s_1, s_2 \in \mathcal{S}$,and $f_2 \in \mathcal{F}$
3. AG(($s_2 \wedge f_4$) $\rightarrow$ EF s_1),where $s_2, s_1 \in \mathcal{S}$,and $f_4 \in \mathcal{F}$
4. AG(($s_2 \wedge f_5$) $\rightarrow$ EF s_3),where $s_2, s_3 \in \mathcal{S}$,and $f_5 \in \mathcal{F}$
5. AG(($s_3 \wedge f_3$) $\rightarrow$ AF s_4),where $s_3, s_4 \in \mathcal{S}$,and $f_3 \in \mathcal{F}$

We tested AG(($s_0 \wedge f_1$) $\rightarrow$ AF s_1), where $s_0, s_1 \in \mathcal{S}$,and $f_1 \in \mathcal{F}$ as follows:

SPEC
AG((sensorVoter.numValid $= 3\wedge$ sensorVoter.outputValid $\wedge f_1$) $\rightarrow$
AF (sensorVoter.numValid = 2 $\wedge$ sensorVoter.outputValid)) where
f_1=(sensor1.fault $\neq$ 0 $\wedge$ sensor2.fault = 0 $\wedge$ sensor3.fault =0) $\vee$
(sensor1.fault=0 $\wedge$ sensor2.fault $\neq$ 0 $\wedge$ sensor3.fault=0) $\vee$
(sensor1.fault=0 $\wedge$ sensor2.fault=0 $\wedge$ sensor3.fault $\neq$ 0).

The choices we made in modeling the environment driving the voter allow this specification to be violated, and a counterexample was identified by SMV. In particular, it was possible in the model for a faulty sensor to never exhibit any observable faulty behavior. After we modified the sensor model to eliminate this possibility, the above SPEC was proved.

Similarly we tested the specification AG(($s_1 \wedge f_2$) $\rightarrow$ AF ($s_2 \vee s_3$)),where $s_1, s_2, s_3 \in \mathcal{S}$,and $f_2 \in \mathcal{F}$ as follows:

SPEC
AG((sensorVoter.numValid $= 2\wedge$ sensorVoter.outputValid $\wedge f_2$ $\rightarrow$
AF((sensorVoter.outputValid $\wedge$ numValid = 1)
$\vee$(!sensorVoter.outputValid $\wedge$ numValid = 2)) where
f_2=(sensor1.fault $\neq$ 0 $\wedge$ sensor2.fault $\neq$ 0 $\wedge$ sensor3.fault =0) $\vee$
(sensor1.fault=0 $\wedge$ sensor2.fault $\neq$ 0 $\wedge$ sensor3.fault $\neq$ 0) $\vee$
(sensor1.fault $\neq$0 $\wedge$ sensor2.fault=0 $\wedge$ sensor3.fault $\neq$ 0).

This specification addresses two situations, the first being when the second sensor failure results in a hardware invalid flag (s_3 is reached), and the other being when the second sensor deviates in signal (s_2 is reached). Testing AG(($s_1 \wedge f_2$) $\rightarrow$ AF (s_3)) yields false; the counterexample, as expected, corresponds to $\delta(s_1, f_2) = s_2$. The state s_2 is quite interesting because it handles the situation in which two sensors miscompare and both sensors have valid hardware flags. In our voter design the number of valid sensors changes from two to one only if one of the two remaining valid sensors has a hardware invalid flag. If, on the other hand, the two valid sensors deviate in signal, then their output is declared invalid, but the two sensors remain in service. These two sensors may agree at a later point in time or the faulty sensor may identify itself via the hardware valid flag and be isolated by the voter.

The specification AG(($s_2 \wedge f_4$) $\rightarrow$ EF s_1) investigates if it is possible for two miscomparing sensors with invalid output to agree in signal and produce valid output. We were able to verify that this specification is correct; the detailed SPEC is below:

SPEC
AG((sensorVoter.numValid = 2 $\wedge \neg$ sensorVoter.outputValid) $\rightarrow$
EF (sensorVoter.numValid = 2 $\wedge$ sensorVoter.outputValid))
The choice of AG(($s_2 \wedge f_4$) $\rightarrow$ EF s_1) and not AG(($s_2 \wedge f_4$) $\rightarrow$ AF s_1) is because we want to verify that s_1 is reachable from s_2 in certain execution paths and not all execution paths.

We use the specification AG(($s_2 \wedge f_5$)$\rightarrow$ EF s_3) to investigate whether s_3 is reachable from s_2 in certain, not all, execution paths. However, an interesting result shows up while testing AG(($s_2 \wedge f_5$) $\rightarrow$ EF s_3) because our second invariant does not allow us to transition from s_2 to s_3.

The following specification produces a counterexample.

SPEC
AG((sensorVoter.numValid = 2 $\wedge \neg$ sensorVoter.outputValid) $\rightarrow$
EF (sensorVoter.numValid = 1 $\wedge$ sensorVoter.outputValid))

The error produced is the following: Sensor1 becomes faulty, miscompares with sensors 2 and 3 and is eliminated. Sensor2 then becomes faulty and miscompares with sensor3 causing outputValid to become false. At this point, numValid + numFaulty = 4. To transition from the current state, we need one of the sensors to produce a hardware invalid flag. However, this is not permitted by our INVAR assumption because the sensor2 fault has not yet been isolated. Further refinements are required to accurately capture the desired fault hypothesis.

5.2 Computation of Output

Our work so far has concentrated on verification of the fault-handling requirements of the voter. We are currently working on verification of the requirements for the voter output signal. The following discussion covers some of the relevant specifications that we are analyzing.

Output Signal The algorithm is required to correctly compute the output signal. The specification below attempts, though weakly, to capture the correctness of this requirement.

SPEC
AG(sensorVoter.outputSignal.out $\neq$ world.out $\rightarrow$
AF (A[sensorVoter.outputSignal.out $\neq$ world.out U
(sensorVoter.outputSignal.out = world.out $\wedge$
sensorVoter.outputValid)] $\vee$ (sensorVoter.outputSignal.out $\neq$
world.out)))

This specification states that when the output signal of the sensors is different than the environment's signal, then either the sensors will eventually stabilize by voting the faulty sensor or it may be the case that the output will never stabilize.

Output Signal Bounds It should always be the case that when the voter outputValid is true, then the voter outputSignal should be within a set error tolerance of the true world value. This tolerance will be a function of the noise introduced by the sensor model and any fault conditions introduced. With no noise and no faults they should agree exactly. The desired specification will be of the form:

SPEC
`AG(sensorVoter.outputValid` $\rightarrow$
$|$ `world.data - sensorVoter.outputSignal` $|$ $<$ `errorThresh)`

Output Transient Bounds The requirements bounding the difference between the voter output and the true signal during a transient are based on establishing a time window around the transient.

The first and second transients should satisfy the following specifications:

SPEC `--first transient`
`AG(sensorVoter.numValid` $=$ `3` $\rightarrow$ `transient.timer` $<$ `3)` was verified to be true.

SPEC `--second transient`
`AG(sensorVoter.numValid` $=$ `2` $\rightarrow$ `transient.timer` $<$ `10)`

This second specification resulted in a counterexample because the number of valid sensors is two in states s_1 and s_2 and it is possible to stay indefinitely in state s_2. Recall that s_2 is the state of invalid output because one of the two valid sensors has deviated in signal and thus the output signal of the voter is different from the true signal of the world.

5.3 Performance

The fault handling specifications typically required 20 Mbytes of memory and approximately 1000 seconds to verify. Detecting the counterexample to the second output transient specification took approximately 14000 seconds and required 30 Mbytes of memory.

6 Conclusion

Our future plans in this study include the following work:

1. Increasing the signal range and checking the specifications using a magnitude threshold greater than 1. We will assess the relationship between the signal range and the performance of the model checker (state space, analysis time).

2. Analysis of additional specifications of the voter behavior and refinement of the environment model.
3. We are also researching automation of the translation process to generate an SMV model from a Simulink model. Wide spread and practical use of model checking in this domain will require automation of this sort.
4. In addition, we plan to use other model checking tools to examine the correctness of the sensor voter algorithm.

References

[1] P. Kurzhals, et al, “Integrity in Electronic Flight Control Systems”, AGARDograph No. 224, April 1977. (available through National Technical Information Service, Springfield, VA) 35

[2] T. Cunningham, et al, “Fault Tolerance Design and Redundancy Management Techniques”, NATO AGARD Lecture Series No. 109. Sept 1980. (available through National Technical Information Service, Springfield, VA) see especially Chapter 3: Computer Based In-flight Monitoring; Chapter 7: Failure Management for Saab Viggen JA-37 Aircraft; Chapter 8: Flight Experience with Flight Control Redundancy Management 35

[3] G. Belcher, D. McIver and K. Szalai, “Validation of Flight Critical Control Systems”, AGARD Advisory Report No. 274, Dec 1991. (available through National Technical Information Service, Springfield, VA) 35

[4] S. Osder, “Practical View of Redundancy Management Application and Theory”, Journal of Guidance and Control, Vol. 22 No. 1 , Jan-Feb 1999. 35

[5] R. P. G. Collinson, Introduction to Avionics, Chapman & Hall, London, 1998. 35

[6] K. McMillan, Symbolic Model Checking , Kluwer Academic Publishers, Boston, Dordrecht, London, 1993. 40

[7] Micheal R A Huth and Mark D Ryan, Logic in Computer Science Modelling and reasoning about systems, University Press, Cambridge, United Kingdom, 2000. 43

[8] SMV web page: `http://www-2.cs.cmu.edu/ modelcheck` 40

[9] sf2smv web page: `http://www.ece.cmu.edu/ webk/sf2smv` 40

[10] Checkmate web page: `http://www.ece.cmu.edu/ webk/checkmate` 40

[11] Simulink weg page: `http://www.mathworks.com/products/simulink` 36

Distributed Explicit Fair Cycle Detection (Set Based Approach)

Ivana Černá and Radek Pelánek*

Department of Computer Science, Faculty of Informatics
Masaryk University Brno, Czech Republic
{cerna,xpelanek}@fi.muni.cz

Abstract. The fair cycle detection problem is at the heart of both LTL and fair CTL model checking. This paper presents a new distributed scalable algorithm for explicit fair cycle detection. Our method combines the simplicity of the distribution of explicitly presented data structure and the features of symbolic algorithm allowing for an efficient parallelisation. If a fair cycle (i.e. counterexample) is detected, then the algorithm produces a cycle, which is in general shorter than that produced by depth-first search based algorithms. Experimental results confirm that our approach outperforms that based on a direct implementation of the best sequential algorithm.

1 Introduction

The fair cycle detection problem is at the heart of many problems, namely in deciding emptiness of ω-automata like generalised Büchi and Streett automata, and in model checking of specifications written in linear and branching temporal logics like LTL and fair CTL.

A generalised Büchi automaton [10] is provided together with several sets of accepting states. A run of such an automaton is accepting if it contains at least one state from every accepting set infinitely often. Accordingly, the language of the automaton is nonempty if and only if the graph corresponding to the automaton contains a reachable *fair cycle*, that is a cycle containing at least one state from every accepting set, or equivalently a reachable *fair strongly connected component*, that is a nontrivial strongly connected component (SCC) that intersects each accepting set. The acceptance condition for Streett automata [34] is more involved and consists of pairs of state sets. The language of the automaton is nonempty if and only if the automaton graph contains a cycle such that for every pair of sets whenever the cycle intersects the first set of the pair then it intersects also the second set. The nonemptiness check for Streett automata can thus be also based on identification of the fair SCCs of the automaton graph. Other types of automata for which the nonemptiness check is based on identification of fair cycles are listed in [15].

* Supported by GA ČR grant no. 201/00/1023.

T. Ball and S.K. Rajamani (Eds.): SPIN 2003, LNCS 2648, pp. 49–73, 2003.

The LTL model checking problem and the LTL model checking with strong fairness (compassion) reduce to language emptiness checking of generalised Büchi automata and Streett automata respectively [36, 26]. Fair cycle detection is used to check the CTL formula **EG**f under the full (generalised) fairness constraints [15]. Hence, the core procedure in many model checking algorithms is the fair cycle detection. These algorithms are in common use in explicit and symbolic LTL model checkers such as SPIN [22] and SMV [29] respectively, in fair-CTL model checkers such as SMV, VIS [7], and COSPAN [19].

Despite the developments in recent years, the main drawbacks of model checking tools are their high space requirements that still limit their applicability. Distributed model checking tackles with the space explosion problem by exploiting the amount of resources provided by parallel environment. Powerful parallel computers can be build of Networks Of Workstations (NOW). Thanks to various message passing interfaces (e.g., PVM, MPI) a NOW appears from the outside as a single parallel computer with a huge amount of memory.

Reports by several independent groups ([33, 28, 17, 4, 3]) have confirmed the usefulness of distributed algorithms for the state-space generation and reachability analysis. Methods for distributing LTL and CTL model checking have been presented in [1, 2, 8] and [6] respectively. However, until today not much effort has been taken to consider distributed algorithms for fair cycle detection. In our search for an effective distributed algorithm let us first discuss diverse sequential algorithms for fair cycle detection.

In *explicit algorithms* the states of a graph are represented individually. The decomposition of the graph into SCC can be solved in linear time by the Tarjan algorithm [35]. With the use of this decomposition it is easy to determine fair components and hence our problem has linear time complexity. Moreover, the nested depth-first search algorithm [23] (NESTEDDFS) optimises the memory requirements and is able to detect cycles *on-the-fly*. This makes NESTEDDFS the optimal sequential algorithm.

The explicit representation allows for a direct distribution of the state space. States of the graph are distributed over particular computers in NOW and are processed in parallel. When necessary, messages about individual states are passed to the neighbour computers. However, the depth-first search crucially depends on the order in which vertices are visited and the problem of depth-first search order is P-complete [31]. Therefore it is considered to be inherently sequential and we cannot hope for its good parallelisation (unless NC equals P).

Symbolic algorithms represent sets of states via their characteristic function, typically with binary decision diagrams (BDDs) [9, 13], and operate on entire sets rather than on individual states. This makes the depth-first approach inapplicable and symbolic algorithms typically rely on the breadth-first search (for surveys see [16, 30]). Unfortunately, the time complexity of symbolic algorithms is not linear; the algorithms contain a doubly-nested fixpoint operator, hence require time quadratic in the size of the graph in the worst case. The main advantage of symbolic algorithms over their explicit counterpart is the fact that BDDs provide a more compact representation of the state space capturing some of the regularity in the space and allow to verify systems with extremely large number of states, many orders of magnitude larger than could be handled by the explicit algorithms [11]. Nevertheless, there are applications where explicit model checkers outperform the others, for examples see [33, 24, 25, 14]

Thank to the fact that symbolic algorithms search the graph in a manner where the order in which vertices are visited is not crucial, these algorithms are directly parallelizable. On the other hand, the distribution of the BDD data structure is rather complicated. A parallel reachability BDD-based algorithm in [20] partitions the set of states into slices owned by particular processes. However, the state space has to be dynamically repartitioned to achieve the memory balance and the method requires passing large BDDs between processes, both for sending non-owned states to their owners and for balancing. This causes a significant overhead.

Bearing all the reported arguments in mind we have tried to set down a parallel algorithm for fair cycle detection combining advantages of both explicit and symbolic approach. Our algorithm is in its nature explicit as the states are represented individually. The state space is well distributable and the parallel computation needs to communicate only information about individual states. The way how the algorithm computes resembles that of symbolic algorithms and thus allows for a good parallelisation of the computation alone.

Since our algorithm is based on symbolic ones, its worst-case complexity is $O(n \cdot h)$ where h is the height of the SCC quotient graph. Previous experiments ([16]) clearly show that this height is in practice very small and thus the algorithm is nearly linear. This observation has been confirmed also by our experiments.

The proposed algorithm is not on-the-fly and the whole state space has to be generated. For this reason the algorithm is meant not to replace but to complement the depth-first search based algorithms used in LTL model checking. The depth-first search based algorithms are of help before spacing out the available memory. On the other hand, our algorithm performs better in cases when the whole state space has to be searched. This distinction has been confirmed also by our initial performance evaluation using several protocols. Our algorithm outperforms that based on a direct implementation of the best sequential algorithm in a distributed environment especially in cases, when a fair cycle is not detected.

In model checking applications, the existence of a fair cycle indicates a failure of the property. In such a case, it is essential that the user is given a fair cycle as a *counterexample*, typically presented in the form of a finite stem followed by a cycle. The counterexample should be as short as possible, to facilitate debugging. Finding the shortest counterexample, however, is NP-complete [21]. The great advantage of our approach is that thanks to the breadth-first search character of the computation the computed fair cycle (counterexample) is very short in comparison with those computed by a depth-first search based algorithm.

Last but not least, we would like to emphasis that the algorithm is compatible with other state-space saving techniques used in LTL model checking. Namely, the algorithm can be applied together with static partial order reduction [27].

Plan of the work Section 2 reviews basic notions and explains the basics of symbolic fair cycle detection algorithms. In Section 3 a new sequential explicit fair cycle detection algorithm is presented together with the proof of its correctness and the analysis of its complexity. The distributed version of the algorithm is described in Section 4. Modifications of the algorithm allowing for a fair cycle detection for generalised Büchi and Streett automata and a simplification for weak ω-automata are presented in Section 5. Section 6 presents experimental results on real examples and compares the performance of our algorithm to a distributed implementation of the best sequential algorithm. Section 7 concludes.

2 Fair Cycle Detection Problem

A directed graph is a pair $G = (V, E)$, where V is a finite set of *states* and $E \subseteq V \times V$ is a set of *edges*. A *path* from $s_1 \in V$ to $s_k \in V$ is a sequence $(s_1, \ldots, s_k) \in V^+$ such that $(s_i, s_{i+1}) \in E$ for $1 \leq i < k$. A *cycle* is a path from a state s to itself. We say that a state r (a cycle c) is *reachable* from a state s if there exists a path from s to r (to a state r on the cycle c). Moreover, every state is reachable from itself. Given a state set U, the graph $G(U) = (U, E \cap (U \times U))$ is the graph *induced* by U.

A *strongly connected component* (SCC) of G is a maximal set of states $C \subseteq V$ such that for each $u, v \in C$, the state v is reachable from u and vice versa. The *quotient graph* of G is a graph (W, H), such that W is the set of the SCCs of G and $(C_1, C_2) \in H$ if and only if $C_1 \neq C_2$ and there exist $r \in C_1, s \in C_2$ such that $(r, s) \in E$. The *height* of the graph G is the length of the longest path in the quotient graph of G (note that the quotient graph is acyclic).

A strongly connected component C is a *trivial* component if $G(C)$ has no edges and *initial* if it is the source of the quotient graph. Let $F \subseteq V$ be a set of *fair states*. An SCC C is a *fair* component if it is nontrivial and $C \cap F \neq \emptyset$. A cycle is *fair* if it contains a fair state.

The *fair cycle detection problem* is to decide, for a given graph G with a distinguished initial state *init_state* and a set of fair states F, whether G contains a fair cycle reachable from the initial state. In the positive case a fair cycle should be provided.

Our goal is to bring in an algorithm for the fair cycle detection problem that is not based on a depth-first search and thus enables effective distribution. Here we take an inspiration in symbolic algorithms for cycle detection, namely in SCC hull algorithms. These algorithms compute the set of states that contains all fair components. Algorithms maintain the approximation of the set and successively remove unfair components until they reach a fixpoint. Different strategies of removal of unfair components lead to different algorithms. An overview, taxonomy, and comparison of symbolic algorithms can be found in independent reports by Fisler at al. [16] and Ravi at al. [30]. As the base for our algorithm we have chosen the *One Way Catch Them Young* algorithm [16]. The reasons for this choice are discussed at the beginning of Section 4.1.

Symbolic algorithms are conveniently described with the help of μ-caluculus formulae. Our algorithm makes use of the following two functions:

$$Reachability(S) = \mu Z.(S \cup image(Z))$$
$$Elimination(S) = \nu Z.(S \cap image(Z))$$

The set $image(Z)$ contains all successors of states from Z in the graph G. The function $Reachability(S)$ computes the set of all states that are reachable from the set S. The function $Elimination(S)$ computes the set of all states q for which either q lies on a cycle in S or q is reachable from a cycle in S along a path that lies in S. The computation of $Elimination(S)$ is performed by successive removal of states that do not have predecessors in S. With the help of these functions the algorithm *One Way Catch Them Young* can be formulated as follows:

```
proc OWCTY(G, F, init_state)
  S := Reachability(init_state);
  old := ∅;
  while (S ≠ old) do
        old := S;
        S := Reachability(S ∩ F);
        S := Elimination(S);
  od
  return (S ≠ ∅);
end
```

The assignment $S := Reachability(S \cap F)$ removes from the set S all initial components of $G(S)$, which do not contain any fair state (in fact only SCCs reachable from a fair component are left in S). The assignment $S := Elimination(S)$ removes from the set S all initial trivial components (besides others). Thus each iteration of the **while** cycle (so called *external iteration*) removes initial unfair components of $G(S)$ until the fixpoint is reached.

The worst-case complexity of the algorithm is $O(n^2)$ steps[1] or more precisely $O(h \cdot n)$), where n is the number of states of the graph and h is the height of G. However, numerous experiments show that the number of external iterations tends to be very low and hence the number of steps is practically linear [16].

3 Sequential Algorithm

In this section we present a new sequential explicit algorithm that computes a hull, that is, a set of states that contains all fair components in a way which resembles the set based algorithm *One Way Catch Them Young*. In the second part an algorithm enumerating a fair cycle is introduced. The correctness of both algorithms is proved, and their complexity is analysed. The distributed version of the algorithm is given in the next section.

[1] The complexity of symbolic algorithms is usually measured in number of steps (*image* computations), since the real complexity depends on the conciseness of the BDD representation.

3.1 Detection of a Fair Cycle

The explicit algorithm DETECT-CYCLE emulates the behaviour of the OWCTY algorithm. The set S is represented explicitly. For each state q the information whether q is in the set S is stored in boolean array *inS*. The emulation of the intersection operation and the *Reachability*(S) function is straightforward (see the procedures RESET and REACHABILITY respectively). The emulation of *Elimination*(S) is more involved: concurrently with the emulation of *Reachability*(S) we count for each state q the number of its predecessors belonging to the set S (array p). On top of that we keep the list L of vertices, which have no predecessors in S, that is, those for which $p[q] = 0$. These vertices are eliminated from S in the procedure ELIMINATION. Data structures used by the algorithm and their initial settings are:

Sequential algorithm for fair cycle detection

```
proc DETECT-CYCLE(G, F, init_state)
  put init_state into queue;
  inS[init_state] := true;
  REACHABILITY;
  while (Ssize ≠ oldSsize ∧ Ssize > 0) do
        RESET;
        REACHABILITY;
        ELIMINATION;
  od
  return(Ssize > 0);
end
```

```
proc RESET
  oldSsize := Ssize;
  Ssize := 0;
  foreach q ∈ V do
    inS[q] := inS[q] ∧ q ∈ F;
    p[q] := 0;
    if inS[q] then Ssize := Ssize + 1;
                   put q in queue;
                   put q in L; fi
  od
end
```

```
proc REACHABILITY
  while queue ≠ ∅ do
        remove q from queue;
        foreach (q, r) ∈ E do
          if (¬inS[r]) then inS[q] := true;
                            Ssize := Ssize + 1;
                            put r in queue; fi
          if p[r] = 0 then remove r from L; fi
          p[r] := p[r] + 1;
        od
  od
end
```

```
proc ELIMINATION
  while L ≠ ∅ do
        remove q from L;
        inS[q] := false;
        Ssize := Ssize − 1;
        foreach (q, r) ∈ E do
           p[r] := p[r] − 1;
           if p[r] = 0 then put r to L fi
        od
  od
end
```

- *inS* is a boolean array and is set to *false* for each state.
- p is an integer array and is set to 0 for each state.
- L is a list of states, initially empty. L is implemented as doubly linked list, hence all necessary operations (insertion, deletion, and removal of a state) can be performed in constant time.
- *Ssize* and *oldSsize* are number variables initially set to 1 and 0 respectively.
- *queue* is an initially empty queue.

Correctness

In what follows we denote S the set of states q such that $inS[q] = true$ and particularly S_l^i the set of states q such that $inS[q] = true$ just before the i-th execution of the line l in DETECT-CYCLE ($l = 6, 7, 8$). Arguments are presented in the manner, which allows their transfer to the distributed algorithm.

Lemma 1. *At the end of* REACHABILITY *the set S is the set of states that are reachable from states which were in the queue at the beginning of the procedure.*

Proof: Whenever the procedure REACHABILITY is called, the *queue* contains exactly all the states for which $inS[q] = true$. REACHABILITY performs the standard breadth-first search and empties the *queue*.

Lemma 2. *The invariant $q \in L \Rightarrow (q \in S \wedge p[q] = 0)$ holds true during the whole computation of* DETECT-CYCLE.

Proof: Only states r with $p[r] = 0$ are put in L in ELIMINATION and RESET. To show $L \subseteq S$ we notice that $queue = S = L$ at the end of RESET and S is the set of states reachable from L at the end of REACHABILITY (Lemma 1). Only states reachable from L are put to L in ELIMINATION but those states are already in S.

Lemma 3. *Immediately after executing* RESET, REACHABILITY *and* ELIMINATION *respectively, the value of Ssize is the size of the set S.*

Proof: Whenever a new state q is added to S in REACHABILITY the variable *Ssize* is changed accordingly. In RESET only those states which are kept in S are counted. Correctness for ELIMINATION follows from the inclusion $L \subseteq S$ (Lemma 2).

Lemma 4. *Immediately after executing* Reachability *and* Elimination *respectively, the value of $p[q]$ is the number of those direct predecessors of the state q, which belong to S.*

Proof: Whenever a state r is attained in Reachability the value $p[r]$ is updated. Whenever a state is deleted from S in Elimination all its direct successors are visited and their respective values are updated.

On the other side, the value of $p[r]$ is changed only when some of its direct predecessors is added to/removed from *queue* (Lemma 2).

Lemma 5. *During one execution of the procedure* Reachability *each state is inserted to and deleted from the queue at most once. During one execution of the procedure* Elimination *each state is removed from L at most once.*

Proof: No state is removed from S in Reachability. Moreover, $q \in queue \Rightarrow q \in S$ and the state q is added to *queue* only if $q \notin S$.

The assertion for Elimination follows from Lemma 2 and the fact that states are removed simultaneously both from L and S.

Lemma 6.
- $S^i_7 = S^i_6 \cap F$.
- S^i_8 *is the set of states reachable from the set* S^i_7.
- S^{i+1}_6 *is the set of all states q for which either q lies on a cycle in $G(S^i_8)$ or q is reachable in $G(S^i_8)$ from a cycle in $G(S^i_8)$.*

Proof: The first equality follows directly from the code of the procedure Reset.

The second fact is a direct consequence of Lemma 1, because the content of *queue* at the beginning of Reachability is S^i_7.

By Lemma 4, value $p[q]$ is the number of direct predecessors of q in $G(S^i_8)$ and only states with none predecessors are removed from S in Elimination. Therefore all states with the required property are in S^{i+1}_6. On the other hand, all predecessors of the state q not satisfying the condition will eventually be removed (this can be formalised by induction on the length of the longest chain of predecessor of a given state), hence eventually $p[q]$ is set to 0, the state q is put in L and removed from the set S afterwards.

Lemma 7. $S^{i+1}_6 \subseteq S^i_6$

Proof: The assertion can be proved by induction on i. For the base case $i = 1$ we argue that S^1_6 is the set of all states reachable from *init_state* and all the states put in S in Reachability (line 7) are reachable from *init_state* and thus $S^2_6 \subseteq S^1_6$.

For the general case we suppose $S^{i+1}_6 \subseteq S^i_6$. Then we can reason with the use of Lemma 6 as follows: $(S^{i+1}_6 \subseteq S^i_6) \Rightarrow (S^{i+1}_6 \cap F \subseteq S^i_6 \cap F) \Rightarrow (S^{i+1}_7 \subseteq S^i_7) \Rightarrow$ each state reachable from S^{i+1}_7 is reachable from S^i_7 as well $\Rightarrow (S^{i+1}_8 \subseteq S^i_8) \Rightarrow$ each state that lies on (or is reachable from) a cycle in S^{i+1}_8 lies on (or is reachable from) a cycle in S^i_8 as well $\Rightarrow (S^{i+2}_6 \subseteq S^{i+1}_6)$.

Theorem 1 (Termination). *The* DETECT-CYCLE *algorithm terminates.*

Proof: The termination of REACHABILITY and ELIMINATION follows from Lemma 5. The termination of RESET is straightforward.

By Lemma 7, $S_6^{i+1} \subseteq S_6^i$ which together with Lemma 3 ensures that the condition on line 5 eventually becomes false and DETECT-CYCLE terminates as well.

Theorem 2 (Completeness). *If G contains a fair cycle reachable from the init_state then* DETECT-CYCLE *returns true.*

Proof: Let C be a fair cycle in G and q a fair state that lies on the cycle C. We prove by induction on i that $q \in S_6^i$. For the base case $i = 1$ we argue that S_6^1 is the set of states reachable from *init_state* and thus $q \in S_6^1$.

Now let $q \in S_6^i$. By Lemma 6, $q \in S_7^i$. The state q as well as all the states reachable from q belong to S_8^i. Namely, the whole cycle C belongs to S_8^i and by Lemma 6 cycle C belongs also to the set S_6^{i+1}.

Hence after executing the **while** loop the state q belongs to S, therefore *Ssize* > 0 (Lemma 3) and DETECT-CYCLE returns true.

Theorem 3 (Soundness). *If* DETECT-CYCLE *returns true, then G contains a fair cycle reachable from the init_state.*

Proof: Let us suppose that DETECT-CYCLE terminates after k iterations of the **while** cycle. Since the algorithm returns *true*, *Ssize* > 0, $S_6^k = S_6^{k-1}$ and S_6^k is nonempty (Lemma 3 and 7).

Let us consider the decomposition of S_6^k into SCCs. Let C be the initial component. We demonstrate that C is fair (that is, C contains a fair state and is nontrivial). This implies the assertion of the theorem.

Let us suppose that $C \cap F = \emptyset$. The set S_8^{k-1} contains only states reachable from $S_6^{k-1} \cap F = S_6^k \cap F$ and because C is initial no state from C is in S_8^{k-1}. Consequently C is not contained in S_6^k (Lemma 6), a contradiction.

If the component C were trivial, it would be removed from the set $S_6^k = S_6^{k-1}$ by the procedure ELIMINATION due to Lemma 6.

Theorem 4 (Complexity). *The worst-case complexity of the algorithm* DETECT-CYCLE *is $O(h \cdot (n + m))$, where n is the number of states in G, m is the number of edges in G, and h is the height of G.*

Proof: The complexity of the procedure RESET is $O(n)$. Both REACHABILITY and ELI- MINATION procedures have complexity $O(m)$ (Lemma 5). Thus it remains to show that the **while** loop in DETECT-CYCLE can iterate at most h times.

For a graph H, let us denote by h_u the length of the longest path in the quotient graph of H starting in an initial unfair component (the unfair height of H). By induction on i we prove that the unfair height of $G(S_i^6)$ is at most

$h - i + 1$. The assertion clearly holds for $i = 1$ as $h_u \leq h$. For the induction step we note that by Lemma 6 in the i-th iteration of the **while** cycle all initial unfair components of S_i^6 are removed from S_i^6. This claim together with the observations that all SCCs of S_{i+1}^6 are also SCCs in S_i^6 and the quotient graph of S_{i+1}^6 is a subgraph of the quotient graph of S_i^6 guarantee that the **while** loop in DETECT-CYCLE iterates at most h times.

3.2 Extraction of a Fair Cycle

In model checking applications a fair cycle corresponds to a counterexample (a trace of a verified system which does not satisfy a given specification). The knowledge of a counterexample helps developers to tune the system. Accordingly, the shortest counterexamples are searched for.

In this section we present an algorithm, which complements DETECT-CYCLE and for graphs with fair cycles returns a particular fair cycle. The algorithm for extraction of a fair cycle makes use of values stored in the boolean array *inS* computed by DETECT-CYCLE. The set S (represented via *inS*) initially contains all fair cycles.

The procedure EXTRACT-CYCLE searches the graph G from the initial state for a fair state s from the set S. A nested search is initialised from s and an existence of a cycle from s to s is checked. In the nested search only the graph $G(S)$ induced by S is searched. Moreover, every state, which has been completely searched by a nested search without discovering a cycle can be safely removed from S. This ensures that each state is visited in nested searches only once and the algorithm has linear complexity.

In both searches the graph is traversed in a breadth-first manner. Nevertheless, the order in which states are visited is not important and this allows for an effective distribution of the computation. The discovered cycle is output with the help of *parent* values.

The great advantage of our approach is that due to the fact that the graph is searched in a breadth-first fashion the counterexamples tend to be much shorter than those generated by depth-first based algorithms (see Section 6).

Sequential algorithm for the extraction of a fair cycle

```
proc EXTRACT-CYCLE(G, F, init_state, inS)
  put init_state into queue;
  while cycle not found do
        remove s from queue;
        if inS[s] ∧ s ∈ F then NESTEDBFS(s); fi
        foreach (s, r) ∈ E do
          if parent[r] = nil then parent[r] := s;
                                  put r in queue; fi
        od
  od
  while s ≠ init_state do output s; s := parent[s]; od
end
```

```
proc NestedBFS(s)
  put s into queue2;
  while cycle not found and queue2 not empty do
        remove q from queue2;
        foreach (q, r) ∈ E do
          if inS[r] ∧ parent2[r] = nil then parent2[r] = q;
                                            put r in queue2 fi
          if r = s then cycle found;
                        r := parent2[r];
                        while r ≠ s do output r; r := parent2[r]; od
          fi
        od
        inS[q] := false;
  od
end
```

Lemma 8 (Soundness). *The sequence of states output by* Extract-Cycle *forms (in the reverse order) a cycle containing a fair state followed by a path from the fair state to the initial state.*

Proof: Each state s visited in the **while** cycle of Extract-Cycle is reachable from the *init_state* and similarly each state r visited in NestedBFS(s) is reachable from s. Since NestedBFS is initialised only from fair states, the lemma follows.

Lemma 9 (Completeness). *The algorithm* Extract-Cycle *finds a fair cycle.*

Proof: Let C be an initial component of the quotient graph of $G(S)$, where S is the set computed by Detect-Cycle(G, F, *init_state*). In NestedBFS only the induced graph $G(S)$ is searched and thus no state from C can be reached (and removed from S) by NestedBFS initialised in a state outside C. By the proof of Theorem 3, the component C is also fair. For that reason it must be the case that either a fair cycle is found somewhere outside C or Extract-Cycle reaches a fair state s in C and consequently NestedBFS(s) discovers a cycle from s to s.

Lemma 10 (Complexity). *The complexity of* Extract-Cycle *is* $O(n+m)$.

Proof: The Extract-Cycle procedure visits each state only once. NestedBFS visits only states in S and once a state is completely searched by NestedBFS it is removed from S. Hence, NestedBFS visits each state at most once too.

4 Distributed Algorithm

Similar to other works devoted to the distributed model checking [6, 3, 8, 33, 4] we assume the MIMD architecture of a network of workstations, which communicate via message passing (no global information is directly accessible). All workstations execute the same program. One workstation is distinguished as a *Manager* and is responsible for the initialisation of the computation, detection of the termination, and output of results.

The set of states of the graph to be searched for fair cycles is partitioned into disjoint subsets. The partition is determined by the function *Owner*, which assigns every state q to a workstation i. Each workstation is responsible for the graph induced by the owned subset of states. The way how states are partitioned among workstations is very important as it has a direct impact on the communication complexity and thus on the runtime of the algorithm. We do not discuss it here because it is itself quite a difficult problem, which moreover depends on a particular application.

4.1 Detection of a Fair Cycle

The procedures RESET, REACHABILITY, and ELIMINATION can be easily transformed into distributed ones. Each workstation performs the computation on its part of the graph. Whenever a state s belonging to a different workstation is reached, the workstation sends an appropriate message to the *Owner*(s). All workstations periodically read incoming messages and perform required commands (*Serve_messages*).

Computations on particular workstations can be performed in parallel. However, some synchronisation is unavoidable. All workstations perform the same procedure (RESET, REACHABILITY, ELIMINATION, or COUNT-SIZE). As soon as a workstation completes the procedure it sends a message to the *Manager* and becomes idle. When all workstations are idle and there are no pending messages the *Manager* synchronises all workstations and the computation continues.

The need of synchronisation after each procedure is the reason why we have chosen the *One Way Catch Them Young* algorithm as a base for our explicit algorithm. The analysis and experiments by Fisler at al. [16] indicates that this algorithm performs less external iterations then for example the well-known Emerson-Lei algorithm[2]. The number of external iteration determines the number of necessary synchronisations.

Distributed algorithm for fair cycle detection

```
proc DETECT-CYCLE(G, F, init_state)
  if init_state is local then put init_state into queue;
                              inS[init_state] := true; fi
  REACHABILITY;
  while continue do
        RESET;
        REACHABILITY;
        ELIMINATION;
```

[2] We note that some other algorithms studied by [16] perform even less external iterations. These algorithms make use of the *preimage* computation (i.e. computation of predecessors), which is usually not available in the explicit model checking.

```
        Count-size; od
  if Manager then return (global_Ssize > 0); fi
end

proc Reset
  local_Ssize := 0;
  foreach q ∈ V, q is local do
    inS[q] := inS[q] ∧ q ∈ F;
    p[q] := 0;
    if inS[q] then local_Ssize := local_Ssize + 1;
                   put q in queue;
                   put q in L; fi
  od
  Synchronization;
end

proc Reachability
  while not finshed do
        Serve_messages;
        if queue ≠ ∅
          then remove q from queue;
               foreach (q, r) ∈ E do
                 if r is local then Visit-state(r);
                              else send(Owner(r), "Visit-state(r)"); fi
               od
          else Synchronization; fi
  od
end

proc Elimination
  while not FINISHED do
        Serve_messages;
        if L ≠ ∅
          then remove q from L;
               inS[q] := false; local_Ssize := local_Ssize − 1;
               foreach (q, r) ∈ E do
                 if r is local then Eliminate-state(r);
                              else send(Owner(r), "Eliminate-state(r)"); fi
               od
          else Synchronization; fi
  od
end

proc Count-Size
  if Manager
    then sum up local_Ssize from all workstations;
         if global_Ssize = old_global_Ssize then send(all, stop);
                                           else send(all, continue); fi
```

```
    else send(Manager, local_Ssize);
         Wait_for_message;
  fi
end

proc SYNCHRONIZATION
  if Manager
    then if all processes are idle and there are no pending messages
           then send(all, finished)
            else Wait_for_message;
         fi
    else send(Manager, I am idle)
         Wait_for_message;
         if message ≠ finished then send(Manager, I am not idle) fi
  fi
end

proc VISIT-STATE(r)
  if ¬inS[r] then inS[r] := true;
                  local_Ssize := local_Ssize + 1;
                  put r in queue; fi
  if p[r] = 0 then remove r from L; fi
  p[r] := p[r] + 1;
end

proc ELIMINATE-STATE(r)
  p[r] := p[r] − 1;
  if p[r] = 0 then put r to L; fi
end
```

The correctness proof is an analog to that for the sequential algorithm. In fact, under a proper modification all lemmas and theorems from Section 3 hold for the distributed algorithm as well.

The number of iterations of the **while** cycle in DETECT-CYCLE is bounded above by the height of the quotient of G. The complexity of all procedures is linear with respect to the size of the owned part of the graph.

4.2 Extraction of a Fair Cycle

The distributed counterpart of the procedure EXTRACT-CYCLE comes by in a similar way as for DETECT-CYCLE. The basic traversal is executed in parallel. Whenever a workstation finds a suitable candidate s for the nested traversal (that is, $s \in S \cap F$) it sends it to the *Manager*. The *Manager* puts the incoming candidates into a queue and successively starts NESTEDBFS from them. The important point is that only one NESTEDBFS can be performed at a time.

The termination detection of the NESTEDBFS in a case that it failed to find a cycle is done in the same way as the detection of the end of procedures in distributed DETECT-CYCLE.

Distributed algorithm for the extraction of a fair cycle

```
proc EXTRACT-CYCLE
  if init_state is local then put init_state into queue; fi
  while not (finished or cycle_found do
          Serve_messages;
          if queue ≠ ∅
             then remove s from queue;
                    if inS[s] ∧ s ∈ F then send(Manager, NESTEDBFS candidate= s); fi
                    foreach (s,r) ∈ E do
                       if r is local then VISIT1(r, s);
                                      else send(Owner(r), VISIT1(r, s)); fi
                    od
          fi
  od
end

proc NESTEDBFS(s)
  put s into queue;
  while not (finshed or cycle_found) do
          Serve_messages;
          if queue ≠ ∅
             then remove q from queue;
                    foreach (q,r) ∈ E do
                       if r is local then VISIT2(r, q, s);
                                      else send(Owner(r), VISIT2(r, q, s)); fi
                    od
                    inS[q] := false;
               else SYNCHRONIZATION;
          fi
  od
end

proc VISIT1(r, s)
  if parent[r] = nil then parent[r] := s;
                          put r in queue; fi
end

proc VISIT2(r, q, s)
  if inS[r] ∧ parent2[r] = nil then parent2[r] = q;
                                      put r in queue2 fi
  if r = s then send(all, cycle_found);
                 PRINT-CYCLE(r, s) fi
end

proc PRINT-CYCLE(at, start)
  flag := cycle;
  while not finished do
          if at is local
```

```
            then output at;
                 if at = start then send(all, (flag := way)); fi
                 if at = init_state then send(all, finished); fi
                 if flag = cycle then at := parent2[at]; else at := parent[at]; fi
                 if at is not local then send(Owner(at), continue from at) fi
             else Wait_for_message;
        fi
  od
end
```

The correctness of the distributed EXTRACT-CYCLE algorithm again follows from that for the sequential one.

5 Modifications

In LTL model checking one often encounters not only Büchi automata for which the non-emptiness problem directly corresponds to a detection of fair cycles, but also their variants called *weak* and *generalised* Büchi automata and *Streett* automata. For these automata the non-emptiness problem corresponds to a slightly different version of the fair cycle detection problem. The advantage of the DETECT-CYCLE algorithm is that it can be easily modified in order to solve these problems.

In this section we provide pseudocodes of set based algorithms for the modified problems. The necessary modifications in both sequential and distributed explicit algorithms straightforwardly reflect changes of the set based algorithm and we do not state them.

5.1 Weak Graphs

We say that a graph G with a set F of fair states is *weak* if and only if each component C in SCC decomposition of G is either fully contained in F ($C \subseteq F$) or is disjoint with F ($C \cap F = \emptyset$).

Our study of hierarchy of temporal properties [12] suggests that in many cases the resulting graph is weak. Thus it is useful to develop specialised algorithms for these graphs. Actually, Bloem, Ravi, and Somenzi [5] have already performed experiments with specialised symbolic algorithms and state-of-the-art algorithms for generation of automaton for an LTL formula [32] include heuristics generating automaton as "weak" as possible.

From the definition of weak graphs it follows that the set F is a union of some SCCs. Thus a fair component exists if and only if some *nontrivial* component is contained in F. These observations lead to the following algorithm:

```
proc WEAK-DETECT-CYCLE(G, F, init_state)
  S := Reachability(init_state);
  S := Elimination(S ∩ F);
  return (S ≠ ∅);
end
```

The algorithm WEAK-DETECT-CYCLEhas several advantages. At first, its complexity of is $O(n+m)$ which is asymptotically better than the complexity of DETECT-CYCLE and is the same as the complexity of the NESTEDDFS algorithm. At second, in the distributed environment, the specialised algorithm needs to synchronise only two times. And finally, this algorithm is easier to implement and provide better possibilities for heuristics and optimisations (especially in the distributed environment) than the depth-search based ones.

Thus one can use the specialised algorithm profitably whenever it is possible. The natural question is how expensive is to find out whether a graph is weak. In model checking applications the graph to be searched for fair cycles is a product of a system description (that is a graph without fair states) and a rather small graph expressing a desired property of the system. The weakness of the graph is determined by the property graph and hence it suffices to put the small graph to the weakness test.

5.2 Generalised Fair Condition

Generalised fair condition $\mathcal{F}$ is a set $\{F_i\}$ of fair sets. A cycle is *fair in respect to a generalised fair condition* $\{F_i\}$ if and only if for each fair set F_i there exists a state q on the cycle such that $q \in F_i$.

In model checking applications, algorithms translating an LTL formula into an automaton usually end up with generalised fair conditions [18]. One can transform (and model checker tools usually do so) the generalised condition into the ordinary one through a "counter construction". But the transformation increases the number of states, which is highly undesirable. Therefore it is more favourable to test directly the generalised condition.

The modification of the DETECT-CYCLE algorithm for generalised condition is rather simple. It suffices to guarantee that states in S are reachable from all fair sets.

```
proc GENERALIZED-DETECT-CYCLE(G, F, init_state)
  S := Reachability(init_state);
  old := ∅;
  while (S ≠ old) do
        old := S;
        foreach F_i ∈ F do
           S := Reachability(S ∩ F_i);
        od
        S := Elimination(S);
  od
  return (S ≠ ∅);
end
```

5.3 Streett Fair Condition

Streett fair condition $\mathcal{F}$ is a set of tuples $\{(P_i, Q_i)\}$. A cycle C is *fair in respect to a Streett fair condition* if and only if for each tuple (P_i, Q_i) it holds $C \cap P_i \neq \emptyset \Rightarrow C \cap Q_i \neq \emptyset$.

Streett fair condition is used to express strong fairness (compassion), that is, intuitively "if there is an infinite number of requests then there is an infinite number of responses". Strong fairness can be expressed in LTL and thus it is possible to use the algorithm for (generalised) Büchi fair condition in order to check properties of system with strong fairness requirements. However, this approach leads to the blowup of the size of formula automaton and thus it is more efficient to check the strong fairness directly (see [26]).

The set based algorithm for the Street fair condition can be formulated as follows:

```
proc STREETT-DETECT-CYCLE(G, F, init_state)
  S := Reachability(init_state);
  old := ∅;
  while (S ≠ old) do
        old := S;
        foreach (P_i, Q_i) ∈ F do
           S := (S − P_i) ∪ Reachability(S ∩ Q_i);
        od
        S := Elimination(S);
  od
  return (S ≠ ∅);
end
```

For the proof of correctness see [26]. Corresponding modification of the explicit algorithm is more technically involved though rather straightforward.

The important fact is that other algorithms like NESTEDDFS or algorithm presented in [8] cannot cope with generalised and Streett condition in such a simple way (in fact the distributed algorithm from [8] cannot be directly modified to cope with generalised and Streett fair cycles).

6 Experiments

We performed series of experiments in order to test the practical usefulness of the proposed algorithm. In this section we mention representative results and discuss conclusions we have drawn from the experiments.

The implementation has been done in C++ and the experiments have been performed on a cluster of twelve 700 MHz Pentium PC Linux workstations with 384 Mbytes of RAM each interconnected with a fast 100Mbps Ethernet and using Message Passing Interface (MPI) library. Reported runtimes are averaged over several executions.

6.1 Examples

Graphs for experiments were generated from a protocol and an LTL formula in advance and programs have been provided with an explicit representation of a graph. This approach simplifies the implementation. However, as discussed later it has an unpleasant impact on the scalability of the distributed algorithm.

For graphs generation a simple model-checking tool has been used allowing us to generate graphs with approximately one million states. The algorithm was tested on several classical model checking examples:

- Absence of a starvation for a simple mutual exclusion protocol and for the Peterson protocol (`Mutex, Peterson`).
- Safety property for the alternation bit protocol (`ABP`).
- Reply properties (with fairness) for a model of an elevator (`Elevator1, Elevator2`).
- Safety and liveness properties for a token ring (`Ring1, Ring2, Ring3, Ring4`).
- Liveness property for the dining philosophers problem (`Philosophers`).

6.2 General Observations

At first, we have compared the sequential version of our algorithm with the sequentially optimal NestedDFS algorithm. We remind that from the theoretical point of view our algorithm is asymptotically worse. Table 1 summarises experiments with graphs without fair cycles and Table 2 covers experiments with graphs with fair cycles.

Table 1. Sequential experiments for graphs without fair cycles

System Size	Algorithm	Time (s)	External Iterations
`Peterson`	NestedDFS	0.02	
376	Detect-Cycle	0.06	18
`ABP`	NestedDFS	0.22	
7 286	Detect-Cycle	0.41	1
`Ring1`	NestedDFS	17.13	
172 032	Detect-Cycle	7.61	1
`Elevator2`	NestedDFS	35.10	
368 925	Detect-Cycle	55.76	30
`Philosophers`	NestedDFS	72.68	
608 185	Detect-Cycle	52.04	1

The following conclusions can be drawn from the experiments:

- The number of external iterations of Detect-Cycle is very small (less than 40) even for large graphs. This observation is supported by experiments in [16] with the symbolic implementation of the set-based algorithm. They obtained similar results for hardware circuits problems.
- The complexity of Detect-Cycle is in practice nearly linear.
- The runtime of our algorithm is comparable to NestedDFS for correct specifications (graphs without fair cycles).

- In the case of an erroneous specification (graphs with fair cycles) the NestedDFS algorithm is significantly faster because it is able to detect cycles "on-the-fly" without traversing the whole graph.
- On the other hand, the counterexamples generated by Detect-Cycle are significantly shorter because of the breadth-first nature of the algorithm. This is practically very important feature as counterexamples consisting of several thousands of states (as those generated by NestedDFS) are quite useless.
- The last observation compares the runtime of the first phase (cycle detection) to the second phase (cycle extraction) of our algorithm. Evidently the time needed for the second phase is significantly shorter than that for the first phase. Thus potential optimisations, heuristics, etc. of the algorithms should be directed at the first phase.

Table 2. Sequential experiments for graphs with a fair cycle. The column time gives the overall time, extract time is the time needed for the extraction of the cycle.

System Size	Algorithm	Time (s)	Extract time (s)	External Iterations	Fair cycle Prefix	 Loop
Mutex 232	NestedDFS Detect-Cycle	0.01 0.02	 0.01	 2	76 2	3 2
Ring3 389 542	NestedDFS Detect-Cycle	2.70 29.07	 1.17	 2	14420 28	3 23
Elevator1 683 548	NestedDFS Detect-Cycle	7.28 99.43	 1.80	 8	304 20	76 22
Ring2 1 027 394	NestedDFS Detect-Cycle	12.82 305.51	 11.31	 40	2754 52	363 14

6.3 Distributed Tests

We note that experiments concerning the distributed version are only preliminary since the current implementation is straightforward and is far from being optimal. For example, it suffers from problems with load-balancing. The only optimisation that we have used is the reduction of communication by packing several messages into one.

We have compared our algorithm to the distributed version of NestedDFS where only one processor, namely the one owning the actual state in the depth-first search, is executing the search at a time. The network is in fact running the sequential algorithm with extended memory. The runtime of NestedDFS increases with the number of workstations thanks to the additional communication. On the other hand, our algorithm can take advantage of more workstations since it exploits parallelism. Hence in the distributed environment our algorithm convincingly outperforms NestedDFS.

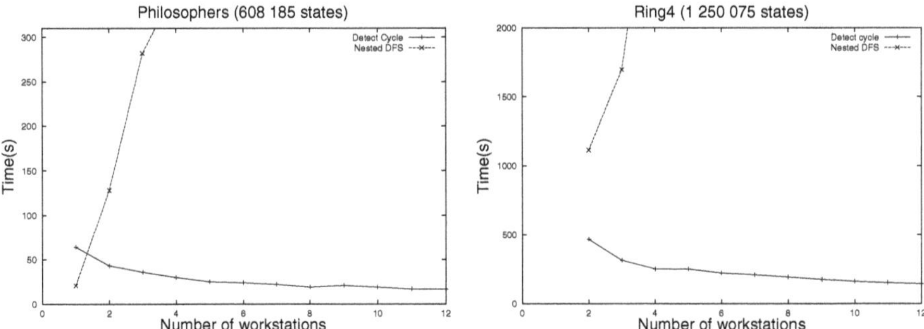

Fig. 1. Comparison of distributed NestedDFS and Detect-Cycle. The system `Ring4` cannot be handled by one computer

The current implementation of Detect-Cycle algorithm is not optimised and does not scale ideally. We identify two main reasons. The first one is the straightforwardness of our implementation. The second, more involved reason, is based on fact that in our experiments we use pre-generated graphs, which however are not too large in comparison to the memory capacity of the NOW. Consequently the local computations are very fast and the slow communication has high impact on the overall runtime. We infer, in a similar way as [6], that if the algorithm computed the graph on-the-fly from the specification language then the communication and synchronisation would have smaller impact on the runtime and the algorithm would achieve better speedup. To support this explanation we have measured besides the real time taken by the computation also the CPU time consumed by particular workstations. Fig. 2 resumes the results. The numbers indicate that the time taken by a local computation (CPU time) really scales well.

We have also implemented the distributed Weak-Detect-Cycle algorithm and performed a comparison of the general and the specialised algorithm on weak graphs. Fig. 3 indicates that the use of specialised algorithm can yield a considerable improvement.

7 Conclusions and Future Work

In this paper, we presented a new *distributed* algorithm for fair cycle detection problem. The demand for such an algorithm becomes visible especially referring to automata-based LTL model checking. This verification method suffers from the state explosion. Distributed model checking allows to cope with the state explosion by reason of allocation of the state space to several workstations in a network.

Our distributed algorithm comes out from a set-based algorithm, which searches the state space in a breadth-first search manner, which makes a distribution possible. On the other hand, the state space is represented explicitly

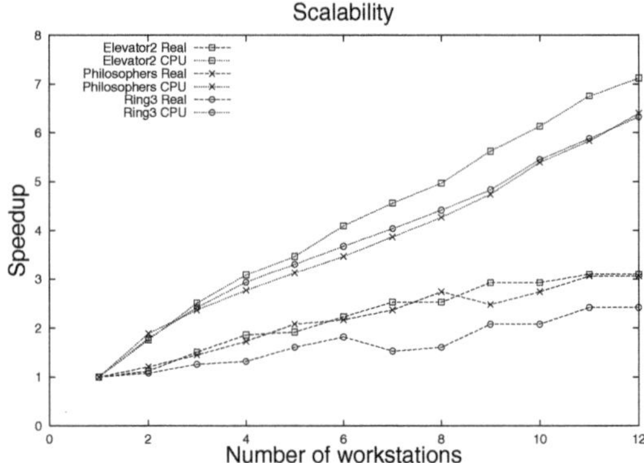

Fig. 2. Dependency of the runtime on the number of workstations. Figure shows the difference between real time taken by the program and the average CPU time used by a workstation

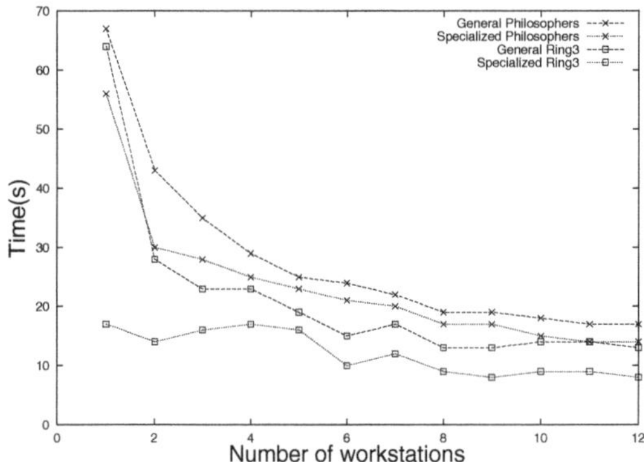

Fig. 3. Detect-Cycle and Weak-Detect-Cycle on weak graphs

and thus can be partitioned very naturally. The algorithm is compatible with other state space saving methods, namely with static partial order reduction. It aims not to replace but to complement the classical nested depth-first search algorithm used in explicit LTL model checkers as it demonstrates its efficiency especially in cases when the searched space does not contain any fair cycle.

We have implemented our approach within an experimental platform. We found out that the complexity of our algorithm is nearly linear. The runtime of the sequential Detect-Cycle algorithm is comparable to that of NestedDFS on correct specifications. For an erroneous specifications counterexamples generated by our algorithm tend to be significantly shorter. The distributed Detect-Cycle algorithm is noteworthy faster than the distributed implementation of NestedDFS for all types of graphs. In the future we plan to implement our approach to an existing tool and to compare its efficiency with other distributed LTL model checking algorithms ([1, 8]).

There are several alternatives to *One Way Catch Them Young* in the literature, for excellent reviews see [30, 16]. The natural question thus is whether similar distributed algorithms for fair cycle detection as the one we have proposed can be build upon other symbolic algorithms for cycle detection.

References

[1] J. Barnat, L. Brim, and J. Stříbrná. Distributed LTL Model-Checking in SPIN. In *Proc. SPIN Workshop on Model Checking of Software*, volume 2057 of *LNCS*, pages 200 – 216. Springer, 2001. 50, 71

[2] J. Barnat, L. Brim, and I. Černá. Property driven distribution of Nested DFS. In *Proc. Workshop on Verification and Computational Logic*, number DSSE-TR-2002-5 in DSSE Technical Report, pages 1 – 10. Dept. of Electronics and Computer Science, University of Southampton, UK, 2002. 50

[3] G. Behrmann. A performance study of distributed timed automata reachability analysis. In *Proc. Workshop on Parallel and Distributed Model Checking*, volume 68 of *Electronic Notes in Theoretical Computer Science*. Elsevier Science Publishers, 2002. 50, 59

[4] S. Ben-David, T. Heyman, O. Grumberg, and A. Schuster. Scalable distributed on-the-fly symbolic model checking. In *Proc. Formal Methods in Computer-Aided Design*, volume 1954 of *LNCS*, pages 390–404, 2000. 50, 59

[5] R. Bloem, K. Ravi, and F. Somenzi. Efficient decision procedures for model checking of linear time logic properties. In *Proc. Computer Aided Verification*, volume 1633 of *LNCS*, pages 222–235. Springer, 1999. 64

[6] B. Bollig, M. Leucker, and M. Weber. Parallel model checking for the alternation free μ-calculus. In *Proc. Tools and Algorithms for the Construction and Analysis of Systems*, volume 2031 of *LNCS*, pages 543–558. Springer, 2001. 50, 59, 69

[7] R. K. Brayton et al. VIS: a system for verification and synthesis. In *Proc. Formal Methods in Computer Aided Design*, volume 1166 of *LNCS*, pages 248 – 256. Springer, 1996. 50

[8] L. Brim, I. Černá, P. Krčál, and R. Pelánek. Distributed LTL model checking based on negative cycle detection. In *Proc. Foundations of Software Technology and Theoretical Computer Science*, volume 2245 of *LNCS*, pages 96–107. Springer, 2001. 50, 59, 66, 71

[9] R. E. Bryant. Graph-based algorithms for boolean function manipulation. In *IEEE Transactions on Computers*, volume C-35(8), pages 677 – 691, 1986. 50

[10] J. R. Büchi. On a decision method in restricted second order arithmetic. In *Proc. International Congress on Logic, Methodology and Philosophy Science*, pages 1 – 11. Stanford university Press, 1960. 49

[11] J. R. Burch, E. M. Clarke, K. L. McMillan, D. L. Dill, and L. J. Hwang. Symbolic model checking: 10^{20} states and beyond. *Information and Computation*, 98(2):142–170, 1992. 51

[12] I. Černá and R. Pelánek. Relating the hierarchy of temporal properties to model checking. Submitted, 2002. 64

[13] E. M. Clarke, O. Grumberg, and D. A. Peled. *Model Checking*. The MIT Press, 1999. 50

[14] C. Eisner and D. Peled. Comparing symbolic and explicit model checking of a software system. In *Proc. SPIN Workshop on Model Checking of Software*, volume 2318 of *LNCS*, page 230 239. Springer, 2002. 51

[15] E. A. Emerson and C.-L. Lei. Modalities for model checking: branching time logic strikes back. *Science of Computer Programming*, 8:275 – 306, 1987. 49, 50

[16] K. Fisler, R. Fraer, G. Kamhi Y. Vardi, and Z. Yang. Is there a best symbolic cycle-detection algorithm? In *Proc. Tools and Algorithms for Construction and Analysis of Systems*, volume 2031 of *LNCS*, pages 420–434. Springer, 2001. 50, 51, 52, 53, 60, 67, 71

[17] H. Garavel, R. Mateescu, and I. Smarandache. Parallel state space construction for model-checking. In *Proc. SPIN Workshop on Model Checking of Software*, volume 2057 of *LNCS*, pages 215+. Springer, 2001. 50

[18] R. Gerth, D. Peled, M. Y. Vardi, and P. Wolper. Simple on-the-fly automatic verification of linear temporal logic. In *Proc. Protocol Specification Testing and Verification*, pages 3–18. Chapman & Hall, 1995. 65

[19] R.H. Hardin, A. Harel, and R.P. Kurshan. COSPAN. In *Proc Conference on Computer Aided Verification*, volume 1102 of *LNCS*, pages 423 – 427. Springer, 1996. 50

[20] T. Heyman, D. Geist, O. Grumberg, and A. Schuster. Achieving scalability in parallel reachability analysis of very large circuits. In *Proc. Conference on Computer Aided Verification*, volume 1855 of *LNCS*, pages 20–35. Springer, 2000. 51

[21] R. Hojati, R.K. Brayton, and R.P. Kurshan. BDD-based debugging using language containment and fair CTL. In *Proc. Conference on Computer Aided Verification*, volume 697 of *LNCS*, pages 41 – 58. Springer, 1993. 51

[22] G. J. Holzmann. The model checker SPIN. *IEEE Transactions on Software Engineering*, 23(5):279–295, 1997. 50

[23] G. J. Holzmann, D. Peled, and M. Yannakakis. On nested depth first search. In *Proc. SPIN Workshop on Model Checking of Software*, pages 23–32. American Mathematical Society, 1996. 50

[24] A. J. Hu. *Techniques for efficient formal verification using binary decision diagrams.* PhD thesis, Stanford University, 1995. 51

[25] A. J. Hu, G. York, and D.L. Dill. New techniques for efficient verification with implicitly conjoined BDDs. In *Proc. Design automation Conference*, pages 276 – 282, 1994. 51

[26] Y. Kesten, A Pnueli, and L. Raviv. Algorithmic verification of linear temporal logic specifications. In *Proc. Automata, Languages and Programming*, volume 1443 of *LNCS*, pages 1–16. Springer, 1998. 50, 66

[27] R. Kurshan, V. Levin, M. Minea, D. Peled, and H. Yenigün. Static partial order reduction. In *Tools and Algorithms for Construction and Analysis of Systems*, volume 1384 of *LNCS*, pages 345 – 357. Springer. 52

[28] F. Lerda and R. Sisto. Distributed-memory model checking with SPIN. In *Proc. SPIN Workshop on Model Checking of Software*, volume 1680 of *LNCS*, Berlin, Germany, 1999. Springer. 50

[29] K.L. McMillan. *Symbolic Model Checking.* Kluwer Academic Publisher, 1994. 50

[30] K. Ravi, R. Bloem, and F. Somenzi. A comparative study of symbolic algorithms for the computation of fair cycles. In *Proc. Formal Methods in Computer-Aided Design*, volume 1954 of *LNCS*, pages 143–160. Springer, 2000. 50, 52, 71

[31] J.H. Reif. Depth-first search is inherrently sequential. *Information Processing Letters*, 20(5):229–234, 1985. 50

[32] F. Somenzi and R. Bloem. Efficient Büchi automata from LTL formulae. In *Proc. Computer Aided Verification*, volume 1855 of *LNCS*, pages 248–263. Springer, 2000. 64

[33] U. Stern and D. L. Dill. Parallelizing the Murφ verifier. In *Proc. Computer Aided Verification*, volume 1254 of *LNCS*, pages 256–267. Springer, 1997. 50, 51, 59

[34] J. R. Streett. Propositional dynamic logic of looping and converse is elementarily decidable. *Information and Control*, 54(1 - 2):121 – 141, 1982. 49

[35] R. Tarjan. Depth first search and linear graph algorithms. *SIAM Journal on computing*, pages 146–160, 1972. 50

[36] M. Y. Vardi. An automata-theoretic approach to linear temporal logic. In *Logics for Concurrency: Structure versus Automata*, volume 1043 of *LNCS*, pages 238 – 266. Springer, 1996. 50

Efficient Model Checking of Safety Properties

Timo Latvala *

Laboratory for Theoretical Computer Science
Helsinki University of Technology
P.O. Box 9205
FIN-02015 HUT
Finland
Timo.Latvala@hut.fi

Abstract. We consider the problems of identifying LTL safety properties and translating them to finite automata. We present an algorithm for constructing finite automata recognising informative prefixes of LTL formulas based on [1]. The implementation also includes a procedure for deciding if a formula is pathologic. Experimental results indicate that the translation is competitive when compared to model checking with tools translating full LTL to Büchi automata.

1 Introduction

Informally, safety properties are properties of systems where every violation of a property occurs after a finite execution of the system. Safety properties are relevant in many areas of formal methods. Testing methods based on executing a finite input and observing the output can only detect safety property violations. Monitoring executions of programs is also an area where safety properties are relevant as monitoring also only can detect failures of safety properties. Naturally, formal specifications are also verified to make sure that a given safety property holds.

All of the above mentioned uses of safety properties can be accomplished by specifying the properties as finite automata. While automata are useful in many cases, a more declarative approach, such as using a temporal logic, is usually preferred. Many model checking tools, such as Spin [2], support linear temporal logic (LTL).

In the automata theoretic approach to verification [3, 4, 5], LTL formulas are verified by translating their negation to Büchi automata, which are then synchronised with the system. If the synchronised system has an accepting execution, the property does not hold. One could benefit from using finite automata instead of Büchi automata if the given LTL property is a safety property. Reasoning about finite automata is simpler than reasoning about Büchi automata. For

* The financial support of Helsinki Graduate School in Computer Science and Engineering, the Academy of Finland (Project 47754), the Wihuri foundation and Tekniikan Edistämissäätiö (Foundation for Technology) is gratefully acknowledged.

T. Ball and S.K. Rajamani (Eds.): SPIN 2003, LNCS 2648, pp. 74–88, 2003.

explicit state model checkers, reasoning about Büchi automata requires slightly more complicated algorithms. In the symbolic context, emptiness checking with BDDs is in practice significantly slower than simple reachability [6]. For model checkers based on net unfoldings, such as [7], handling safety is much easier than full LTL [8].

Unfortunately, there are some complexity related challenges in translating LTL formulas to finite automata. A finite automaton specifying every finite violation of a LTL safety property can be doubly exponential in the size of the formula [1]. Formulas, for which every failing computation has an *informative* bad prefix, or alternatively called the non-pathological formulas, have singly exponential finite automata recognising their finite violations [1]. Deciding if an LTL formula is pathologic is a PSPACE-complete problem [1]. Pathological LTL formulas are not needed for expressiveness, as a pathological formula always can be expressed with an equivalent non-pathological one [1].

We present an efficient translation algorithm from LTL safety properties to finite automata based on [1]. The resulting finite automata can be used by explicit state model checkers and they can be fairly easily adapted to partial order semantics methods too [8]. The translation has been implemented in a tool and is experimentally evaluated. Experiments show that our approach is competitive and can result in significant gains when used. We have also implemented a decision procedure to decide if an LTL formula is pathologic. To our knowledge, this is the first time an implementation for checking if a formula is pathologic has been evaluated.

Other authors have also considered the problem of model checking of LTL safety properties. Kupferman and Vardi [1] present many complexity theoretical results and an algorithm on which the algorithm presented in this paper is based on. Some of the results are generalisations of results by Sistla [9]. Geilen [10] presents a tableau algorithm which essentially is a forward direction version of the algorithm of Kupferman and Vardi, which is described in the backward direction. Model checking safety properties expressed using past temporal operators has been considered at least by [11, 12].

The rest of this paper is structured as follows. Section 2 introduces the necessary theory. In Sect. 3 we present our translation from LTL to finite automata. We also discuss the relevant complexity issues. Section 4 covers issues related to implementation and the experiments are presented in Sect. 5. Finally, in Sect. 6 we discuss some implications of the results and consider avenues for further research.

2 Preliminaries

This section introduces the necessary theory and some notations presented in [1].

Let $w = \sigma_0\sigma_1\sigma_2 \ldots \in \Sigma^\omega$ be an infinite word over the finite alphabet Σ. We denote the i:th position of the word by $w(i) = \sigma_i$ and the suffix $\sigma_i\sigma_{i+1}\ldots$ is denoted by w^i. A *Büchi* automaton is a tuple $\mathcal{A} = \langle \Sigma, Q, \delta, Q_0, F\rangle$, where Σ is the *alphabet*, Q is a finite set of *states*, $\delta \subseteq Q \times \Sigma \times Q$ is the *transition relation*,

$Q_0 \subseteq Q$ the set of *initial states*, and $F \subseteq Q$ is a set of *final states*. A *run* of the automaton $\mathcal{A}$ on a word $w \in \Sigma^\omega$ is a mapping $\rho : \mathbb{N} \to Q$ such that $\rho(0) \in Q_0$ and $(\rho(i), \sigma_i, \rho(i+1)) \in \delta$ for all $i \geq 0$. We use $inf(\rho)$ to denote the set of states occurring infinitely often in the run. A word w is accepted if it has a run ρ such that $inf(\rho) \cap F \neq \emptyset$. Finite automata differ from Büchi automata only in the acceptance condition. An automaton on finite words accepts a finite word $w = \sigma_0\sigma_1 \ldots \sigma_n \in \Sigma^*$ if it has a run ρ on w such that $\rho(n+1) \in F$. The set of words accepted by an automaton $\mathcal{A}$, its *language*, is denoted $\mathcal{L}(\mathcal{A})$. Deciding if $\mathcal{L}(\mathcal{A}) = \emptyset$ is referred to as doing an emptiness check.

Let $L \subseteq \Sigma^\omega$ be a language on infinite words over an alphabet Σ. We say that a finite word $x \in \Sigma^*$ is a *bad prefix* for language L, if for every $y \in \Sigma^\omega$ we have that $x \cdot y \notin L$. Given a language L, if all $w \in \Sigma^\omega \setminus L$ have a bad prefix we call L a *safety language*. We denote the set of bad prefixes of a language L by $pref(L)$.

2.1 LTL

The syntax of LTL consists of atomic propositions, the normal boolean connectives, and *temporal operators*. Let AP be a set of atomic propositions. Well-formed formulae of LTL are constructed in the following way:

- **true**, **false** and every $p \in AP$ are well-formed formulae
- If ψ and φ are well-formed formulae, then so are $\psi \wedge \varphi$, $\psi \vee \varphi$, $\psi\, U\, \varphi$, $\psi\, V\, \varphi$, $\neg\varphi$ and $X\varphi$.

LTL is interpreted over infinite sequences of atomic propositions, i.e. infinite words in $(2^{AP})^\omega$. A model (or word) $\pi = \sigma_0\sigma_1\sigma_2\ldots$, where $\sigma_i \subseteq AP$, is a mapping $\pi : \mathbb{N} \to 2^{AP}$. By π^i we denote the suffix $\pi^i = \sigma_i\sigma_{i+1}\sigma_{i+2}\ldots$ and π_i denotes the prefix $\pi_i = \sigma_0\sigma_1\ldots\sigma_i$. For an LTL formula ψ and a model π, we write $\pi^i \models \psi$, "the suffix π^i is a model of ψ". The semantics of the models relation $\models$ is defined inductively in the following way.

- For all π^i we have that $\pi^i \models$ **true** and $\pi^i \not\models$ **false**.
- For atomic propositions $p \in AP$, $\pi^i \models p$ iff $p \in \sigma_i$
- $\pi^i \models \psi_1 \vee \psi_2$ iff $\pi^i \models \psi_1$ or $\pi^i \models \psi_2$.
- $\pi^i \models \psi_1 \wedge \psi_2$ iff $\pi^i \models \psi_1$ and $\pi^i \models \psi_2$.
- $\pi^i \models X\psi$ iff $\pi^{i+1} \models \psi$.
- $\pi^i \models \neg\psi$ iff $\pi^i \not\models \psi$.
- $\pi^i \models \psi_1\, U\, \psi_2$ iff there exists $k \geq i$ such that $\pi^k \models \psi_2$ and for all $i \leq j < k$ $\pi^j \models \psi_1$.
- $\pi^i \models \psi_1\, V\, \psi_2$ iff for all $k \geq i$, if $\pi^k \not\models \psi_2$, then there is $i \leq j < k$ such that $\pi^j \models \psi_1$.

Usually we do not write $\pi^0 \models \psi$ but simply $\pi \models \psi$. LTL formulas which are in positive normal form (PNF) only have negations in front of atomic propositions. Any LTL formula can be rewritten into PNF using the duality between U and V. We use $cl(\psi)$ to denote the set of subformulas of ψ. The size of a formula, denoted $|\psi|$, is defined as the cardinality of $cl(\psi)$.

An LTL formula ψ specifies a language $\mathcal{L}(\psi) = \{\pi \in (2^{AP})^\omega \mid \pi \models \psi\}$. We say that an LTL formula is a safety formula if its language is a safety language.

3 Model Checking LTL Safety Properties

In the automata theoretic approach to LTL model checking the negation of the LTL specification is translated into a Büchi automaton $\mathcal{A}_{\neg\psi}$. The system is then viewed as an automaton and synchronised with the property automaton. If the property holds, the language of the synchronised automaton is empty.

Our goal is to construct a finite automaton which detects the bad prefixes for $\mathcal{L}(\psi)$. The resulting finite automata can be used e.g. for model checking, real-time monitoring [12] or as a specification for testing [13]. In the context of model checking treating safety as a special case has some benefits. One benefit is that fairness need not be taken into account, if we know we are dealing with a safety specification. Another benefit is that reasoning about finite automata is simpler. For instance, dealing with finite automata is much simpler than dealing with Büchi automata for model checkers based on net unfoldings [7]. For explicit state model checkers the algorithm for checking emptiness of Büchi is slightly more complicated than checking the emptiness for a finite automaton. When model checking with finite automata, we do not need to proceed in a depth-first order. Instead, we can e.g. apply a heuristic and do a best-first search to possibly obtain shorter counterexamples.

There are two major obstacles to using finite automata for LTL safety formulas. First of all, we must be able recognise safety formulas. This problem is unfortunately PSPACE-complete in the size of the formula [9]. A partial solution to this is that Sistla [9] has introduced a syntactic fragment of LTL which can only express safety properties. The fragment includes all LTL formulas which in PNF only contain the temporal operators V and X. The second problem is that translating an LTL safety formula to a finite automaton is hard in the general case. The worst case complexity of an automaton for $\mathit{pref}(\mathcal{L}(\psi))$ is doubly exponential in the size of ψ [1]. It turns out, however, that for well behaved formulas a singly exponential automaton is possible [1]. The notion of a well behaved formula is formalised through *informativeness.*

3.1 Informativeness

We consider LTL formulae in positive normal form. The notion of informativeness tries to formalise when a bad prefix for the formula can demonstrate completely why the formula failed. Let ψ be an LTL formula and π a finite computation $\pi = \sigma_0\sigma_1 \dots \sigma_n$. The computation π is *informative* for ψ iff there exists a mapping $L : \{0, \dots, n+1\} \to 2^{cl(\neg\psi)}$ such that the following conditions hold:

- $\neg\psi \in L(0)$,
- $L(n+1)$ is empty, and
- for all $0 \leq i \leq n$ and $\varphi \in L(i)$, the following hold.
  - If φ is a propositional assertion, it is satisfied by σ_i.
  - If $\varphi = \varphi_1 \vee \varphi_2$ then $\varphi_1 \in L(i)$ or $\varphi_2 \in L(i)$.
  - If $\varphi = \varphi_1 \wedge \varphi_2$ then $\varphi_1 \in L(i)$ and $\varphi_2 \in L(i)$.
  - If $\varphi = X\varphi_1$, then $\varphi_1 \in L(i+1)$.

- If $\varphi = \varphi_1 \, U \, \varphi_2$ then $\varphi_2 \in L(i)$ or $[\varphi_1 \in L(i)$ and $\varphi_1 \, U \, \varphi_2 \in L(i+1)]$.
- If $\varphi = \varphi_1 \, V \, \varphi_2$ then $\varphi_2 \in L(i)$ and $[\varphi_1 \in L(i)$ or $\varphi_1 \, V \, \varphi_2 \in L(i+1)]$.

If π is informative for ψ, the mapping L is called the *witness* for $\neg\psi$ in π. Using the notion of informativeness, safety formulae can be classified into three different categories [1]. A safety formula ψ is *intentionally* safe iff all the bad prefixes for ψ are informative. The formula ψ is *accidentally* safe iff every computation that violates ψ has an informative prefix. In other words, ψ can have bad prefixes which are not informative. Every computation is, however, guaranteed to have at least one informative prefix. A safety formula ψ is *pathologically* safe if there is a computation that violates ψ and has no informative bad prefix.

Accidentally safe and pathologically safe formulas always contain redundancy. It is, however, an open problem if there are feasible ways to remove these redundancies. As previously mentioned, it is possible to construct a singly exponential finite automaton which detects all informative prefixes of a formula. This means that as long as the given formula is not pathologic, using this construct will return a correct result if used in model checking. For pathologic formulas we must either remove the redundancy, do model checking with a Büchi automaton, or use a doubly exponential construct. However, any counterexample returned by the singly exponential construction is a valid counterexample, even for pathological formulas.

Deciding if an LTL formula ψ is pathologic is a PSPACE-complete problem in the size of the formula [1]. The problem can be decided in the following way. It is possible to construct an alternating Büchi automaton $\mathcal{A}_{\psi}^{true}$ with a linear number of states in $|\psi|$ which accepts exactly all computations which have informative prefixes [1]. We can also construct an alternating Büchi automaton $\mathcal{A}_{\neg\psi}$ where $\mathcal{L}(\mathcal{A}) = \mathcal{L}(\psi)$ [5]. Pathologic formulas have violating computations which are not informative. Thus, a formula is not pathologic if every computation that satisfies $\neg\psi$ is accepted by $\mathcal{A}_{\neg\psi}^{true}$ This can be verified by checking the containment of $\mathcal{L}(\mathcal{A}_{\neg\psi})$ in $\mathcal{L}(\mathcal{A}_{\neg\psi}^{true})$. The above check has the nice property that if ψ is not a safety formula it will automatically rejected as pathological. Thus, in our intended application there is no need for a separate check if ψ is a safety formula.

3.2 Translation Algorithm

The finite automaton for informative prefixes of Kupferman and Vardi [1] is suboptimal for explicit model checkers. It will almost always have a state for every subset of $cl(\psi)$. While Geilen's procedure [10] is not as inefficient, it will still produce big automata. A more efficient construction will only consider some subsets. We define the restricted closure $rcl(\psi)$ of a formula ψ as the smallest set with the following properties.

- All temporal subformulas $\varphi \in cl(\psi)$, i.e. formulas with a temporal operator at the root of their parse tree, belong to $rcl(\psi)$.
- If a formula $X\varphi$ belongs to $rcl(\psi)$ then $\varphi \in rcl(\psi)$.
- If no other rule applies, then the top-level formula ψ belongs to $rcl(\psi)$.

The restricted closure defines which sets of subformulas must be considered when constructing a finite automaton for an LTL formula. Temporal subformulas must belong to the restricted closure because they refer to other than the current state. There are two special cases when other formulas are also included. The first case is the immediate subformula of a next-operator. In this case the subformula must be kept to ensure that it will be true in the next state. The second case is when ψ is a propositional expression when the reason is that $rcl(\psi)$ cannot be empty, because this will result in an automaton with no states.

Let S be a subset of $cl(\psi)$. We define $sat(\psi, S)$ in the following way:

- $sat(\mathbf{true}, S) = \mathbf{true}$
- $sat(\mathbf{false}, S) = \mathbf{false}$
- $sat(\psi, S) = \mathbf{true}$ if $\psi \in S$.
- $\psi = \psi_1 \vee \psi_2$: $sat(\psi, S) = \mathbf{true}$ if $sat(\psi_1, S)$ or $sat(\psi_2, S)$.
- $\psi = \psi_1 \wedge \psi_2$: $sat(\psi, S) = \mathbf{true}$ if $sat(\psi_1, S)$ and $sat(\psi_2, S)$.
- Otherwise $sat(\psi, S) = \mathbf{false}$

We can now present our algorithm, which is an optimisation of the construction presented in [1]. The general idea of both algorithms is to start from an empty set of requirements and by going backwards compute all possible informative prefixes. The algorithm as it is presented here will produce an automaton where there are many transitions from one state to another state. In an implementation these arcs would of course be joined to conserve memory.

```
Input: A formula ψ in positive normal form.
Output: A finite automaton A = ⟨Σ, Q, δ, Q0, F⟩.
proc translate(ψ)
F := {∅}; Σ := 2^AP;
Q := X := F;
while(X ≠ ∅) do
    S :="some set in X"; X := X \ {S}
    for each σ ∈ 2^AP do
        S' := σ;
        for each φ ∈ rcl(ψ) do //in increasing subformula order
            switch(φ) begin
                case φ = ψ1 ∨ ψ2:
                if (sat(ψ1, S') or sat(ψ2, S')) then  S' := S' ∪ {φ};
                case φ = ψ1 ∧ ψ2:
                if (sat(ψ1, S') and sat(ψ2, S')) then S' := S' ∪ {φ};
                case φ = Xψ1:
                if (ψ1 ∈ S) then S' := S' ∪ {φ};
                case φ = ψ1 U ψ2:
                if (sat(ψ2, S') or (sat(ψ1, S') and φ ∈ S)) then S' := S' ∪ {φ};
                case φ = ψ1 V ψ2:
                if (sat(ψ2, S') and (sat(ψ1, S') or φ ∈ S)) then S' := S' ∪ {φ};
            end
            if σ ∉ rcl(ψ) then S' := S' \ {σ};
```

od
if$(sat(\psi, S'))$ **then** $Q_0 := Q_0 \cup \{S'\}$;
$\delta = \delta \cup \{(S', \sigma, S)\}$;
$X := X \cup \{S'\}$; $Q := Q \cup \{S'\}$
od
od

The resulting non-deterministic automaton can easily be determinised. Although this can theoretically result in an exponential blow up, according to our experiments this does not usually occur. The deterministic automaton is, in fact, in most cases smaller than the original.

The correctness of the algorithm is quite easy to justify using the same arguments as Kupferman and Vardi [1]. There is technical report which considers these questions in more depth [14].

Theorem 1. *[14] Given an LTL formula ψ, the algorithm translate(ψ) constructs a finite automaton which accepts exactly the informative prefixes of $\neg\psi$.*

The theoretical bound achieved by our algorithm is in most cases better than the ones presented in [1, 10].

Theorem 2. *[14] The number states of the automaton is bounded by $2^{rcl(\psi)}$.*

For LTL formulas without the next-operator the bound is equal to $max(2^{tf(\psi)}, 2)$, where $tf(\psi)$ denotes the temporal subformulas of ψ.

4 Implementation

We have implemented the optimised translation algorithm for safety LTL formulae and also the check for determining if a formula is pathologic.

The implementation is BDD-based. BDDs are used to represent sets of formulas efficiently. Especially the translation algorithm heavily employs manipulation of sets, which can easily be implemented with BDDs. However, BDDs can also incur a certain overhead making the algorithm slower in some cases compared to algorithms using simpler set representations.

The tool, *scheck*, has been implemented using ANSI C++ and it should compile on most platforms where a C++-compiler supporting templates is available. It is available online from `http://www.tcs.hut.fi/~timo/scheck` under the terms of the GNU general public license (GPL). It easy to use *scheck* with Spin. *scheck* uses the neverclaim facility together with "-DSAFETY" and a failing assertion to stop Spin when a counterexample has been found.

The implementation of the translation algorithm is split into four separate stages. The first stage simply parses the input formula and transforms it into positive normal form. Optionally it can also perform some simple checks such as check for syntactic safety of the formula. The next stage builds a symbolic transition relation characterising the given formula. The third stage optionally performs some automata theoretic transformations, such as determinisation of the automaton. The fourth and the last stage outputs the automaton to the desired file or stream.

The basic idea of the second stage is to construct a symbolic transition relation which adheres to the translation rules given in the previous section. Symbolic reachability analysis is used to construct the automaton. To represent the states, $2 * N$ BDD variables are reserved, where N is the number of subformulas, i.e. $|cl(\psi)| = N$. One variable describes if the subformula belongs to the current state and one variable is for the next state. By using quantification it is easy remove state bits not in $rcl(\psi)$.

The third stage of the translation is an optional determinisation of the automaton. Early experiments showed that in almost all cases determinisation makes the automaton smaller. A deterministic automaton also has shorter model checking times, because it causes less branching in the product automaton. See the section on experiments for more details. If the automata are to be used for monitoring executions of software, determinisation is mandatory, although it can be performed on-the-fly while monitoring. Before the third stage, the automaton is converted to an explicit representation. Determinisation is easier when the automaton is in an explicit form. The arcs are still represented as BDDs since this allows easy manipulation of the arcs.

The last stage of the translation outputs the automaton to a file or a stream. Here, the only challenge is to output the arc labelling, represented as BDDs, succinctly using $\wedge$, $\vee$ and negation in front of the propositions.

4.1 Checking Pathologic Safety

Implementing, a check for if a formula is pathologic involves implementing an emptiness check for the intersection of two automata. Recall that an LTL formula ψ is pathologic iff $\mathcal{L}(\mathcal{A}_{\neg\psi}) \not\subseteq \mathcal{L}(\mathcal{A}^{true}_{\neg\psi})$. This is equivalent to that $\mathcal{L}(\mathcal{A}_{\neg\psi} \times \bar{\mathcal{A}}^{true}_{\neg\psi}) \neq \emptyset$.

Our implementation does not directly follow the procedure described in [1]. We perform the following steps when we are given an LTL formula ψ.

1. Construct a Büchi $\mathcal{A}_{\neg\psi}$ automaton corresponding to the negation of ψ.
2. Construct a *deterministic* finite automaton $\mathcal{B}_{\neg\psi}$, which accepts all informative bad prefixes of ψ.
3. Interpret $\mathcal{B}_{\neg\psi}$ as a deterministic Büchi automaton and construct the complement $\bar{\mathcal{B}}_{\neg\psi}$.
4. Construct the product automaton $\mathcal{C} = \mathcal{A}_{\neg\psi} \times \bar{\mathcal{B}}_{\neg\psi}$.
5. Check if $\mathcal{L}(\mathcal{C}) = \emptyset$.

The reason we require that $\mathcal{B}_{\neg\psi}$ is deterministic is that complementing a nondeterministic Büchi automaton is complicated and has an exponential time lower bound [15], while complementing a deterministic Büchi automaton can be done in linear time. The procedure outlined above is not optimal in the complexity theoretical sense but it works quite well when the size of $\mathcal{B}_{\neg\psi}$ does not explode. An optimal approach could use alternating automata, as outlined in [1].

We have presented how all steps can be performed except the complementation of the deterministic Büchi automaton. We follow the presentation Vardi given in his lecture notes [16]. Let $\mathcal{A} = \langle \Sigma, Q, \delta, s_0, F \rangle$ be a deterministic Büchi automaton. The complement $\bar{A} = \langle \Sigma, \bar{Q}, \bar{\delta}, \bar{s_0}, \bar{F} \rangle$ can be computed with the following operations.

- $\bar{Q} = (Q \times \{0\}) \cup ((Q - F) \times \{1\})$,
- $\bar{s_0} = s_0 \times \{0\}$,
- $\bar{F} = (S - F) \times \{1\}$, and
- for all states $q \in Q$ and symbols $a \in \Sigma$:

$$\bar{\delta}((q,0),a) = \begin{cases} \{(\delta(q,a),0)\}, & \text{if } \delta(q,a) \in F \\ \{(\delta(q,a),0),(\delta(q,a),1)\}, & \text{if } \delta(q,a) \notin F \end{cases}$$
$$\bar{\delta}((q,1),a) = \{(\delta(q,a),1)\},\ \delta(q,a) \notin F$$

The size of the complement is at most twice the size of the original automaton.

In the implementation we first compute explicit state representations of $\mathcal{A}_{\neg\psi}$ and $\mathcal{B}_{\neg\psi}$. Next, the deterministic automaton $\mathcal{B}_{\neg\psi}$ is complemented using the procedure above. Finally the product is computed and an emptiness check is performed using Tarjan's algorithm for finding strongly connected components. The tool has an interface for using an external translator to construct the Büchi automaton $\mathcal{A}_{\neg\psi}$, to benefit from more optimised Büchi translators than the simple one of the tool.

5 Experiments

In order to evaluate the implementation, *scheck*, we conducted some experiments. Four experiments were performed. The two first experiments measured the performance of the tool for random formulae, while for the third experiment we used the formulas in the specification pattern system [17]. In the fourth experiment *scheck* was interfaced with the model checker Spin to measure performance on practical models. We have collected the models used and other relevant files to a webpage: `http://www.tcs.hut.fi/~timo/spin2003`.

We used three LTL to Büchi translators as reference: a state of the art tool by Paul Gastin and Dennis Oddoux [18], the translator packaged with the Spin tool [2], and an efficient implementation of the algorithm described in [19] by Mäkelä, Tauriainen and Rönkkö [20]. In the following we refer to the tool of Gastin and Oddoux as *ltl2ba*, to the tool of Mäkelä et al. as *lbt* and to the translator of Spin simply as *spin*. The two first tests were conducted on a machine with a 266 MHz Pentium II processor with 128 MB of memory. The third and fourth tests were conducted on a machine with a 1 GHz AMD Athlon processor with 1 GB of memory.

For the two first tests which involve random formulae and random state-spaces we have used the LTL to Büchi translator test bench by Tauriainen and Heljanko [21]. The tool includes facilities for randomly generating LTL formulae and measuring different statistics such as the size of the generated automaton and generation time.

The first test generates random syntactically safe formulae. Most safety formula encountered in practice will probably be of this form. The idea is to measure how well the tools can cope with typical safety formulae. Statistics measured are the number of states and transitions in the automata produced, the time to generate the automata and the size of the product of a random state space of twenty states and the automaton. The number states and transitions in the generated automaton and generation give an indication of the general performance of the translator while the size of the product statespace depends on both the size of the generated automaton and the structure of the automaton. Automata which have small product statespaces can potentially at an early stage 'decide' if the current sequence under inspection cannot satisfy the given formula.

We generated one thousand formulas of fixed length between five and 22, three times. For *lbt* and *spin* we stopped the generation at 15 because we started to run out of memory. We set *scheck* to generate deterministic automata, as preliminary experiments indicated that this improved performance. To compare to the other tools we computed the mean $E(M(proc, L))$ over the three times for each procedure *proc*, formula length L and measure M. The ratio of the means $\frac{E(M(scheck,L))}{E(M(proc,L))}$ have been computed in Figure 1.

When we compare the size of the automatons generated, i.e. number of states and transitions, *scheck* seems to be very competitive when formula sizes grow. Especially the procedures based on [19] cannot compete well. When the formulas are short *spin* and *ltl2ba* are able to compete, but when the length of the formulas grows, *scheck* clearly scales better than the other tools. At the time when the measurements were made *scheck* did not check for a "sink state" in its deterministic automata. If the tests were rerun, *scheck* would probably narrow down the small lead *spin* and *ltl2ba* have in short formulae. Long formulae are not affected as much by the removal of one sink state. Note that in the number of transitions *scheck* scales even better compared to the other tools. One reason is probably that *scheck* generates deterministic automata.

Generation time gives a different picture of how well the tools perform. The tools based on [19] have an advantage with short formulae but do not scale as well. *ltl2ba* is however much faster than *scheck* in all cases. It scales better and it is faster for short formulae. It is possible that the implementation of *scheck* using BDDs gives the other tools an competitive advantage. This is supported by the fact that *scheck* produces smaller or as small automata as the other tools but is still in some cases significantly slower.

We expected *scheck* to have smaller product statespaces, because the automata it generates are deterministic. When the automaton is deterministic, the branching factor should be smaller. The results also confirm this. *scheck* generates smaller product statespaces than all three other tools.

The second test is in a sense a generalisation of the first. Now we randomly generate any type of LTL formula and use the implemented check for pathologic formulae to see if its a safety formula which can be used in the tests. This test

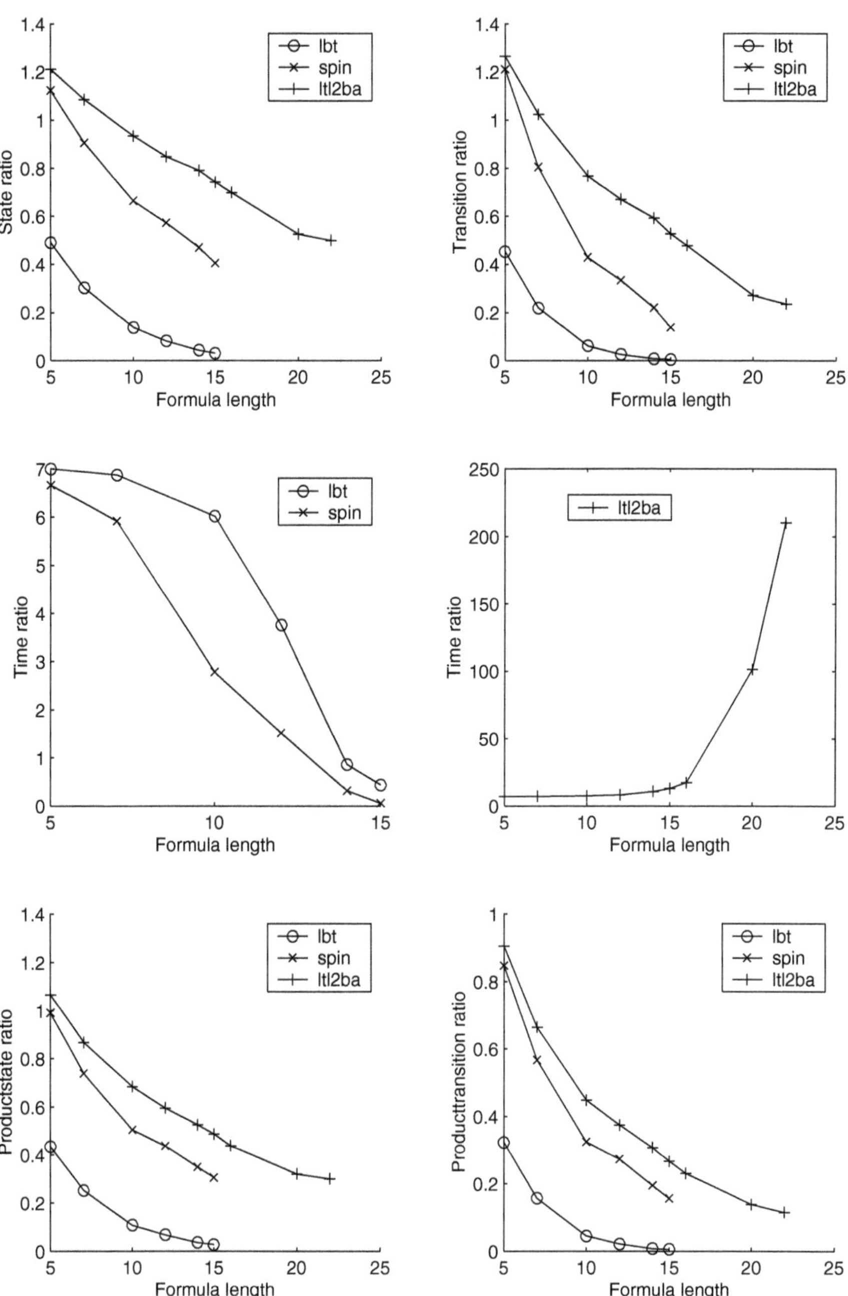

Fig. 1. Comparison of the tools with syntactically safe formulae

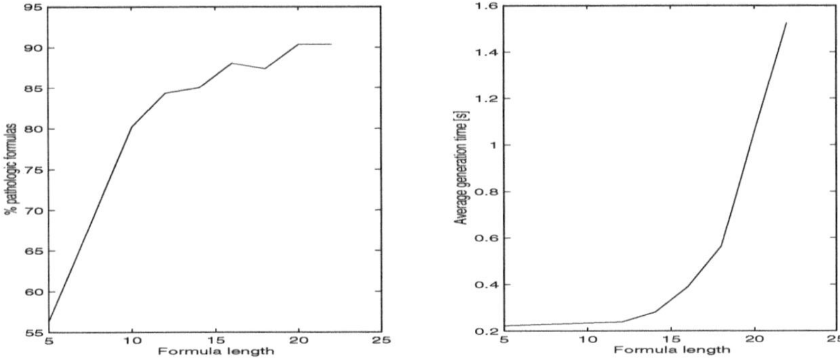

Fig. 2. *scheck* performance for general formulae

is only performed for *scheck*, as none of the other tools can check if a formula is pathologic.

One hundred formulas and their negation were generated for each length ranging from five to 22. As can been seen from the first plot, most of the generated pathologic or liveness formulas and the percentage grows when formula length increases. This is of course not surprising as the temporal operators often describing liveness properties are more likely to occur. The generation time, which includes the time to check if the formula is pathologic, for formulas which are not pathologic shows the familiar exponential increase which usually manifests itself sooner or later when solving PSPACE-complete problems. Our suspicion is that why *scheck* can require exponential time but not generate exponential automata is due to inefficiencies in implementation when using BDDs in *scheck*. One conclusion which is not affected by high rejection ratio of the formulas is that *scheck* can clearly scale well when identifying pathologic formulas. We refer the interested reader to [14] for more statistics.

The third test measures the same statistics as the two first but here we use the formulas from the specification pattern system [17]. Of the 60 patterns for LTL, 36 patterns are safety formulas to which we applied the translators. As *spin* ran out of memory for some of the formulas it was excluded from the test. The results can be found in Table 1.

For the fourth test we used five models of distributed algorithms. We used the model checker Spin, using "-DSAFETY" with *scheck* and normal LTL model checking with the others, to check a safety property on each model. Because the

Table 1. Statistics for the specification pattern formulas (36 formulas)

	states	arcs	time [s]	product states	product arcs
ltl2ba	160	348	0.5	3037	15406
lbt	1915	31821	1.2	25134	763203
scheck	144	316	2.1	2481	9806

Table 2. Experiments on practical models. A '-' means out of memory

model	*scheck*			*spin*			*ltl2ba*			
	states	arcs	t [s]	states	arcs	t [s]	states	arcs	t [s]	$\|\psi\|$
peterson(3)	17476	32343	0.06	21792	45870	0.09	21792	45870	0.09	10
peterson(4)	3254110	709846	20.8	4216030	10315000	37.3	4216030	10315000	37.5	10
sliding(1,1)	130799	407238	0.9	258456	890026	2.2	258432	890386	2.2	21
sliding(1,2)	518050	1670120	3.9	1027130	3604660	9.8	1027120	3604410	9.8	21
sliding(2,1)	5447700	18271400	534.7	10794100	39649800	1097.4	10794000	39645700	1097.6	21
erathostenes(50,1)	522	522	0.03	522	522	0.03	678	678	0.03	7
erathostenes(60,2)	324	324	0.02	357958	647081	4.0	794322	1319710	8.4	10
erathostenes(70,3)	522	522	0.04	2047030	4407400	48.5	3110700	6474410	76.6	13
erathostenes(80,4)	789	789	0.04	-	-	-	-	-	-	16
erathostenes(80,5)	847	847	0.04	-	-	-	-	-	-	19
iprot	7095180	20595400	377.0	16011900	46288600	1006.2	16011900	46288600	1003.7	21
giop	146646	215640	1.8	255105	524493	4.8	255105	524493	4.6	9

tool *lbt* did not have a Spin interface it did not participate in the tests. The property for *peterson*, *sliding*, *iprot*, and *giop* is a property which holds while the property for *erathotenes* does not hold. Additionally, the specification for *erathotenes* was parametric (the second parameter of the model). The statistics compared are size of the product statespace, which gives an indication of the memory use of the model checker, and the time used for model checking. Table 2 contains the results.

It would seem that the advantage of using finite automata for safety properties is very significant when debugging models. The fact that the algorithm can stop immediately when the error has been discovered without completing an infinite loop can result in significant gains. If the property holds the gain is smaller, but still there. It would appear that *scheck* causes less branching in product statespace. These results are of course preliminary and to get a clearer picture of the situation more tests are required.

6 Discussion

The implementation of the translation procedure presented in this work, *scheck*, produces smaller automata than the state of the art of the LTL to Büchi automata translators. In some cases the difference is exponential, while in other times it is negligible. The resulting product statespaces are also smaller for *scheck*. This is probably because *scheck* produces deterministic automata. The fact that determinising would result in much smaller automata came as a pleasant surprise. It is a well-known that determinising a non-deterministic automaton can result in an exponentially larger automaton. Safety properties can be expressed using reverse deterministic automata [1]. Apparently, the succinctness of non-determinism is not needed in the forward direction, when using random formulae. Currently *scheck* (version 1.0) does not apply a minimisation algorithm to the deterministic automata produced. This would be simple to add but we leave this to further work. Automata generation time was the one area where the results for *scheck* were disappointing. Although *scheck* generates the automaton for almost any formula used the tests in a few seconds, this is quite slow compared ltl2ba which in most cases would only use a few hundreths of a second. One of the reasons could be that *scheck* uses BDDs to manage sets, which sometimes can cause overhead even when the sets are small. A non-BDD implementation would probably perform better. To produce even smaller automata faster than *scheck*, another approach is probably required. It would be interesting to see if starting from alternating automata as in [18] could facilitate an efficient translation.

For practical models it would seem that using *scheck* gives the most gain when debugging models, especially if the properties are complex. The gain will not manifest itself if we are model checking a formula of the form $\mathbf{G}p$ as most LTL to Büchi automata translators handle this case optimally. More experiments are needed to get a clearer picture of the situation.

In order to be able to benefit from treating safety properties as a special case we must be able to recognise safety formulae. There are two ways in which this can be done. Either we only use the syntactically safe subset of LTL, which is easy to recognise or we implement pathologic checking in the tool. Experiments seem to confirm that pathologic checking is feasible. This means that both options for recognising safety properties are available and can be used. In some cases, as many probably have noticed, it is possible to interpret the Büchi automaton produced by a normal translator as a finite automaton, and use it directly for model checking. This could be confirmed by interpreting the produced finite automaton as the output of *scheck* and check if it is pathologic. In this way, a normal LTL to Büchi automata translator could in some cases be used to output finite automata. The construction of Geilen [10] has the advantage that it can provably produce correct Büchi and finite automata for informative prefixes with very small changes.

The results of Geilen [10] indicate that there is tight relationship between the Büchi automata and the finite automata for LTL formulas. In the future it would seem reasonable that a translator tool could produce both small finite automata and small Büchi automata.

scheck is available online from `http://www.tcs.hut.fi/~timo/scheck` and ready to be used with Spin.

Acknowledgements

The author is grateful to Keijo Heljanko for fruitful discussions and comments on drafts of the paper.

References

[1] Kupferman, O., Vardi, M.: Model checking of safety properties. Formal Methods in System Design **19** (2001) 291–314 74, 75, 77, 78, 79, 80, 81, 86
[2] Holzmann, G.: The model checker Spin. IEEE Transactions on Software Engineering **23** (1997) 279–295 74, 82
[3] Kurshan, R.: Computer-Aided Verification of Coordinating Processes: The Automata-Theoretic Approach. Princeon University Press (1994) 74
[4] Vardi, M. Y., Wolper, P.: Automata-theoretic techniques for modal logic of programs. Journal of Computer and System Sciences **32** (1986) 183–221 74

[5] Vardi, M.: An automata-theoretic approach to linear temporal logic. In: Logics for Concurrency: Structure versus Automata. Volume 1043 of LNCS. Springer (1996) 238–266 74, 78
[6] Hardin, R., Kurshan, R., Shukla, S., Vardi, M.: A new heuristic for bad cycle detection using BDDs. In: Computer Aided Verification (CAV'97). Volume 1254 of LNCS., Springer (1997) 268–278 75
[7] Esparza, J., Heljanko, K.: Implementing LTL model checking with net unfoldings. In: SPIN 2001. Volume 2057 of LNCS., Springer (2001) 37–56 75, 77
[8] Heljanko, K.: Combining Symbolic and Partial Order Methods for Model Checking 1-Safe Petri Nets. PhD thesis, Helsinki University of Technology, Department of Computer Science and Engineering (2002) 75
[9] Sistla, A.: Safety, liveness, and fairness in temporal logic. Formal Aspects in Computing **6** (1994) 495–511 75, 77
[10] Geilen, M.: On the construction of monitors for temporal logic properties. In: RV'01 - First Workshop on Runtime Verification. Volume 55 of Electronic Notes in Theoretical Computer Science., Elsevier Science Publishers (2001) 75, 78, 80, 87
[11] Berard, B., Bidoit, M., Finkel, A., Laroussinie, F., Petit, A., Petrucci, L., Schnoebelen, P.: Systems and Software Verication. Model-Checking Techniques and Tools. Springer (2001) 75
[12] Havelund, K., Rosu, G.: Synthesizing monitors for safety properties. In: Tools and Algorithms for the Construction and Analysis of Systems. Volume 2280 of LNCS., Springer (2002) 342–356 75, 77
[13] Helovuo, J., Leppänen, S.: Exploration testing. In: Application of Concurrency in System Design (ACSD'2001), IEEE (2001) 201–210 77
[14] Latvala, T.: On model checking safety properties. Technical Report 80, 85 HUT-TCS-A76, Helsinki University of Technology (2002) Available from `http://www.tcs.hut.fi/Publications`
[15] Safra, S.: Complexity of Automata on Infinite Objects. PhD thesis, The Weizmann Institute of Science (1989) 81
[16] Vardi, M.: Automata-theoretic approach to design verification. Webpage (1999) `http://www.wisdom.weizmann.ac.il/~vardi/av/notes/lec2.ps` 82
[17] Dwyer, M., Avrunin, G., Corbett, J.: Property specification patterns for finite-state verification. In: Workshop on Formal Methods in Software Practice, ACM Press (1998) 7–15 82, 85
[18] Gastin, P., Oddoux, D.: Fast LTL to Büchi automata translation. In: Computer Aided Verification (CAV'2001). Volume 2102 of LNCS., Springer (2001) 53–65 82, 87
[19] Gerth, R., Peled, D., Vardi, M., Wolper, P.: Simple on-the-fly automatic verification of linear temporal logic. In: Protocol Specification, Testing, and Verification, Warsaw, Chapman & Hall (1995) 3–18 82, 83
[20] Mäkelä, M., Tauriainen, H., Rönkkö, M.: lbt: LTL to Büchi conversion (2001) `http://www.tcs.hut.fi/Software/maria/tools/lbt/` 82
[21] Tauriainen, H., Heljanko, K.: Testing LTL formula translation into Büchi automata. STTT - International Journal on Software Tools for Technology Transfer **4** (2002) 57–70 82

A Light-Weight Algorithm for Model Checking with Symmetry Reduction and Weak Fairness

Dragan Bošnački

Eindhoven University of Technology
PO Box 513, 5600 MB Eindhoven, The Netherlands
dragan@win.tue.nl

Abstract. We present an algorithm for (explicit state) model checking under weak fairness that exploits symmetry for state space reduction. It is assumed that the checked properties are given as Büchi automata. The algorithm is based on the Nested Depth First Search (NDFS) algorithm by Courcoubetis, Vardi, Wolper and Yannakakis. The weak fairness aspect is captured by a version of the Choueka flag algorithm. As the presented algorithm allows false positives, it is mainly intended for efficient systematic debugging. However, we show that for this more modest goal our algorithm has significant advantages over the existing full-fledged model checking algorithms that exploit symmetry under weak fairness. The prototype implementation on top of Spin showed encouraging results.

1 Introduction

Symmetry reduction (c.f. [11, 7]) is one of the most effective weapons against the state space explosion problem in model checking [7].

Many systems, like mutual exclusion algorithms, cache coherence protocols, or bus communication protocols, exhibit significant degree of symmetry. In order to grasp the idea behind symmetry reduction, consider a typical mutual exclusion protocol. The (im)possibility for processes to enter their critical sections simultaneously will stay the same if the process identities are permuted. As a consequence, when during state-space exploration a state is visited that is the same, up to a permutation of pids, as some state that has already been visited, the search can be pruned. More formally, the symmetry of the system is represented by a given group G of permutations that act on the global states of the system. It turns out that two states s and s' are behaviorly equivalent if there exists a permutation $\pi \in G$ such that s' can be obtained by applying π on s. Thus, the system state space T is partitioned into equivalence classes. We define a selection function h which selects a unique representative from each equivalence class. Next, the quotient state space $h(T)$ is constructed that contains only these representatives and the property is checked using $h(T)$ instead of T. As $h(T)$ is in general much smaller than T, the gain in memory and time needed for the verification algorithms can be significant.

T. Ball and S.K. Rajamani (Eds.): SPIN 2003, LNCS 2648, pp. 89–103, 2003.

In this paper we confine our attention to the notion of weak fairness on process level. Thus, in a quite standard way we assume that the system is specified as a collection of concurrent (sequential) processes. Under this assumption we require that for every execution sequence of the system, if some process becomes continuously enabled at some point of time (i.e. can always execute some of its statements), then at least one statement from that process will eventually be executed. This kind of fairness is most often associated with mutual exclusion algorithms, busy waiting, simple queue-implementations of scheduling, resource allocation, etc. Weak fairness will guarantee the correctness of properties like eventually entering the critical region for every process which is continuously trying to do this (in the mutual exclusions) or eventually leaving the waiting queue for each process that has entered it (in the scheduling) [14].

Thus, combining the algorithms for model-checking under weak fairness with reduction techniques, and in particular symmetry, is a prerequisite for the verification of many interesting properties in practice. However, when coupling the two concepts special care should be taken, because of the possible incompatibilities between the particular algorithms.

The main contribution of this paper is an algorithm for model checking under weak fairness (in the sense described above) that exploits symmetry reduction. We assume that the properties that are checked are specified as Büchi automata [20]. As a consequence the problem of checking whether some given property holds for the system under consideration can be reduced to the problem of finding acceptance cycles (i.e., cycles that contain acceptance states) in the graph representing the product of the system state space with the property automaton (c.f. [8, 7]).

Our basic idea is conceptually simple. We apply a (symmetry) reduction algorithm in order to reduce the state space and on the reduced state space we run an algorithm for detecting weakly fair acceptance cycles. (In accord with what was said above, along these cycles each process must be either disabled or contribute a transition to the cycle.) The main challenge is how to combine the symmetry and weak fairness algorithms efficiently. This means that we want the two algorithms to be run simultaneously (instead of sequentially) and on-the-fly (i.e. the state space is generated only on demand). The on-the-fly feature is very important in debugging because it often happens that there is not enough memory or time to deal with the whole state space although it can still be easy and useful to detect possible erroneous executions with the existing resources. Unfortunately, with our symmetry reduction algorithm it is not guaranteed (at least in theory) that if there exists a fair acceptance cycle in the original state space, it will also exists one in the reduced state space. As a consequence, the combined algorithm can give false positives, i.e., it can miss some acceptance cycles. As such, our algorithm is mainly intended for debugging.[1]

---

[1] At this stage it is not clear for what kind of acceptance cycles (i.e. models and properties) our algorithm will fail. The counterexample [3] (an idea of Dennis Dams) was quite contrived and we were not able to produce a corresponding Promela model on which our algorithm should fail. For all examples on which the algorithm was

The algorithms which are presented in this paper are based on the so-called nested depth first search (NDFS) algorithm by Courcoubetis, Vardi, Wolper and Yannakakis [8] for detecting acceptance cycles in the state space.

As a stepping stone toward the final goal, we first describe an NDFS based algorithm for model checking under weak fairness without symmetry reduction. This algorithm is a minor modification of the weak fairness algorithm of the model checker Spin, as implemented by Holzmann. The last algorithm is actually a version of the Choueka flag algorithm [6]. The idea of this upgrade of NDFS for weak fairness is to do the search for an acceptance cycle in an extended state space in which it is guaranteed that each cycle which is detected is a fair one. The final algorithm which features both fairness and symmetry is a merge of the weak fairness algorithm with a NDFS based algorithm for symmetry reduction from [4]. The main idea behind the resulting algorithm is to find a path in the original state space for which it can be proved that it is a fragment of a weakly fair cycle. Along such a fragment each process has already been disabled or contributed a transition. In fact the weakly fair cycle can be obtained by concatenating symmetric images of the fragment.

The algorithms for combining symmetry with (weak) fairness that we found in the literature [12, 15] are based on finding maximal strongly connected components (MSCC) in the state space graph. Because of that our algorithm has the advantages that standard NDFS has over the MSCC based algorithms. More precisely, we argue that in practice both the time and space complexities of our algorithm are better. Also, unlike the algorithms from [12, 15], our algorithm is compatible with the approximative verification techniques from [16, 22], which are important in the context of debugging. Shortly before the submission of this paper it was suggested to the author that an efficient model checking algorithm that exploits symmetry with fairness based on the LTL model checking algorithm from [9] can be designed. It is quite difficult to compare the efficiency of our algorithm with such a hypothetical algorithm. However, as the algorithm of [9] is also based on MSCC, it is evident that it is not going to be compatible with the above mentioned approximative verification techniques from [16, 22].

2 Preliminaries

2.1 Labeled Transition Systems

In the sequel we adopt the automata theoretic approach to model checking [21]. In particular, we assume that the properties that are checked are given as Büchi automata. As it was mentioned in the introduction, we work with the graph obtained as a product of the state space graph representing the system (more precisely: the system model) with the automaton (graph) representing the (negation of the) property. The algorithms to obtain the product state space are quite standard (c.f. [8, 7]). In the sequel we assume that the product state space is

tested, if an acceptance cycle existed, the algorithm successfully reported an error. Of course, this is not enough to draw any definite conclusions.

given. (An on-the-fly integration of the algorithms for obtaining the product state space with the algorithms presented in this paper should be trivial (c.f. [7]).)

Because we deal with weak process fairness it is natural to assume that we model the system as a collection of processes. To capture this in the semantics we assume a finite sequence of processes $P_1, P_2, \ldots, P_N$, $N \geq 1$, which are represented by their indices (process IDs, pids) from the set $I = \{1, 2, \ldots, N\}$. For our purposes, we represent the final state space graph as a *labeled transition system* formally defined as follows:

Definition 1. *Let* Prop *be a set of atomic propositions. A* labeled transition system *(LTS) is a 7-tuple* $T = (S, A, I, R, L, \hat{s}, F)$, *where*

- S *is a finite set of* states,
- A *is a finite set of actions,*
- I *is a finite set of processes (process IDs),*
- $R \subseteq S \times A \times I \times S$ *is a* transition relation *(we write* $s \stackrel{a,i}{\rightarrow} s' \in R$ *for* $(s, a, i, s') \in R$*),*
- $L : S \rightarrow 2^{Prop}$ *is a* labeling function *which associates with each state a set of atomic propositions that are true in the state,*
- $\hat{s}$ *is the* initial state,
- $F \subseteq S$ *is the set of* acceptance states.

Unless stated differently, we fix T to be $(S, A, I, R, L, \hat{s}, F)$ for the rest of the paper.

Intuitively, if a transition is labeled by the pid i, this means that it is obtained as a result of a statement executed by the process P_i. An action a is *enabled* in a state $s \in S$ iff $s \stackrel{a,i}{\rightarrow} s' \in R$ for some $s' \in S$ and $i \in I$. We say that the process P_i is *enabled* in $s \in S$ iff there exists $a \in A, s' \in S$, such that $s \stackrel{a,i}{\rightarrow} s' \in R$. An *execution sequence* or *path* is a finite or infinite sequence of subsequent transitions, i.e., for $s_i \in S$, $a_i \in A$, $j_i \in I$ the sequence $s_0 \stackrel{a_0,j_0}{\rightarrow} s_1 \stackrel{a_1,j_1}{\rightarrow} s_2 \ldots$ is an execution sequence in T iff $s_i \stackrel{a_i,j_i}{\rightarrow} s_{i+1} \in R$ for all $i \geq 0$. An infinite execution sequence is said to be *accepting* iff there is an acceptance state $s \in F$ that occurs infinitely many times in the sequence. A finite execution sequence $c = s_0 \stackrel{a_0,j_0}{\rightarrow} s_1 \stackrel{a_1,j_1}{\rightarrow} \ldots \stackrel{a_{n-1},j_{n-1}}{\rightarrow} s_n, n \geq 1$ is a *cycle* iff the start and end states coincide, i.e. $s_0 = s_n$. Given a finite or infinite execution sequence $\sigma = s_0 \stackrel{a_0,j_0}{\rightarrow} s_1 \stackrel{a_1,j_1}{\rightarrow} s_2 \ldots$, a process P_i, $1 \leq i \leq N$, and a state s_j from the execution sequence, we say that P_i is *executed* in σ in s_j iff $s_j \stackrel{a,i}{\rightarrow} s_{j+1}$ is a transition in σ. A state s is *reachable* iff there exists a finite execution sequence that starts at $\hat{s}$ and ends in s. A cycle c is *reachable* iff there exists a state in c which is reachable. A cycle c is an *acceptance cycle* if it contains at least one acceptance state.

2.2 The Standard Nested Depth-First Search Algorithm

The algorithms presented in this paper are based on the algorithm of [8] for memory efficient verification of LTL [10] properties, called nested depth first search (NDFS) algorithm. The standard NDFS algorithm is given in Fig. 1.

```
1  proc dfs1(s)
2     add {s,0} to States
3     for each process i := 1 to N do
4        for each transition (s,a,i,s')  do
5           if {s',0} not in States then dfs1(s') fi
6        od
7     od
8     if accepting(s) then seed:={s,1}; dfs2(s) fi
9  end
10
11 proc dfs2(s) /* the nested search */
12    add {s,1} to States
13    for each process i := 1 to N do
14       for each transition (s,a,i,s')  do
15          if {s',1} == seed  then report cycle
16          else if {s',1} not in States then dfs2(s') fi
17       od
18    od
20 end
```

Fig. 1. Nested depth first search (NDFS) algorithm

The algorithm consists of two depth first search (DFS) procedures: `dfs1` which implements the "basic" DFS and `dfs2` which performs the "nested" DFS. In order to detect possible acceptance cycles, at each acceptance cycle the basic DFS is temporarily suspended and the nested DFS is launched (by calling `dfs2` in line 8), with the current (acceptance) state as a `seed`. The procedures `dfs1` and `dfs2` work in separate state spaces. If `dfs2` matches the `seed`, this means that an acceptance cycle is found. In this case the cycle is reported and the program is stopped (line 16). If, however, the nested DFS ends without matching the `seed`, the basic DFS (`dfs1`) is resumed until a possible new acceptance state is encountered. It should be emphasized that, although it might look quadratic, the NDFS algorithm is linear in the number of states in the state space [8]. (See also [4].)

The fact that for each state s of the original state space the copies in the first and second DFS differ only in the second (bit) component can be used to save memory space [18]. The states $(s, 0)$ and $(s, 1)$ can be stored together as (s, b_1, b_2), where b_1 (respectively b_2) is a bit which is set to 1 iff $(s, 0)$ (resp. $(s, 1)$) has been already visited during the first (resp. second) DFS. Thus in this way, the (doubled) state space used by NDFS takes, for realistic systems, virtually the same amount of memory as the original state space.

The following claim (essentially Theorem 1 from [8]) establishes the correctness of the algorithm:

Theorem 1 ([8]). *Given an LTS T, the* NDFS algorithm *in Fig. 1, when called on $\hat{s}$, reports a cycle iff there is a reachable acceptance cycle in T.*

2.3 Symmetry Reduction

Given a LTS $T = (S, A, I, R, L, \hat{s}, F)$ let $Perm(I)$ and $Perm(S)$ be the groups of permutations of the sets $I = \{1, \ldots, N\}$ of pids and S of states, respectively. Both $Perm(I)$ and $Perm(S)$ are groups under the functional composition $\circ$ defined as: For any two permutations π_1, π_2, $(\pi_1 \circ \pi_2)(x) \stackrel{def}{=} \pi_1(\pi_2(x))$. We assume that each permutation $\pi \in Perm(I)$ can be lifted into the permutation π^* on the state set S. This assumption is quite natural regarding the way symmetry reduction is handled in practice (see for instance [19, 11, 5]). Formally, we require that there exists a mapping $()^* : Perm(I) \rightarrow Perm(S)$ which maps each $\pi \in Perm(I)$ into $\pi^* \in Perm(S)$.

Definition 2. *Given a LTS $T = (S, A, I, R, L, \hat{s}, F)$ and a mapping $()^* : Perm(I) \rightarrow Perm(S)$, a subgroup G of $Perm(I)$ is called a* symmetry group *of T iff for all $\pi \in G$*

- $s \stackrel{a,i}{\rightarrow} s' \in R$ *iff* $\pi^*(s) \stackrel{a,\pi(i)}{\rightarrow} \pi^*(s') \in R$.
- *For all* $s \in S$ $\pi^*(s) = \hat{s}$ *iff* $s = \hat{s}$
- *For all* $s \in S$ $L(s) = L(\pi^*(s))$.
- $s \in F$ *iff* $\pi^*(s) \in F$.

We say that the states $s_1, s_2 \in S$ are in the same *orbit* iff there exists $\pi \in G$ such that $\pi^*(s_1) = s_2$. The symmetry group G induces the *orbit* relation $\Theta_G \subseteq S \times S$ defined as $\Theta_G = \{(s_1, s_2) \mid s_1 \text{ and } s_2 \text{ are in the same orbit}\}$. It is trivial to show that Θ_G is an equivalence relation. It is convenient to work with representatives of these equivalence classes (orbits). To this end we introduce the function $h : S \rightarrow S$ which maps a given state s of T into its representative. More precisely, given $s_1, s_2 \in S$, s_1 and s_2 are in the same orbit iff $h(s_1) = h(s_2)$.

Directly from Def. 2 above we have:

Corollary 1. *Let $\rho = s_0 \stackrel{a_0,j_0}{\rightarrow} s_1 \stackrel{a_1,j_1}{\rightarrow} \ldots \stackrel{a_{n-1},j_{n-1}}{\rightarrow} s_n$, $n \geq 1$, be a path in T and π a permutation in G. Then the path $\pi(\rho) = \pi^*(s_0) \stackrel{a_0,\pi(j_0)}{\rightarrow} \pi^*(s_1) \stackrel{a_1,\pi(j_1)}{\rightarrow} \ldots \stackrel{a_{n-1},\pi(j_{n-1})}{\rightarrow} \pi^*(s_n)$ is also in T.*

We can exploit the symmetry for state space reduction by pruning the state space search from the currently visited state, if some symmetric state (i.e. from the same equivalence class) has already been visited. An adaptation of the NDFS algorithm that employs symmetry is given in Fig. 2.

The only changes compared to the standard NDFS from Fig. 1 are in lines 2, 5, 8, 12, 15, and 16, where s and s' are replaced with their representatives $h(s)$ and $h(s')$, respectively. (Notice though that the procedures `dfs1` and `dfs2` are called with s and s' as parameters, instead of $h(s)$ and $h(s')$ respectively.) The net effect is the same as if we do the exploration of the state space instead in the original state space T in a reduced LTS $h(T)$. The states of $h(T)$ are representatives of the symmetry equivalence classes from T obtained by means of the function h.

```
proc dfs1(s)
   add {h(s),0} to States
   for each porcess i := 1 to N do
      for each transition (s,a,i,s')  do
         if {h(s'),0} not in States then dfs1(s') fi
      od
   od
   if accepting(s) then seed:={h(s),1}; dfs2(s) fi
end

proc dfs2(s) /* the nested search */
   add {h(s),1} to States
   for each porcess i := 1 to N do
      for each transition (s,a,i,s')  do
         if {h(s'),1} == seed  then report cycle
         else if {h(s'),1} not in States then dfs2(s') fi
      od
   od
end
```

Fig. 2. Nested depth first search (NDFS) algorithm with symmetry reduction

In [4] it is shown that the algorithm in Fig. 2 reports a cycle iff there is an acceptance cycle in the original LTS T. Notice though that the preservation of fair acceptance cycles is not guaranteed. In other words, given a fair acceptance cycle c in T, the acceptance cycle which is detected (and reported) in the reduced state space $h(T)$, and which corresponds to c, is not necessarily weakly fair. Intuitively this is because in general the cycles in $h(T)$ can be shorter and the process indices are "scrambled".

It is worth emphasizing again that the in order to exploit symmetry the state space must be symmetric. As we assume that we work with state spaces which incorporate the property (originally given as a Büchi automaton), this means that implicitly we require that the property which is checked is also symmetric, i.e., invariant under the permutations from G applied on pids from I.

2.4 Weak Fairness

We consider weak fairness with regard to processes, i.e. we say that a given execution sequence is fair if for each process that becomes continuously enabled starting at some point in the execution sequence, a transition belonging to this process is executed infinitely many times. Formally:

Definition 3. *An infinite execution sequence* $s_0 \stackrel{a_0,p_0}{\rightarrow} s_1 \stackrel{a_1,p_1}{\rightarrow} s_2 \ldots$ *is* (weakly) fair *iff for each process* $P_l, 1 \leq l \leq N$*, the following holds: If there exists* $i \geq 0$ *such that* P_l *is enabled in* s_j *for all* $j \geq i$*, then there are infinitely many* $k \geq 0$ *such that* P_l *is executed in* s_k*.*

A cycle $c = s_0 \overset{a_0,p_0}{\rightarrow} s_1 \overset{a_1,p_1}{\rightarrow} \ldots s_{n-1} \overset{a_{n-1},p_{n-1}}{\rightarrow} s_0$ *is* (weakly) fair *iff whenever a process* P *is enabled in all states* s_i, $0 \leq i < n$, *then* P *is executed in some state* s_j, $0 \leq j < n$.

When solving the model-checking problem under the (weak) fairness assumption we are interested only in fair accepting execution sequences. As we work with finite LTSs, it is obvious that, translated in terms of acceptance cycles, the fairness assumption means that we require that the acceptance cycles we detect in the state space are fair.

3 Combining Weak Fairness with Symmetry Reduction

3.1 Model Checking under Weak Fairness without Symmetry

In the sequel we informally discuss an algorithm for model checking with weak fairness (WF) without symmetry reduction. The algorithm which is described below is is a variant of Choueka's flag algorithm [6], based on the version implemented in the model checker Spin by Holzmann.

In order to capture weak fairness, one also has to modify the standard NDFS algorithm. This is because the latter only guarantees that it will find some acceptance cycle, if there exists one, but not all of them. Thus, one cannot use the straightforward idea to just ignore the detected cycles which are not fair until one finds a fair one, or there are no more cycles.

To bypass this limitation of the NDFS, we apply it not to the original state space, but to an extended state space. The latter is constructed such that the existence of a fair acceptance cycle in the original state space implies that there exists an acceptance cycle in the extended state space, and vice versa. We first give the intuition behind the extended state space and the modified NDFS algorithm. The set of states of the extended state space consists of $N + 1$ copies of the original state set, where N is the number of processes. The extended state space and its relation to the original state space are shown in Figure 3.

T and F denote the original state space and its acceptance states, respectively. The extended state space is denoted with $\mathcal{F}(T)$, the set of its acceptance states with F_f, while $T_i, 0 \leq i \leq N$, are the copies of the original state space T. With $T_0 - F_f$ we denote copy 0 of the original state space without the acceptance states F_f. The label a, l $(a, i \neq l)$ on the arrows between the copies express the fact that we can pass between the copies l and $l+1$ (resp. stay inside copy l) by executing a transition belonging to process l.

The intuition behind the copies of T is that when the algorithm works in the i-th copy of the state space ($1 \leq i \leq N$), this means that it waits for process i to contribute a transition or to become disabled. (In order to treat these two cases uniformly, we will assume that when process i is disabled in the original state space, in the extended state space it executes a *default transition*, labeled with a special action ϵ_i.) When the algorithm is in copy i and process i executes a transition, then the algorithm passes to copy $i + 1$. From copy N it goes back to the special copy 0.

All acceptance states of $\mathcal{F}(T)$ (i.e. the set F_f) reside in copy 0. When the algorithm comes across an acceptance state of $\mathcal{F}(T)$ it jumps immediately via a special ϵ_0-transition to copy 1. (The ϵ_0-transitions can be considered as meta transitions which do not belong to any process and do not correspond to any transition from the original system.) The algorithm stays inside copy 0 as long as transitions originating from a non-acceptance state are explored. The ϵ_0-transitions are the only possible transitions from an acceptance state. Thus, from the structure of $\mathcal{F}(T)$ it is obvious that in order to get back to the acceptance state one has to pass through all N copies of T. This implies that each process i has contributed a transition (ordinary or ϵ) along the cycle, and therefore the latter is weakly fair.

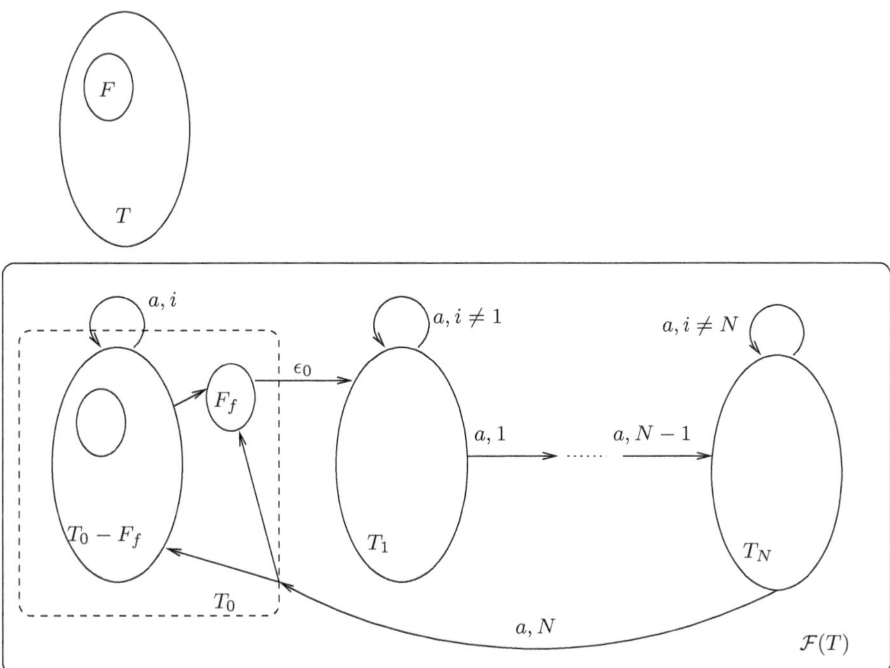

Fig. 3. The extended state space for the weak fairness algorithm

3.2 Weak Fairness and Symmetry Together On-the-Fly

The most direct way to model check under weak fairness is to first unfold the original state space T into the corresponding weakly fair extension $\mathcal{F}(T)$ and then to apply the NDFS algorithm on $\mathcal{F}(T)$. Instead, for efficiency reasons, we do the unfolding of the state space and the NDFS simultaneously. In this way we keep the advantage of the on-the-fly approach that, if there exists a fair acceptance cycle, usually we do not have to generate the whole $\mathcal{F}(T)$. Once NDFS is adapted to generate the extended state space, it remains to add the symmetry reduction part. We do this by merging the obtained on-the-fly NDFS with weak fairness with the NDFS based symmetry reduction algorithm from [4], given in Fig. 2. Thus, the state space search is pruned from the current state s if a symmetric state has already been saved in the state space. The pseudo-code of the algorithm is given in Figure 4.

We represent the states of the extended state space as triples of the form (s, C, b). They are obtained in a straightforward way by extending each state s, apart from the bit b discriminating between the first and second DFS, also with the integer counter C that keeps track of the current copy of the original state space.

There are several changes in the standard NDFS algorithm which are needed for the generation of $\mathcal{F}(T)$. The ϵ_0-transitions are generated with the true branch of the outermost `if` statement (lines 3 and 4, and 23 and 24). The increment of the counter component by 0 or 1, depending on whether the counter C matches the pid of the currently considered process or not, takes place in lines 7 and 27. The ϵ_i-transitions corresponding to the disabled processes are implemented with the true branch of the corresponding `if` statements in lines 8 and 9, and 28-30). Notice that also the transition between the sates in copy 0, i.e., when the current state is in copy 0 and it is not an acceptance state, is also implicitly implemented through line 7 and 27. As variable `i` is never 0, if `C` is 0, then the assignment `C' = C` is executed, which leaves the counter component unchanged.

The symmetry reduction part is implemented analogously to the algorithm in Fig. 2, i.e., by replacing some occurrences of states with their representatives.

The correctness of the algorithm is given with the following claim:

Theorem 2. *Given an LTS T, if the algorithm from Fig. 4, started with arguments $\hat{s}$ and 0 reports a cycle, then there exists a reachable weakly fair acceptance cycle in T.*

Proof. Suppose that the algorithm reports a cycle. The intuition is that in that case it has detected a path $\rho^0 = s_0^0 \stackrel{a_0,j_0}{\rightarrow} s_1 \stackrel{a_1,j_1}{\rightarrow} \ldots \stackrel{a_{n-1},j_{n-1}}{\rightarrow} s_0^1$, $n \geq 1$, which can be extended into a weakly fair cycle in the original state space T. More precisely ρ^0 is such that

- $h(s_0^0) = h(s_0^1)$, and
- ρ^0 is a "fair fragment", i.e., for each process i it holds that there exists on ρ^0 a state s_k such that i is disabled in s_k or executed in s_k.

This is implied by the following reasoning. Let s_0^0 be the acceptance state from which we have obtained (in line 17) the seed state which is matched by the algorithm. Thus, $(h(s_0^0), C, 1) = seed$. (Recall that we consider that our algorithm works in the extended state space $\mathcal{F}(T)$, where each state in the extended state space is a triple of the form (s, C, b).) The algorithm can make a move, i.e., generate a transition in $\mathcal{F}(T)$ from the currently visited state (s, C, b) in the extended state space only in the following cases:

```
proc dfs1(s,C)
   add {h(s),C,0} to States
   if C == 0 and accepting(s) then
      if {h(s),1,0} not in States then dfs1(s,1) fi
                                                      /* epsilon_0 move */
   else
      for each process i := 1 to N do
         if C == i then C' := (C+1) mod (N+1) else C' := C fi
         if process i is disabled then /* epsilon_i move */
            if {h(s),C',0} not in States and C == i then dfs1(s,C') fi
         else
            for all (s,a,i,s') do
               if {h(s'),C',0} not in States then dfs1(s',C') fi
            od
         fi
      od
   fi
   if C == 0 and accepting(s) then seed := {h(s),C,1}; dfs2(s,C) fi
 end


proc dfs2(s,C) /* the nested search */
   add {h(s),C,1} to States
   if C == 0 and accepting(s) then
      if {h(s),1,1} not in States then dfs2(s,1) fi
                                                      /* epsilon_0 move */
   else
      for each process i := 1 to N do
         if C == i then C' := (C+1) mod (N+1) else C' := C fi
         if process i is disabled then /* epsilon_i move */
           if {h(s),C',1} == seed then report cycle
           else
            if {h(s),C',1} not in States and C == i then dfs2(s,C') fi
         else
           for all (s,a,i,s') do
             if {h(s'),C',1} == seed then report cycle
             else if {h(s'),C',1} not in States then dfs2(s',C') fi
           od
         fi
       od
   fi
end
```

Fig. 4. An Algorithm that combines weak fairness and symmetry reduction

- s is an acceptance state and $C = 0$ (lines 3 and 4, and 23 and 24 – ϵ_0-transition), or
- Process i is disabled in s and $C = i$ (lines 8 and 9, and 28-30 – ϵ_i-transition), or
- there exists a transition in T from s to s' (lines 12–34).

The first two cases (the ϵ-transitions) do not correspond to "real" transitions that exist in T. We obtain ρ^0 by removing such transitions from the sequence of moves (transitions) taken by the algorithm. This can be done because the source and target states of the ϵ-transitions always have the same s-component. By omitting these transitions no state (of the original LTS T) is lost. The states s_0^0 and s_0^1 belong to the same symmetry equivalence class because also $h(s_0^1, C, 1) = seed$, and therefore $h(s_0^0) = h(s_0^1)$. Thus, by omitting the C and b components of the states in the transition sequence which the algorithm generates in $\mathcal{F}(T)$ without the ϵ-transitions, we obtain the desired path ρ^0 which exists in T.

Now we show the "fairness" of ρ^0. From the structure of the algorithm it is clear that the counter C is increased first from 0 to 1 (line 4, 24), then from 1 to N (lines 7, 27), and then reset back to 0 (again lines 7, 27). The increment of the counter C from value i to $i+1$ (or reset to 0, if $C = N$) is possible only if process i is disabled in the current state or a transition is taken that belongs to process i (code fragments between lines 7 and 14, and 27 to 34.) The increment from 0 to 1 is immediate in case s is an acceptance state. This means that the algorithm generates a sequence of $N+1$ states $s_{j_0}, \ldots, s_{j_N}$ which are on ρ^0, and for each process i it holds that in s_{j_i} process i is disabled or contributes a transition along ρ^0.

It remains to show that the "fair fragment" ρ can be extended to obtain a fair cycle. If ρ^0 is a cycle, i.e., $s_0^0 = s_0^1$, then we are done. So, suppose that $s_0^0 \neq s_0^1$. Consequently, there exists a permutation π_1 such that $s_0^1 = \pi_1(s_0^0)$. If we now apply the permutation π_1 to each transition in ρ^0 we will obtain the path $\pi_1(\rho^0) = \rho^1$. By Corollary 1 this path exists in T. (Notice that the end state of ρ^0 is the same with the start state of ρ^1.) In an obvious way we can continue this procedure to obtain new paths $\rho^{i+1} = \pi_{i+1}(\rho^i)$. From the finiteness of the equivalence class to which the starting states s_0^i belong, it follows that sooner or later one of the states s_0^k will repeat itself. In other words, there exists $0 \leq k < l$ such that $s_0^k = s_0^l$. From the discussion above, it is obvious that the cycle which is obtained as a concatenation of the paths ρ^k to ρ^{l-1} is a weakly fair cycle in T. □

Comparison with Related Work. We compare our algorithm with the algorithms of Emerson and Sistla (ES95) [12] and Gyuris and Sistla (GS97) [15]. These were the only algorithms for combining weak fairness and symmetry that we could find in the literature. GS97 is an improved version of ES95, so we will refer to the former for comparison. The GS97 algorithm is on-the-fly and it is based on the graph algorithm for finding all maximal strongly connected components (MSCC) from [1]. Unlike our algorithm, ES95 and GS97 are model checking algorithms that work in both directions, i.e., they do not report false positives.

However, in the sequel we argue that if one considers only systematic debugging, our algorithm is more efficient in general. This is mainly because the algorithm in Fig. 4 has the usual advantages that NDFS have over the algorithms that work with MSCCs.

Regarding the time complexity it is assumed that finding a representative can be done in an efficient way, more precisely, in our calculations we assume a constant time. Unfortunately, this is the case only for some special systems and symmetries. In general, no polynomial algorithm is known to compute a unique representative of a symmetry equivalence class. There are however efficient heuristics that work reasonably well in practice(c.f. [19, 5]). The same assumption is made also for the complexity calculations for the GS97 algorithm, therefore, this feature does not have any impact on the comparison.

Under the above assumption our algorithm and GS97 have the same worst case time complexity $O(N \cdot |h(T)|)$, where N is the number of processes in the system and $|h(T)|$ is the size (in number of transitions) of the reduced LTS $h(T)$.

In practice we reduce the space complexity of our algorithm by using a similar trick which allowed us to avoid doubling of the state space in the case of the standard NDFS algorithm as described in Section 2.2. Namely, instead of using $N+1$ copies of the state space $h(T)$ we can extend the state description with $2 \times (N+1)$ bits, each corresponding to the $(N+1)$ copies of $h(T)$ in the basic and nested DFS, respectively. (Factor 2 comes because of the two NDFS copies.) This overhead per state is less than the overhead required by GS97. Namely, the MSCC algorithm from [1] keeps two long integers per state as state identifiers. The bottom line is that it can be shown by simple calculation that in practice our algorithm requires less memory in the worst case than GS97.

If a fair acceptance cycle is reported, our algorithm has an obvious advantage regarding both time and space because it does not have to finish finding the whole MSCC. GS97 has to construct the whole MSCC in order to detect a violation of the property. This means that the whole MSCC is kept in the memory in contrast to our algorithm which keeps only a part of it – in the best case only the acceptance cycle. Also, exploring a bigger portion of the state space takes more time.

An important practical advantage of our algorithm is that, unlike the two existing algorithms, it is compatible with the memory efficient approximate verification techniques like bit-state hashing [16] and hash-compact [22]. This is not the case with GS97, because of the above mentioned two integers per state needed in the MSCC computation. Finally, for practical reasons our algorithm is also easier to implement because it has a simpler theory basis behind it and does not require some complex structures which are used in GS97.

4 Experiments

A prototype implementation of the algorithm is included in SymmSpin [5], an extension of the model checker Spin [16] with symmetry reductions. We tried it on the case studies from [5] with encouraging results. The obtained reductions

Table 1. Results for Peterson's mutual exclusion protocol

N	2		3		4		5	
	+SR	-SR	+SR	-SR	+SR	-SR	+SR	-SR
nr. of states	81	153	636	2295	4150	84707	77064	out of memory
time [min:sec]	0.1	0.1	0.2	0.6	2.1	1:51.4	5:06.3	—

for correct properties were usually of several orders of magnitude, very similar with the results for the same examples for safety properties, reported in [5]. Also significant reductions were obtained for incorrect properties, i.e., when a fair acceptance cycle was reported. Due to space constraints we give only the results for one of the examples, which is nevertheless quite illustrative. Table 1 gives the results for Peterson's mutual exclusion algorithm for an incorrect property of bounded response type (LTL formula: $\Box(p \rightarrow \Diamond q)$). (SR+ and SR- mean with and without symmetry reduction, respectively.) The symmetry reduction algorithm used a selection function h which corresponds to the "pc-segmented" heuristic from [5]. One can see t the reduction factor significantly improves as N increases, which is typical for symmetry reduction.

5 Conclusion and Future Work

In this paper we presented an algorithm for efficient debugging of properties under weak fairness while exploiting symmetry reduction. It was argued that, compared with the similar algorithms that exist in the literature, our algorithm has advantages regarding the time and memory efficiency, and the compatibility with other verification (debugging) techniques. The efficiency of the algorithm was further supported with some encouraging experiments with a prototype implementation on top of the model checker Spin.

A natural avenue for future work is to design an NDFS-based algorithm for full-fledged model checking, i.e., to avoid false positives. Further, it would be interesting to combine our algorithm with other state space reduction techniques, like, for instance, partial order reduction (POR), [7]. In the literature there are successful attempts [13] of combining symmetry and POR. Despite the seemingly widespread belief that weak fairness and partial order are inherently irreconcilable, we believe that this is not true. We are confident that the POR algorithm from [17] can be adapted so that it becomes compatible with fairness. A previous attempt in that direction is described in [2].

References

[1] A. V. Aho, J. E. Hopcroft, J. D. Ulmann, *The design and Analysis of Computer Algorithms*, Addison Wesley, 1974. 100, 101

[2] D. Bošnački, *Partial Order Reduction in Presence of Rendez-vous Communications with Unless Constructs and Weak Fairness*, Theoretical and Practical Aspects of SPIN Model Checking, 5th and 6th International SPIN Workshops, LNCS 1680, pp. 40–56, Springer, 1999. 102

[3] D. Bošnački, *Enhancing State Space Reduction Techniques for Model Checking*, p. 146, Ph.D. Thesis, Eindhoven University of Technology, ISBN 90-386-0951-5, 2001. 90

[4] D. Bošnački, *A Nested Depth First Search Algorithm for Model Checking with Symmetry Reduction*, Proc. of FORTE'02, LNCS, Springer, 2002. 91, 93, 95, 98

[5] D. Bošnački, D. Dams, L. Holenderski, *Symmetric Spin*, 7th Int. SPIN Workshop on Model Checking of Software SPIN 2000, pp. 1-19, LNCS 1885, Springer, 2000. 94, 101, 102

[6] Y. Choueka, *Theories of Automata on ω-tapes: a Simplified Approach*, Journal of Computer and System Science, Vol. 8, pp. 117-141, 1974. 91, 96

[7] E. M. Clarke, Jr., O. Grumberg, D. A. Peled, *Model Checking*, The MIT Press, 2000. 89, 90, 91, 92, 102

[8] C. Courcoubetis, M. Vardi, P. Wolper, M. Yannakakis, *Memory Efficient Algorithms for the Verification of Temporal Properties*, Formal Methods in System Design I, pp. 275-288, 1992. 90, 91, 92, 93

[9] J.-M. Couvreur, *On-the-fly Verification of Linear Temporal Logic*, Proc. of FM'99, pp. 253–271, LNCS 1708, 1999. 91

[10] E. A. Emerson, *Temporal and Modal Logic*, in J. van Leeuwen (ed.), Formal Models and Semantics, pp. 995–1072, Elsevier, 1990. 92

[11] E. A. Emerson, A. P. Sistla, *Symmetry and model checking*, Proc. of CAV'93 (Computer Aided Verification), LNCS 697, pp. 463–478, Springer, 1993. 89, 94

[12] E. A. Emerson, A. P. Sistla, *Utilizing Symmetry when Model Checking under Fairness Assumptions: An Automata Theoretic Approach*, Proc. of CAV'95 (Computer Aided Verification), LNCS 697, pp. 309–324, Springer, 1995. 91, 100

[13] E. A. Emerson, S. Jha, D. Peled, *Combining partial order and symmetry reductions*, in Ed Brinksma (ed.), Proc. of TACAS'97 (Tools and Algorithms for the Construction and Analysis of Systems), LNCS 1217, pp. 19–34, Springer, 1997. 102

[14] N. Francez, *Fairness*, Springer, 1986. 90

[15] V. Gyuris, A. P. Sistla, *On-the fly model checking under fairness that exploits symmetry*, in O. Grumberg (ed.), Proc. of CAV'97 (Computer Aided Verification), LNCS 1254, pp. 232–243, Springer, 1997. 91, 100

[16] G. J Holzmann, *Design and Validation of Communication Protocols*, Prentice Hall, 1991. Also: `http://netlib.bell-labs.com/netlib/spin/whatispin.html`. 91, 101

[17] G. Holzmann, D. Peled, *An Improvement in Formal Verification*, FORTE 1994, Bern, Switzerland, 1994. 102

[18] G. Holzmann, D. Peled, M. Yannakakis, *On Nested Depth First Search*, Proc. of the 2nd Spin Workshop, Rutgers University, New Jersey, USA, 1996. 93

[19] C. N. Ip, D. L. Dill, Better verification through symmetry. *Formal Methods in System Design*, Vol. 9, pp. 41–75, 1996. 94, 101

[20] W. Thomas, *Automata on Infinite Objects*, in J. van Leeuwen (ed.), Formal Models and Semantics, pp. 995–1072 Elsevier, 1990. 90

[21] M. Vardi, P. Wolper, *Automata Theoretic Techniques for Modal Logics of Programs*, Journal of Computer and System Science, 32(2), pp. 182–221, 1986. 91

[22] P.Wolper, D. Leroy, *Reliable Hashing without Collision Detection*, Proc. of CAV'93 (Computer Aided Verification), LNCS 697, pp. 59–70, Springer, 1993. 91, 101

A SAT Characterization of Boolean-Program Correctness

K. Rustan M. Leino

Microsoft Research
One Microsoft Way, Redmond, WA 98052, USA
leino@microsoft.com

Abstract. Boolean programs, imperative programs where all variables have type boolean, have been used effectively as abstractions of device drivers (in Ball and Rajamani's SLAM project). To find errors in these boolean programs, SLAM uses a model checker based on binary decision diagrams (BDDs). As an alternative checking method, this paper defines the semantics of procedure-less boolean programs by weakest solutions of recursive weakest-precondition equations. These equations are then translated into a satisfiability (SAT) problem. The method uses both BDDs and SAT solving, and it allows an on-the-fly trade-off between symbolic and explicit-state representation of the program's initial state.

Introduction

Boolean programs are imperative computer programs where all variables have type boolean. They have been found to be useful abstractions of low-level systems software. In particular, boolean programs have been used as abstractions of device drivers in the SLAM project [3]. In this paper, I show how to translate a procedure-less boolean program into a logical formula that (a) is satisfiable if and only if there is a path from the beginning of the program to an error and (b) can be used as input to a satisfiability (SAT) solver.

The translation starts with the semantics of the procedure-less boolean program, which I define as the weakest solution to a set of weakest-precondition equations. The main challenge is then to transform the second-order fixpoint characterization into a first-order propositional formula. I present an algorithm for doing so. The algorithm is founded on three mathematical ingredients, which I explain.

The translation into a SAT formula uses binary decision diagrams (BDDs) [7]. A simple mathematical equality allows the symbolic representation of the program's initial values to be changed, on the fly, into a representation that models these boolean values explicitly. Because of this explicit representation, the BDDs used can be made arbitrarily simple.

Initial experience with an implementation (called Dizzy) of the method has exhibited poor performance. An unknown portion of this is due to that Dizzy inlines procedures rather than summarizing them (which SLAM's model checker

T. Ball and S.K. Rajamani (Eds.): SPIN 2003, LNCS 2648, pp. 104–120, 2003.

$$
\begin{array}{rcl}
\mathit{Prog} & ::= & \textbf{var}\ \mathit{Id}^*\ ;\ \mathit{Block}^+ \\
\mathit{Block} & ::= & \mathit{LabelId}\text{: } \mathit{Stmt}^*\ [\ \textbf{goto}\ \mathit{LabelList}\ ;\ ] \\
\mathit{Stmt} & ::= & \mathit{Id}^+ := \mathit{Expr}^+\ ; \\
 & | & \textbf{assume}\ \mathit{Expr}\ ; \\
 & | & \textbf{assert}\ \mathit{Expr}\ ;
\end{array}
\qquad
\begin{array}{rcl}
\mathit{LabelList} & ::= & \mathit{LabelId} \\
 & | & \mathit{LabelList}\ \textbf{or}\ \mathit{LabelId} \\
\mathit{Expr} & ::= & \textbf{false} \mid \textbf{true} \mid \mathit{Id} \\
 & | & \neg \mathit{Expr} \mid \mathit{Expr} \vee \mathit{Expr} \\
 & | & \mathit{Expr} \wedge \mathit{Expr}
\end{array}
$$

Fig. 1. Grammar of the boolean programs in this paper

Bebop [2] does). I hope the method presented here stimulates further research, perhaps where the method is used as an intraprocedural component of another checker.

Section 1 defines boolean programs and their weakest-precondition semantics. Section 2 presents the three mathematical ingredients on which the translation is based. Section 3 shows the translation algorithm. Section 4 discusses the complexity of the algorithm, brings out its symbolic-versus-explicit-state trade-offs, and reports on some preliminary experiments.

1 Boolean Programs and Their Semantics

Boolean programs in SLAM can have procedures [2]. In this paper, I use a procedure-less language. Procedures can be inlined at call sites (as indeed they are in Dizzy), since recursion is not prevalent in the device drivers that SLAM checks.

1.1 Syntax

In this paper, a boolean program has the form given in Figure 1. A program consists of a set of boolean variables and a set of named blocks. Each block consists of a sequence of statements followed by a **goto** statement that declares a set of successor blocks (the absence of a **goto** statement indicates the empty set of successor blocks).

The execution of a program fragment may *terminate* (in some state), *loop forever*, *go wrong*, or *idle*. Going wrong indicates undesirable behavior. A program is erroneous if an execution of it can go wrong; otherwise, it is correct. Idling indicates points in the execution beyond which we are not interested in the program's behavior, such as the beginning of infeasible paths.

Program execution begins in the first given block. Upon termination of the statements in a block, a successor block is picked arbitrarily (nondeterministically) and execution continues there. If the set of successor blocks is empty, execution idles.

In addition to ordinary assignment statements, there are **assume** and **assert** statements. Executing these statements when their conditions evaluate to **true** is equivalent to a no-op. That is, their execution terminates in the same state in which it started. If the condition evaluates to **false**, the **assert** statement goes wrong whereas the **assume** statement idles.

For the purpose of checking the program for errors, this simple language is sufficiently expressive to encode common conditional and iterative statements. For example, an if statement **if** E **then** S **else** T **end** is encoded as:

0: **goto** 1 **or** 2 ;
1: **assume** E ; S ; **goto** 3 ;
2: **assume** $\neg E$; T ; **goto** 3 ;
3:

and a loop **while** E **do** S **end** is encoded as:

0: **goto** 1 **or** 2 ;
1: **assume** E ; S ; **goto** 0 ;
2: **assume** $\neg E$; **goto** 3 ;
3:

Here is a simple example program, which I use as a running example throughout the paper:

var x, y ;
A : $x :=$ **true** ; **goto** B ;
B: **assert** x ; $x := x \wedge y$; **goto** B **or** C ; (1)
C:

The program contains an error, because if y is initially **false**, then x will be **false** in a second iteration of block B, causing the **assert** statement to go wrong.

1.2 Semantics

I define the semantics of a boolean program in terms of *weakest preconditions* [8]. (The connection between operational semantics and weakest preconditions has been studied elsewhere, *e.g.* [11] and [9].) For any sequence of statements S and postcondition Q (that is, Q characterizes some set of post-states of S), $wp(S, Q)$ characterizes those pre-states from which execution of S is guaranteed:

- not to go wrong, and
- either the execution does not terminate or it terminates in a state satisfying Q.[1]

Pictorially (see Figure 2), $wp(S, Q)$ is the largest set of pre-states from which execution of S never goes wrong and terminates only in Q.

The weakest preconditions of statement sequences are defined as follows, for any expression E, statement sequences S and T, and postcondition Q:

$$\begin{array}{rcl} wp(\epsilon, Q) & = & Q \\ wp(S\ T, Q) & = & wp(S, wp(T, Q)) \end{array} \qquad \begin{array}{rcl} wp(x := E;, Q) & = & Q[x := E] \\ wp(\textbf{assume}\ E;, Q) & = & E \Rightarrow Q \\ wp(\textbf{assert}\ E;, Q) & = & E \wedge Q \end{array} \qquad (2)$$

[1] Unlike Dijkstra's original definition of weakest preconditions, I distinguish between looping forever and going wrong, and only the latter makes a program erroneous.

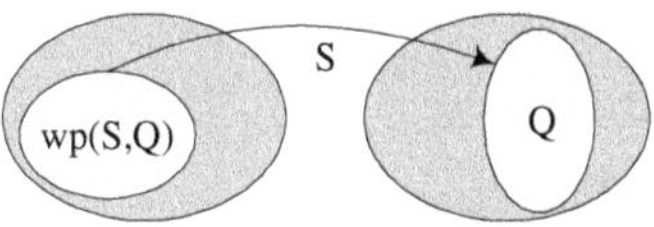

Fig. 2. $wp(S, Q)$ denotes the largest set of pre-states with the following property: starting from any state in $wp(S, Q)$, execution of S does not go wrong, and, if the execution terminates, it does so in a state satisfying Q

where ϵ denotes the empty statement sequence, $S\ T$ is the sequence S followed by sequence T, and $Q[x := E]$ denotes the capture-free substitution of E for x in Q.

The semantics of a block is defined by the weakest precondition of the block statements with respect to the semantics of the block's successor blocks. To formalize the definition, I introduce for each block a boolean function on the block's pre-state, a function whose name I take to be the same as the name of the block. The function represents the semantics of the block. Formally, for any block B, the equation defining the function B is, for any w:

$$B(w) \quad = \quad wp(S, \bigwedge_{G \in \mathcal{G}} G(w)) \tag{3}$$

where w denotes the program variables, S is the sequence of statements of block B, and $\mathcal{G}$ is the set of successor blocks of B. That is, $B(w)$ is defined as $wp(S, Q)$ where Q is the conjunction of $G(w)$ for every block G in $\mathcal{G}$. Thus, for any pre-state w of B (that is, for any value of the program variables w), $B(w)$ is **true** if and only if execution of the program beginning at block B from state w is guaranteed not to go wrong.

Example program (1) gives rise to three functions, A, B, C, defined as follows, for any x, y:

$$\begin{array}{lcl} A(x,y) & = & wp(x := \mathbf{true},\ B(x,y)) \\ B(x,y) & = & wp(\mathbf{assert}\ x\,;\ x := x \wedge y,\ B(x,y) \wedge C(x,y)) \\ C(x,y) & = & wp(\epsilon,\ \mathbf{true}) \end{array}$$

which, after expanding the wp and making the quantification over x, y explicit, gives:

$$\begin{array}{lcl} (\forall x, y :: A(x,y) & = & B(\mathbf{true}, y)\ ) \\ (\forall x, y :: B(x,y) & = & x \wedge B(x \wedge y, y) \wedge C(x \wedge y, y)\ ) \\ (\forall x, y :: C(x,y) & = & \mathbf{true}\ ) \end{array} \tag{4}$$

The set of equations formed by the definitions of the boolean functions may not have a unique solution, a fact that arises from the presence of loops in boolean programs. For example, these two closed-form definitions of A, B, C

both satisfy equations (4):

$$\begin{array}{ll} (\forall x, y :: A(x,y) = \textbf{false}\,) & (\forall x, y :: A(x,y) = y\,) \\ (\forall x, y :: B(x,y) = \textbf{false}\,) & (\forall x, y :: B(x,y) = x \wedge y\,) \\ (\forall x, y :: C(x,y) = \textbf{true}\,) & (\forall x, y :: C(x,y) = \textbf{true}\,) \end{array} \tag{5}$$

To be precise about the semantics equations, let us indicate which variables are the unknowns, which I shall do by writing them in front of the equations. For the example, the unknowns are A, B, C, so from now on I write (4) as:

$$\begin{array}{llcl} A, B, C: & (\forall x, y :: A(x,y) & = & B(\textbf{true}, y)\,) \\ & (\forall x, y :: B(x,y) & = & x \wedge B(x \wedge y, y) \wedge C(x \wedge y, y)\,) \\ & (\forall x, y :: C(x,y) & = & \textbf{true}\,) \end{array} \tag{6}$$

Of the various solutions to the equations we have set up, which solution do we want? The weakest solution. That is, the largest solution. That is, the solution where the unknowns are functions that return **true** as often as possible. The reason for this is that we want these weakest-precondition equations to characterize *all* the pre-states from which executions do not go wrong, that is, the *largest* set of pre-states from which executions do not go wrong.

To illustrate, consider the second line of the left-hand solution in (5). This line says that *if* the program is started from block B in a state satisfying **false** [2], then any resulting execution will be correct. However, since this is not the *weakest* solution, the line says nothing about starting executions from states *not* satisfying **false**. The second line of the right-hand solution in (5) says that if the program is started from block B in a state satisfying $x \wedge y$, then any resulting execution will be correct. Since this happens to *be* the weakest solution, we also have that if the program is started from B in a state *not* satisfying $x \wedge y$, then there exists an execution that goes wrong.

In summary, the semantics of a boolean program is the weakest solution to the set of equations prescribed, for every block B in the program, by (3).

Weakest Solution versus Weakest Fixpoint Before going on, let me take the opportunity to clear up a possible confusion, namely the issue of weakest *solution* versus weakest *fixpoint*. The distinction between the two is analogous to the distinction between the result of a function and the function itself. The weakest solution (in the unknown a) to $a: a \ = f(a)$ is the weakest fixpoint of f. Likewise, the weakest solution to a set of equations:

$$\begin{array}{lcl} a, b, c: \ a & = & f(a,b,c) \\ b & = & g(a,b,c) \\ c & = & h(a,b,c) \end{array} \tag{7}$$

is the weakest fixpoint of f, g, h. [3]

[2] An impossibility, but never mind that.

[3] That is, the fixpoint of the tuple function $[f, g, h]$, defined for any 3-tuple w as $[f, g, h](w) = \langle f(w), g(w), h(w) \rangle$, with the partial order of tuples defined pointwise as $\langle a, b, c \rangle \sqsubseteq \langle a', b', c' \rangle \ \equiv \ a \ \leq a' \wedge b \leq b' \wedge c \leq c'$.

To view the semantics of a boolean program as a weakest fixpoint, we formulate equations (6) equivalently as:

$$A,B,C: \quad \begin{array}{rcl} A &=& \mathcal{F}(A,B,C) \\ B &=& \mathcal{G}(A,B,C) \\ C &=& \mathcal{H}(A,B,C) \end{array} \tag{8}$$

where $\mathcal{F},\mathcal{G},\mathcal{H}$ are defined as follows, for any functions A,B,C :

$$\begin{array}{rcl} \mathcal{F}(A,B,C) &=& (\,\lambda\, x,y :: \; B(\mathbf{true},y)\,) \\ \mathcal{G}(A,B,C) &=& (\,\lambda\, x,y :: \; x \wedge B(x \wedge y, y) \wedge C(x \wedge y, y)\,) \\ \mathcal{H}(A,B,C) &=& (\,\lambda\, x,y :: \; \mathbf{true}\,) \end{array}$$

That is, $\mathcal{F}$, $\mathcal{G}$, and $\mathcal{H}$ are defined to take three functions (here called A,B,C) as arguments and to return one function (here denoted by λ -expressions). Since we are now dealing with functions that map functions to functions, it may sometimes be confusing as to which kind of function I'm referring to; therefore, I shall refer to $\mathcal{F},\mathcal{G},\mathcal{H}$ as *functional transformations* when doing so provides clarification. Under formulation (8), the semantics of the boolean program is the weakest fixpoint of $\mathcal{F},\mathcal{G},\mathcal{H}$.

According to a celebrated theorem by Knaster and Tarski (see, *e.g.*, [9]), a unique weakest fixpoint to the functional transformations $\mathcal{F},\mathcal{G},\mathcal{H}$ exists (equivalently, a unique weakest solution to (6) exists), provided $\mathcal{F},\mathcal{G},\mathcal{H}$ are monotonic. To see that the functional transformations are indeed monotonic, we just need to remember that they come from the right-hand side of (3). In particular, in the right-hand side of (3), the arguments to the functional transformations (that is, the functions G) occur conjoined in the second argument of the *wp* . And indeed, *wp* is monotonic in its second argument (see definition (2) or [8]).[4]

Program Correctness Given the semantics of a boolean program, as defined above, the program is correct if and only if $(\,\forall\, w :: \; start(w)\,)$ is a valid formula, where *start* is the program's start block and w denotes the program's variables. That is, the program is correct if, for every initial state w , its executions are guaranteed not to go wrong. Conversely, the program contains an error if and only if $(\,\exists\, w :: \; \neg start(w)\,)$, that is, if $\neg start(w)$ is satisfiable.

Applying SAT Now that we have defined the semantics and correctness criterion of boolean programs, we may get the feeling that the problem of checking the program for correctness can be performed by a SAT solver. This is an enticing prospect, given the recent impressive progress in producing efficient SAT solvers, for example like GRASP [12] and Chaff [13]. Indeed, the equations that define the

[4] Note that the existence of a weakest fixpoint requires the *functional transformations* ($\mathcal{F},\mathcal{G},\mathcal{H}$) to be monotonic. In particular, the existence of the weakest fixpoint does not rely on the *arguments* of the functional transformations (the functions A,B,C) to be monotonic. That's good, because the functions A,B,C are generally not monotonic.

program semantics are boolean formulas, and the existence of an error boils down to the satisfiability of a boolean formula. However, the problem also involves components not addressed by SAT solvers, namely the fact that the semantics is defined in terms of the weakest solution to the set of equations and the fact that the equations involve functions.

In the next section, I go through the mathematical ingredients that let us overcome these roadblocks to applying SAT techniques.

2 Three Mathematical Ingredients

2.1 Eliminating Quantifications: Equations over a Closed Set of Function Terms

The first mathematical ingredient, computing a set of equations over a closed set of function terms, allows us to eliminate the universal quantifications in the semantics equations.

To eliminate the quantifications in a set of equations like:

$$\begin{array}{lllll} A,B,C: & (\forall\, x,y :: & A(x,y) & = & \ldots) \\ & (\forall\, x,y :: & B(x,y) & = & \ldots) \\ & (\forall\, x,y :: & C(x,y) & = & \ldots) \end{array}$$

we can form a new set of equations by appropriate instantiations of the universal quantifications. In general, we need to instantiate the quantifications with all possible values, but if we are interested in evaluating only some particular expression, then we may be able to do with fewer instantiations. Let's do only as many instantiations as required for every mentioned function instantiation, or *function term* as I shall call them, to appear as the left-hand side of some equation. That is, let's instantiate the equations until we get a set of quantifier-free equations over a closed set of function terms.

For example, suppose for (6) that we have an interest in the expression $\neg A(k,m)$, as indeed we do if k and m denote initial values of the program variables x and y. Then, we instantiate the first quantification of (6), the one that defines A, with $x,y := k,m$, producing $A(k,m) = B(\mathbf{true},m)$. This equation mentions two function terms, $A(k,m)$ and $B(\mathbf{true},m)$, but the second of these does not appear as a left-hand side. Therefore, we continue the closure computation and instantiate the second quantification of (6) with $x,y := \mathbf{true},m$:

$$B(\mathbf{true},m) \;=\; \mathbf{true} \;\wedge\; B(\mathbf{true} \wedge m, m) \;\wedge\; C(\mathbf{true} \wedge m, m)$$

This in turn requires two more instantiations:

$$\begin{array}{lll} B(\mathbf{true} \wedge m, m) & = & \mathbf{true} \wedge m \;\wedge \\ & & \qquad B(\mathbf{true} \wedge m \wedge m, m) \;\wedge\; C(\mathbf{true} \wedge m \wedge m, m) \\ C(\mathbf{true} \wedge m, m) & = & \mathbf{true} \end{array}$$

Observe that the function terms appearing in the right-hand sides of these equations also appear as left-hand sides of the equations we've produced so far. This observation hinges on the fact that the function arguments of the new right-hand function terms for B and C, namely $\mathbf{true} \wedge m \wedge m$ and m, are the same as the arguments $\mathbf{true} \wedge m$ and m, respectively, for which we already have instantiations of B and C. Thus, we have now reached a closed set of function terms. Summarizing the example, if we are interested in the solution to (6) only to evaluate $\neg A(k, m)$, then we can equivalently consider the solution to the following quantifier-free equations:

$$\begin{array}{lrcl} A, B, C: & A(k,m) & = & B(\mathbf{true}, m) \\ & B(\mathbf{true}, m) & = & B(m,m) \wedge C(m,m) \\ & B(m,m) & = & m \wedge B(m,m) \wedge C(m,m) \\ & C(m,m) & = & \mathbf{true} \end{array} \tag{9}$$

where I have allowed myself to simplify the boolean expressions involved. In particular, the value of $\neg A(k, m)$ according to the weakest solution of (6) is the same as the value of $\neg A(k, m)$ according to the weakest solution of (9). What we have achieved is a projection of the original equations onto those values relevant to the expression of interest, akin to how *magic sets* can identify relevant instantiations of Horn clauses in logic programs [4].

In general, there may be more solutions to the computed quantifier-free set of equations than to the original set of equations. For example, (9) leaves $B(\mathbf{false}, \mathbf{true})$ unconstrained, whereas (6) constrains it to be **false** (see (5)). However, the function term $B(\mathbf{false}, \mathbf{true})$ is apparently irrelevant to the value of $\neg A(k, m)$, which we took to be the only expression of interest.

It is important to note that, unlike the bound x and y in (6), the occurrences of k and m in (9) are *not* bound. Rather, k and m are free variables in (9).

Another thing to note is that we could have terminated the closure computation above earlier if we had had particular boolean values for k and m. For example, if m had the value **true**, then the function term $B(m, m)$ would be the same as $B(\mathbf{true}, m)$, so we could have stopped the closure computation earlier. But if we are interested in representing k and m symbolically, like we did in this example so they can represent *any* initial program state, then we treat these function terms as potentially being different.

To actually perform this closure computation mechanically, we need to be able to compare two function terms for (symbolic) equality. This can be done by comparing (the names of the functions and) the arguments, which in turn can be done using BDDs [7], because BDDs provide a canonical representation of boolean expressions. The closure computation does terminate, because the number of function terms to be defined is finite: there is one function name for each block, and each function argument is a purely propositional combination of the variables k and m representing the initial program state (function-term arguments never contain nested function terms, see (3) and (2)). Section 4 takes a closer look at the actual complexity.

2.2 Eliminating Functions: Point Functions

The second mathematical ingredient, viewing a function as the union of a collection of point functions, allows us to eliminate functions from the semantics equations.

Any function $f\colon W \to U$ can be viewed as the union of $|W|$ nullary functions that I shall refer to as *point functions.* For every value w in the domain of f, we define a point function $f_w\colon () \to U$ by $f_w() = f(w)$. In principle, we can think of f as being defined by a table with two columns with elements from W and U, respectively. Each row of the table gives the value of f (shown in the right column) for a particular argument (shown in the left column). Each row then corresponds to what I'm calling a point function. By the way, being nullary functions, point functions are essentially just variables, so let's just drop the parentheses after them.

Symbolically, a recursive function (or set of recursive functions) can be defined as the weakest (say) solution of a set of equations; equivalently, the function (or set of functions) can be defined by its (their) point functions, which in turn are defined as the weakest solution to a set of equations where the point functions are expressed in terms of each other. For example, if f is a function on booleans, then the weakest solution to:

$$f: \quad (\forall w :: f(w) \quad = \quad f(\mathbf{false}) \vee f(w)) \tag{10}$$

can equally well be expressed as the weakest solution to:

$$\begin{array}{rrcl} f_{\mathbf{false}}, f_{\mathbf{true}}: & f_{\mathbf{false}} & = & f_{\mathbf{false}} \vee f_{\mathbf{false}} \\ & f_{\mathbf{true}} & = & f_{\mathbf{false}} \vee f_{\mathbf{true}} \end{array}$$

Note that these equations have two unknowns, $f_{\mathbf{false}}$ and $f_{\mathbf{true}}$, whereas (10) has only one unknown, f.

The set of equations that we arrived at in the previous subsection (the ones over a closed set of function terms) can be viewed as constraining a set of point functions. That is, we can think of each function term as being a point function. Viewing function terms as point functions, the equations (9) take the form:

$$\begin{array}{rrcl} A_{k,m}, B_{\mathbf{true},m}, B_{m,m}, C_{m,m}: & A_{k,m} & = & B_{\mathbf{true},m} \\ & B_{\mathbf{true},m} & = & B_{m,m} \wedge C_{m,m} \\ & B_{m,m} & = & m \wedge B_{m,m} \wedge C_{m,m} \\ & C_{m,m} & = & \mathbf{true} \end{array} \tag{11}$$

Before leaving the topic of point functions, there's another issue worth analyzing. Because we allow variables like k and m in the instantiations of the functions, the conversion into point functions may produce several variables for what is really the same point function. For example, equations (9) contain the function terms $B(\mathbf{true}, m)$ and $B(m, m)$. From the fact that B is a function, we immediately know that if m happens to have the value $\mathbf{true}$, then these two function terms evaluate to the same value. But by representing the two function terms as two separate variables, the point functions $B_{\mathbf{true},m}$ and $B_{m,m}$,

$$
\begin{array}{lrcl}
J,L,M: & J(k) & = & L(k) \wedge M(k) \\
& L(k) & = & M(\mathbf{true}) \\
& M(k) & = & k \wedge M(k) \\
& M(\mathbf{true}) & = & M(\mathbf{true})
\end{array}
\qquad
\begin{array}{lrcl}
J_k, L_k, M_k, M_{\mathbf{true}}: & J_k & = & L_k \wedge M_k \\
& L_k & = & M_{\mathbf{true}} \\
& M_k & = & k \wedge M_k \\
& M_{\mathbf{true}} & = & M_{\mathbf{true}}
\end{array}
$$

Fig. 3. Sets of equations in function-term form (left) and point-function form (right), illustrating that the conversion into point functions can enlarge the solution set

we no longer have the guarantee that $B_{\mathbf{true},m}$ and $B_{m,m}$ are equal if m and **true** are. Indeed, because we may have introduced several point functions for a function term, the conversion from function terms into point functions may have enlarged the set of solutions to the equations. Suppose a boolean program with one variable and start block J gives rise to the set of quantifier-free equations to the left in Figure 3. Then the corresponding point-function equations, shown to the right in Figure 3, admit the solution where J_k and M_k are **false** and L_k and $M_{\mathbf{true}}$ are **true**, independent of the value of k.[5] In contrast, the *function-term* equations admit this solution *only* if k does not have the value **true**.

Luckily, the fact that our conversion into point functions may produce several names for the same point function, which may, as we've just seen, enlarge the set of solutions to our equations, need not bother us. The reason is that we are interested only in the *weakest* solution, which has not changed. Here's why it has not changed: The quantifier-free equations are produced as instantiations of *one* set of semantics equations. Therefore, if the function for a block B is instantiated in more than one way, say like $B(w')$ and $B(w'')$, then the quantifier-free equations will constrain $B(w')$ and $B(w'')$ in the same way for the case where w' and w'' have the same value. Because the function terms $B(w')$ and $B(w'')$ have the same constraints, the corresponding point functions $B_{w'}$ and $B_{w''}$ also have the same constraints (again, in the case where w' and w'' have the same value). And since the point functions $B_{w'}$ and $B_{w''}$ have the same constraints, the set of solutions for each of these point functions is the same, and, in particular, the weakest solution of each is then the same.

2.3 Eliminating Non-weakest Solutions: Abbreviated Way of Computing Fixpoints

The third mathematical ingredient, an abbreviated way of computing an expression for a fixpoint, allows us to eliminate all but the weakest of the solutions to the set of equations.

[5] The letter k occurs in the subscripts of the point functions, but these occurrences do not denote the *variable* k. Rather, the subscripts are just part of the *names* of the four point-function variables.

Let's review the standard way of computing the weakest fixpoint of a function. If a function F on a complete lattice is *meet-continuous* —that is, if it has no infinite descending chains, or, equivalently, if it distributes meets over any nonempty, linear set of elements— then the weakest fixpoint of F is $F^d(\top)$ for some sufficiently large natural number d, where $\top$ is the top element of the lattice. Stated differently, the weakest fixpoint can be computed by iteratively applying F, starting from $\top$. The number d, which I shall call the *fixpoint depth* of F, is bounded from above by the *height* of the lattice, that is, the maximum number of strictly-decreasing steps required to get from $\top$ to $\bot$, the bottom element of the lattice. In general, the height of a lattice may be infinite. But *if* the lattice itself is finite, then the height is also finite. For a finite lattice, any monotonic function is also meet-continuous, because monotonicity is equivalent to the property of distributing meets over any nonempty, linear, *finite* set of elements [9]. For the particular case of the lattice of booleans, $(\{\mathbf{false}, \mathbf{true}\}, \Rightarrow)$, the height is 1, and so for any monotonic function F on the booleans, $F(\mathbf{true})$ always gives the weakest fixpoint of F.

The functional transformations implicit in our set of equations (11) all return point functions, which in our application are nullary boolean functions, that is, booleans. Suppose there are n equations in the set ($n = 4$ for the set of equations (11)). The height of the lattice of n-tuples of booleans (ordered pointwise, see footnote 3) is n. Hence, the standard way of computing fixpoints tells us that we can obtain the weakest solution to the set of equations by iteratively applying the n functional transformations n times starting from $\mathbf{true}$.

The standard way does compute the weakest fixpoint. However, there is opportunity to compute it a bit faster. According to the standard way, the weakest solution of a for boolean functions f, g, h constrained as in (7) is:

$$\begin{array}{l} f(f(f(\top,\top,\top),\ g(\top,\top,\top),\ h(\top,\top,\top)), \\ \quad g(f(\top,\top,\top),\ g(\top,\top,\top),\ h(\top,\top,\top)), \\ \quad h(f(\top,\top,\top),\ g(\top,\top,\top),\ h(\top,\top,\top))), \end{array} \tag{12}$$

where, for brevity, I have written $\top$ for $\mathbf{true}$. But in fact, nested applications of the functions can be replaced by $\top$, which yields a smaller formula:

$$f(\top,\ g(\top,\top,h(\top,\top,\top)),\ h(\top,g(\top,\top,\top),\top)) \tag{13}$$

In the standard way (12), the tuple top element $\top,\top,\top$ occurs in the formula when the fixpoint depth (namely, 3) of the tuple function $[f, g, h]$ has been reached. In the abbreviated way (13), the boolean top element $\top$ occurs in the formula as soon as the fixpoint depth (namely, 1) of any single function (f, g, or h) has been reached. A proof due to Kuncak shows the standard and abbreviated forms to yield the same value [10].

Let's apply the abbreviated computation of fixpoints to our example (11). Uniquely labeling the subexpressions, we get:

$$\begin{array}{rcl@{\qquad}rcl} 0{:}A_{k,m} & = & 1{:}B_{\mathbf{true},m} & 3{:}C_{m,m} & = & \mathbf{true} \\ 1{:}B_{\mathbf{true},m} & = & 2{:}B_{m,m} \wedge 3{:}C_{m,m} & 4{:}B_{m,m} & = & \mathbf{true} \\ 2{:}B_{m,m} & = & m \wedge 4{:}B_{m,m} \wedge 5{:}C_{m,m} & 5{:}C_{m,m} & = & \mathbf{true} \end{array} \tag{14}$$

Notice how the subexpression $4{:}B_{m,m}$ is set to **true**, because $4{:}B_{m,m}$ is an inner application of the point function $B_{m,m}$, enclosed within subexpression $2{:}B_{m,m}$. Notice also how these equations define a unique value of $0{:}A_{k,m}$; there are no more recursive definitions. By treating the symbolic initial values (here, m) and subexpression labels (like $0{:}A_{k,m}$ and $1{:}B_{\mathbf{true},m}$) as propositional variables, we have now produced a SAT formula for the semantics of the starting block of program (1). Thus, by conjoining $\neg\, 0{:}A_{k,m}$, we get a formula that is satisfiable if and only if program (1) is erroneous. And $\neg\, 0{:}A_{k,m} \wedge (14)$ *is* satisfiable, reflecting the presence of an error in program (1).

3 Algorithm

The algorithm, which is based on the three mathematical ingredients, computes a set of equations, the conjunction of which is satisfiable if and only if the program contains an error. For any block b and arguments u for function b, I write the pair $\langle b, u \rangle$ to represent the mathematical expression $b(u)$, that is, function b applied to the arguments u. In order to check when the fixpoint depth has been reached, the context of an occurrence of such a pair is taken into account, and different occurrences of the same pair may need to be represented by differently named point functions.[6] Therefore, the algorithm labels each pair $\langle b, u \rangle$ with a discriminating value, say s, and I write the labeled pair as a triple $\langle b, u, s \rangle$. The equations computed by the algorithm have these triples (and the symbolic initial values) as their propositional variables.[7]

The algorithm is shown in Figure 4. It outputs the set Eqs, given: a program with start block $start$, (symbolic) initial values w of the program's variables, and a procedure *Instantiate* that for any program block b and argument list u returns the right-hand side of the weakest-precondition equation for b, instantiated with u. For example, for the running example, $Instantiate(B, \langle \mathbf{true}, m \rangle)$ would return the formula $\mathbf{true} \wedge \langle B, \langle \mathbf{true} \wedge m, m \rangle \rangle \wedge \langle C, \langle \mathbf{true} \wedge m, m \rangle \rangle$ simplified to taste.[8] To facilitate the simple generation of discriminating values, the algorithm keeps a counter cnt of the number of different triples produced so far. The algorithm keeps a work list W of pairs $\langle t, cntxt \rangle$, where t is a triple that is used but not defined in Eqs, and where the set $cntxt$ of function terms gives the context in which t is used in Eqs.

The first branch of the if statement is taken when the fixpoint depth for $\langle b, u \rangle$ has been reached in the context $cntxt$. In this case, I shall refer to $\langle b, u, s \rangle$

[6] This is a way in which the algorithm differs from ordinary forward-reachability model checking algorithms.

[7] Depending on the SAT solver used to check the satisfiability of the resulting equations, the equations may first need to be converted into conjunctive normal form.

[8] It seems prudent to apply constant folding to simplify these expressions, since that's simple to do and may reduce the number of function terms that ever make it onto the work list, causing the algorithm to converge more quickly. In my initial experiments, I found constant folding to make a significant difference in the number of equations generated.

$$
\begin{array}{l}
cnt := 0\,; \quad t, cnt := \langle start, w, cnt \rangle, cnt + 1\,; \quad Eqs, W := \{\neg t\}, \{\langle t, \epsilon \rangle\}\,; \\
\textbf{while } W \neq \emptyset \textbf{ do} \\
\quad \textbf{pick } b, u, s, cntxt \textbf{ such that } \langle \langle b, u, s \rangle, cntxt \rangle \in W\,; \\
\quad W := W \setminus \{\langle \langle b, u, s \rangle, cntxt \rangle\}\,; \\
\quad \textbf{if } \langle b, u \rangle \in cntxt \textbf{ then } \quad Eqs := Eqs \cup \{\langle b, u, s \rangle = \textbf{true}\}\,; \quad \textbf{else} \\
\quad\quad rhs := Instantiate(b, u)\,; \\
\quad\quad \textbf{foreach } \langle c, v \rangle \in rhs \textbf{ do} \\
\quad\quad\quad t, cnt := \langle c, v, cnt \rangle, cnt + 1\,; \quad \textbf{replace } \langle c, v \rangle \textbf{ with } t \textbf{ in } rhs\,; \\
\quad\quad\quad W := W \cup \{\langle t, cntxt \cup \{\langle b, u \rangle\} \rangle\}\,; \quad G := G \cup \{\langle b, u, s \rangle \mapsto t\}\,; \\
\quad\quad \textbf{end}\,; \\
\quad\quad Eqs := Eqs \cup \{\langle b, u, s \rangle = rhs\}\,; \\
\quad \textbf{end}\,; \\
\textbf{end}\,;
\end{array}
$$

Fig. 4. The algorithm for computing a set of boolean equations Eqs whose conjunction is satisfiable if and only if the boolean program under consideration is erroneous

as a *fixpoint triple* (like ${}_{4:}B_{m,m}$ in (14)). In my *implementation* (Dizzy) of the algorithm, I use BDDs for the arguments u when comparing $\langle b, u \rangle$ to other pairs $\langle b, \cdot \rangle$ in $cntxt$. The second branch of the if statement attaches a discriminating value to each function term in rhs and adds the resulting triples to the work list.

Variable G represents the edges in a graph whose vertices are the triples produced so far. An edge $t \mapsto t'$ indicates that the equation for t requires a definition for t'. By restricting graph G to vertices corresponding to negative variables in a satisfying assignment, one can produce an execution trace from the initial state to an error.

The algorithm in Figure 4 has the effect of constructing G to be a tree of triples. As an important optimization, Dizzy shares common triples when possible, resulting in a directed acyclic graph. In my experience, this sharing can reduce the number of triples (and thus propositional variables) by more than 4 orders of magnitude.

An interesting possibility that calls for future investigation is the prospect of periodically, or even immediately, passing to the SAT solver the equations added to Eqs (maybe using an incremental SAT solver like Satire [1]). This has the advantage that, if the program is correct, unsatisfiability may be detected before the fixpoint depth has been reached everywhere.

4 Complexity

The complexity of the algorithm depends crucially on the number of function terms generated, because each function term (or, more precisely, each function-term triple) gives rise to a propositional variable. In a program with K variables, a function term consists of a function symbol followed by K boolean-expression arguments in K variables. In a program with N blocks, there are then $N \cdot (2^{2^K})^K$ different function terms. The triple-sharing implementation of the algorithm can therefore produce a doubly-exponential number of different function terms.

There is a simple way to change the worst-case number of function terms generated: replace the symbolic initial values by a complete set of explicit boolean values. For the example, we would then start with $\neg A(\mathbf{false}, \mathbf{false}) \wedge \neg A(\mathbf{false}, \mathbf{true}) \wedge \neg A(\mathbf{true}, \mathbf{false}) \wedge \neg A(\mathbf{true}, \mathbf{true})$ instead of $\neg A(k, m)$. This would cause all subsequently produced function-term arguments also to be explicit boolean values, so there would only be $N \cdot 2^K$ different function terms, a *single* exponential. However, this representation suffers from always producing *at least* 2^K function terms, because that's how many function terms we get for the start block alone.

Interestingly enough, we can adjust the degree to which we use the two argument representations, by using the following simple equality: for any function b, expression e, and lists of expressions E_0 and E_1, we have:

$$b(E_0, e, E_1) \quad = \quad (\neg e \;\wedge\; b(E_0, \mathbf{false}, E_1)) \;\wedge\; (e \;\wedge\; b(E_0, \mathbf{true}, E_1)) \qquad (15)$$

Thus, if e is an expression other than an explicit boolean value, then the procedure *Instantiate* called in Figure 4 can heuristically use (15) in lieu of (3) to return a definition of $b(E_0, e, E_1)$. For example, (15) may be used whenever the argument e is "too complicated", as perhaps when the number of variables in e exceeds some threshold, or when e is anything but the symbolic initial value of the program variable corresponding to this function argument. By using this latter heuristic, the number of different function terms is $N \cdot 3^K$, a single exponential as in the case of using only explicit boolean values; yet, by using this heuristic, the algorithm begins with just one negated start block function, not an exponential number of them as in the case of using only explicit boolean values. (I have yet to experiment with the symbolic-versus-explicit argument representations in my implementation.)

In practice, I expect most boolean programs to generate fewer equations than the worst case. But initial experiments with Dizzy have not been rosy. SLAM's BDD-based model checker Bebop [2] outperforms Dizzy on most, but not all, examples I've tried from the SLAM regression test suite and actual device drivers for the Microsoft Windows operating system. In too many cases to be practical, Dizzy spends so much time it might as well be looping forever.

It may be that the present method reaches fixpoints too slowly to receive a net benefit from speedy SAT solvers. But straightforward measurements don't compare Dizzy with just the BDD-based aspect of Bebop, because Bebop generates procedure summaries, which enable sharing of work between different procedure invocations, whereas Dizzy inlines procedures, which forsakes work sharing and also dramatically increases the effective number of program variables. Since I don't know how to incorporate procedure summarization in Dizzy, I instead tried crippling Bebop by feeding it the inlined-procedure version of a smallish program. This increased Bebop's running time from 37 seconds to 64 minutes. Dizzy practically loops forever on this program, but the big impact of procedure summarization suggests there's room for further innovation in Dizzy.

5 Related Work and Conclusion

The presented method of doing model checking is perhaps, in the end, most reminiscent of a standard forward reachability algorithm where weakest-precondition equations give the next-state relation of blocks. In the present method, each function term corresponds to *one* state (the program counter plus the variables in scope at the beginning of the block), as a function of the *arbitrary* initial state represented symbolically. The method uses both BDDs (in the phase that produces the SAT formula, see Figure 4) and SAT solving (in the phase that checks the resulting formula). In particular, the conditions in **assume** and **assert** statements, which determine whether or not execution proceeds normally, are not used in the first phase (except as mentioned in footnote 8). Instead, these conditions are encoded into the final SAT formula, which puts the responsibility of wrestling with path feasibility and errors onto the SAT solver. Consequently, the boolean expressions that the BDD package sees are much simpler; indeed, by applying equation (15), one can make them arbitrarily simple. The cost of this partitioning of work between BDDs and SAT solving is that the first phase may over-approximate the set of function terms; that is, it may produce some function terms that do not correspond to any reachable state. As I've mentioned, the first phase may also need to produce several copies of a function term, since the decision of when a function-term triple is a fixpoint triple depends on the path leading to the function term (*cf.* footnote 6). In contrast, standard forward reachability algorithms represent a state only once, because they consider path feasibility and errors with each step of the algorithm.

Another technique of model checking is *bounded model checking* [5], which seeks to find errors by investigating only prefixes of the program's execution paths. This allows the technique to continue the forward simulation without checking if the next states have already been explored, a check that can lead to large BDDs. Indeed, bounded model checking has been targeted especially for SAT solvers, avoiding BDDs altogether. By iteratively increasing the prefix length used, bounded model checking can, at least in principle, establish the correctness of a given program. The incremental nature of the technique and the efficiency of modern SAT solvers have let bounded model checking find many errors quickly. The present method can also avoid large BDDs for determining reachability, but does so without missing any errors. It is also interesting to note that the incremental version of the present method mentioned at the end of Section 3 can, in contrast to bounded model checking, establish *correctness* early, whereas finding the presence of errors requires running the present algorithm to completion.

Other SAT-based model checking techniques include the use of induction, which can be used with bounded model checking to make up for the fact that only prefixes of executions are used [15]. Also, standard algorithms for symbolic reachability can be performed using SAT solving rather than BDDs (see, *e.g.*, [6]).

Podelski has considered the characterization of model checking as a system of constraints [14]. In a different context, Tang and Hofmann convert a second-order problem into a first-order problem [16].

In conclusion, I have presented a (sound and complete) method for mechanically checking the correctness of boolean programs. Based on three mathematical ingredients, the method attempts to capitalize on recent advances in SAT solving. The implementation Dizzy shows the method to succeed in using BDDs lightly. Perhaps too lightly, because Dizzy often spends an impractically long time reaching fixpoints, exasperated (caused?) by the act of inlining procedures.

An appealing piece of future work is to consider using the method with some form of procedure summarization. I also hope that the theoretical techniques presented will inspire other future work.

Acknowledgements

I'm grateful to Sriram Rajamani for inspiring discussions about this problem. I have personally benefited, and so has this work, from discussions with Byron Cook about SAT solving, with Jakob Lichtenberg about BDD implementations, and with Ernie Cohen about the complexity of the problem. I'm also grateful to the audiences of a talk I gave on this subject at the Eindhoven Technical University and at the IFIP WG 2.4 meeting at Schloß Dagstuhl, for their comments have helped me improve the presentation of the subject. Viktor Kuncak devised a proof of correctness for the abbreviated way to compute fixpoints [10], and John Dunagan helped me design the triple-sharing algorithm alluded to in Section 3. Byron, Jakob, Viktor, and the referees provided thoughtful and valuable comments on earlier drafts of this paper.

References

[1] Fadi Aloul. Satire. `http://www.eecs.umich.edu/~{}faloul/Tools/satire/`, 116
April 2002.

[2] Thomas Ball and Sriram K. Rajamani. Bebop: A symbolic model checker for boolean programs. In *SPIN 7*, *LNCS* #1885, pp. 113–130. Springer, 2000. 105, 117

[3] Thomas Ball and Sriram K. Rajamani. Automatically validating temporal safety properties of interfaces. In *SPIN 8*, *LNCS* #2057, pp. 103–122. Springer, 2001. 104

[4] François Bancilhon, David Maier, Yehoshua Sagiv, and Jeffrey D. Ullman. Magic sets and other strange ways to implement logic programs. In *PODS 5*, pp. 1–15. ACM Press, 1986. 111

[5] Armin Biere, Alessandro Cimatti, Edmund Clarke, and Yunshan Zhu. Symbolic model checking without BDDs. In *TACAS '99*, *LNCS* #1579, pp. 193–207. Springer, 1999. 118

[6] Per Bjesse and Koen Claessen. SAT-based verification without state space traversal. In *FMCAD 2000*, *LNCS* #1954, pp. 372–389. Springer, 2000. 119

[7] Randal E. Bryant. Graph-based algorithms for boolean function manipulation. *IEEE Transactions on Computers*, 35(8):677–691, 1986. 104, 111

[8] Edsger W. Dijkstra. *A Discipline of Programming*. Prentice Hall, 1976. 106, 109

[9] Edsger W. Dijkstra and Carel S. Scholten. *Predicate Calculus and Program Semantics*. Texts and Monographs in Computer Science. Springer-Verlag, 1990. 106, 109, 114

[10] Viktor Kuncak and K. Rustan M. Leino. On computing the fixpoint of a set of boolean equations. Technical Report MSR-TR-2003-08, Microsoft Research, 2003. 114, 119

[11] M. S. Manasse and C. G. Nelson. Correct compilation of control structures. Technical report, AT&T Bell Laboratories, September 1984. 106

[12] João P. Marques-Silva and Karem A. Sakallah. GRASP: A search algorithm for propositional satisfiability. *IEEE Transactions on Computers*, 48(5):506–521, 1999. 109

[13] Matthew W. Moskewicz, Conor F. Madigan, Ying Zhao, Lintao Zhang, and Sharad Malik. Chaff: Engineering an efficient SAT solver. In *DAC 2001*, pp. 530–535. ACM, 2001. 109

[14] Andreas Podelski. Model checking as constraint solving. In *SAS 2000*, *LNCS* #1824, pp. 22–37. Springer, 2000. 119

[15] Mary Sheeran, Satnam Singh, and Gunnar Stålmarck. Checking safety properties using induction and a SAT-solver. In *FMCAD 2000*, *LNCS* #1954, pp. 108–125. Springer, 2000. 119

[16] Francis Tang and Martin Hofmann. Generation of verification conditions for Abadi and Leino's logic of objects. In *FOOL 9*, 2002. Electronic proceedings. 119

What Went Wrong: Explaining Counterexamples

Alex Groce[1] and Willem Visser[2]

[1] Department of Computer Science, Carnegie Mellon University
Pittsburgh, PA, 15213
[2] RIACS/NASA Ames Research Center, Moffett Field, CA 94035-1000

Abstract. One of the chief advantages of model checking is the production of counterexamples demonstrating that a system does not satisfy a specification. However, it may require a great deal of human effort to extract the essence of an error from even a detailed source-level trace of a failing run. We use an automated method for finding multiple versions of an error (and similar executions that do not produce an error), and analyze these executions to produce a more succinct description of the key elements of the error. The description produced includes identification of portions of the source code crucial to distinguishing failing and succeeding runs, differences in invariants between failing and non-failing runs, and information on the necessary changes in scheduling and environmental actions needed to cause successful runs to fail.

1 Introduction

In model checking [4], algorithms are used to systematically determine whether a system satisfies a specification. One of the major advantages of model checking in comparison to such methods as theorem proving is the production of a *counterexample* that provides a detailed example of how the system violates the specification when verification fails. However, even a detailed trace of how a system violates a specification may not provide enough information to easily understand (much less remedy) the problem with the system. Model checking is particularly effective at finding subtle errors that can elude traditional testing, but consequently the errors are also difficult to understand, especially from a single error trace. Furthermore, when the model of the system is in any sense abstracted from the real implementation, simply determining whether an error is indeed a fault in the system or merely a consequence of modeling assumptions or incorrect specification can be quite difficult.

We attempt to extract more information from a single counterexample produced by model checking in order to facilitate understanding of errors in a system (or problems with the specification of a system). We focus in this work on finite executions demonstrating violation of safety properties (e.g. assertion violations, uncaught exceptions, and deadlocks) in Java programs. The key to this approach is to first define (and then find) multiple variations on a single counterexample (other versions of the "same" error). From this definition naturally arises that of a set of executions that are variations in which the error does not occur. We

T. Ball and S.K. Rajamani (Eds.): SPIN 2003, LNCS 2648, pp. 121–136, 2003.

call the first set of executions *negatives* and the second set *positives*. Analysis of the common features of each set and the differences between the sets may yield a more useful feedback than reading (only) the original counterexample.

One approach to analysis would be to define the negatives as all executions that reach a particular error state (all deadlocks, all assertion violations, etc.). This definition has major drawbacks. A complex concurrent program, for example, may have many deadlocks that have different causes. Attempts to extract any common features from the negatives are likely to fail or be computationally expensive (for example, requiring clustering) in this case. The second problem is that positives would presumably be any executions not ending in the error state, again making comparison difficult. In software, at least, we usually think of errors as occurring at a particular place—e.g., a deadlock at a particular synchronization, or a failure of a particular assertion or array-out-of-bounds error at a particular point in the source code. We define negatives, therefore, as executions that not only end in the same error state, but that reach it from the same *control location*. Rather than analyzing all deadlocks, our definition focuses analysis on deadlocks that occur after the same attempt to acquire a lock, for example. We believe that our definition formally captures a simplified version of the programmer's notion of "the same error." Positives are the executions that pass through that control location without proceeding to an error state.

We present three different analyses that can be automatically extracted from a set of negatives and positives. The first is based on the transitions appearing in the set. The second is based on data invariants over the executions. The last analysis discovers minimal transformations between negatives and positives.

This paper is organized as follows: in Section 2 we discuss related work. The definitions of negative and positive executions are then formalized in Section 3, followed by a presentation of an algorithm for generating executions to analyze in Section 4. The various analyses currently applied and their implementations are discussed in Section 5 and Section 6, respectively. We then present experimental results in Section 7, followed by conclusions and future work.

2 Related Work

The most closely related work to ours is that of Ball, Naik, and Rajamani [1]. They find successful paths to the control location at which an error is discovered in order to find the cause of the error. Once a cause is discovered, they model check a restricted model in which the system is restricted from executing the causal transitions to discover if other causes for the error are possible. The analysis provided is similar to our *transition analysis*; no method analogous to invariant or transformation analysis is provided, nor are concurrent programs analyzed. This error analysis has been implemented for the SLAM [2] tool.

Sharygina and Peled [13] propose the notion of the *neighborhood* of a counterexample and suggest that an exploration of this region may be useful in understanding an error. However, the exploration, while aided by a testing tool, is essentially manual and offers no automatic analysis. No formal notion of other versions of the same error is presented. Dodoo, Donovan, Lin and Ernst [5] use the Daikon invariant detector to discover differences in invariants between passing and failing test cases, but propose no means to restrict the cases to similar executions relevant for analysis or to generate them from a counterexample.

Jin, Ravi and Somenzi [11] proceed from the same starting point of analyzing counterexamples produced by a model checker. Their goal is also similar: providing additional feedback in addition to the original counterexample in order to deal with the complexity of errors. *Fate* and *free will* are terms in a game in which a counterexample is broken into parts depending on whether the environment (attempting to force the system into an error state) or the system (attempting to avoid error) controls it. This approach produces a different kind of explanation (an alternation of fated and free segments).

The work of Andreas Zeller was also an important influence on this work. *Delta debugging* is a technique for minimizing error trails that works by conducting a modified binary search between a failing run and a succeeding run of a program [17]. Zeller has extended this notion to other approaches to automatic debugging, including modifying portions of a program's state to isolate cause-effect chains [16] and discovering the minimal difference in thread scheduling necessary to produce a concurrency-based error [3]. Our computation of transformations between positive and negative executions was inspired by this approach, particularly in that we look for minimal transformations.

3 Definitions

The crucial definitions are those of *negatives* and *positives*, the two classes of executions we use in our analysis. While manual exploration of paths near a counterexample can be useful [13], a formal definition of a variation on a counterexample is necessary before proceeding to the more fruitful approach of automatic generation and analysis of relevant executions. Intuitively, we examine the full set of finite executions in which the program reaches the control location immediately proceeding the error state.

A labeled transition system (LTS) is a 4-tuple $\langle S, S_0, Act, T\rangle$, where S is a finite non-empty set of states, $S_0 \subset S$ is the set of initial states, Act is the set of actions, and $T \subset S \times Act \times S$ is the transition relation. We assume that S contains a distinguished set of error states (with no outgoing transitions), $\Pi = \{\pi_0, \cdots, \pi_n\}$ (representing, e.g. deadlock, assertion violation, uncaught exception...). We also introduce a set C of control locations and a set D of data valuations, such that $S = (C \times D) \cup \Pi$, and introduce partial projection functions $c : S \rightarrow C$ and $d : S \rightarrow D$. We write $s \xrightarrow{\alpha} s'$ as shorthand for $(s, \alpha, s') \in T$.

A *finite transition sequence* from $s_0 \in S$ is a sequence $t = s_0 \xrightarrow{\alpha_1} s_1 \xrightarrow{\alpha_2} \cdots \xrightarrow{\alpha_k} s_k$, where $0 < k < \infty$. We refer to k as the length of t, also denoted by $|t|$. We say that a finite transition sequence $t = s_0 \xrightarrow{\alpha_1} s_1 \xrightarrow{\alpha_2} \cdots \xrightarrow{\alpha_k} s_k$ is a *prefix* of a finite transition sequence $t' = s'_0 \xrightarrow{\alpha'_1} s'_1 \xrightarrow{\alpha'_2} \cdots \xrightarrow{\alpha'_{k'}} s_{k'}$ if $0 < k < k'$ and $\forall i \leq k \;.\; (i \geq 0 \Rightarrow s_i = s'_i) \wedge (i > 0 \Rightarrow \alpha_i = \alpha'_i)$. We say that a finite transition sequence $t = s_0 \xrightarrow{\alpha_1} s_1 \xrightarrow{\alpha_2} \cdots \xrightarrow{\alpha_k} s_k$ is a *control suffix* of a finite transition sequence $t' = s'_0 \xrightarrow{\alpha'_1} s'_1 \xrightarrow{\alpha'_2} \cdots \xrightarrow{\alpha'_{k'}} s_{k'}$ iff $0 < k < k'$ and $\forall i \leq k \,.\, (i \geq 0 \Rightarrow c(s_{k-i}) = c(s'_{k'-i})) \wedge (i > 0 \Rightarrow \alpha_{k-i} = \alpha'_{k'-i})$. We also define the empty transition sequence, *emp* as consisting of no states or actions, where $|emp| = 0$.

We consider the class of counterexamples that are finite transition sequences from $s_0 \in S_0$. Given an initial counterexample $t = s_0 \xrightarrow{\alpha_1} s_1 \xrightarrow{\alpha_2} \cdots \xrightarrow{\alpha_k} s_k$, where $s_k \in \Pi$, we define a *negative* as an execution that results in the same error state from the same control location (the original counterexample is itself a negative). Formally:

Definition: Negative: A negative (with respect to a particular t, as noted above) is a finite transition sequence from $s'_0 \in S_0$, $t' = s'_0 \xrightarrow{\alpha'_1} s'_1 \xrightarrow{\alpha'_2} \cdots \xrightarrow{\alpha'_{k'}} s'_{k'}$, where $0 < k' < \infty$, such that:

1. $c(s_{k-1}) = c(s'_{k'-1}) \wedge \alpha_k = \alpha'_{k'}$ and
2. $s_k = s'_{k'}$.

We then define $neg(t)$ as the set of all negatives with respect to a counterexample t. The original counterexample itself is one such negative, and is used as such in all analyses.

Definition: Positive: A positive (with respect to t) is a finite transition sequence from $s'_0 \in S_0$, $t' = s'_0 \xrightarrow{\alpha'_1} s'_1 \xrightarrow{\alpha'_2} \cdots \xrightarrow{\alpha'_{k'}} s'_{k'}$, where $0 < k' < \infty$ such that:

1. $c(s_{k-1}) = c(s'_{k'-1}) \wedge \alpha_k = \alpha'_{k'}$,
2. $s'_{k'} \notin \Pi$, and
3. $\forall t'' \in neg(t) \,.\, t'$ is not a prefix of t''.

We define $pos(t)$ as the set of all positives with respect to a counterexample t, and $var(t)$ as $neg(t) \cup pos(t)$, the set of all *variations* on the original counterexample. We will henceforth refer to *neg* and *pos*, omitting the implied parameterization with respect to t.

Figure 1 shows an example. The numbers inside states indicate the control location of the state, $c(s)$, and the letters beside the arrows are the labels of actions (in this case drawn from the alphabet $\{a, b\}$). The original counterexample ends in the state $A \in \Pi$, indicating an assertion violation. The negative shown takes a different sequence of actions but also passes through the control location 3, takes an a action, and transitions to the error state A. The positive reaches control location 3 but in a data state such that taking an a action transitions to a non-error state.

These basic definitions, however, give rise to certain difficulties in practice. First, the set of negatives is potentially infinite, as is the set of positives. On the other hand, the set of positives may be empty, as an error in a reactive system is

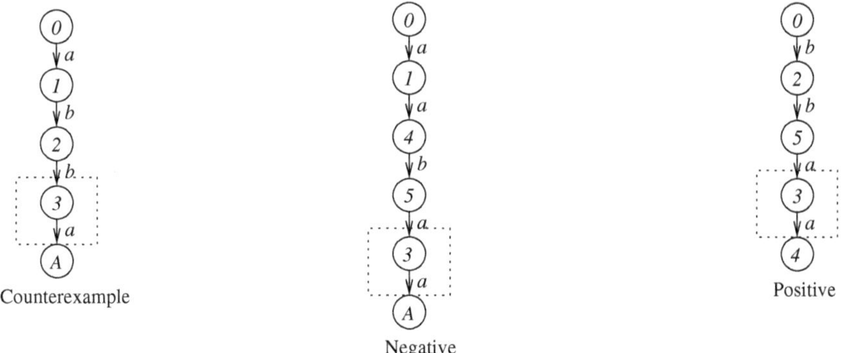

Fig. 1. A counterexample, a negative, and a positive

often reachable from any other state. For reasons of tractability we generate and analyze subsets of the negatives and positives. When only a subset of negatives are known the third condition in the definition of positives cannot be checked; we therefore replace it with the weaker requirement that t' not be a prefix of any negative we generate.

4 Generation of Positives and Negatives

The algorithm for generating a subset of the negatives (and a set of potential positives, per the modified prefix condition) uses a model checker to explore backwards from the original counterexample. We describe an explicit state algorithm, but are investigating a SAT-based approach.

We assume that the model checker (MC) can be called as a function during generation with an initial state s from which to begin exploration, a maximum search depth d, a control state to match c, an error state π, and a visited set v. The model checker returns two (possibly empty) sets: n (negatives) and p (potential positives) and a new visited set v'. The check for whether a state is the last in a positive or negative is a simple safety property relying only on a state's control location and the preceeding control location and action (see the above definitions), and should not pose difficulties. Removal of prefixes of negatives is done in a final stage and need not be taken into account by the model checker.

The generation algorithm (Figure 2) takes as input an initial counterexample $t = s_0 \xrightarrow{\alpha_1} s_1 \xrightarrow{\alpha_2} \cdots \xrightarrow{\alpha_k} s_k$ and a search depth d.

The model checking algorithm used is not specified, but we make a few assumptions about its behavior. If a depth limit is not given each call to the model checker will only terminate upon exploring the full reachable state space from s_i, so we assume that the model checker allows the use of depth limits. We also require that the model checker be able to report multiple counterexamples (paths to all states satisfying the properties for defining negatives and positives). Both of these assumptions can easily be met by various explicit state

```
generate (t, d)
  v := neg := pos := ∅
  i := k − 1
  while i >= 0
    (n, p, v) := MC(s_i, t, d, v)
    neg := neg ∪ n
    pos := pos ∪ p
    i := i − 1
  for all t ∈ pos
    for all t' ∈ neg
      if t is a prefix of t'
        pos := pos \ t
return (neg, pos)
```

Fig. 2. Algorithm for generation of negatives and positives

model checkers—e.g. SPIN supports depth limits as well as multiple counterexamples. The counterexamples can be split into negatives and positives after being returned, if necessary.

To provide more negatives and positives to analyze we also propose one alteration to the internal behavior of the model checker. When the depth limit is reached, we attempt to extend the execution to match the original counterexample. This causes the depth limit to behave as an edit-distance from the original counterexample: negatives and positives may deviate from the original execution for a number of actions limited by d. The algorithm for extension, proceeding from a state s at depth i is given in Figure 3. Briefly, the algorithm checks the state at which exploration terminates due to depth limiting to see if it matches control location with any state further along the original counterexample. For all matches, the actions taken in the original counterexample are repeated if enabled in order to reach either a negative or a positive. The extension algorithm is depth-first, but can be integrated into both breadth-first and heuristic-based model checking algorithms.

```
j := i
while j < k
  if c(s_j) = c(s)
    s' := s
    l := j + 1
    broken := false
    while l < k ∧ ¬ broken
      if ∃ s'' . s' --α_l--> s'' ∧ c(s'') = c(s_l) ∧ s'' ∉ v
        s' := s''
      else
    broken := true
      l := l + 1
    if ¬ broken
      if s' --α_k--> s''
    if s'' ∈ Π
          add transition sequence to s'' to current set of negatives
        else
      add transition sequence to s'' to current set of positives
  j := j + 1
```

Fig. 3. Algorithm for extension

Table 1. Transition analysis set definitions

Transition Analysis Set	Definition
$trans(neg)$	$\langle c, \alpha \rangle \vert \exists t \in neg \ . \ t$ contains $\langle c, \alpha \rangle$
$trans(pos)$	$\langle c, \alpha \rangle \vert \exists t \in pos \ . \ t$ contains $\langle c, \alpha \rangle$
$all(neg)$	$\langle c, \alpha \rangle \vert \forall t \in neg \ . \ t$ contains $\langle c, \alpha \rangle$
$all(pos)$	$\langle c, \alpha \rangle \vert \forall t \in pos \ . \ t$ contains $\langle c, \alpha \rangle$
$only(neg)$	$trans(neg) \setminus trans(pos)$
$only(pos)$	$trans(pos) \setminus trans(neg)$
$cause(neg)$	$all(neg) \cap only(neg)$
$cause(pos)$	$all(pos) \cap only(pos)$

We use *neg* and *pos* below to denote the sets returned by this generation algorithm, not the true complete sets of negatives and positives.

5 Analysis of Variations

Once the negatives and positives have been generated, it remains to produce from them useful feedback for the user. Even without such analysis, the traces may prove useful, but our experience shows that even tightly limited searches will produce large numbers of traces that are as difficult to understand in isolation as the original counterexample. It is not the traces in and of themselves that provide leverage in understanding the error; any negative could have generally been substituted for the original counterexample, and a positive simply shows an instance of the program reaching a control location without error.

5.1 Transition Analysis

The various analyses we employ are designed to characterize (1) the common elements of negatives/positives and (2) the difference between negatives and positives. For this analysis, we examine the presence of transitions in the executions in each set. In particular we compute sets containing projected transitions, pairs $\langle c, \alpha \rangle$, where $c \in C$ is a control location and $\alpha \in Act$ is an action. We say that the finite transition sequence $t = s_0 \xrightarrow{\alpha_1} s_1 \xrightarrow{\alpha_2} \cdots \xrightarrow{\alpha_k} s_k$ *contains* $\langle c, \alpha \rangle$ iff $\exists n < k \ . \ c(s_n) = c \wedge \alpha_{n+1} = \alpha$. The analysis below can also be computed using only projected control locations, ignoring actions (or also projecting on some portion of a composite action, when this is possible).

In transition analysis, we compute a number of sets of transitions, listed in Table 1. $trans(neg)$ and $trans(pos)$ are complete sets of all transitions appearing in negatives and positives, respectively. The sets $all(neg)$ and $all(pos)$ (transitions appearing in all negatives or positives) are reported directly to the user. These may be sufficient to explain an error, either by indicating that certain code is faulty or that execution of certain code prevents the error from appearing. Also reported to the user are the transitions appearing only in negatives/positives, $only(neg)$ and $only(pos)$. Finally, potentially *causal* transition sets are reported.

```
1   int got_lock = 0;
2   do {
3     if (Verify.chooseBool ()) {
4       lock ();
5       got_lock++;
6     }
7     if (got_lock != 0) {
8       unlock ();
9     }
10    got_lock--;
11  } while (Verify.chooseBool ());
```

```
public static void lock () {
  Verify.assertTrue (LOCK == 0);
  LOCK = 1;
}

public static void unlock () {
  Verify.assertTrue (LOCK == 1);
  LOCK = 0;
}
```

Fig. 4. Example 1

The rationale for computing causal sets is that in many cases $all(neg)$ and $all(pos)$ will contain a number of common elements, due to common initialization code and aspects of execution unrelated to the error. $only(neg)$ and $only(pos)$ may also be large sets if the error induces differing behavior in the system before the point at which the error is detected. When non-empty, $cause(neg)$ and $cause(pos)$ denote sets that are potentially much smaller and denote precisely the common behavior that differentiates the negative and positive sets. The error cause localization algorithm used in SLAM is comparable to reporting either $cause(neg)$ or $only(neg)$, as SLAM analyzes one error trace at a time [1].

Example of Transition Analysis The Java code in Figure 4 (adapted from a BLAST example [10]) calls `lock` and `unlock` methods that assert that the lock is not held and the lock is held, respectively. `Verify.chooseBool ()` indicates a nondeterministic choice between `true` and `false` (see Section 6). The bug (line 10 should be inside the scope of the `if` starting at line 7) can appear as a violation of either the lock or unlock assertion. Depth-30 analysis from a counterexample in which the `unlock` assertion is violated ($1 \longrightarrow 2 \longrightarrow 3 \xrightarrow{F} 7 \longrightarrow 10 \longrightarrow 11 \xrightarrow{T} 3 \xrightarrow{F} 7 \longrightarrow 8 \longrightarrow A$) discovers two positives and two negatives.

In this case $cause(neg)$ is unchanged by our use of the weaker prefix constraint for positives (there are no real positives in this program: the error can occur in an extension of every trace ending at line 8). Here $cause(neg)$ notes the key points of the unlocking error: the system chooses not to lock ($\langle 3, F \rangle$), which means that the decrement of `got_lock` (10) is incorrect (the lock's status

Table 2. Transition analysis example results

Transition Analysis Set	Elements
$all(neg)$	$\{1, 2, \langle 3, F \rangle, 7, 8, 10, \langle 11, T \rangle\}$
$all(pos)$	$\{1, 2, \langle 3, T \rangle, 4, 5, 7, 8\}$
$only(neg)$	$\{\langle 3, F \rangle, 10, \langle 11, T \rangle\}$
$only(pos)$	$\emptyset$
$cause(neg)$	$\{\langle 3, F \rangle, 10, \langle 11, T \rangle\}$
$cause(pos)$	$\emptyset$

has not been changed this time through the loop). Reiterating the loop ($\langle 11, T\rangle$) makes it possible to try to unlock when the lock has not been acquired.

5.2 Invariant Analysis

Transition analysis is useful when the control flow or action choices independent of ordering are sufficient to explain an error. However, the same actions from the same control locations may be present in both negatives and positives; it may be that the choice of an action with respect to $d(s)$ rather than $c(s)$ is crucial. A set-based approach projected on $d(s)$ rather than $c(s)$ faces the problem that only certain data values are likely to be relevant, rather than the full state.

Instead, we compute data invariants over the negatives and compare them to the invariants over the positives. Specifically, the user may choose certain control locations as instrumentation points. The value of $d(s)$ (or some projection over certain variables of the data state) is recorded for each transition sequence every time the control flow reaches the instrumentation locations. We then compute invariants using Daikon [6] (see Section 6 for details) with respect to each of the instrumentation points over all negatives and all positives. The invariants for negatives are then compared to the invariants for positives, and the user is presented with this difference. Daikon's analysis is dynamic and thus unsound; however, the invariants reported over a set of traces (which is precisely what we are concerned with here) are always correct *for those traces*. Choosing instrumentation points and how deeply to instrument (by default all local primitive-typed variables, but JPF can also report on object fields and other frames) is not automated and must be guided by user knowledge the other analyses.

Example of Invariant Analysis The code in Figure 5 is intended to sort the variables `a`, `b`, `c` and `d` in ascending order. The last line asserts that the variables are ordered. However, the comparisons are not sufficient to ensure ordering. `Verify.instrumentPoint` indicates a point at which $d(s)$ is recorded (and a name for that instrumentation point). Applying invariant analysis with a search depth of 30 yields the following differences (values after sorting, at the instrumentation point `post-sort`, are indicated by primed variable names):

```
int a˜= Verify.choose(4); int b = Verify.choose(4); // nondeterministic 0-4
int c = Verify.choose(4); int d = Verify.choose(4); // nondeterministic 0-4
int temp = 0;
Verify.instrumentPoint("pre-sort");
if (a > b) {
  temp = b; b = a; a˜= temp; } // Swap
if (b > c) {
  temp = c; c = b; b = temp; } // Swap
if (c > d) {
  temp = d; d = c; c = temp; } // Swap
if (b > c) {
  temp = c; c = b; b = temp; } // Swap
Verify.instrumentPoint("post-sort");
Verify.assertTrue((a <= b) && (b <= c) && (c <= d));
```

Fig. 5. Example 2

Table 3. Invariant analysis example results

Instrumentation Point	Positive Invariant	Negative Invariant
pre-sort	`a >= 0`	`a >= 1`
	`b <= d`	
		`a <= b`
		`a > c`
		`b > c`
post-sort	`a' >= 0`	`a' >= 1`
	`a' <= b'`	`a' > b'`
	`a' <= c'`	
	`b' <= d'`	`b' < d'`
	`d' >= temp`	`d' > temp`

We observe from the negative invariants that `a'` may be greater than `b'`. Because invariant analysis is complete over the negative and positive runs, the absence of an `a' <= c'` invariant for negatives also indicates that `a'` is greater than `c'` in at least one negative. Adding only the `a, b` comparison to the code before again model checking and analyzing the resulting counterexample gives the remaining crucial invariant difference: `b' <= c'` (positive) vs. `b' > c'` (negative). Adding this comparison results in code that satisfies the sorting assertion.

5.3 Transformation of Positives into Negatives

Our final analysis is based on the intuition that when both negatives and positives exist, we can imagine "breaking" a positive by changing the least number of actions required to produce a negative. If a positive and a negative follow the same path for a long sequence of states and actions, then diverge for a period before again rejoining paths, the difference in actions in the divergent section may give important insights into the cause of the error. Our extension algorithm (Figure 3) is intended to find such pairs of negatives and positives. A *transformation* is a pair of smaller finite transition sequences, demarcating precisely the diverging portions of the negative and positive (the portions before and after the transformation segments in each are identical until the point of error).

The *largest prefix* of a finite transition sequence t is the prefix p of t that maximizes $|p|$, or, more simply, t with its final action and state removed. The largest prefix of a set of finite transition sequences T is the finite transition sequence that is a prefix of all elements of T with the largest $|p|$. We say that there is a *transformation* of a positive $t = s_0 \xrightarrow{\alpha_1} s_1 \xrightarrow{\alpha_2} \cdots \xrightarrow{\alpha_k} s_k$ into a negative $t' = s'_0 \xrightarrow{\alpha'_1} s'_1 \xrightarrow{\alpha'_2} \cdots \xrightarrow{\alpha'_{k'}} s'_{k'}$ when:

1. $\exists p \,.\, p$ is a finite transition sequence which is a prefix of both t and t'.
2. $\exists u \,.\, u$ is a finite transition sequence which is a control suffix of both the largest prefix of t and the largest prefix of t'.

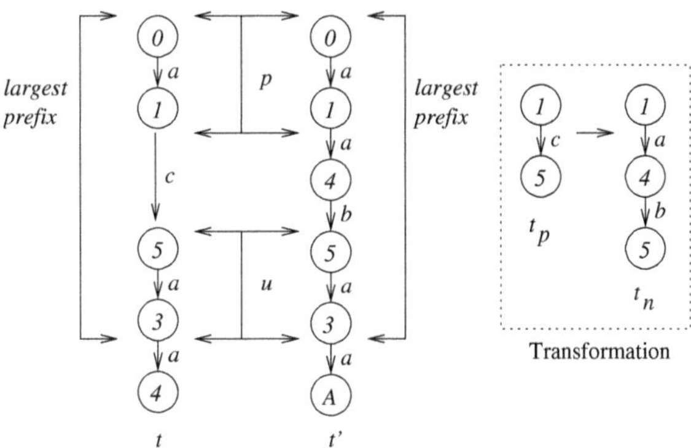

Fig. 6. Transforming a positive into a negative

As the final states of t and t' do not share a control location, we must take the largest prefixes of both in order to allow for the existence of u.

A *minimal transformation* from t to t' always exists when there is a transformation from t to t'. We define the minimal transformation as a 3-tuple $\langle k_t, t_p, t_n \rangle$ where $0 \le k_t < |t|$ and t_p and t_n are either finite transition sequences or the empty transition sequence, *emp*. We may also write $(t_p) \rightarrow (t_n)$ when we are considering only the actual sequences replaced and not the location from which they begin (discarding k_t allows us to see when the same alteration of actions from different positions causes an error in a number of positives).

1. Find the p such that p is largest prefix of the set $\{t, t'\}$.
2. Find the u such that u is the largest finite transition sequence which is a control suffix of both the largest prefix of t and the largest prefix of t' and u satisfies the constraint that $|u| + |p| \le min(|t|, |t'|)$.
3. $k_t = |p|$.
4. $t_p = s_{k_t} \overset{\alpha_{k_t+1}}{\longrightarrow} \cdots s_{k-|u|}$. If $k_t > k - |u|$ then $t_p = emp$.
5. $t_n = s'_{k_t} \overset{\alpha'_{k_t+1}}{\longrightarrow} \cdots s_{k'-|u|}$ If $k_t > k' - |u|$ then $t_n = emp$.

The last two definitions select the diverging portions of t and t' as the positive (t_p) and negative (t_n) portions of the transformation (see Figure 6).

When S_0 contains a single state, there will exist a minimal transformation for every pair in *pos* $\times$ *neg*. Sorting this set by a metric of transformation size ($|t_p| + |t_n|$ is one reasonable choice, though this ignores similarities within the transformation) yields a description of increasingly complex ways to cause a successful execution to fail. This set (along with the associated positive(s) and negative(s) for each transformation) can aid understanding of aspects of an error (such as timing or threading issues) that are not expressible by either transition or invariant analysis. For example, if a positive can be transformed into a negative by changing actions that represent thread/process scheduling choices only, an error can be immediately classified as a concurrency problem. Additionally, we reapply the transition analysis with the values of t_p replacing *pos* and the values of t_n replacing *neg*. This may yield causal transitions when none are discovered by the first analysis (because the context in which the transitions are executed is important).

Returning to the example in Figure 4, running transformation analysis gives us two distinct minimal transformations: $(3 \xrightarrow{T} 4 \longrightarrow 5 \longrightarrow 7) \rightarrow (3 \xrightarrow{F} 7 \longrightarrow 10 \longrightarrow 11 \xrightarrow{T} 3 \xrightarrow{F} 7)$ and $(3 \xrightarrow{T} 4 \longrightarrow 5 \longrightarrow 7) \rightarrow (3 \xrightarrow{F} 7 \longrightarrow 10 \longrightarrow 11 \xrightarrow{T} 3 \xrightarrow{T} 4 \longrightarrow 5 \longrightarrow 7 \longrightarrow 10 \longrightarrow 11 \xrightarrow{T} 3 \xrightarrow{F} 7 \longrightarrow 8 \longrightarrow 10 \longrightarrow 11 \xrightarrow{T} 3 \xrightarrow{F} 7)$. The first of these can be read as "the error will occur in this execution if, rather than choosing to acquire the lock (t_p), the system, in a state where `get_lock == 0`, decrements `get_lock`, then chooses to loop around and again chooses not to acquire the lock (t_n)." The second example produces the negative in which the lock is acquired once—only on the second iteration through the loop does `get_lock`'s value become incorrect with respect to the guard in line 7.

6 Implementation

We implemented our algorithm for generating and analyzing variations inside the Java PathFinder model checker [15]. Java PathFinder (JPF) is an explicit state on-the-fly model checker that takes compiled Java programs (i.e. bytecode class-files) and analyzes all paths through the program for deadlock, assertion violations and linear time temporal logic (LTL) properties. In this implementation we only consider safety properties. We hope to consider the analysis of LTL counterexamples in future work. Actions of an environment not under the control of the Java program are represented in JPF as nondeterministic choices, introduced with special `Verify.chooseBool()` or `Verify.choose(int i)` calls which are trapped by the model checker. For example, `Verify.choose(2)` will nondeterministically return a value in the range 0–2, inclusive. In terms of the LTS model used above, $Act = (t \times n)$, where t is a non-negative integer identifying the thread executing in the step, and n is either a non-negative integer indicating a nondeterministic choice resulting from a `Verify` call (or -1, indicating no such call was made). Π is the set $\{deadlock, assertion, exception\}$ indicating that there is a deadlock, an assertion was violated, or that an uncaught exception was raised. States are the various states of the JVM (including states for each member of Π). $c(s)$ returns a set of control locations (bytecode positions), one for each thread in the current state, allowing for further projection of the control location along each thread.

Our implementation of error explanation makes use of JPF's various search capabilities to provide a wide range of possible searches during the generation of variations, including heuristic searches [8].

We have added the ability to produce Daikon [6] trace files to JPF. Daikon is a tool that takes trace files generated by instrumented code and discovers invariants over the set of traces. We use Daikon for invariant analysis. The other analysis techniques are implemented inside JPF. In JPF, all executions start from the same initial state of the JVM, so the full transformation set always exists. For transition analysis JPF allows various projections on actions, such as ignoring nondeterministic choice or selected thread, as well as analysis based only on control location. In the JPF implementation, we universally use, rather than the $c(s)$ defined above, a projection that produces only the control location of the thread that is executed from a state ($c(s, \alpha)$), an improvement in almost all cases where there are well-defined control locations for threads or processes.

7 Experimental Results

We applied error explanation to determine the cause of a subtle error in an early version of the DEOS real-time operating system used by Honeywell in small business aircraft. We studied this system originally [12] knowing only that an error was present. When we found the error it took us hours to determine that the counterexample given was non-spurious (a time abstraction was used) and showed the error sought. Given this experience and the fact that the DEOS error is very subtle we believed this to be a good test of the error explanation approach. We analyzed a 1500 line Java translation of (a slice of) the original C++ system.

DEOS is a real-time operating system based on rate-monotonic scheduling that allows user-threads to make kernel calls during their execution; for example, they can *yield* the CPU by making a `WaitUntilNextPeriod` call or remove themselves by making a `Delete` call. Since threads can have different priority they can be interrupted by a higher priority thread when a `SystemTick` happens (indicating a new scheduling period starting), or they can use up all their allotted time, indicated by a `TimerInterrupt`. We were checking a safety property asserting time-partitioning—a thread always gets the amount of time it asked for—checked whenever a new thread is to be scheduled.

JPF found the original error in 52 seconds (on a 2.2Ghz Pentium with 2GB of memory), and then spent another 102 seconds performing a depth-limit 30 analysis (finding 131 variations on the error in the process). The resulting output indicated the following key points:

- The `Delete` call is present in all negatives, but also in some positives.
- The shortest transformations from positive runs to negatives are:
  - replacing a `WaitUntilNextPeriod` with a `Delete` call;
  - inserting a `TimerInterrupt` and a `SystemTick` before a `Delete` call.

This shows that the `Delete` call is essential to the error, but only in specific circumstances. This matches the cause of the known error, where a `Delete` call is performed after a specific amount of time has elapsed. Note that making a `Delete` call by itself is not sufficient to cause the error, since there are positives containing this call. It took approximately 15 minutes to analyze the output file produced from the error explanation to determine the cause.

One difficulty with the DEOS example is that we were already familiar with the code and the problem. We applied error analysis to a mode-confusion in an autopilot system [14]. In this case, a user unfamiliar with the code and error was able to describe (relying primarily on the transformation analysis) the problem and generalize to the sequences of actions in which it arises.

We also applied error analysis to concurrency errors such as those in the Remote Agent [9] and the executive planner of a Mars planetary rover. Transformation analysis identified concurrency errors in both cases and showed how minimal scheduling changes resulted in error.

8 Conclusions and Future Work

We propose definitions for two kinds of variations on a counterexample discovered during model checking and present an algorithm for generating a subset of these variations. These successful and failing executions are then used by various analysis routines to provide users with a variety of indications as to the important aspects of the original counterexample. The analyses suggested provide feedback on (1) control locations and actions key to the error (2) data invariant differences key to the error and (3) means of transforming successful executions into counterexamples. While further experiments are needed, our results demonstrate that this analysis can be useful in understanding complex errors.

An important feature of our approach is that we do not have to assume we can compute the full set of reachable states in order to perform analysis—unlike in the related approaches of [1] and [11]. In our experience, when a counterexample can be found, error explanation to a useful search depth is also feasible. In particular, we could find and explain concurrency errors in the Mars rover (8K lines of code with a complicated control structure involving seven threads and complicated exception handling) although it has a very large state space that cannot be fully explored by JPF. Note that since we cannot always explore the complete state space of a system, we might not be able to show that an error is no longer present in a corrected system. In this case, however, we can use the set of negatives for the original counterexample during regression testing.

The exploration algorithm used to generate negatives and positives can also be used to find a counterexample by searching "close to" a path the user suspects could lead to an error. As an example we used JPF's race detection feature [15] to find race conditions in the Remote Agent (without finding any deadlocks or property violations), then fed the path to a race violation to the error explanation facility as the "counterexample" and found a property violation (a deadlock).

The most important area of further research should be improving the methods of analysis both to provide more useful feedback and to do more automatic classification of errors. While the goal of routinely reporting "change line i in the following manner" is unlikely ever to be reached, we believe that better methods than the rudimentary ones presented here may exist. In particular, automatic analysis of the transformations between positives and negatives should be taken a step further than merely noting concurrency-only differences. Another possibility is to generate from the negatives an automaton for an environment that avoids reproducing the error as in the work of Giannakopoulou, Păsăreanu, and

Barringer [7]. It is possible that in some instances such an assumption might succinctly characterize the error, although as an assumption it would only be an approximation of the most general environment for the program.

References

[1] T. Ball, M. Naik, and S. Rajamani. From Symptom to Cause: Localizing Errors in Counterexample Traces. In *Principles of Programming Languages*, 2003. 122, 128, 134

[2] T. Ball and S. K. Rajamani. Automatically Validating Temporal Safety Properties of Interfaces. In *SPIN Workshop on Model Checking of Software*, pages 103–122, 2001. 122

[3] J. Choi, and A. Zeller. Isolating Failure-Inducing Thread Schedules. In *International Symposium on Software Testing and Analysis*, 2002. 123

[4] E.M. Clarke, O. Grumberg, and D. Peled. *Model Checking.* MIT Press, 2000. 121

[5] N. Dodoo, A. Donovan, L. Lin and M. Ernst. Selecting Predicates for Implications in Program Analysis. `http://pag.lcs.mit.edu/~mernst/pubs/invariants-implications-abstract.html`. March 16, 2000. Viewed: September 6th, 2002. 123

[6] M. Ernst, J. Cockrell, W. Griswold and D. Notkin. Dynamically Discovering Likely Program Invariants to Support Program Evolution. In *International Conference on Software Engineering*, pages 213–224, 1999. 129, 132

[7] D. Giannakopoulou, C. Păsăreanu, and H. Barringer. Assumption Generation for Software Component Verification. In *Automated Software Engineering*, 2002. 135

[8] A. Groce and W. Visser. Model Checking Java Programs using Structural Heuristics. In *International Symposium on Software Testing and Analysis*, 2002. 132

[9] K. Havelund, M. Lowry, S. Park, C. Pecheur, J. Penix, W. Visser and J. White. Formal Analysis of the Remote Agent Before and After Flight. In *Proceedings of the 5th NASA Langley Formal Methods Workshop*, June 2000. 134

[10] T.A. Henzinger, R. Jhala, R. Majumdar and G. Sutre. Lazy Abstraction. In *ACM SIGPLAN-SIGACT Conference on Principles of Programming Languages*, 2002. 128

[11] H. Jin, K. Ravi and F. Somenzi. Fate and Free Will in Error Traces. In *Tools and Algorithms for the Construction and Analysis of Systems*, pages 445–458, 2002. 123, 134

[12] J. Penix, W. Visser, E. Engstrom, A. Larson and N. Weininger. Verification of Time Partitioning in the DEOS Scheduler Kernel. In *International Conference on Software Engineering*, pages 488–497, 2000. 133

[13] N. Sharygina and D. Peled. A Combined Testing and Verification Approach for Software Reliability. In *Formal Methods for Increasing Software Productivity, International Symposium of Formal Methods Europe*, pages 611–628, 2001. 122, 123

[14] O. Tkachuk, G. Brat and W. Visser Using Code Level Model Checking To Discover Automation Surprises In *Digital Avionics Systems Conference*, Irvine CA, October 2002. 134

[15] W. Visser, K. Havelund, G. Brat and S. Park. Model Checking Programs. In *Automated Software Engineering (ASE)*, pages 3–11, 2000. 132, 134

[16] A. Zeller. Isolating Cause-Effect Chains from Computer Programs. In *International Symposium on the Foundations of Software Engineering (FSE-10)*, 2002. 123

[17] A. Zeller and R. Hildebrandt. Simplifying and Isolating Failure-Inducing Input. In *IEEE Transactions on Software Engineering*, 28(2), February 2002, pages 183–200. 123

A Nearly Memory-Optimal Data Structure for Sets and Mappings

Jaco Geldenhuys and Antti Valmari

Tampere University of Technology, Institute of Software Systems
PO Box 553, FIN-33101 Tampere, FINLAND
{jaco,ava}@cs.tut.fi

Abstract. A novel, very memory-efficient hash table structure for representing a set of bit vectors — such as the set of reachable states of a system — is presented. Let the length of the bit vectors be w. There is an information-theoretic lower bound on the average memory consumption of any data structure that is capable of representing a set of at most n such bit vectors. We prove that, except in extreme cases, this bound is within 10% of $nw - n\log_2 n + n$. In many cases this is much smaller than what typical implementations of hash tables, binary trees, etc., require, because they already use nw bits for representing just the payload. We give both theoretical and experimental evidence that our data structure can attain an estimated performance of $1.07nw - 1.05n\log_2 n + 6.12n$, which is close to the lower bound and much better than nw for many useful values of n and w. We show how the data structure can be extended to mappings while retaining its good performance. Furthermore, our data structure is not unduly slow.

1 Introduction

The greatest obstacle faced by automated verification techniques based on state exploration is the *state explosion problem*: the number of states grows exponentially in the number of components. Unfortunately, typical explicit state enumeration approaches store the set of reachable states.

In this paper we consider the case where the number of states is much smaller than the size of the universe from which the states are drawn, as is typical in state exploration. We address the question *how close can we come to the absolute lower bound on the memory needed in this kind of situation, without an unbearable increase in the running time?*

The literature contains many approaches that attempt to strike a balance between optimal use of available memory and reasonable runtime costs. Examples include state compaction [2] and byte masking, run-length encoding, and Huffman encoding [6], closed (rehashing) hash tables, open (chaining) hash tables [3], bit-state hashing [5], hash compaction [13, 16], recursive indexing [7, 15], minimized automata-based techniques [8], sharing trees (or GETSs) [4], and difference compression [11].

T. Ball and S.K. Rajamani (Eds.): SPIN 2003, LNCS 2648, pp. 136–150, 2003.

Many of these methods rely on a certain degree of regularity in the structure of the reachable states. For example, recursive indexing relies on the fact that various subparts of the state take on only a few distinct values, resulting in a distribution with "clusters".

Some of the data structures store the entire state vectors. This means that their memory consumption is subsumed by that of *linear storage*, a data structure that stores states consecutively as a string of bits. It is, however, possible to significantly reduce memory consumption below that of linear storage. Due to lack of space, the relative performance of data structures that represent states implicitly (e.g., BDDs) are not addressed in this paper. One could argue that, as some simulation experiments have also suggested, BDDs are not particularly well-suited to storing small subsets of big sets.

We describe a novel data structure that minimizes the memory overhead associated with the management of its data, and makes no assumptions about its distribution. It is therefore not application-specific. The design of the data structure emphasizes memory efficiency over time efficiency. Our approach is a variant of closed hashing with linked lists for collision handling [9, Section 6.4]. To minimize memory usage, we (1) use a hashing function that makes it unnecessary to store whole elements (see [9, Exercise 6.4.13]), and (2) allocate memory in two kinds of blocks that can hold several entries, thus eliminating the need for most pointers.

The data structure is perhaps not as fast as many of its competitors, but not woefully slow either. It can also save time by allowing an analysis that would otherwise require the use of slow disk memory, to complete in fast central memory. Saving memory can mean saving time if it reduces the amount of swapping performed by the operating system. The primary objective of the design then, is to make optimal use of available memory to store as many states as possible; making the operations as fast as possible is only a secondary objective.

In Section 2 we discuss the information-theoretic lower bound on the memory required for representing a set of reachable states, and introduce approximations that we use later on. Section 3 describes the data structure and its operations, Section 4 relates a series of simulations we performed to investigate the parameters for optimal performance, and Section 5 analyses the memory consumption of the data structure theoretically. A test implementation of the data structure inside an existing tool for parallel composition is described in Section 6 and measurements obtained from actual models are presented. Lastly, conclusions are presented in Section 7.

2 Information-Theoretic Bounds

It is possible to derive an absolute information-theoretic lower bound for the amount of memory needed for representing a small subset of a large set U (called the universe). The number of subsets of size n of U is $\binom{|U|}{n}$. A data structure that can represent each of these subsets must use at least

$$M_{low} = \log_2 \left(\frac{|U|!}{n!(|U|-n)!} \right)$$

bits on the average. Some sets of size n may have shorter representations, but, if that is the case, then some others need more than M_{low} bits.

In many applications, such as explicit state space construction, the set grows to its final size in several steps. It is therefore also interesting to consider a data structure that is able to represent all subsets that have at most n elements. Then the number of bits it uses on the average is at least

$$M_{opt} = \log_2 \left(\sum_{k=0}^{n} \frac{|U|!}{k!(|U|-k)!} \right) .$$

However, when $n \ll |U|$, the value of M_{opt} differs very little from M_{low}. So, in practice, M_{low} is a valid limit also in this case.

While these formulations allow us to compute lower bounds numerically, they are cumbersome to manipulate. Therefore, we derive a simple but reasonably precise estimate that will allow us greater flexibility. Let w be the number of bits in the representation of an individual element of the set U. There are therefore $|U| = 2^w$ possible elements in the universe.

Let $w' = w - \log_2 n$. We shall use the following estimate for the information-theoretic lower bound: $M_{est} = nw' + n$.

Before discussing the accuracy of this estimate, let us give it an intuitive meaning. Storing the n elements as such in an array would take n locations of w bits each, totalling nw bits. We call this technique *linear storage*. If the elements are explicitly stored in a hash table, binary tree or other similar structure, then nw bits are needed for them, and additional bits are needed for pointers, etc. We see that nw is a lower bound for any data structure that stores each element of the set explicitly. However, when n is large, $nw' + n \ll nw$. This means that it should be possible to represent large sets much more densely than linear storage does.

We claim the following about the accuracy of our estimate, namely that the absolute lower bound is within 10% of the estimate, when $w' \geq 5$ and $n \geq 7$.

Theorem 1. *$0.9M_{est} \leq M_{low} \leq M_{opt} \leq 1.1M_{est}$ when $w' \geq 5$ and $n \geq 7$.*

Proof. First we show that $M_{low} \geq 0.9M_{est}$. Making use of the fact that

$$\begin{aligned} \log_2 \left[(2^w)!/(2^w-n)!\right] &= \log_2 \left[2^w(2^w-1)\cdots(2^w-n+1)\right] \\ &\geq \log_2 (2^w-n)^n \\ &= \log_2 (n(2^{w'}-1))^n \\ &= n\log_2 n + n\log_2(2^{w'}-1) \\ &= n\log_2 n + nw' - \varepsilon n \end{aligned}$$

where $\varepsilon = \log_2(2^{w'}/(2^{w'}-1)) < 0.1$ for all $w' \geq 4$, and the fact that $\log_2 n! \leq n(\log_2 n - 0.5)$ when $n \geq 2$, we find that

$$\begin{aligned} M_{low} &= \log_2\left[(2^w)!/\left(n!(2^w-n)!\right)\right] \\ &\geq n\log_2 n + nw' - \varepsilon n - \log_2 n! \\ &\geq n\log_2 n + nw' - \varepsilon n - n\log_2 n + 0.5n \\ &= nw' + \kappa n \ . \end{aligned}$$

Since $\varepsilon < 0.1$ when $w' \geq 4$, we know that $\kappa = 0.5 - \varepsilon \geq 0.4$. Now, if $w' \geq 5$, $0.9M_{est} = 0.9nw' + 0.9n = nw' - 0.1nw' + 0.9n \leq nw' - 0.5n + 0.9n \leq M_{low}$.

The second inequality follows directly from the definitions of M_{low} and M_{opt}. Due to lack of space, we will not go into the details of proving the last inequality here, except to mention that it relies on the fact that $\log_2 n! \geq n(\log_2 n - \log_2 e)$ (based on Stirling's approximation), and on the proximity of M_{opt} and M_{low}. □

3 The Data Structure

We now describe a data structure, which we call a very tight hash table. Often state space exploration techniques rely on information about only the presence or absence of states, and then the data structure can be used to implement a set. Sometimes, however, tools also need to store associated data for each state; we discuss how very tight hash tables can be used to implement such mappings.

The data structure is called "very tight" because the primary objective is to get the most out of the available memory and come as close to the theoretical lower bound as possible. This goal is approached in two ways: first, only a part of each state is stored, and second, the design minimizes the overhead needed for the organization of the data.

The data structure was designed for the case where the elements are drawn from the uniform distribution. This assumption does *not* result in hash lists being roughly the same length; rather, they are distributed according to the binomial distribution. Because this assumption does not automatically hold in practice, a function may have to be applied to the elements to "randomize" them. The purpose of the function is to have as many bits of the element as possible affect the bits that are eventually used as the index. Many such functions are available; one example is described in Section 6.1. In the rest of this section we assume that the assumption *does* hold.

3.1 The Implementation of Sets

A data structure D for representing a subset of U must support at least the following dictionary operations on the elements $s \in U$:

- $D.Add(s)$: Adds s to the subset.
- $D.Find(s)$: Determines whether s is in the subset.
- $D.Delete(s)$: Removes s from the subset.

Let each element $s \in U$ be represented in w bits. The basis of our proposal is to break an element $s = s_1 s_2 \cdots s_w$ into two parts: the *index* $s_1 \cdots s_i$ and the *entry* $s_{i+1} \cdots s_w$. The index contains $i = \mathsf{bii}$ (bits in index) bits and the entry contains $w - i = \mathsf{bie}$ (bits in entry) bits.

$$\begin{aligned} \textit{capacity} = \quad & 2^{\mathsf{bii}} \cdot \mathsf{sib} && \text{basic block slots} \\ & + \mathsf{nob} \cdot \mathsf{sio} && \text{overflow block slots} \end{aligned}$$

slots. They are numbered from 0 to *capacity* − 1. The practical capacity of the data structure is less than *capacity*, because some blocks may be partially empty when the overflow blocks are exhausted. According to our experiments in Section 4, the practical capacity varies from 80 to 98% of the theoretical capacity.

The available memory is partitioned into two parts. The greater part, called the *basic region* is subdivided into 2^{bii} *basic blocks*. An element's index determines the basic block where the element's entry is stored, if possible. Each basic block contains sib (slots in basic block) slots where up to sib entries can be stored.

A basic block may of course fill up, and this is where the second part of the memory, the *overflow region* comes into the picture. It, too, is subdivided

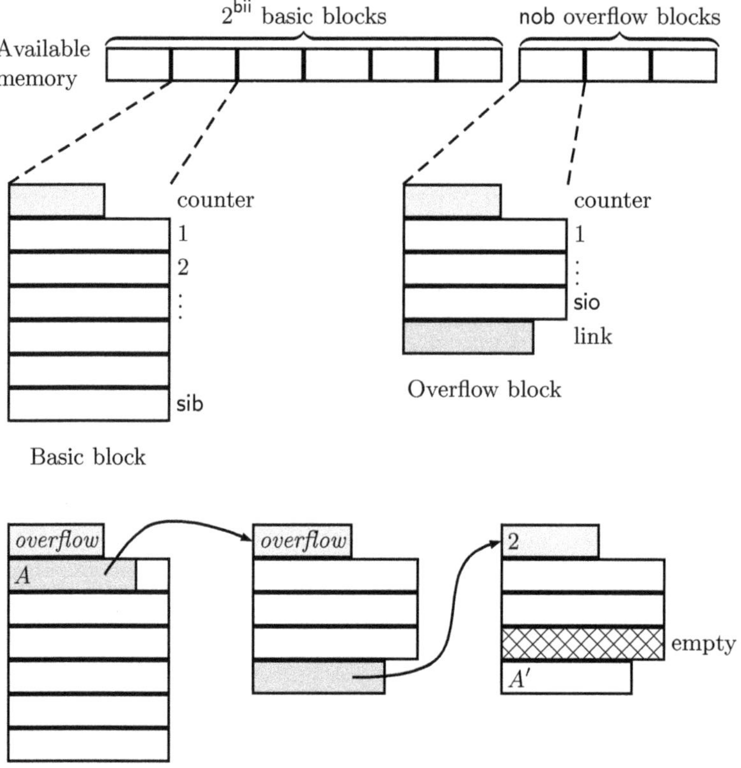

Fig. 1. Organization of very tight hash tables. The three blocks at the bottom show a hash list that overflows into two overflow blocks. The initial bits (A) of the basic block are moved to the link field of the last block (A') of the list to make room for a link

into blocks: there are nob (number of overflow blocks) blocks, containing sio (slots in overflow block) slots. The overflow blocks are allocated as needed to accommodate those entries that cannot fit into their basic blocks. When an overflow block fills up, another overflow block is allocated to store the extra entries. A basic block together with its overflow blocks constitute a *hash list.*

The very tight hash table is fully specified by the values of the five parameters: bii, bie, sib, nob, and sio. This organization of memory (depicted in Fig. 1) was selected to expend as few bits as possible on the organization of the data structure. Given the parameters, a very tight hash table has altogether

The parameters have a critical effect on the memory consumption. Each basic block contains $\mathsf{sib} \cdot \mathsf{bie}$ bits. In addition, a counter of $\lceil \log_2(2+\mathsf{sib})\rceil$ bits is needed to indicate the number of entries in the block along with two special conditions: that the block is empty and that it overflows. Overflow blocks contain $\mathsf{sio} \cdot \mathsf{bie}$ bits and a counter of $\lceil \log_2(1+\mathsf{sio})\rceil$ bits. It is unnecessary to indicate that an overflow block is empty; it is either unallocated or contains at least one entry.

Overflow blocks further contain a link of $\lceil \log_2 \mathsf{nob}\rceil$ bits that indicates the number of the overflow block into which it overflows (if it does). Basic blocks do not have such a link since those bits would be wasted in blocks that do not overflow. Instead, an overflowing basic block stores its overflow link in the first bits of the block. The entry bits overwritten by the link are moved to the as yet unused link bits of the overflow block. When it, in turn, overflows, the bits are moved to link bits of the next overflow block, and so on. Consequently, the last link field in a hash list always stores entry bits that correspond to the first slot(s) of the basic block. Unused overflow blocks are linked together in a free list using the link bits as a pointer to the next block in the list. When an overflow occurs, the first block of the free list is allocated and removed from the list.

In total, the data structure uses

$$
\begin{aligned}
& 2^{\mathsf{bii}} \cdot (\mathsf{sib} \cdot \mathsf{bie} && \text{basic block entries}\\
& \qquad + \lceil \log_2(2+\mathsf{sib})\rceil) && \text{basic block counter}\\
& + \mathsf{nob} \cdot (&& \\
& \qquad \mathsf{sio} \cdot \mathsf{bie} && \text{overflow block entries}\\
& \qquad + \lceil \log_2(1+\mathsf{sio})\rceil && \text{overflow block counter}\\
& \qquad + \lceil \log_2 \mathsf{nob}\rceil) && \text{overflow block link}\\
& + \lceil \log_2(1+\mathsf{nob})\rceil && \text{free list start link}
\end{aligned}
$$

bits of memory. We will address the selection of parameters in Section 4.

The workings of the *Find*, *Add*, and *Delete* operations are very similar: given an element, a linear search is performed through the hash list until the entry part of the element is located, or the end of the list is reached. *Find* simply reports the outcome of the search, while *Add* adds the entry if it wasn't located (possibly causing an overflow). When *Delete* finds an entry it moves the last entry of the hash list into the position of the deleted entry and decreases the size of the last block. If this block is an overflow block that becomes empty, it is deallocated and returned to the free list, and the appropriate adjustments are made to the new last block of the hash list.

All three operations have an average case asymptotic time complexity of $\Theta(n/2^{\mathsf{bii}})$, where n is the number of elements stored in the data structure. As with linked lists, *Find* can be made faster, at the cost of making *Add* and *Delete* slower, by maintaining the hash lists in order.

3.2 The Implementation of Mappings

For mappings, there is a second set A of associated data items. In this paper we treat the elements of A as opaque. The operations a data structure E for a mapping needs to support are very similar to those for a set:

- $E.Add(s, a)$: Adds the association (s, a) to the mapping.
- $E.Find(s)$: Returns the element a associated with s, or NIL if there is none.
- $E.Delete(s)$: Removes s from the mapping (i.e., maps it to NIL).

An obvious possibility for implementing a mapping is to store the associated data along with each entry either in the same array, or in a separate array in the place determined by the slot number of the entry. Because the practical capacity is less than the theoretical, a part of the array will be wasted. If the associated data items are large, it is of course possible to allocate them dynamically and store only pointers to them in the array, to reduce the wasted memory.

Alternatively, one can delegate the storage of the associated data to the user of the data structure, by returning the slot number after each *Add* and *Find* operation. A complication arises, however. If an element is deleted in the way described earlier, the last entry in the hash list is moved into the now empty position. The slot number of the last element therefore changes.

This problem can be circumvented by marking deleted entries with a special entry value, e.g., all zeros or all one's, instead of moving the last entry. This means that the special value is not usable as a regular entry. To compensate for this, it suffices to add just one extra bit to each basic block. This bit will indicate whether the special value is present in the hash list as a regular entry, even though it is never stored as such. Also, the special value must be given a special slot number that corresponds to no slot. Only 2^{bii} extra bits are needed to implement this scheme. An overflow block can be deallocated, when all its entries have been deleted. Because of this possibility, the performance penalty caused by deleted entries is less than with open addressing hash tables.

4 Simulations

To gain an understanding of how the choice of parameters influences the performance of the very tight hash tables, we ran two sets of simulations. In the first, random data is generated and the behaviour of our data structure is simulated, while the second simulation analyses the behaviour of the data structure given a theoretical distribution of the hash list lengths.

Table 1. Simulations (with random data) for varying element and memory sizes

w	Memory	bii	sio	sib	Theoretical capacity	Practical capacity	Performance	Basic/overflow boundary
24	10	7	3	24	4562	4327	143%	78%
	100	12	3	17	59823	54106	159%	78%
	500	14	3	16	375246	332885	181%	79%
	2000	17	3	13	2090544	1715022	217%	80%
32	10	6	3	32	3027	2919	128%	81%
	100	10	3	23	35219	33290	134%	79%
	500	13	3	28	196239	185013	139%	81%
	2000	15	3	33	874837	822803	146%	83%
48	10	5	2	40	1841	1799	116%	84%
	100	8	3	52	19730	19320	119%	81%
	500	11	3	34	105862	102220	121%	80%
	2000	13	3	37	447053	431128	123%	82%
60	10	5	2	49	1426	1401	113%	81%
	100	8	3	53	15068	14801	115%	79%
	500	10	3	51	78903	77223	116%	81%
	2000	12	3	54	328167	321073	117%	82%

4.1 Simulation with Random Data

The first set of simulations consists of about ten thousand simulation experiments. In each experiment, random data items between 0 and $2^{\mathsf{bii}} - 1$ were generated. Counters were maintained to keep track of the length of each simulated hash list. Whenever a counter reached a value that corresponds to overflow, an extra counter that kept track of the number of simulated free overflow blocks was decremented. When this counter underflowed (reached -1), the simulation was terminated and the number of random data items was returned.

Each simulation experiment consisted of three simulation runs, of which the results of the best and worst were discarded. Simulation experiments were made with a wide range of combinations of values for bii, sio, and sib. The value of bie was equal to $w-$bii by definition, and nob was made as large as the given memory allowed. For each data width w and amount of memory, the average parameter values and performance results of the best five parameter combinations were reported. A representative sample of the results is given in Table 1. Memory is measured in 1000 bytes, and performance is M/M_{est}, where M is the amount of memory used.

Some interesting observations were made from the simulation results. Firstly, 3 proved to be an almost universally good value for sio. Very small values of sio lead to many links and large values result in many unused slots, so a "smallish" optimal value was expected. Another apparently universal observation is that about 80% of the available memory should be devoted to slots in basic blocks. The last column shows measured values for this percentage, that is, $2^{\mathsf{bii}} \cdot \mathsf{bie} \cdot \mathsf{sib}/\mathit{total\ memory}$. When reading the column, one should note that when sib grows by one, the figure changes by several percentage units.

These observations can be used as guidelines when picking parameter values for a practical implementation. Of course, one should remember that they are not necessarily valid outside the data width and memory amount range of the simulations. Furthermore, the simulation ignores the fact that in reality a long list has a slightly smaller probability of growing than a short list, because only $|U|/2^{\mathsf{bii}}$ items can fall into each list. This effect is small when 2^{bie} is large compared to the list length.

4.2 Simulation with Ideal Distribution

To verify the results above, we ran a second set of simulations. Instead of generating random data, hash list lengths were calculated using the Poisson distribution, which is the limit of the binomial distribution when the number of elements grows large relative to the number of lists [10, 12]. If n elements are thrown into n/h lists at random with equal probability, the average list length becomes h, and the expected proportion of lists of length k is

$$\frac{n!}{k!(n-k)!}\left(\frac{h}{n}\right)^k\left(1-\frac{h}{n}\right)^{n-k} \approx_{(\text{when } n \gg k)} \frac{h^k}{k!}e^{-h}.$$

Given the number of elements and the data width w, the simulation calculated those values of bii, sio, and sib that result in the best performance.

Table 2 shows the outcome of the second set of simulations. Specifically, each row of the table describes a simulation experiment with the same data width and number of states (i.e., practical capacity) as that of its counterpart in Table 1. The third, fourth and fifth columns contain the calculated values of bii, sio, and sib that yield the best performance. Column six contains the average list length $h = n/2^{\mathsf{bii}}$. The memory (in 1000 byte units) needed by a very tight hash table with these parameters is given in column seven, and the last column gives the corresponding performance.

Once again, several interesting observations can be made. The values of bii and sio correspond closely to those of the first experiments, but the same is not true for sib. We hypothesize that the precise value of sib is not crucial, and that average list length can be used as a heuristic. In all cases the memory requirements are less than the available memory of the first experiment, and, most importantly, the performance figures match those of Table 1 to within three percentage points.

Not only does this second set of simulations confirm the results of the first set, but it also provides us with a convenient tool to derive parameters when the number of states is known, as is the case in the next section. Moreover, it is much faster to generate the hash list length distribution (in the order of 2^{bii} operations), than to produce the random data. This allows us not only to quickly find "good" parameters for the data structure, but also to estimate the expected performance for larger numbers of states.

Table 2. Simulations (with Poisson distribution) for varying element and memory sizes

w	States	bii	sio	sib	h	Memory	Performance
24	4327	8	2	15	16.9	10	142%
	54106	12	3	12	13.2	100	158%
	332885	15	3	10	10.2	497	179%
	1715022	18	3	7	6.54	1973	214%
32	2919	7	2	20	22.8	10	127%
	33290	10	3	28	32.5	100	133%
	185013	13	3	20	22.6	498	139%
	822803	15	3	23	25.1	1986	145%
48	1799	6	2	22	28.1	10	116%
	19320	9	2	31	37.7	100	119%
	102220	11	3	43	49.9	499	121%
	431128	13	3	46	52.6	1994	122%
60	1401	5	2	37	43.8	10	112%
	14801	9	2	23	28.9	100	114%
	77223	10	3	65	75.4	499	115%
	321073	12	3	68	78.4	1997	116%

5 An Approximation of Memory Consumption

We are now able to derive an approximative formula for the memory consumption for very tight hashing, subject to the following assumptions: We fix $\mathsf{sio} = 3$ as suggested by the simulations, and we assign a value to bii such that the average list length $h = n/2^{\mathsf{bii}}$. Once bii is fixed, we set the value of sib to $\lfloor h \rfloor = h - \varepsilon$, where $0 \leq \varepsilon < 1$. Since $\mathsf{bii} = \log_2 n/h$, we know that $\mathsf{bie} = w - \mathsf{bii} = w - \log_2 n + \log_2 h = w' + \log_2 h$.

Let p_h be the proportion of lists that are shorter than or equal to the average length (i.e., lists of length $\leq h$), and let q_h be the proportion of elements in such lists.

Theorem 2. *Setting* $\mathsf{sio} = 3$, *the memory consumption of the very tight hashing data structure for an average set is*

$$M_{vth} < c_1 n w' + c_2 n \log_2 n + c_3 n,$$

where $r_h = 1 - q_h - (\lfloor h \rfloor - 2)(1 - p_h)/h$, *and*

$$\begin{aligned} c_1 &= \lfloor h \rfloor / h + r_h, \\ c_2 &= r_h/3, \text{ and} \\ c_3 &= c_1 \log_2 h + 1/h \lceil \log_2(\lfloor h \rfloor + 2) \rceil + c_2(3 + \log_2 c_2). \end{aligned}$$

Proof. Consider the graph in Figure 2. It shows the n/h lists of a hypothetical distribution arranged according to their lengths. Area B contains all those elements that are in underflow basic blocks, while area A represents the wasted

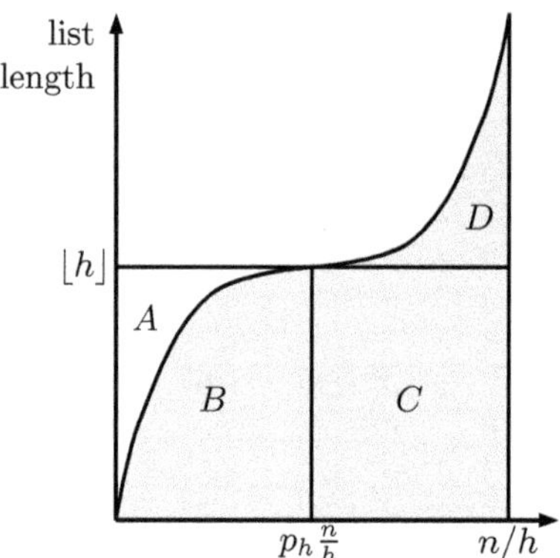

Fig. 2. The n/h lists of a typical distribution arranged according to length

slots of basic blocks. Area C contains those elements that fill their basic blocks and spill into overflow blocks represented by area D. By simple arithmetic we know that $C = \lfloor h \rfloor (1 - p_h)n/h$, and that $B = q_h n$, and, since $B + C + D = n$, that $D = n - (B + C) = n - n(q_h + \lfloor h \rfloor (1 - p_h)/h) = n(1 - q_h - \lfloor h \rfloor (1 - p_h)/h)$.

The number of slots in overflow blocks is the number of overflow elements plus the number of wasted slots. Since $\mathsf{sio} = 3$, each overflow list contains at most 2 wasted slots. Let v denote the number of overflow slots. Then

$$\begin{aligned} v &= D + \text{wasted slots} \\ &\leq n(1 - q_h - \lfloor h \rfloor (1 - p_h)/h) + 2 \cdot (\text{number of overflow lists}) \\ &= n(1 - q_h - \lfloor h \rfloor (1 - p_h)/h) + 2(1 - p_h)n/h \\ &= n r_h \end{aligned}$$

The total memory consumption is therefore

$$\begin{aligned} M_{vth} = & \quad (\text{slots in basic blocks}) \cdot (\mathsf{bie}) \\ & + (\text{number of basic blocks}) \cdot (\text{basic block counter size}) \\ & + (\text{slots in overflow blocks}) \cdot (\mathsf{bie}) \\ & + (\mathsf{nob}) \cdot (\text{2-bit counter size}) \\ & + (\mathsf{nob}) \cdot (\lceil \log_2 \mathsf{nob} \rceil) \\ = & \quad (\lfloor h \rfloor n/h) \cdot (w' + \log_2 h) + (n/h) \cdot \lceil \log_2(\lfloor h \rfloor + 2) \rceil \\ & + (v) \cdot (w' + \log_2 h) + (v/3) \cdot 2 + (v/3) \cdot \lceil \log_2(v/3) \rceil \\ < & \quad c_1 n w' + c_2 n \log_2 n + c_3 n \end{aligned}$$

□

While this theorem talks about the memory consumption of an average set, and not the average memory consumption of all sets, it still provides a good indication of the space needed. Table 3 lists the values of the constants for selected values of h. If the value of h is too small and the lists are too short, the performance of the data structure is poor, partly due to the ratio of data to overhead. On the other hand, if the lists are too long, too much time will be taken by linearly searching through them.

Table 3. M_{vth} upper bounds for various values of h

h	Upper bound
10	$1.21nw' + 0.07n\log_2 n + 4.31n$
20	$1.13nw' + 0.04n\log_2 n + 5.05n$
50	$1.07nw' + 0.02n\log_2 n + 6.12n$
100	$1.05nw' + 0.02n\log_2 n + 6.99n$
150	$1.04nw' + 0.01n\log_2 n + 7.52n$
200	$1.03nw' + 0.01n\log_2 n + 7.90n$

As in the last simulation, the Poisson distribution was used to compute the values of p_h and q_h:

$$p_h = \sum_{k=0}^{\lfloor h \rfloor} \frac{h^k}{k!} e^{-h} \qquad \text{and} \qquad q_h = \frac{1}{h} \sum_{k=0}^{\lfloor h \rfloor} k \frac{h^k}{k!} e^{-h}.$$

We have also computed p_h and q_h using the precise distribution for a wide range of n and w'. The values obtained were usually close to those in Table 3, and in almost all cases the differences were in such a direction that the precise distribution predicts a smaller memory consumption than Table 3.

The memory used for storing the payload is nw'. Thus, $c_1 - 1$ is the ratio of wasted slots to used slots. We see that the proportion of wasted slots becomes small as h grows. Unless n is unrealistically large (like 2^{60}), the $c_2 n \log_2 n$ term is insignificant.

6 Measurements with a Test Implementation

To demonstrate the feasibility of the data structure, we have incorporated it into an existing toolset, TVT [14] for the verification of concurrent systems. One of its components, `tvt.parallel`, computes the set of reachable states of a system. We have modified this program to make use of very tight hashing for storing the set of reachable states.

6.1 Implementation Details

The modified `tvt.parallel` tool uses very tight hashing to represent a mapping from states to auxiliary information about states. Of the previously discussed operations, only *Add* is required. In the implementation, *Add* returns a flag to indicate whether the state was really added or already present in the set. Since *Delete* is not used, the implementation need not maintain a free list of overflow blocks and it returns slot numbers with which the tool manages associated data. Overflow blocks are simply allocated from the first to the last.

The tool imposes a new requirement: it needs a *Retrieve* operation that, given the slot number, returns the original state. This is not a problem when the slot number is in the basic region, since a simple calculation yields the index part. However, when the slot number is in the overflow region there is no way to calculate the index short of scanning through all hash lists. For this reason, the index for each overflow block is stored in an extra field inside the block.

The implementation aligns the entries, counters and links on bit boundaries, thereby saving memory that might otherwise be lost to alignment.

States are randomized in the following way [1, p. 234]: Given the index and entry parts (s_I, s_E) of a state, a replacement index is computed as

$$s'_I = s_I \oplus ((a \cdot s_E + b) \bmod p),$$

where $\oplus$ represents the exclusive or operation, p is the smallest prime larger than 2^{bii}, and both a and b are chosen from the the range $\{1, 2, \ldots, p-1\}$.

6.2 The Results

The results of running the `tvt.parallel` program on four different models are shown in Table 4. The first column specifies a model parameter, such as the number of components. The second and third columns give the number of bits in the state and the number of states for each system. The fourth, fifth and sixth columns give the memory (in units of 1000 bytes and rounded to the nearest unit) and time (in seconds) used by the standard version of the tool, and its performance relative to the lower bound estimate (M/M_{est}). In the next few columns are the memory consumption when using very tight hash tables with and without the extra memory needed for the *Retrieve* operation, followed by the time and performance figures. The last column gives the value of nw/M_{est}.

The standard version of the tool stores states using an open hash table, in which each node in a hash list stores a state and a pointer to the next node. In addition to the set itself, a tool for computing the set of reachable states needs memory for other things, most notably for keeping track of incomplete work. The amount of memory needed depends on many factors, including the nature of additional services provided by the reachable state set data structure, like the *Retrieve* mentioned earlier. To keep the comparison to the theoretical lower bound straightforward, only the memory needed for representing the set is taken into account in the performance figures.

Following the considerations discussed after the proof of Theorem 2, bii was chosen so that the average list length h falls between 32 and 64. The other parameters were selected systematically according to the results of the simulations: sio was set to 3, and sib was set to $\lfloor h \rfloor$. Even better results were obtained by handtuning the parameters and the randomization function, but they are not presented here since they would not be feasible in a practical setting.

Very tight hashing clearly outperforms the original data structure with respect to memory use. More importantly, the new data structure also outperforms the linear storage for all the models. As far as time consumption is concerned,

Table 4. Memory and time consumption experiments

	Param.	Bits	States	Original Mem.	Original Time	Original Perf.	Very Tight Hashing Mem.R.	Very Tight Hashing Mem.	Very Tight Hashing Time	Very Tight Hashing Perf.	Linear Perf.
Dining philosophers	8	24	6560	72	0.42	714%	15	15	0.53	148%	194%
	9	27	19682	156	1.38	461%	49	48	1.74	142%	196%
	10	30	59048	409	4.66	365%	158	156	5.96	139%	198%
	11	33	177146	1956	16.25	533%	521	514	19.81	140%	199%
Pipeline sort	7	36	2234	55	0.12	759%	9	9	0.15	126%	139%
	8	50	6469	98	0.41	314%	38	37	0.56	120%	130%
	9	56	18545	223	1.43	224%	120	119	1.83	120%	130%
	10	62	52746	809	5.17	259%	377	375	6.61	120%	131%
Sliding window protocol	11	27	3654	54	5.22	735%	11	10	5.38	140%	167%
	12	28	4622	61	13.33	622%	13	13	13.36	133%	166%
	13	29	5748	67	32.97	534%	17	17	33.35	132%	165%
	14	30	7044	75	82.51	468%	22	22	83.23	136%	164%
Rubik's cube model	3	15	5670	67	0.32	2671%	6	6	0.47	244%	424%
	4	20	68040	512	4.98	1216%	100	95	6.45	225%	404%
	5	25	612360	4865	55.24	938%	1216	1137	67.13	219%	368%
	6	30	3674160	31946	398.79	756%	8254	7893	467.65	186%	326%

very tight hashing fares slightly worse, but the difference does not appear to be significant.

7 Conclusions

In this paper we have described very tight hashing — a variant of open hashing for representing sets and mappings. Its primary objective is to make optimal use of available memory and it does so in two ways: first, only the entry part of each element is stored, while the index part is discarded without compromising the integrity of the elements stored. Second, overhead costs are kept low by allocating blocks of slots, instead of individual slots, at a time.

It is instructive to compare the estimate of the information-theoretic absolute lower bound, the average set upper bound for very tight hashing (when $h = 50$), and the memory consumption of linear storage:

$$\begin{array}{lrcl} \text{Lower bound} \approx & nw' & + & n \\ \text{Very tight hashing} & 1.07nw' + 0.02n\log_2 n & + & 6.12n \\ \text{Linear storage} & nw' + \quad n\log_2 n & & \end{array}$$

We can see from the formulae that very tight hashing performs significantly better than linear storage for a wide range of n and w'. For instance, very tight hashing consumes only half of the memory consumed by linear storage when $h = 50$, $w' = 5$ and $n \geq 5 \cdot 10^5$. On the other hand, the theoretical limit does not allow any data structure to consume much less than half of the memory consumed by very tight hashing while $h = 50$, $n \leq 10^7$ and $w' \geq 5$.

As the simulations, experimental results and the above calculations show, very tight hashing comes closer to the theoretical limit than linear storage which represents a zero-overhead representation. Moreover, the runtime costs of very tight hash tables in our test implementation are not much inferior to those of the open hash tables used by the original version of our tool.

Acknowledgments

Thanks to Antti Puhakka for comments, and Juha Nieminen for help with the implementation. The work of J. Geldenhuys was funded by the Academy of Finland and by the TISE graduate school.

References

[1] T. M. Cormen, C. E. Leiserson, R. L. Rivest & C. Stein. *Introduction to Algorithms, 2nd edition.* The MIT Press. 2001. 148

[2] J. Geldenhuys & P. J. A. de Villiers. Runtime efficient state compaction in SPIN. In *Proc. 5th* SPIN *Workshop*, LNCS #1680, pp. 12–21. Springer-Verlag. 1999. 136

[3] P. Godefroid, G. J. Holzmann & D. Pirottin. State space caching revisited. In *CAV'92: Proc. of the 4th Intl. Conf. on Computer-Aided Verification*, LNCS #663, pp. 175–186. Springer-Verlag. 1992. 136

[4] J. C. Grégoire. State space compression with GETSs. In *Proc. 2nd* SPIN *Workshop*, Held Aug 1996, DIMACS Series No. 32, pp. 90–108. AMS. 1997. 136

[5] G. J. Holzmann. On limits and possibilities of automated protocol analysis. In *PSTV'87: Proc. 7th Intl. Conf. on Protocol Specification, Testing, and Verification*, pp. 339–344. Elsevier. 1987. 136

[6] G. J. Holzmann, P. Godefroid & D. Pirottin. Coverage preserving reduction strategies for reachability analysis. In *PSTV'92: Proc. 12th Intl. Conf. on Protocol Specification, Testing, and Verification*, pp. 349–363. Elsevier. 1992. 136

[7] G. J. Holzmann. State compression in SPIN: recursive indexing and compression training runs. In *Proc. 3rd* SPIN *Workshop*. 1997. 136

[8] G. J. Holzmann & A. Puri. A minimized automaton representation of reachable states. *Software Tools for Technology Transfer*, 2(3), pp. 270–278. Springer-Verlag. 1999. 136

[9] D. E. Knuth. *The Art of Computer Programming, Vol. 3: Searching and Sorting.* Addison-Wesley. 1973. 137

[10] A. Papoulis. Poisson Process and Shot Noise. Ch. 16 in *Probability, Random Variables, and Stochastic Processes*, 2nd ed., pp. 554–576. McGraw-Hill. 1984. 144

[11] B. Parreaux. Difference compression in SPIN. In *Proc. 4th* SPIN *Workshop*. 1998. 136

[12] P. E. Pfeiffer & D. A. Schum. *Introduction to Applied Probability.* Academic Press. 1973. 144

[13] U. Stern & D. L. Dill. Improved probabilistic verification by hash compaction. In *CHARME'95: Advanced Research Working Conf. Correct Hardware Design and Verification Methods*, LNCS #987, pp. 206–224. Springer-Verlag. 1995. 136

[14] http://www.cs.tut.fi/ohj/VARG/TVT/ 147

[15] W. C. Visser. Memory efficient storage in SPIN. In *Proc. 2nd* SPIN *Workshop*, Held Aug 1996, DIMACS Series No. 32, pp. 21–35. AMS. 1997. 136

[16] P. Wolper & D. Leroy. Reliable hashing without collision detection. In *CAV'93: Proc. of the 5th Intl. Conf. on Computer-Aided Verification*, LNCS #697, pp. 59–70. Springer-Verlag. 1993. 136

Checking Consistency of SDL+MSC Specifications*

Deepak D'Souza and Madhavan Mukund

Chennai Mathematical Institute
92 G N Chetty Road, Chennai 600 017, India
{deepak,madhavan}@cmi.ac.in

Abstract. We consider the problem of checking whether a distributed system described in SDL is consistent with a set of MSCs that constrain the interaction between the processes. In general, the MSC constraints may be both positive and negative. The system should execute all the positive scenarios "sensibly". On the other hand, the negative MSCs rule out some interactions as illegal. We would then like to verify that all the remaining legal interactions satisfy a desired global property, specified in linear-time temporal logic. We outline an approach to solve this problem using Spin, building in a modular way on existing tools.

1 Introduction

A distributed system involves several modules that interact with each other to produce a global behaviour. The specification of each module in the system describes its local data structures and control flow. At each step, a module either executes an internal action to update its local data or communicates and exchanges data with another module.

The interaction between modules is usually described in terms of scenarios, using mechanisms such as use-cases and message sequence charts. In general, it is difficult to exhaustively analyze all possible interaction scenarios and arrive at a distributed implementation that permits precisely the set of desired scenarios.

A more realistic approach is to iteratively maintain two sets of scenarios, positive and negative. Positive scenarios are those that the system is designed to execute—for instance, these may describe a handshaking protocol to set up a reliable communication channel between two hosts on a network. Negative scenarios indicate undesirable behaviours that the designer is aware of, such as a situation when both hosts simultaneously try to set up the channel, leading to a collision. In general, the set of positive and negative scenarios is not likely to be exhaustive—an interaction may not be ruled out by the set of negative scenarios, even though it is not explicitly one of the positive scenarios.

A reasonable expectation at each stage in the iterative design of the system is the following:

* Partly supported by a grant from Tata Research Development and Design Centre, Pune, India.

T. Ball and S. K. Rajamani (Eds.): SPIN 2003, LNCS 2648, pp. 151–166, 2003.

– The system should be able to execute every positive scenario in at least one way. Each such execution should leave the system in a specified safe state.
– All legal behaviours of the system—those that do not exhibit any of the negative scenarios—should satisfy a desired global property.

If the system fails the first test, the existing design has a major flaw that must be fixed. On the other hand, failure to pass the second test probably reveals an incomplete understanding on the part of the system designer of which interaction scenarios are undesirable. In either case, the test provides some insight into how the design should be refined in the next iteration.

When the system passes both tests, the designer can concentrate on cutting out the current set of negative scenarios to complete the design. The interactions permitted by the system at this point may exceed the positive scenarios required by the original design, but this relaxation on its own does not violate the global specification. One virtue of this approach is that the designer naturally arrives at a less constrained, simpler implementation of the specification, rather than a precise implementation that may be unnecessarily complex.

To make the problem more concrete, we fix the following context: individual modules are described using the visual specification language SDL [11, 14]. Scenarios involving specific subsets of modules are specified using collections of message sequence charts (MSCs) [10, 16]. The global specification is a formula in linear-time temporal logic (LTL) [15, 12].

We propose a solution to the problem using the model-checking system Spin [9]. The tools described in [4, 3] jointly provide an automated framework for translating a large class of SDL specifications into Promela, the process description language used by Spin. Our approach is to add an extra *monitor* process to the Promela translation of an SDL specification. Each of the Promela processes arising out of the translation is modified so that it synchronizes with the monitor process whenever it sends or receives a message. The monitor process can thus track the communication pattern executed by the original set of processes.

One complication is that we interpret the positive and negative MSC specifications as templates that may embed loosely in the actual communication graph of the processes [13]. The monitor process has to determine how the template is embedded. For positive specifications, it suffices to guess the embedding. To deal with negative specifications, however, we need to check embedability deterministically. We establish a graph-theoretic property of embeddings that permits us to construct a deterministic monitor process. After constructing an appropriate monitor process, depending on whether we are checking the positive or negative scenarios, we enhance the original temporal logic specification for the system with a temporal logic assertion about the monitor to form a more complex formula that can be automatically converted into a Spin *never claim*.

The paper is organized as follows. We begin with a description of how we interpret positive and negative MSC specifications. The next section provides some background on synthesizing finite-state automata from MSCs. Section 4 is the heart of the paper, describing how we tackle the consistency problem in Promela. We conclude with a summary and discussion of future work.

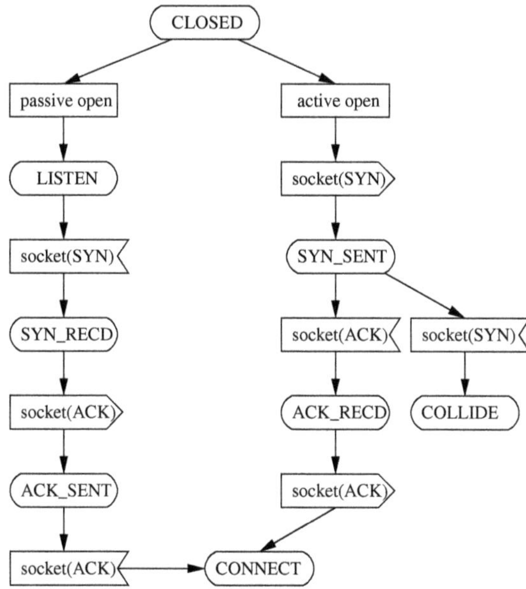

Fig. 1. A simple TCP-like connection establishment protocol

2 Positive and Negative MSC Specifications

We assume that the processes in the distributed system specified in SDL are connected by one-way, point-to-point, FIFO channels. In general, a pair of processes may be connected by more than one such channel.

A sequence of messages transmitted between the processes can be described graphically using a message sequence chart (MSC). We do not formally define either SDL or MSCs in this paper—both notations are reasonably intuitive and we will explain the notation through some representative examples.

In Figure 1, a simplified version of the connection phase of the TCP protocol is specified in SDL. The system has two identical copies of this process. One of the copies is expected to be passive (the *server*) while the other is active (the *client*). The server performs a passive open and waits in state LISTEN. The client performs an active open and sends a SYN to the server, who responds with an ACK. The client then replies with another ACK and both client and server move into the state CONNECT. If the client receives SYN after an active open, it aborts the connection and goes into the state COLLIDE, indicating that a collision has occurred with an active open of another client.

The desired global property for this run is that whenever both processes have moved off the CLOSED state and at least one of them is the client, a connection is established—that is, both processes reach the state CONNECT. However, it is easy to observe that the property fails if both processes simultaneously perform an active open. This will lead to both processes moving to the state COLLIDE.

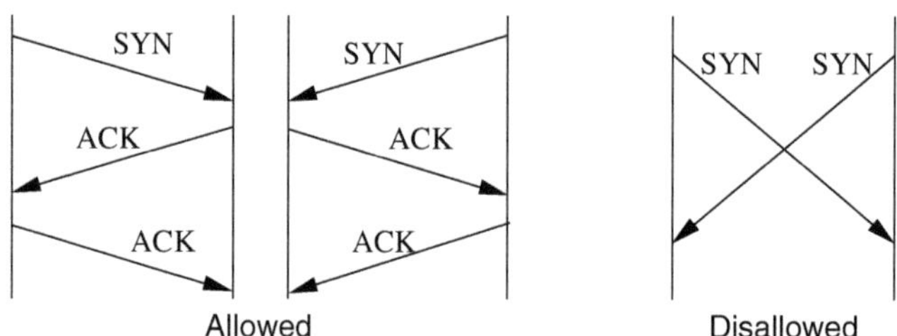

Fig. 2. MSC specifications for the connection establishment protocol

We can rule out such a deadlock with the positive and negative MSC specifications in Figure 2. The positive MSC specifications are given by the MSCs Allowed while the negative MSC specification is given by the MSC Disallowed. The positive MSCs describe the two symmetric desirable scenarios where one process acts as a client and the other as a server. The negative MSC describes an undesirable scenario where both processes simultaneously start off as clients. Notice that the positive and negative scenarios in this case are matched *exactly* in the communication pattern of the system being analyzed.

We shall assume, in general, that both the sets Allowed and Disallowed are finite—this is a reasonable assumption because most real world system specifications do, in fact, enumerate only a finite set of scenarios. We suggest how to deal with a relaxation of this finiteness requirement in Section 5.

As we have remarked, in the first example, the MSCs in Allowed and Disallowed are matched *exactly* by the communication pattern between the processes. In general, we relax the interpretation of the sets Allowed and Disallowed and regard them as templates that may be *embedded* in the system behaviour.

The notion of one MSC being embedded in another is the usual one—there is an injective function mapping the messages in the first MSC into the messages in the second MSC that preserves the partial order between the events of the first MSC. (The next section describes how to represent MSCs as labelled partial orders. For a more formal definition of MSC embedding, see [13].)

For positive scenarios, embeddings permit the implementation to use auxiliary messages to implement the specification. Suppose we enhance our connection establishment protocol to permit the processes to handle a collision as shown in Figure 3. Nondeterministically, one of the processes decides to remain a client and requests the other process to exchange roles by sending an XCH message. If exactly one of the processes sends the XCH message, a connection is established.

The communication patterns exhibited by the enhanced protocol are shown in Figure 4. Observe that two new patterns lead to connection. Both of these embed the original positive specifications in Figure 2 (the embedded pattern is shown using larger arrowheads). The negative behaviours can be characterized by the occurrence of crossing pairs of ACK messages or XCH messages. This yields a revised set Disallowed—see Figure 5. Observe that both the positive and negative scenarios in this case must be interpreted as templates to be embedded.

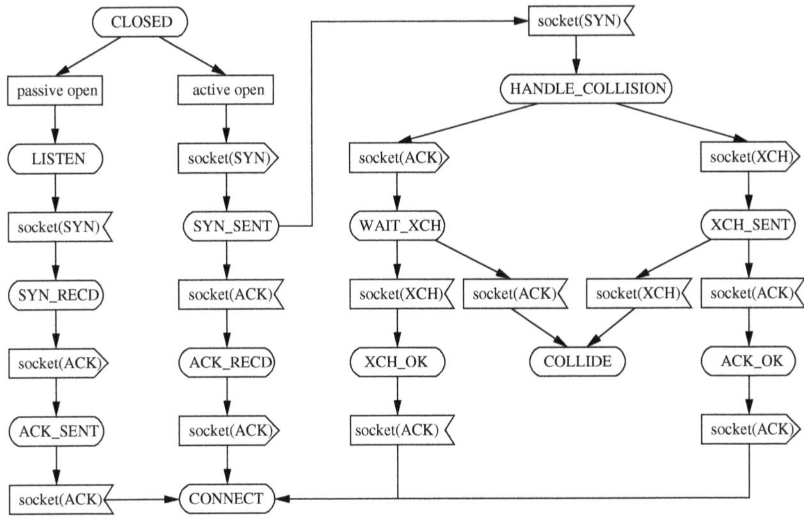

Fig. 3. An enhanced connection protocol

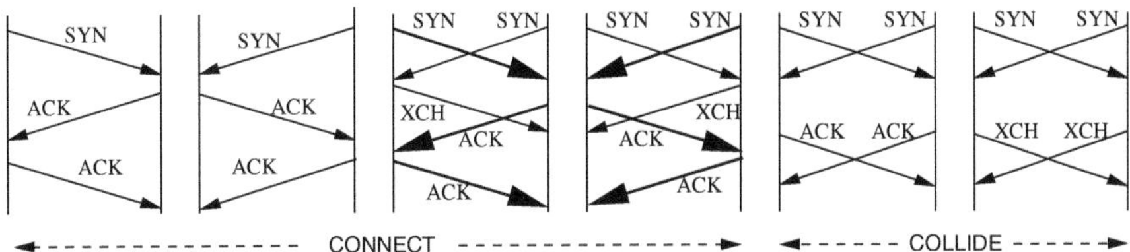

Fig. 4. MSCs exhibited by the enhanced protocol

The example in Figure 6 illustrates another aspect of treating scenarios modulo embedding. The free behaviour of these two processes permits communication patterns like the k-MSC shown in the centre of Figure 7. The variable n in the first process keeps track of the number of messages in the channel $c2$ that are yet to be read by it.

If we impose the constraint Disallowed shown at the left of Figure 7, we rule out k-MSCs for all $k > 1$. Effectively, the only legal communication pattern is the one shown on the right of Figure 7. In other words, the MSC constraint Disallowed guarantees that the system satisfies the property that in every reachable global state, the value of n is bounded by 1. If we demanded an exact match of the MSCs in Disallowed we would have to generate an infinite family of incomparable MSCs, one for each k, to achieve the same effect.

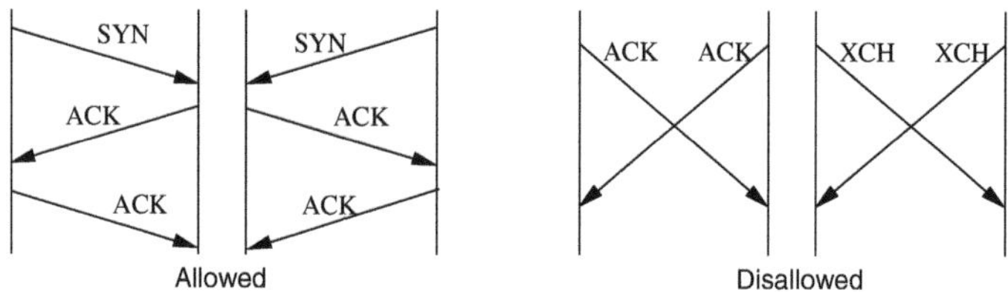

Fig. 5. Positive and negative MSC specifications for the enhanced protocol

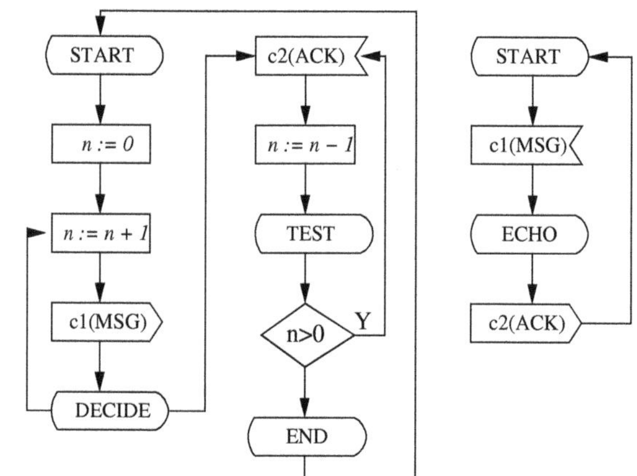

Fig. 6. A counting process

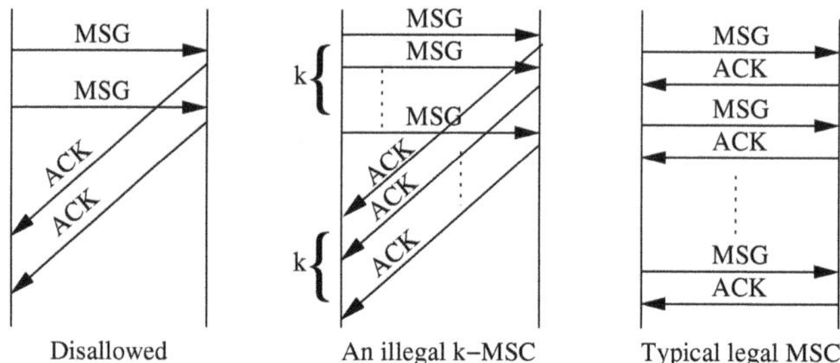

Fig. 7. MSC specifications for the counting process

3 From MSCs to Finite-State Automata

Each message in an MSC can be broken up into two events, one where the message is sent and the other where it is received. Let $\mathcal{P} = \{p, q, \ldots\}$ denote the set of processes, $Ch = \{c, c', \ldots\}$ the set of channels and $\Delta = \{m, m', \ldots\}$ a finite set of message types. Each channel is a point-to-point FIFO link between a pair of processes. Thus, we have functions $src : Ch \rightarrow \mathcal{P}$ and $tgt : Ch \rightarrow \mathcal{P}$ that uniquely identify the source and target process of each channel. The transfer of a message m from p to q on channel c generates a matching pair of events; the send event $c!m$ and the receive event $c?m$. We need not mention the processes p and q because these can be unambiguously recovered as $src(c)$ and $tgt(c)$, respectively.

The MSC defines a labelled partial order on these events. The partial order on events is obtained from the two basic orders implicit in the MSC:

- The send event for a message precedes the corresponding receive event.
- All events executed by a single process are linearly ordered.

An MSC can be uniquely recovered from the set of linearizations of its events. (In fact, a single linearization determines the structure of the MSC.) Stated differently, each MSC has a canonical representation as a finite language over the alphabet $\{c!m, c?m \mid c \in Ch, m \in \Delta\}$. We can thus associate with an MSC M a finite-state automaton $\mathcal{A}_M$ that recognizes the set of its linearizations.

We can extend this framework to define *regular* collections of MSCs. We say that a set $\mathcal{M}$ of MSCs is regular just in case the set of linearizations generated by the MSCs in $\mathcal{M}$ forms a regular language. If we look at the minimum deterministic finite-state automaton (DFA) $\mathcal{A}_\mathcal{M}$ associated with a regular collection of MSCs $\mathcal{M}$, we can uniquely associate with each state s in $\mathcal{A}_\mathcal{M}$ a vector of values indicating the number of messages pending (that is, as yet undelivered) in each channel at that state. This vector is an *invariant* property of the state—no matter which linearization takes us to this state, the channel contents at the state will be according to the given vector [8].

A useful formalism for presenting sets of MSCs is that of a hierarchical message sequence chart (HMSC). The most basic form of an HMSC is a message sequence graph (MSG). An MSG is a finite, directed graph in which each vertex is labelled by a single MSC. A path through the MSG traces out a single MSC obtained by concatenating the MSCs observed at the vertices that lie along the path. The MSG has a start vertex and a set of final vertices. The set of MSCs generated by the MSG is the set traced out by paths that originate at the start vertex and end at one of the final vertices. In general, an HMSC is like an MSG except that the annotation of a vertex can, in turn, be an HMSC, with the restriction that the overall level of nesting be bounded.

It is not difficult to show that HMSCs can define collections of MSCs that are not regular. A sufficient condition is that the HMSC satisfy a structural condition called *boundedness* [2]. Unfortunately, boundedness is not a necessary condition for regularity—in general, it is undecidable whether an HMSC defines a regular language [7]. However bounded HMSCs do satisfy a completeness property. It turns out that bounded HMSCs can describe all finitely-generated regular collections of MSCs—that is, collections that are generated by concatenating MSCs from a finite set of "atomic" MSCs [7].

In this paper, we restrict our attention to finite collections of MSCs, which are always regular. For reasons that we shall make clear in the next section, we will treat each MSC separately. In Section 5, we will discuss the possibility of extending our work to deal with infinite regular collections of MSCs.

4 Monitoring Communications in Promela

As we mentioned in the Introduction, the tools described in [4, 3] provide a mechanism for translating SDL processes into Promela, the process description language used by the Spin system. We add a *monitor process* to the Promela translation of the SDL code and modify the code of every other process p to synchronize with the monitor process each time p communicates with another process q in the system. Before describing how to construct such a monitor process, we show how we use it to solve the problem of checking that the given SDL specification is consistent with the positive and negative MSC scenarios.

4.1 Verification Using the Monitor Process

Let M be an MSC scenario. We assume that we can construct a monitor process with a local boolean variable `good` that is initially false and becomes true when the monitor detects that a run of the system embeds the MSC M.

Positive Specifications For a positive scenario M, the problem of checking consistency can be broken up into two subgoals:

- *Liveness:* Show that it is possible for the system to exhibit the scenario M (in an embedded form).
- *Safety:* Show that whenever the system exhibits the scenario M, it satisfies a desirable global property. For instance, in Figure 1, the desirable property is that the two processes reach the state CONNECT. In general, we may assume that this desired property is specified by an LTL formula φ_M.

The LTL formula $\Diamond$`good` specifies that the monitor process detects an embedding of M. To check the *liveness* condition, we can do conventional LTL model-checking for the formula $\neg\Diamond$`good`. If the system *does* satisfy this specification, then no execution of the system embeds the MSC M and the system under test fails the liveness condition.

To verify the *safety condition*, we check that the modified system incorporating the monitor process satisfies the LTL formula $\Diamond$`good` $\Rightarrow \varphi_M$. This formula asserts that any execution that embeds M must satisfy φ_M.

Thus, both the conditions that we need to verify reduce to model-checking formulas of LTL, which is built in to Spin. An important observation is that we do not need to reimplement the translation from LTL formulas into Spin *never claims*—we can use any standard translation, such as the algorithm from [6] that is built in to Spin or the newer translation described in [5].

Negative Specifications Let M be a negative scenario and let ψ denote a desirable global property of the system. The goal is to show that any run of the system that does *not* embed M satisfies ψ. Equivalently, we have to show that every run either embeds M or satisfies ψ. This is captured by the LTL formula $\Diamond$`good` $\vee\, \psi$. Thus, verifying the consistency of negative scenarios also reduces to conventional LTL model-checking.

Nondeterminism in the Monitor There is an important distinction between the positive and negative cases. The natural approach to detect whether M can be embedded in the communication pattern of the current run is to use nondeterminism. However, because of the nondeterminism, there will, in general, be runs of the system where the main computation does embed M but the monitor does not reach the state `good`.

This does not matter for positive specifications. For the liveness condition we use the negated formula $\neg\Diamond$`good` which checks that *no* run of the monitor reaches the state `good`. For the safety formula $\Diamond$`good` $\Rightarrow \varphi_M$, for every execution of the system that embeds M, there will be at least one run of the monitor that enters the state `good` and it is sufficient to verify that φ_M holds for such runs.

In the negative case, however, for the LTL formula to correctly capture the property we wish to verify, we must ensure that the monitor process reaches the state `good` *whenever* the current interleaving embeds M. For this, we need a more restrictive monitor process. One way to achieve the stronger requirement is to make the monitor deterministic.

4.2 Constructing the Monitor Process

Let `mon` be a new Promela process type and let `snoop` be a new channel shared by all the Promela process types, including `mon`, defined as: `snoop = chan[0] of (chan,byte,bit)`. The channel `snoop` is synchronous and each rendezvous exchanges a channel name, a message type and a bit indicating send/receive.

We assume that the SDL specification is written so that whenever p sends a message to q, the first component of the message designates one of the finite message-types used in the scenario specifications. We modify the Promela code of every process p in the SDL translation so that each statement of the form `c!m(a1,...,ak)` is replaced by `atomic{snoop!c,m,0; c!m(a1,...,ak)}`. In a similar fashion, each statement `c?m(x1,...,xk)` is replaced by `atomic{snoop!c,m,1; c?m(x1,...,xk)}`.

The messages on `snoop` inform the monitor process about the messages being exchanged by the main Promela processes. The `atomic` construct ensures that the sequence of communications observed by the monitor process is identical to the actual communication pattern in the current interleaved execution of the Promela processes. In the third parameter sent via `snoop`, 0 indicates a send and 1 a receive. The parameters `(a1,...,ak)` and `(x1,...,xk)` associated with message-type `m` are not relevant and hence ignored by `snoop`.

This transformation of the Promela processes generated automatically from the original SDL specification by the tools described in [4, 3] is completely uniform and can be achieved using a simple edit script.

A Nondeterministic Monitor Recall that the goal of the monitor is to detect whether the system specification embeds M. As we saw in Section 3, a regular MSC language is one for which we can construct a finite-state automaton over the alphabet $\{c!m, c?m \mid c \in Ch, m \in \Delta\}$ that recognizes the set of linearizations of all the MSCs in the language.

A single MSC M is a trivial example of a regular MSC language for which it is very simple to construct a recognizing automaton. If we project the events of M onto a process p, the semantics of MSCs guarantees that these p-events are linearly ordered. Thus, we can represent the MSC M in a canonical way in terms of the sequences of p-events that it generates, for each process $p \in \mathcal{P}$.

Clearly, for each sequence of p-events, we can construct a DFA that checks that its input matches this sequence—for the sequence $a_1 a_2 \ldots a_m$, the automaton has $m{+}1$ states $s_0, s_1, \ldots, s_m$ with initial state s_0, accepting state s_m and transitions $s_{i-1} \xrightarrow{a_i} s_i$, $i \in \{1, 2, \ldots, m\}$. We can then run the DFAs for all the p-projections of M in parallel as a (free) product automaton to obtain a DFA $\mathcal{A}_M$ that recognizes all the linearizations of M.

The monitor process simulates $\mathcal{A}_M$ to decide whether the system run exhibits the MSC M. Since we are looking for embeddings, rather than faithful copies, of M, the monitor nondeterministically decides which send and receive events to include in the embedding. For this to work correctly, the monitor must ensure that whenever it includes a send (respectively, receive) event in the embedding, it also includes the matching receive (respectively, send) event.

To make a consistent nondeterministic choice across matching events, the monitor maintains as auxiliary data a list Marked of pairs of type `(chan,int)`. If a pair (c, i) is present in Marked, it means that the message at position i in channel c has been included in the embedding.

The monitor process executes an infinite loop that consists of receiving an event on the channel `snoop` and then dealing with it as follows.

- If the new event is a send event $c!m$, the monitor decides (nondeterministically) whether to include the new message in the embedding.

  If it decides not to include the message, there is no further work to be done and the monitor returns to the head of the loop to await the next event on channel `snoop`.

  If the monitor does include the message in the embedding, it performs the following steps:
  - Add the pair $(c, len(c)+1)$ to the list Marked, where *len* is the built-in Promela function that returns the length of the queue on channel c.
  - Simulate $\mathcal{A}_M$ for one step on the action $c!m$.
- If the new event is a receive event $c?m$, the monitor deterministically performs the following action:
  - For each pair (c', i') in Marked, if $c' = c$ then decrement i'.
  - After the decrement, if the pair $(c, 0)$ appears in Marked, delete it and simulate $\mathcal{A}_M$ for one step on the action $c?m$.

Thus, the monitor decides the fate of each message when it sees the send event. If the message is included in the embedding it is marked and tracked as it progresses through the queue. When it reaches the head of the queue, the corresponding receive event is also included in the embedding.

Note that the state space of the monitor consists of the state space of the DFA $\mathcal{A}_M$ augmented with the list Marked. We can maintain Marked as an array.

A trivial upper bound for the number of entries in Marked is the sum of the capacities of the channels as declared in the Promela specification. A much better upper bound is the maximum of the channel capacities assigned to the states of the DFA $\mathcal{A}_M$ (as described in Section 3). Further, each entry in Marked is bounded by the channel capacities in the Promela specification. Thus, the monitor process always has a bounded state space.

A Deterministic Monitor As we noted earlier, to check the consistency of a negative scenario M, we need to construct a deterministic monitor for M. An obvious approach is to apply the subset construction to the nondeterministic monitor described above. This will blow up the state space of the monitor by an unacceptable amount since the set of possible states includes all possible configurations of the list Marked.

A more realistic approach is to use a greedy algorithm to discover the shortest embedding of the negative scenario in the system run. To explain this approach we need to establish a result about MSC embeddings.

Recall that an MSC M can be equipped with a partial order $\leq_M$ on the events in M (see Section 3). Let m_1 and m_2 be two messages in M, on channels c_1 and c_2, respectively. We can extend the partial order $\leq_M$ from events to messages, as follows: $m_1 \leq_M m_2$ if $c_1!m_1 \leq_M c_2!m_2$ and $c_1?m_1 \leq_M c_2?m_2$. Notice that if m_1 and m_2 are both messages on the same channel then the FIFO semantics for channels ensures that either $m_1 \leq_M m_2$ or $m_2 \leq_M m_1$.

We can now order embeddings of MSCs. Let $f_1 : M_1 \to M_2$ and $f_2 : M_1 \to M_2$ be two embeddings of MSC M_1 into MSC M_2. We say that $f_1 \leq f_2$ if for each message m in M_1, $f_1(m) \leq_{M_2} f_2(m)$.

Theorem 1. *Let M_1, M_2 be MSCs such that M_1 can be embedded into M_2. Then, there is a unique minimum embedding (with respect to $\leq$) of M_1 into M_2.*

Proof Sketch: For any pair of embeddings f_1, f_2, we construct a new embedding f' such that for each message m, $f'(m)$ is the minimum of $f_1(m)$ and $f_2(m)$. Clearly $f' \leq f_1$ and $f' \leq f_2$. To complete the proof, we have to show that f' is indeed an embedding. We omit the details due to lack of space. □

We can now program the monitor process to recognize the minimum embedding of M_1 into M_2 in a greedy manner. The monitor records a finite history of the messages exchanged by the system that it has heard about via the channel `snoop`. This history is recorded as a (possibly partial) MSC in terms of the projections of the MSC onto each process p (see Section 3).

We say that an MSC M is atomic if it cannot be written as a concatenation of smaller MSCs [7]. For instance, in Figure 2, the MSC on the right is atomic, while both MSCs on the left can be decomposed into three atomic MSCs.

Let M be a negative scenario to be matched against the system. Let $M_1 \cdot M_2 \cdots M_k$ be a decomposition of M into atomic MSCs. Then, we can sequentially search for embeddings of the atomic MSCs M_1, M_2, ..., M_k. Thus, we may assume, without loss of generality, that at each stage we are trying to detect an embedding of an atomic MSC M.

Suppose, then, that we want to check whether the scenario M can be embedded into the (possibly partial) MSC M', where M and M' are both atomic. We may assume that M' consists of only those message types that occur in M—we need not record messages that will never be matched. Our strategy is to check the embedding at the level of sequences, for canonical linearizations of M and M'. To fix a canonical linearization, we specify an arbitrary linear order on the channels. There is then a unique linearization of the events of the MSC such that e precedes e' in the linearization if (i) $e < e'$ in the underlying partial order on events or (ii) e and e' are unordered but the channel on which e occurs is below the channel on which e' occurs or (iii) e is a send event and e' is a (non-matching) receive event along on the same channel.

In [13], a naïve one pass algorithm is used to check the embedding of one MSC in another. Essentially, this algorithm checks that the linearization of the template M is a subsequence of the linearization of the system behaviour M'. The correctness of this algorithm crucially relies on closure with respect to *race conditions* [1]. In this semantics, along a process line, if a send event is immediately followed by a receive event, the two events can also occur transposed. This would imply that a template where two messages cross (for instance, the SYN messages in Figure 2) would be matched by an execution where the first message is received by the second process before it despatches the second message. This does not seem reasonable, so we interpret scenarios literally.

If we do not implicitly close scenarios with respect to race conditions, we need to use backtracking for template matching. Consider Figure 8. Let the channels corresponding to m and m' be c and c', respectively, with c less than c' in the linear order on channels. Then, the canonical linearizations of the two MSCs are $c!m\ c'!m'\ c?m\ c'?m'$ and $c!m\ c!m\ c?m\ c'!m'\ c?m\ c'?m'$. The naïve greedy subsequence algorithm will incorrectly try to match the event $c!m$ from the template on the left to the first occurrence of $c!m$ on the right.

The backtracking algorithm proceeds as follows. Let $\sigma = e_0 e_1 \dots e_n$ be the canonical linearization of the template M and $\sigma' = e'_0 e'_1 \dots e'_\ell$ be the canonical linearization of the system history M' (which may not be a complete MSC). For each index $j \in \{0, \dots, \ell\}$, we maintain a pointer $\mu(j)$ into the set $\{-1, 0, 1, \dots, n\}$. If event e'_j has already been matched to event e_i, then $\mu(j) = i$. Otherwise e'_j is unmatched and $\mu(j) = -1$. Initially, we set $\mu(j) = -1$ for all j.

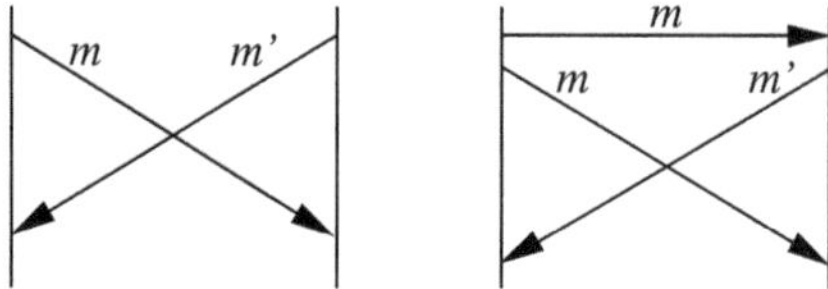

Fig. 8. Template matching requires backtracking

We now scan σ and σ' from left to right. Assume that we are currently scanning e_i and e'_j and the partial embedding constructed so far is reflected in the values of $\mu(k)$, for $k < j$.

- If $e_i = e'_j = c!m$, set $\mu(j) = i$ and increment both i and j.
- If $e_i = e'_j = c?m$, let $e'_k = c!m$ be the matching send event in σ'. If $\mu(k) \neq -1$, set $\mu(j) = i$ and increment both i and j. Otherwise, set $\mu(j) = -1$ and increment j.
- If $e_i \neq e'_j$ and $e'_j = c'!m'$, set $\mu(j) = -1$ and increment j.
- If $e_i \neq e'_j$ and $e'_j = c'?m'$, let $e'_k = c'!m'$ be the matching send event in σ'. If $\mu(k) = -1$, set $\mu(j) = -1$ and increment j. Otherwise, backtrack by setting i to $\mu(k)$, $\mu(k')$ to -1 for all $k' \in \{k, k+1, \ldots, j\}$ and j to $k+1$.

Thus, backtracking occurs when we try to skip over a receive event whose corresponding send has been matched.

We now describe the deterministic monitor. Each time the monitor receives a new event via `snoop`, it does the following:

- If the message type does not occur in the pattern to be matched, do nothing.
- If the message is a send event, the event is added to the history.
- If the event is a receive event, the event is added to the history and we apply the backtracking algorithm described above to check if the current history embeds M.

  If the algorithm succeeds, we move onto to the next (atomic) MSC to be embedded.

  If the backtracking algorithm fails but the current history is a (complete) atomic MSC, we discard the atomic MSC and start a fresh history.

  If the backtracking algorithm fails but the current history is an incomplete MSC, we can discard any minimal event in the history that was bypassed by the backtracking algorithm *before* reaching the end of the current history. (Since backtracking is deterministic, such an event will *always* be skipped, even after the history is extended.) This prunes the history.

Spin permits `hidden` global variables. The value of such a variable is always undefined when enumerating the state space. Thus, hidden variables do not increase the number of reachable states. All the auxiliary variables used by the monitor for the backtracking algorithm can thus be declared to be `hidden`.

Our tactic for pruning histories does not, per se, guarantee that the history is bounded. It is possible to do a more careful analysis and develop a criterion to discard useless events from the history in such a way that the history size is always bounded. However, it seems more pragmatic to fix a reasonable upper bound on the history size based on the size of the template to be matched and live with the possibility of false negatives rather than add further complexity to the deterministic monitor process.

In the worst-case, our backtracking algorithm takes exponential time. However, in practice we believe that it is relatively efficient because it matches one atomic MSC at a time, and atomic MSCs are generally quite small.

5 Discussion

The monitor processes described here have been constructed by hand for some examples, including the ones described in this paper. However, we still have to automate the process of generating the monitor process directly from the positive and negative scenarios.

It is worth noting that at a theoretical level, the problem we have addressed is relatively straightforward. The system specification S can be modelled as a system of communicating finite-state processes. We can abstract away from internal actions and obtain a corresponding *message-passing automaton* $\mathcal{A}_S$ describing its communication patterns [8]. Similarly, we can represent the single positive and negative MSC scenario specifications by message-passing automata $\mathcal{A}_{pos}$ and $\mathcal{A}_{neg}$, respectively. Checking the positive specification amounts to checking whether the language $L(\mathcal{A}_{pos})$ has a nonempty intersection with $L(\mathcal{A}_S)$, while checking the negative specification amounts to checking whether $L(\mathcal{A}_S)\setminus L(\mathcal{A}_{neg})$ is contained in the set of models $L(\varphi)$ of the property φ.

An important aspect of our work is that our approach to solve the problem uses an existing verification system. The solution builds on existing work in a modular way. At one end, we use the SDL to Promela translation from [4, 3]. At the other end, we use the standard translation from LTL to *never claim* processes in Spin [5, 6]. Our contribution is to augment the Promela specification with a monitor process that synchronizes with every other process in the system. This requires us to modify the Promela code produced by the translation from SDL, but the modification is uniform and and hence not difficult to implement.

Another important contribution is the way we combine branching-time and linear-time specifications, using MSC constraints in conjunction with LTL formulas. In our setup, the MSC constraints describe those runs of the system that are "interesting", which is a branching-time assertion. The LTL formula is then treated as a conventional linear-time specification that has to hold universally along all the selected runs. This method of combining of branching-time and linear-time specifications does not appear to have been studied and seems to be of independent interest.

An interesting question is how to generalize the analysis to the case where the set of scenarios is infinite, but regular (in the sense of Section 3). For positive scenarios, we can still construct a nondeterministic monitor, so checking safety is a simple extension of what is done for finite sets of MSCs. However, the strategy for establishing liveness of positive scenarios no longer works. If we check for the satisfiability of the formula $\neg\Diamond\texttt{good}$, where the boolean condition `good` denotes that one of a set $\mathcal{M}$ of MSCs has been observed, what we capture is a situation where the system cannot execute *any* of the scenarios in $\mathcal{M}$. Thus, the situation where the system can execute some, but not all, of the scenarios in $\mathcal{M}$, would not be caught by this approach. This problem does not appear to admit an obvious solution even at a theoretical level, using automata.

The analysis for negative scenarios is also complicated when we have an infinite set of scenarios. There does not appear to be an obvious way to construct an unambiguous monitor in this case. Without this, as we indicated earlier, the formula good $\vee\, \psi$ no longer captures the property that we are trying to check.

Yet another theoretical issue that remains to be resolved is the exact complexity of the problem of detecting when one MSC embeds into another. As we mentioned earlier, a naïve linear-time greedy algorithm is presented in [13], but with respect to a semantics where MSC events may be reordered in the presence of race conditions. Without this relaxation on the order of events, it is not clear that a deterministic polynomial-time algorithm exists.

References

[1] R. Alur, G. Holzmann and D. Peled: An analyzer for message sequence charts. *Software Concepts and Tools*, **17(2)** (1996) 70–77. 162

[2] R. Alur and M. Yannakakis: Model checking of message sequence charts. *Proc. CONCUR'99*, LNCS **1664**, Springer-Verlag (1999) 114–129. 157

[3] D. Bosnacki, D. Dams, L. Holenderski and N. Sidorova: Model checking SDL with Spin, *Proc TACAS 2000*, LNCS **1785**, Springer-Verlag (2002) 363–377. 152, 158, 159, 164

[4] M. Bozga, J-C. Fernandez, L. Ghirvu, S. Graf, J.P. Karimm, L. Mounier and J. Sifakis: If: An intermediate representation for SDL and its applications, *Proc. SDL-FORUM '99*, Montreal, Canada, 1999. 152, 158, 159, 164

[5] P. Gastin and D. Oddoux: Fast LTL to Büchi automata translation, *Proc. CAV 2001*, LNCS **2102**, Springer-Verlag (2001) 53–65. 158, 164

[6] R. Gerth, D. Peled, M.Y. Vardi and P. Wolper: Simple on-the-fly automatic verification of linear temporal logic, *Proc PSTV 95*, Warsaw, Poland, Chapman & Hall (1995) 3–18. 158, 164

[7] J.G. Henriksen, M. Mukund, K. Narayan Kumar and P.S. Thiagarajan: On Message Sequence Graphs and Finitely Generated Regular MSC Languages, *Proc. ICALP 2000*, LNCS **1853**, Springer-Verlag (2000) 675–686. 157, 161

[8] J.G. Henriksen, M. Mukund, K. Narayan Kumar and P.S. Thiagarajan: Regular Collections of Message Sequence Charts', *Proc. MFCS 2000*, LNCS **1893**, Springer-Verlag (2000) 405–414. 157, 164

[9] G.J. Holzmann: The model checker SPIN, *IEEE Trans. on Software Engineering*, **23**, 5 (1997) 279–295. 152

[10] ITU-T Recommendation Z.120: *Message Sequence Chart (MSC)*. ITU, Geneva (1999). 152

[11] ITU-T Recommendation Z.100: *Specification and Description Language (SDL)*. ITU, Geneva (1999). 152

[12] Z. Manna and A. Pnueli: *The Temporal Logic of Reactive and Concurrent Systems*, Springer-Verlag, Berlin (1991). 152

[13] A. Muscholl, D. Peled, and Z. Su: Deciding properties for message sequence charts. *Proc. FOSSACS'98*, LNCS **1378**, Springer-Verlag (1998) 226–242. 152, 154, 162, 165

[14] A. Olson *et al*: *System Engineering using SDL-92*, Elsevier, North-Holland (1997). 152

[15] A. Pnueli: The Temporal Logic of Programs, *Proc. 18th IEEE FOCS* (1977) 46–57. 152

[16] E. Rudolph, P. Graubmann and J. Grabowski: Tutorial on message sequence charts, *Computer Networks and ISDN Systems—SDL and MSC*, Volume **28** (1996). 152

Model Checking Publish-Subscribe Systems

David Garlan, Serge Khersonsky, and Jung Soo Kim

Carnegie Mellon University, School of Computer Science
5000 Forbes Avenue, Pittsburgh, PA 15213 USA
+1 412 268-5056
garlan@cs.cmu.edu

Abstract. While publish-subscribe systems have good engineering properties, they are difficult to reason about and to test. Model checking such systems is an attractive alternative. However, in practice coming up with an appropriate state model for a pub-sub system can be a difficult and error-prone task. In this paper we address this problem by describing a generic pub-sub model checking framework. The key feature of this framework is a reusable, parameterized state machine model that captures pub-sub run-time event management and dispatch policy. Generation of models for specific pub-sub systems is then handled by a translation tool that accepts as input a set of pub-sub component descriptions together with a set of pub-sub properties, and maps them into the framework where they can be checked using off-the-shelf model checking tools.

1 Introduction

An increasingly common architectural style for component-based systems is publish-subscribe (pub-sub). In this style components "announce" (or "publish") events, which may be "listened to" (or "subscribed to") by other components. Components can be objects, processes, servers, applications, tools or other kinds of system runtime entities. Events may be simple names or complex structures.

The key feature of such systems is that components do not know the name, or even the existence, of listeners that receive events that they announce. The consequent loose coupling between components in a pub-sub system makes it relatively easy to add or remove components in a system, introduce new events, register new listeners on existing events, or modify the set of announcers of a given event. Thus implicit invocation systems support the ability to compose and evolve large and complex software systems out of independent components [17].

However, there is a downside to pub-sub systems: they are hard to reason about and to test. In particular, given the inherent non-determinism in the order of event receipt, delays in event delivery, and variability in the timing of event announcements, the number of possible system executions becomes combinatorially large. There have been several attempts to develop formal foundations for specifying and reasoning about pub-sub systems [1, 3, 10, 7, 8], and this

T. Ball and S.K. Rajamani (Eds.): SPIN 2003, LNCS 2648, pp. 166–180, 2003.

area remains a fertile one for formal verification. Unfortunately, existing notations and methods are difficult to use in practice by non-formalists, and require considerable proof machinery to carry out.

An attractive alternative to formal reasoning is the use of model checking. A model checker finds bugs in systems by exploring all possible execution states of an approximating finite state model to search for violations of some desired property (often described as a temporal logic formula). Model checking has had great success in hardware verification, and is starting to be used by researchers to find errors in software systems [5].

While model checking is a powerful technique, one of the stumbling blocks to using it is the creation of appropriate finite state models for the systems being checked. Since most software systems are infinite-state, one must first find suitable abstractions that reduce the system to a finite state model, without eliminating the class of errors that one wants to pinpoint.

A related problem is finding a suitable *structure* for the state model so that properties of interest can be easily expressed in terms of the state machine, and further, so that when errors are found, they can be easily related back to the original system. In general, this abstraction and structuring process is highly system- and domain-specific: techniques for deriving models from one class of software system may be completely inappropriate for another. This means that the person creating a model often has to develop a new set of structures from scratch for each system.

One step towards improving this situation would be to provide generic structured models for certain classes of systems that can be easily tailored to the needs of a particular system within class. In this paper we do just that for pub-sub systems. The key idea is to provide a generic, parameterized pub-sub model-checking framework that factors the problem into two parts: (a) reusable model components that capture run-time event management and dispatch, and (b) components that are specific to the pub-sub application being modeled.

Since much of the complexity of modeling pub-sub systems is in the run-time event mechanisms, the cost of building a checkable model is greatly reduced. For example, within our framework event delivery policy becomes a pluggable element in the framework, with a variety of pre-packaged policies that can be used "off-the-shelf." To further reduce costs of using a model checker, we also provide a tool that translates pub-sub application component descriptions (specified in an XML-like input language) and properties into the a lower-level form where they can be checked using standard model checking tools.

2 Related Work

Publish-subscribe systems have received considerable attention in commercial products and standards (e.g., [20, 18]), as well as academic research systems (e.g., [4, 19]). Most of these efforts have focused on the problem of constructing systems that exhibit desirable run time qualities, such as scalability, efficiency, adaptability, and security, rather than the problem of reasoning about the correctness of such systems, as in this paper.

There has been some foundational research on formal reasoning for pub-sub systems [1, 3, 10, 7, 8]. While these efforts provide a formal vehicle for reasoning about pub-sub systems, at present they require an expert in formal specification and theorem proving to use them effectively. Our research builds on those underpinnings, but aims to make reasoning more accessible by leveraging automated property checking afforded by today's model checkers.

Model checking of software systems is an extremely active area of research at present. Like our research, much of this effort aims to make model checking easy for practitioners to use, for example by allowing the input language to be a standard programming language (e.g., [14, 11]), and by providing higher-level languages for specifying properties to check (e.g., [6]). However, to the best of our knowledge, none of these efforts has focused on exploiting the regularities of a particular component integration architecture, as we do for publish-subscribe systems.

Finally, there have been several previous efforts at providing formal, checkable models for software architectures. Some of these even use model checkers (e.g., [2, 12]) to check properties of event-based systems. However, none has been tailored to the specific needs of pub-sub systems development.

3 Modeling Pub-Sub Systems

How should one go about modeling a pub-sub system as a checkable finite state model? Answering this question is difficult in general because pub-sub systems vary considerably in the way they are designed. Although all share the basic principals of loose component coupling and communication via multi-cast events, specific details differ from system to system [15]. However, a typical system can generally be described as consisting of the following structural elements:

- **Components:** Components encapsulate data and functionality, and are accessible via well-defined interfaces. Interface "methods" are invoked by the pub-sub run-time system as a consequence of event announcements, and each method invocation may result in more events being announced in the system.
- **Event Types:** The types of events indicate what can be announced in the system. Events may have substructure including a name, parameters, and other attributes such as event priorities, timestamps, etc. In some systems, event types are fixed; in others they can be user-specified.
- **Shared Variables:** In addition to event announcement, most event systems support some form of shared variables. For example, in an object-oriented implementation, the methods of a class would have access to the local shared variables of that class.
- **Event Bindings:** Bindings define the correspondence between events and components' methods that are to be invoked in response to announcing these events.

- **Event Delivery Policy:** Delivery policy defines the rules for event announcement and delivery. From an implementation point of view, policies are typically encoded in an event dispatcher, a special run-time component that brokers events between other components in the system according to the event bindings. Event delivery policy dictates such factors as event delivery order (whether or not to deliver events in the order announced), whether events can be lost, the ability to deliver events to recipients in parallel, use of priorities, etc.
- **Concurrency Model:** The concurrency model determines which parts are assigned separate threads of control (e.g., one for the whole system, one for each component, or one for each method).

Given this architectural structure, there are two main stumbling blocks to creating a state model for an pub-sub system that is suitable for model checking. One is the construction of finite-state approximations for each of the component behaviors (methods). In the case of our prototype system we have adopted the following restrictions: all data has a finite range; the event alphabet and the set of components and bindings are fixed at runtime; there is a specified limit on the size of the event queue and on the length of event announcement history maintained by the dispatcher; there is a limit on the size of invocation queues (pending method invocations as a result of event delivery).

A second problem is the construction of the run-time apparatus that glues the components together, mediating their interaction via event announcements. This involves developing state machines that maintain pending event queues, enforce dispatch regimes (correctly modeling non-deterministic aspects of the dispatch), and providing shared variable access. In principle, this part of the modeling process could be done afresh for each system using brute force. Unfortunately modeling pub-sub systems involves a fair amount of state machinery, and is not trivial to get right. Moreover, once built, it is hard to experiment with alternative run time mechanisms. For example, one might want to investigate the consequences of using a dispatcher in which events could be lost, or one in which causal ordering for events is guaranteed.

In our research we have factored out this second effort, by providing reusable run-time model checkable infrastructure for the run-time mediation. To account for variability in the dispatch mechanisms we provide pluggable state modules that allow a modeler to choose from one of several possible run-time models.

Figure 1 illustrates the resulting model structure. The user provides a specification of (a) the component methods (as state machines), (b) an optional set of shared variables, (c) the list of events, (d) the event-method bindings, (e) a model of the environment (or a specification of its behavior), and (f) a set of properties to check. In addition, the user picks the specific dispatch policy (from the options listed in Figure 2), and the concurrency (or synchronization) model (from the options also listed in Figure 2). Using a model generation tool that we built, these parts are then translated into a set of interacting state machine descriptions and properties that are checked using a commercial model checker.[1]

[1] We use the Cadence SMV model checker [13].

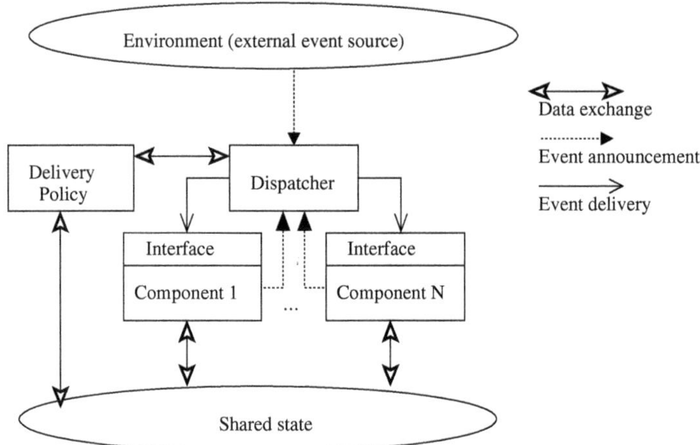

Fig. 1. Structure of a pub-sub system model

In the remaining sections we detail the design of each of these parts and provide examples of their use.

4 The Run-Time State Model

In our approach the run-time infrastructure supporting pub-sub communication has two parts: (a) the mechanisms that interact with the components of the system to handle event announcement, event buffering, and method invocation; and (b) the mechanisms that implement event dispatch and event delivery policy.

Delivery Policies:
- *Asynchronous:* immediate return from announcement
  - *Immediate:* immediate invocation of destination
  - *Delayed:* accumulate events before announcement
- *Synchronous:* no return until event completely processed

Synchronization Options:
- *Separate threads of control:*
  - Single thread per component
  - Multiple threads per component
    - Concurrent invocation of different methods
    - Concurrent invocation of any method
- *Single thread of control*

Fig. 2. Delivery policies and synchronization options

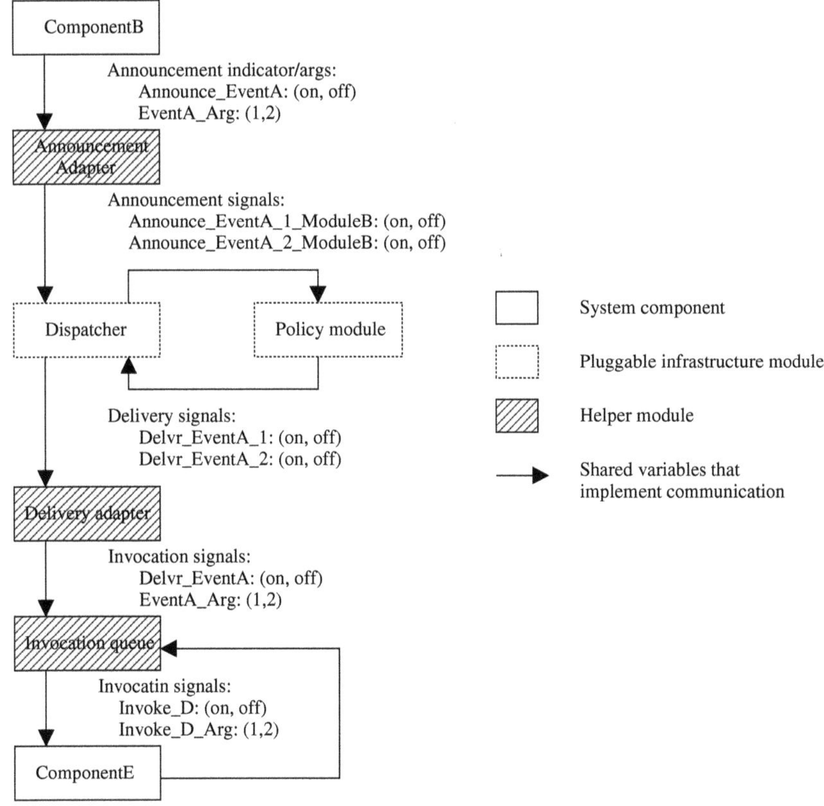

Fig. 3. Event dispatch structures

In more detail, the first part must provide state machine structures that faithfully model:

- Event announcements by the system components.
- Storage of event announcements by the run-time infrastructure in preparation for dispatch.
- Event delivery to the system components, after the dispatch mechanism has selected the event(s) for dispatch (described below).
- Invocation of the methods bound to the delivered events.
- Invocation acknowledgement, which indicates that a method has completed its execution.

Our state model generation method implements this communication in terms of the following shared state variables (see also Figure 3):

- Event announcement: each component announcing a particular event indicates the announcement via a binary *announcement indicator* and a set of corresponding *announcement attributes* such as arguments, priority, etc. For

example, if Announce_EventA has one argument that can assume values 1 or 2, and ComponentB can announce this event, then ComponentB announces the event by writing to two shared variables: the 'on/off' flag EventA and a $\{1,2\}$-valued variable EventA_Arg.
- Announcement acceptance: for each event type, there is a binary-valued *announcement signal* for each possible combination of the event's attributes, such as argument values, source component, priority, etc. For example, a set of binary announcement signals for EventA, explained as above, would be Announce_EvtA_1_ModuleB, and Announce_EvtA_2_ModuleB (assuming that the event's argument is the only attribute of interest). An adapter mechanism (the *announcement adapter* in Figure 3) is used to assign values to these four flags based on corresponding announcement indicator and announcement attribute values written by ComponentB. The announcement signals for each event/attribute combination are then fed directly into the pending event accounting mechanism in the dispatcher (see below).
- Event delivery: implementation of event *delivery signals* is similar to event announcement. To continue the previous example, the set of delivery signal flags generated for EventA might be Delvr_EventA_1 and Delvr_EventA_2.
- Method invocation: method invocation is implemented via binary *invocation signals* and (optionally) *invocation arguments* derived from event arguments. If EventA is bound to method MethodD in ComponentE, and MethodD takes an argument, then the corresponding generated state variables will be a binary flag Invoke_D and a {1, 2}-valued argument variable Invoke_D_Arg. There is a translation mechanism (a *delivery adapter*) that sets up the correspondence between event delivery notification and method invocation variables (i.e., makes sure that Invoke_D is 'on' whenever either Delvr_EventA_1 or Delvr_EventA_2 is 'on', and assigns the appropriate value to Invoke_D_Arg).
- Invocation acknowledgment: this is implemented simply by shared binary state variables that are written by component methods and read by invocation queues described above.

The second aspect of the run-time infrastructure is the dispatcher/delivery policy pair that is positioned between event announcement acceptance and event delivery notification (see Figure 3). This portion of the infrastructure is responsible for immediate announcement acceptance and does not keep track of whether the event delivery notification has been properly processed (the invocation queues take care of that).

The dispatcher state machine performs the role of reading the announcement signals, immediately updating the data structure that reflects the set of pending events (the active events history), and assigning delivery signals as directed by the delivery policy. The delivery policy executes by continuously reading the pending event information from the dispatcher and generating another data structure (the delivery directive) that marks events to be delivered during a particular cycle.

The data structures maintained and shared by dispatcher and delivery policy may vary in complexity, depending on how much information about the set of pending events is required by the delivery policy. The most general mechanism maintains all of the attributes of pending events and also keeps track of the temporal announcement information for each event. We have found that this mechanism is most easily modeled with the aid of distinct announcement signals as described above.

The modularization and separation of delivery and synchronization models make it easy to substitute different dispatchers and delivery policies to examine their effects on the system behavior without changing any other portions of the state model; in many cases interesting behavior can be explored by replacing just those modules. For example, one might investigate the effects of moving from a single address space implementation using synchronous delivery and a single thread of control, to a distributed version of the system by changing the delivery policy to asynchronous, and allowing each component to be a separate thread..

5 Example

To illustrate the approach we use a simple example, introduced in [16] and elaborated in [7]. The target system includes two components: a set and a counter. Elements may be added to or removed from the set. The counter may be incremented or decremented. Elements are added/removed from the set upon the receipt of insert(v) or delete(v) events from the environment; when the insertion or deletion is successful (insertion fails if element is in the set already; deletion fails if element is not in the set), the set announces update(ins) or update(del) events which are dispatched to invoke corresponding increment and decrement events in the counter. The goal is to determine if the system preserves the "invariant" that the counter is equal to the size of the set.

Figure 4 shows the state model structure and the shared state variables used for communication. Note that in this case no announcement/delivery adapters are required for Delete and Insert events because they have no arguments and can simply be represented by single binary signals. An appendix to this paper contains additional details of the SMV model, and in particular shows two different delivery policies.

To check the model for properties of interest we use a model checker. In the case of Cadence SMV we can exploit a feature that allows us to assert certain properties of the model, and then use those assumptions in verifying other properties. For example, to avoid buffer overflow in the finite event queues, we assert that the environment will not generate an overflow. We also assert that the environment will eventually stop, in order to verify that even though Counter may get out of sync with the Set contents, it will eventually catch up).[2]

```
ConsiderateEnvironment :
  assert (G (~disp.evtBuffOverflow &~updateInvQueue.error));
```

[2] In this example, properties are expressed in the logical notation of LTL, using "F" to represent "eventually," "G" to represent "globally," and tilda to represent "not."

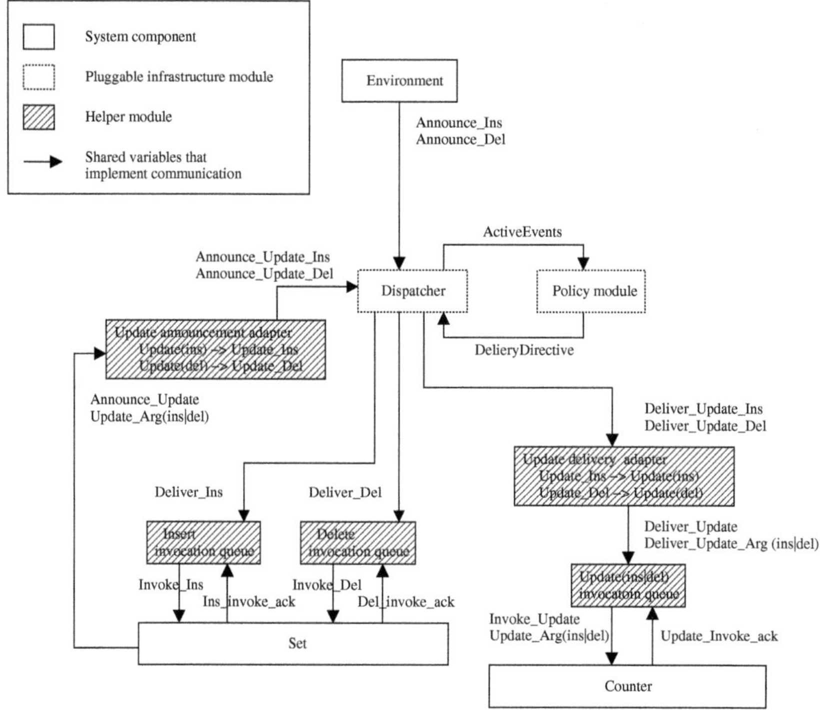

Fig. 4. Generated Set-and-Counter model

```
StoppingEnvironment :
  assert(F G (~announceUpdt));
```

The fact that the environment does eventually stop is used to verify that the counter indeed eventually catches up with the set contents:

```
CounterCatchesUp :
  assert(G F (set.setSize = counter.count));

using StoppingEnvironment, ConsiderateEnvironment
prove CounterCatchesUp;
```

Other interesting properties of the model are obtained via counter examples. For example the following property demonstrates that the counter can actually be negative. (This can happen if, by the whim of the delivery policy, insert events headed for the counter are held up while delete events are allowed through for a number of cycles.)

```
CounterNeverNegative :
  assert(G (~counter.count = -1));
```

The generated SMV code is about 184 lines (excluding comments). Of this, 147 lines (about 80%) is automatically-generated run-time structure, produced by our tool. While this percentage would go down for larger examples, nonetheless it represents a significant reduction in modeling effort, and one that is non-trivial to get right.

6 A More Interesting Example

To investigate the applicability of the approach to more realistic situations, we applied it to the problem of reasoning about dynamic resource allocation for tasks in a mobile computing environment.

The system in question contains components of three types: resources, tasks, and schedulers. Task components represent units of meaningful computation for mobile device users, such as voice call, ftp download, and mp3 play. Resource components represent assignable system resources, such as battery, CPU, memory, and network bandwidth. They are targets for competition between task components. Scheduler components lie between these two groups and arbitrate competition between tasks for available resources.

Communication between components uses publish-subscribe. As illustrated in Figure 5, task components are triggered by environment events requesting their execution. These tasks then announce resource request events, and wait for either grant or reject events. At the same time, resource components announce their resource levels and prices. Resources can also receive events notifying them that some of their capacity has been consumed or replenished. Scheduler components mediate resource assignment, listening for resource requests and resource status, then making decisions about which tasks are to be granted which resources, and how much they are granted.

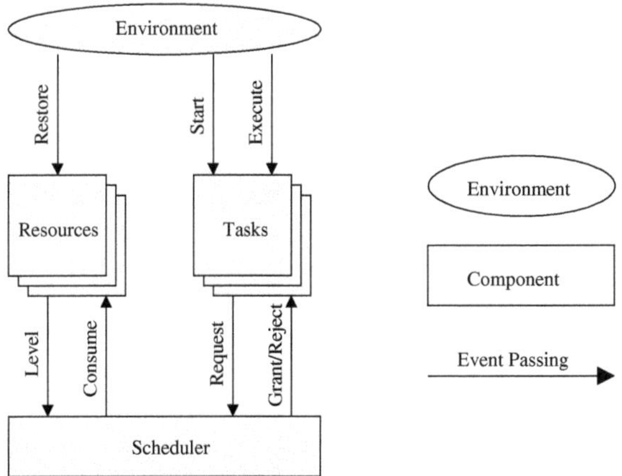

Fig. 5. Mobile resource allocation system

The primary goal of the modeling exercise was to verify that the loosely coupled behavior of publish-subscribe was consistent with the need for a scheduler to be able to accurately assign resources. To test this we initially restricted the system to use a single resource, a single task, and a single scheduler. We also abstracted away the application-specific behavior of the tasks, modeling their behavior simply in terms of units of work yet to be accomplished. A representative sample of the kinds of properties that can be checked include:

1. When started, a task component will eventually finish its work.
   `assert(G ((TASK.Work > 0) -> F (TASK.Work = 0)));`
2. The scheduler will always eventually have an accurate representation of resource levels.
   `assert(G F (RESOURCE.Level = SCHEDULER.Level));`
3. The scheduler must be able to know when resources are exhausted.
   `assert(G((RESOURCE.Level = 0) -> F (SCHEDULER.Level = 0)));`

As a result of verification, the second property turned out to be false. Because there is no assumption of a stopping environment, similar to the one used in set-counter example, it is possible for the level of a resource component to continuously change in response to incoming consume and restore events, leading to a situation in which the scheduler will never catch up with resource components. The first and third properties proved to hold.

7 Discussion and Future Work

We have outlined an approach to model checking pub-sub systems that factors out and parameterizes the run-time mechanisms that support component integration. We then illustrated the idea for two examples, showing how interesting properties could be checked, and the fact that the tool automatically generates a significant body of model checking code.

The more general idea behind the approach is to exploit regularities and known variabilities in architectural structure so that common checking infrastructure can be built once and then used by anyone designing systems in the corresponding architectural style. Not only does this approach reduce the cost of building the models to be checked, but it greatly simplifies the technology since the modeler need only worry about the application-specific aspects of the problem (in this case, the behavior of the components). Naturally, a similar approach could be applied to other architectural styles, with similar gains in cost reduction and ease of use — promising avenue for future research.

One of the drawbacks to such an approach is that because the models are generic and machine-generated, they may be less efficient than hand-crafted models. By “efficient,” we mean that they can be represented by a more compact state representation. In some cases, given today’s model checking technology, this may be the difference between a tractable and intractable model. Understanding when such fine-tuning and extra effort is required represents another important area of future work.

Additionally, the approach is partially hampered by the need to use temporal logic to represent properties of interest, in many cases requiring the modeler to have a detailed understanding of the generated structures in order to specify those properties. An attractive avenue of research would be to develop a set of common pub-sub specific properties that could be easily specified and automatically checked. We are currently working on this, using an extension of the Bandera Specification Language [6]. We are also developing a component specification language that provides a closer link to code than the current SMV-oriented XML-based input language.

Finally, for a complete solution to the problems of checking pub-sub systems, there are several other complementary advances that must be made. Given the translation step, there must be mechanisms to relate counterexamples back to the input model. A hard problem in general, it is even more difficult for us, since the details of the run-time mechanism are hidden from the user of the tool, and so explaining how a series of event announcements leads to an anomalous result is problematic. Another place requiring additional attention is the general problem of developing component models from source code, ensuring that the models are adequate approximations of the actual implementation.

Acknowledgements

This paper is an expanded version of a previously-published, short workshop paper [9]. The research grew out of work on formal reasoning about pub-sub systems, conducted jointly with Juergen Dingel, David Notkin, and Somesh Jha. Goran Momiroski developed an early prototype of the translation tool. This paper also has benefited from discussions with Bill Griswold, Matthew Dwyer, Kevin Sullivan, and Mary Shaw. Partial funding for this research was provided by NSF (CCR-9633532), DARPA (F30602-97-2-0031 and F30602-96-1-0299) and the Army Research Office (ARO) (DAAD19-01-1-04). Views and conclusions contained in this document are those of the authors and should not be interpreted as representing the official policies, either expressed or implied, of the sponsor institution or the US Government, NASA, or the Department of Defense.

References

[1] Gregory Abowd, Robert Allen, and David Garlan. Using style to understand descriptions of software architecture. In *Proceedings of SIGSOFT'93: Foundations of Software Engineering*, Software Engineering Notes 18(5), pages 9–20. ACM Press, December 1993. 166, 168

[2] Robert Allen and David Garlan. Formalizing architectural connection. In *Proceedings of the 16th International Conference on Software Engineering*, pages 71–80, Sorrento, Italy, May 1994. 168

[3] Daniel J. Barrett, Lori A. Clarke, Peri L. Tarr, and Alexander E. Wise. A framework for event-based software integration. *ACM Transactions on Software Engineering and Methodology*, 5(4):378–421, October 1996. 166, 168

[4] A. Carzaniga, D. S. Rosenblum, and A. L. Wolf. Achieving expressiveness and scalability in an internet-scale event notification service. *Proc. 19th ACM Symposium on Principles of Distributed Computing*, July 2000. 167

[5] E. Clarke and J. Wing. Formal methods: State of the art and future directions. *ACM Computing Surveys*, 24(4), December 1996. 167

[6] James Corbett, Matthew Dwyer, and John Hatcliff. Bandera : Extracting finite-state models from java source code. *Proceedings of the 22nd International Conference on Software Engineering*, June 2000. 168, 177

[7] Jürgen Dingel, David Garlan, Somesh Jha, and David Notkin. Reasoning about Implicit Invocation. In *Proceedings of the Sixth International Symposium on the Foundations of Software Engineering (FSE-6)*, Lake Buena Vista, Florida, November 1998. ACM. 166, 168, 173

[8] Jürgen Dingel, David Garlan, Somesh Jha, and David Notkin. Towards a formal treatment of implicit invocation. *Formal Aspects of Computing*, 10:193–213, 1998. 166, 168

[9] David Garlan and Serge Khersonsky. Model checking implicit invocation systems. In *Proceedings of the 10th International Workshop on Software Specification and Design*, San Diego, CA, November 2000. 177

[10] David Garlan and David Notkin. Formalizing design spaces: Implicit invocation mechanisms. In *VDM'91: Formal Software Development Methods*, pages 31–44, Noordwijkerhout, The Netherlands, October 1991. Springer-Verlag, LNCS 551. 166, 168

[11] K. Havelund and T. Pressburger. Model checking java programs using Java Pathfinder. *International Journal on Software Tools for Technology Transfer, STTT*, 2(4), April 2000. 168

[12] Jeff Magee and Jeff Kramer. *Concurrency: state models & JAVA programs.* John Wiley & Son, April 1999. 168

[13] Ken McMillan. *Cadence SMV.* 169
http://www-cad.eecs.berkeley.edu/ kenmcmil/smv/.

[14] Microsoft. Slam. http://research.microsoft.com/slam. 168

[15] David Notkin, David Garlan, William G. Griswold, and Kevin Sullivan. Adding implicit invocation to languages: Three approaches. In S. Nishio and A. Yonezawa, editors, *Proceedings of the JSSST International Symposium on Object Technologies for Advanced Software*, pages 489–510. Springer-Verlag LNCS, no. 742, November 1993. 168

[16] Kevin J. Sullivan and David Notkin. Reconciling environment integration and software evolution. In *Proceedings of SIGSOFT '90: Fourth Symposium on Software Development Environments*, Irvine, December 1990. 173

[17] Kevin J. Sullivan and David Notkin. Reconciling environment integration and software evolution. *ACM Transactions on Software Engineering and Methodology*, 1(3):229–268, July 1992. 166

[18] Sun Microsystems. JavaBeans. http://java.sun.com/products/javabeans. 167

[19] Richard N. Taylor, Nenad Medvidovic, Kenneth M. Anderson, Jr. E. James Whitehead, Jason E. Robbins, Kari A. Nies, Peyman Oreizy, and Deborah L. Dubrow. A component- and message-based architectural style for GUI software. *IEEE Transactions on Software Engineering*, 22(6):390–406, June 1996. 167

[20] TIBCO The Power of Now. Tibco hawk. http://www.tibco.com/solutions/. 167

APPENDIX: Set-Counter Details

In the Set-and-Counter model, information about pending events is kept in the SMV data structure shown in Figure 6. Note that the events announced in the system are (a) update with an 'insert' or 'delete' argument, (b) insert, and (c) delete.

The dispatcher module (not shown here) maintains the above event counts by correctly updating them during every execution cycle. The dispatcher also receives directives from the delivery policy and generates delivery signals.

Figure 7 shows an example of a simple delivery policy that instructs the dispatcher to deliver all events immediately. With this delivery policy, the Counter component always remains in sync with the Set. (In fact, the counterNeverNegative property described before is true.)

A more interesting delivery policy, while making use of the same communication infrastructure, may decide to randomly delay the events as long as the event buffers do not overflow. This is shown in Figure 8. With this delivery policy, the counterNeverNegative property is false and model checker generates a counterexample illustrating how the Counter may get out of sync with the Set.

```
/*****************************************************************/
/* ActiveEventsHistory holds information about pending events.    */
/* For each event count number of steps ago that it was announced, */
/* and if events of this kind are still pending.                  */
/*****************************************************************/
typedef ActiveEventsHistory struct {
 Update_Ins_Pending: boolean;
 Update_Ins_Recent : array 1..EVENT_Q_SIZE+1 of boolean;
 Update_Ins_Oldest : 0..EVENT_Q_SIZE+1;
 Update_Del_Pending: boolean;
 Update_Del_Recent : array 1..EVENT_Q_SIZE+1 of boolean;
 Update_Del_Oldest : 0..EVENT_Q_SIZE+1;
 Insert_Pending: boolean;
 Insert_Recent : array 1..EVENT_Q_SIZE+1 of boolean;
 Insert_Oldest : 0..EVENT_Q_SIZE+1;
 Delete_Pending: 0..boolean;
 Delete_Recent : array 1..EVENT_Q_SIZE+1 of boolean;
 Delete_Oldest : 0..EVENT_Q_SIZE + 1;
}
```

Fig. 6. Pending events

```
module EventDeliveryPolicy(activeEvents, delivery) {
    input activeEvents   : ActiveEventsHistory;
    output delivery      : EventsDeliveryDirective;

    /* Simple policy: just deliver events as they arrive */
    delivery.Deliver_Update_Ins := activeEvents.Update_Ins_Pending;
    delivery.Deliver_Update_Del := activeEvents.Update_Pending;
    delivery.Deliver_Insert := activeEvents.Insert_Pending;
    delivery.Deliver_Delete := activeEvents.Delete_Pending;
}
```

Fig. 7. Event delivery policy 1

```
module EventDeliveryPolicy(activeEvents, delivery) {
    input activeEvents: ActiveEventsHistory;
    output delivery: EventsDeliveryDirective;
    /* Deliver events with random delays, as long as events are not
       delayed forever */
    /* If no pending events, or pending events are old ==>> -1
       (i.e., deliver oldest pending event if any)
       Else randomly decide to deliver oldest pending event (if any)
       or stall delivery */
    delivery.Deliver_Update_Ins :=
        (activeEvents.Update_Ins_Oldest=0 |
         activeEvents.Update_Ins_Oldest=EVENT_Q_SIZE+1 ? -1:{0,-1});
    delivery.Deliver_Update_Del :=
        (activeEvents.Update_Del_Oldest=0 |
         activeEvents.Update_Del_Oldest=EVENT_Q_SIZE+1 ? -1:{0,-1});
    delivery.Deliver_Insert :=
        (activeEvents.Insert_Oldest = 0 |
         activeEvents.Insert_Oldest = EVENT_Q_SIZE + 1 ? -1 : { 0, -1 });
    delivery.Deliver_Delete :=
        (activeEvents.Delete_Oldest = 0 |
         activeEvents.Delete_Oldest = EVENT_Q_SIZE + 1 ? -1 : { 0, -1 });
}
```

Fig. 8. Event delivery policy 2

A Methodology for Model-Checking Ad-hoc Networks

Irfan Zakiuddin[1], Michael Goldsmith[2,3], Paul Whittaker[2], and Paul Gardiner

[1] QinetiQ, Malvern, UK
I.Zakiuddin@eris.QinetiQ.com
[2] Formal Systems (Europe) Ltd.
{michael,paulw}@fsel.com
http://www.fsel.com
[3] Worcester College, University of Oxford

Abstract. Wireless networks, specifically *ad-hoc* networks, are characterised by rapidly changing network topologies. The dynamic nature of ad-hoc networks makes protocol design and assessment particularly challenging. We present a methodology, based on CSP and the FDR model-checker, to validate critical properties of ad-hoc networks, properties like self-stabilisation. Our work started by applying CSP/FDR to a tactical internet (a military mobile network). The techniques developed there were generalised to our methodology for model-checking ad-hoc networks, and more general self-configuring systems. We first give an overview of the results of model-checking the tactical internet, then we describe the methodology on an ad-hoc network case study, namely the Cluster-Based Routing Protocol. The methodology is quite generic, but it enables the complex dynamic properties of ad-hoc networks to be captured quickly and easily, in models that are ususally readily tractable. We end with a brief discussion of some of its other applications.

1 Introduction

The ARPANET bug [1] showed how critical it is to design correct networking protocols. There, one faulty router issued a few corrupt topology update messages before crashing, and that was sufficient to livelock the entire ARPANET. To break the livelock, every single router in the ARPANET had to be manually re-booted. The problem was that the network management protocols in the ARPANET were not *self-stabilising*. Perlman [1] defines a network as self-stabilising when, after some fault, it is able to return to a normal state in a 'reasonable' amount of time, without human intervention. She also requires that the fault does not recur. Perlman's notion of self-stabilisation is related to Dijkstra's [2], but is more informal and focused on networking protocols. Her more pragmatic notion served as a useful starting point for our investigations.

Modern networks are increasingly mobile, using wireless communications. An extreme class are *M*obile *A*d-hoc *NET*works, MANETs, [3], which do not even rely on a fixed infrastructure to serve nodes that are potentially moving very

T. Ball and S. K. Rajamani (Eds.): SPIN 2003, LNCS 2648, pp. 181–196, 2003.

fast. Rather, a MANET is required to form and maintain itself spontaneously. Self-stabilisation for these networks is particularly challenging. Protocols for MANETs are prone to get caught in a cycle of perpetual self-configuration - even in the absence of faults, and merely as a consequence of a dynamic topology.

This paper describes work done at QinetiQ (formerly part of DERA) and Formal Systems (Europe) Ltd, to apply CSP and FDR [4] to study protocols for self-configuring networks. The driving case study for that work was a 'tactical internet'; in effect this is a MANET for deployment in the theatre of battle. Studying the tactical internet produced techniques of significant interest and value. However, the tactical internet is commercially confidential (not to mention its military sensitivity!). To further advance the techniques and to enable their exposure we applied them to some public domain systems, *viz.*:

- the Cluster Based Routing Protocol (CBRP) [5], which is a MANET
- Mobile IP

These studies yielded, in effect, a methodology for model-checking ad-hoc networks, and more generally for self-configuring systems. Further use was made of this methodology in our wider research work on:

- a self configuring key hierarchy, for group key management, [6]
- a link reversal routing algorithm, for MANETs.

And these various items confirmed to us the value and the interest of our approach. In all of the above examples the challenge is to capture the dynamism of the subject, specifically its complex dynamic interactions, in models that are easy to code and tractable to analyse. We believe the methodology delivers a capability for this challenge; it derives its power from flexible and simple concepts, which are supported by CSP_M's powerful programming facilities.

Of course our models are limited to a small finite number of principals, typically about 5, but this is often sufficient locate undesirable behaviour (section 2, on the tactical internet, discusses examples as far as possible). To *verify* systems like these, with a model-checker, requires some form of inductive reasoning. In a CSP and FDR context, they will typically be based on data independent induction, [7]. Techniques for data independent induction establish the base and step case for infinitely many inductions, at the same time. In effect, results are proved for an unbounded number of principals.

The methodology we present is intended as a precursor to the use of data independent induction. The idea being that the complex dynamic behaviour of ad-hoc protocols can be validated quickly and easily using the methodology. The models that have been thus created can then be the basis for subsequent inductive reasoning.

1.1 Plan of the Paper

The rest of this paper presents an overview of modelling the tactical internet, and the results achieved, this is section 2. We then discuss the general methodology in section 3. In section 4 we give a brief introduction to CBRP, which is the second case study. The description of CBRP is a basis for illustrating the methodology in section 5. The conclusion discusses some of the other applications, very briefly.

2 Applying CSP/FDR to a Tactical Internet

2.1 The First Attempt

We had access to descriptions of a tactical internet technology; this was being developed by a leading networking firm and it was tendered as one component of the UK Army's next generation communications system. The technology was required to create and to maintain a radio network across highly mobile nodes, in another words it was a MANET.

The descriptions covered various aspects of the network, but of greatest interest, to us, were the networking protocols. Our first attack on the problem was to code the networking protocols in CSP_M. This was challenging because the descriptions available were somewhat incomplete. Nevertheless, we were able to produce CSP_M models of the system. The models were, in essence, a direct translation, of the networking protocols. Of course, data types were limited to small finite types and continuous parameters were discretised to small finite ranges, but, apart from that, not much abstraction was applied. As such, we created *high fidelity* models of the system.

Unfortunately, the state space of these models was too large to perform much meaningful analysis. While FDR is equiped with a number of state reduction operators [4], these were not able to improve matters significantly. The models of the networking protocols were simply too complex.

2.2 Results with Abstract Models

While the high fidelity models were being developed, another thread of work had been studying routers exchanging link state data. Link state routing is one of the major types of routing protocol [1]. In a link state protocol, each router maintains a database of the state of all links in the network.

To study link state routing CSP_M was used to describe link state routers, in a network of variable topology, trying to agree on the network topology. This work was the basis for the CSP_M specifications of self-stabilisation described below. These models were very abstract; they did not attempt to model any specific protocol. Instead, they simply had routers exchanging time-stamped information about the state of specific links.

The tactical internet used link state routing protocols which were closely related to IP standards. Some state changes, in its networking protocols, were decided according to nodes' views of the network topology. It was possible to upgrade our CSP_M models of routers with a representation of some of these node states. In effect, this yielded an abstract model of aspects of the tactical internet's functionality. Analysing these models proved to be interesting, it showed that the network could partition itself, furthermore some partitions could fail to be detected - some of these behaviours were not at all obvious. We discussed this first phase of the work with the designers of the tactical internet. These behaviours were known to them (in fact an extra layer of protocol coped with some of them), but they were impressed by an automated capability to find protocol flaws and they were very positive about this work. Thus the primary benefit of this phase was to provide us with an encouraging proof-of-concept.

We had found that the high fidelity models were largely intractable, and that starting with very abstract models (of routers exchanging link state data) and adding selected features was promising. This led us to model the mobile network, as a whole, at an abstract level. The essential idea behind the abstraction was to represent a sub-protocol, which caused a set of nodes to change their states with a single CSP event. Such events are synchronised across nodes and they change the nodes' states according to the effects of the sub-protocol. In essence, nodes are given the capability to update states of other nodes directly. This modelling was the basis for the powerful and generic techniques discussed in Section 4, below.

The more abstract modelling started with the simplest possible representation of the substates of a node, with single events controlling transitions between substates. This model was refined incrementally, the pattern was that an abstract CSP network model would be found to have some CSP divergence (some cycle of internal events). This corresponded to the potential for part of the network to continually re-configure itself. This is a type of self-stabilisation failure, and it could be removed by refining the model by adding more system features.

This type of modelling soon developed into an interesting analysis. The models were gradually refined to contain a representation of most of the networks behaviour. In these quite rich models FDR found complex configurations of network topology and node state, which in conjunction could cause the network to perpetually re-configure itself.

Figure 1, attempts to give a flavour of the type of behaviours found by FDR in our models of the tactical internet. Each node decides its state change on the basis of:

- its own state
- the state of its neighbours
- its knowledge of the network topology

In effect FDR explores all possible combinations of these factors, which can lead either to cycles of re-configuration, or to the network configuring itself incorrectly (see section 5.3). In our simple example, the nodes in state *White* decide, on the basis of the above factors to change to state *Black*; and *vice-versa*. The result is a global configuration that is symmetric to the previous state. Each node, will

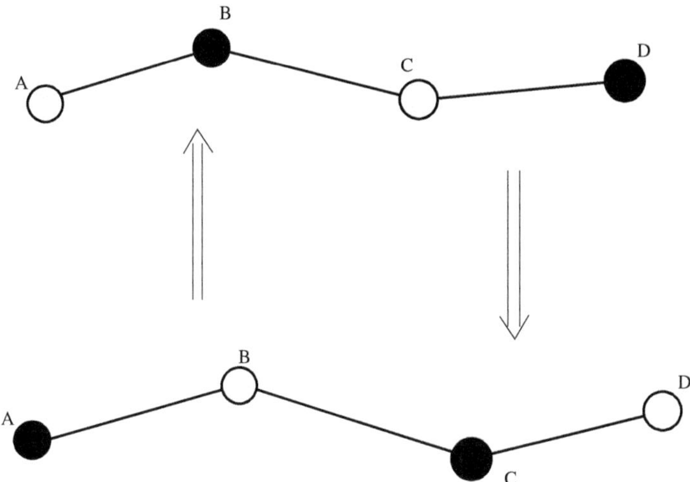

Fig. 1. Simple example of cyclic re-configuration in a MANET

then make corresponding state changes that return the network to the original configuration, and so on.

The result of this modelling was to identify the need for a number of randomising elements in the network specification. Certain state changes in the protocols were guarded by a randomised delay. These delays were found at a few, very select, places in the network description. Initially, we simply ignored them, we could not guess their purpose. However, as our abstract models developed, we found that these randomising elements were necessary to preclude possibilities of perpetual re-configuration, such as alluded to by our fig 1. Returning to our example, if either pairs of nodes A and C, or B and D are forced to wait a random amount of time, before changing their states, then the simultaneity that engenders the cycle is broken.

We subsequently discovered that using a randomised delay is a standard technique for avoiding these potential self-stabilisation failures. However, *finding* the very select places to put these randomised delays is difficult. Current methods are based on a combination of expertise and extensive simulation.

3 Principles of the Methodology

The methodology for modelling mobile networks, that was inspired by the tactical internet study, is simple in concept and powerful in applicability; it also has the benefit of not suffering, very much, from the state explosion. The driving idea is to capture the states of the system's components simply and then to map interactions between components onto their states. The methodology depends on two features of CSP_M, *viz.*:

1. CSP_M's programming support for renaming processes through a relation - this is used to program the way nodes interact.
2. CSP's, hence CSP_M's, model of shared event communication - this is used to implement interactions between nodes in our models.

Renamings are a very powerful programming construct in CSP_M. If P is a process and R is a relation on sets of events, then renaming P through R, written $P[[R]]$, maps P to its relational image under R. So, if a is one of the events performed by P, then $P[[R]]$ will offer the external choice of all the events in $\{x \mid aRx\}$, instead of a. Furthermore, if a set, E, of events are renamed, by R, to the single event e, then the occurrence of e in $P[[R]]$ corresponds to the nondeterministic choice of the E-events in P. In general, events can be renamed in many ways and in this work we primarily use one-to-many renamings.

CSP uses a handshake model of communication. If processes P and Q communicate on an event a, then both P and Q perform a single a together. Furthermore, communication is multiway, so many processes can synchronise on events in the same way as two processes.
The methodology has three parts:

1. **The Local View.** The base of the model are CSP_M processes that capture the state transitions of the units of the subject; crucially this includes processes for links as well as nodes. These basic processes only capture *local* states and state transitions.
2. **Promoting Local to Global.** The CSP_M renamings that map interactions onto the states of the basic processes. In other words the local states of the node and link processes are promoted to the ways they can affect each other. In effect renamings promote a *local view* to a *system view.*
3. **Specifying Properties.** In FDR properties are also specified in CSP_M, but CSP has no built in notion of time or temporality. Nevertheless, we require our subjects to be eventually 'correct' (*cf.* Perlman's notion of self-stabilisation). In fact, we can code the requisite properties of eventual 'correctness', quite elegantly, in CSP.

An important part of our approach is to condense as much protocol as possible into a single shared event. It is also important to make the 'local view' processes as simple as possible. Clearly, the extent to which this is possible will vary from problem to problem, and it will also vary according to the skill of the CSP_M programmer. To illustrate the three parts of the methodology on CBRP we first need a brief description of it.

4 A Short Description of CBRP

The Cluster-Based Routing Protocol [5] is a networking and routing protocol designed for use in MANETs. It uses distributed algorithms to organise nodes into clusters. Each cluster has one, and only one, head, and a number of member nodes. Thus the states of a node are either a cluster *Head*, or a cluster *Member*, but, in certain circumstances, a node can have a third *Undecided* state, before deciding to become a *Head* or a *Member*. The clusters are identified by the ID of their *Head*, and a node is deemed to be a *Member* of a cluster if and only if it has a bidirectional link to the *Head*. So a node can be a *Member* of several clusters simultaneously.

Nodes detect the presence of other nodes and organise themselves into clusters by using regular broadcasts known as 'HELLO' messages. These are periodically broadcast from each node. As a node receives these messages, it builds up a table of the nodes which it is able to hear, and the state of these neighbouring nodes (*i.e. Head*, *Member*, or *Undecided*). The HELLO messages are made up of the state of the broadcasting node together with the neighbour table. By observing whether or not its own ID appears in a neighbour table, a node can determine whether it has a unidirectional or a bidirectional link the sender of the HELLO message.

Cluster formation is also centred around the HELLO messages. Initially, all nodes are in the *Undecided* state, and all nodes commence their HELLO message broadcasts. A timer is also started at each node. If a node receives a broadcast from a *Head* before the time-out, then it becomes a *Member*. If it times out without hearing such a broadcast, then it can automatically go from the *Undecided* to *Head*. If several non-*Head* nodes are in bidirectional contact with each other, then the node with the lowest ID becomes the *Head*. To assist nodes in moving from *Undecided* to *Member*, a *Head* node will, in addition to its periodic broadcasts, send out a triggered HELLO message whenever it receives a broadcast from an *Undecided* node. Once all nodes are in either *Head* or *Member* states, cluster formation is complete.

CBRP is intended for operation in a dynamic environment and the network of clusters must be maintained as connectivity changes; thus nodes states are also liable to change, as radio connectivity changes. Cluster maintainence follows much the same pattern as cluster formation. If a *Member* node loses its last bidirectional connection to a *Head* node, then it will revert to the *Undecided* state and follow the initial procedure. Also, if a *Head* gains a bidirectional link with another *Head*, for longer than a predetermined length of time, then the node with the lower ID remains a *Head*, and the other becomes one of its *Member* nodes. Furthermore, if several non-*Head* nodes come into contact with each other, then the node with the least ID in the peer group becomes a *Head*.

Let us note that network formation and maintenence in CBRP is rather simpler than in the tactical internet. For instance, in CBRP state changes in a node are decided by its own state and that of its peer group; but in the tactical internet, a node's knowledge of the network topology is an additional factor in nodes deciding state changes. The motivation for creating the clusters is to support efficient routing; but we are not going to discuss that, instead we will concentrate on how our methodology enables us to model CBRP's dynamic cluster formation and maintenence.

5 Modelling CBRP

We are now ready to describe how CBRP can be modelled. Abstraction is an important part of our methodology; modelling CBRP starts with the following abstractions:

- We assume that links are always bi-directional (this can easily be rectified, but our presentation will make this assumption).
- We do not store and communicate the neighbour table, but it is possible to access neighbour information implicitly, through the link processes.
- We make a node always receptive to any communication that will change its state (instead of modelling the time triggered and event triggered broadcast of 'HELLO' messages).

5.1 State Transitions of the Basic Processes

The Basic Node. A node will have a number of states. In the case of CBRP, these states are *Head*, *Member* and *Undecided*; so we have the CSP_M type declaration:

$datatype\ NodeState = Head \mid Member \mid Undecided$

The basic node process is parameterised by the current *NodeState*. It performs two types of event: the *stay* event identifies the *current* state the node is in, and it does not change the node's state; with a *move* event the node changes its state, and the event carries its *current* state and its *new* state (the *diff* function is simply set difference and the appendix explains the ? notation as well channels, types and name bindings).

$channel\ stay : NodeState$
$channel\ move : NodeState.NodeState$

$$
\begin{aligned}
&BASICNODE(current) = \\
&\quad stay.current \rightarrow BASICNODE(current) \\
&\quad\quad \Box \\
&\quad move.current?new : diff(NodeState, \{current\}) \rightarrow BASICNODE(new)
\end{aligned}
$$

The Basic Link. We capture a lot of interesting dynamic behaviour by having a simple two state process for a link, these states are *Up* and *Down*. Transition between these two states is controlled by the *make* and *break* events and *linkstate* events report whether the link is *Up* or *Down*.

$channel\ make, break$
$channel\ linkstate : LinkState$

$$
\begin{array}{l}
BASICLINK = \\
\quad let \\
\quad\quad DOWN = \\
\quad\quad\quad make \qquad\qquad\quad \rightarrow UP \\
\quad\quad\quad\quad \Box \\
\quad\quad\quad linkstate.Down \ \rightarrow DOWN \\
\quad\quad UP = \\
\quad\quad\quad break \qquad\qquad\quad \rightarrow DOWN \\
\quad\quad\quad\quad \Box \\
\quad\quad\quad linkstate.Up \qquad \rightarrow UP \\
\quad within \\
\quad\quad DOWN
\end{array}
$$

BASICLINK has *UP* and *DOWN* as its local states, with *DOWN* being the initial state.

BASICNODE and *BASICLINK* are the fundamental units of the system's model; but to build the model these processes need to interact and the node and link identifiers need to be added. The interactions are programmed by renaming the basic processes according to the ways they can affect each others state, and, as such, these renamings also carry the node and link identifiers. The interactions are then implemented by making the renamed CSP_M processes communicate.

5.2 Renaming and Connecting Processes

Renaming and synchronisation are used to create the model of the network in a number of ways and the principal techniques are summarised here. We assume that nodes are named A, B, etc. and that this defines the type *NodeId*. Elements of this type are ordered alphabetically. We can then identify a link by the pair of nodes it connects, *viz.*: $\{A, B\}$,$\{B, D\}$, etc.

Causing State Changes. A local event can be renamed to a cause of a state change, in another node. The local event will typically capture the local state of the node. In the CBRP example the *stay.x* event, in the *BASICNODE*, is renamed to cause all state changes that are a consequence of state x. For instance, suppose we want to program the way a node, A, can affect other nodes when it is a *Head*. For this we use the channel:

channel announce : *NodeState.NodeId*

to rename *stay.Head* to *announce.Head.A*, in the code for node A. But to complete mapping the effects of a node being a *Head* we need to make local state changes, in other nodes, receptive to all events of type *announce.Head*.

Allowing Local States to be Changed. A local state change is marked by the appropriate event and this event must be renamed to allow other nodes to activate the state change. So if a node, B, is *Undecided*, then it will become a *Member* when its link with a *Head* node becomes *Up*. To implement this the *move.Undecided.Member*, in node B, has to be renamed to:

$$\{announce.Head.x \mid x \in diff(NodeId, \{B\})\}$$

To iterate, applying this renaming means that in node C the external choice of both the above events will be offered. So in the *Undecided* state C will synchronise with either *announce.Head.A* or *announce.Head.B* to become *Member*.

Modelling Synchronised Broadcast. Network connectivity is another factor in deciding how nodes affect each other and this determines the various ways the *BASICLINK* process (or its analogue) is renamed.

To continue our example of the interactions between *Head* and *Undecided* nodes, to allow A to broadcast that it is a *Head* all links in the set:

$$\{\{A, n\} \mid n \in diff(NodeId, \{A\})\}$$

will have their *linkstate.Up* event renamed to *announce.Head.A*. This in renaming, in conjunction with the two former renamings, allows a *Head* node to change all *Undecided* nodes, of lower id, into *Member*. In effect we have implemented a synchronised broadcast by parameterising the *announce.Head* event with only the sender.

Modelling Pointwise Interactions. *Undecided* nodes also broadcast their state to solicit a respose from a neighbouring *Head*; the response is, in effect, a point-to-point communication. To model the reponse from a *Head*, we need a new channel:

$$channelpt2pt : Sender.Receiver.NodeState$$

where both *Sender* and *Receiver* are equal to *NodeId*. Taking the instance where A is *Head* and B is *Undecided*, renaming each of:

- *stay.Head* in the process for node A,
- *move.Undecided.Member* in the process for node A,
- *linkstate.Up* in the process for link $\{A, B\}$

to *pt2pt.A.B.Head*, will implement this part of the protocol. In general pointwise interactions are modelled by parameterising the 'global view' event with both sender and receiver.

Note that the sub-protocol we have described is condensed into the single *pt2pt* event. Finally, note that the *Undecided* broadcast does not cause any node's state to change and an *Undecided* node is always receptive to a change to *Member* by a *pt2pt* event. This means we can omit the *Undecided* broadcast and condense this sub-protocol into the single *pt2pt* event.

Capturing Effects of Losing Connectivity. The renamings we have discussed above have depended on links being *Up*. We can capture the consequences of loosing connectivity with renamings as well, here are two brief examples.

When a *Member*, say C, loses its last link to a *Head* it becomes *Undecided*. This can be implemented by declaring:

channel losehead : *NodeId*

and renaming C's *move.Member.Undecided* event to a *losehead*.C event. Also all *linkstate.Down* events in C's links must be renamed to the same *losehead* event. Thus if node C is a *Member* and it has lost all its links to its *Head*'s, then it will synchronise on a *losehead* event, with its link processes, to become *Undecided*.

The *linkstate.Down* event can also be used to simulate a timeout. If an *Undecided* node does not get a link to a *Head*, then it times out and becomes a *Head*. Maintaining our nomenclature, if the *move.Undecided.Head* event is also renamed to *losehead*.C, then this will synchronise with the *losehead*.C events in C's links to make C a *Head*.

Using Multiway Synchronisation. Multiway synchronisation can be used to condense a complex interaction across nodes into an atomic global state transitions. In the case of CBRP, multiway synchronisation can be used to model, with a single transition, when a group of mutually audible *Undecided*'s elect the one with the lowest ID as a new *Head*, while the rest become its *Member*.

One might imagine that this would require accumulating state at each node to make this decision. However, the flexibility of synchronisation in CSP allow this to be achieved in a single multi-way communication; but this multiway communication involves not only the nodes in the connected component of the network in question, but those isolated from it as well.

When a link is *Down*, the link process prevents its nodes from being elected, but it permits any other node to be made the *Head*. When the link is *Up*, the nodes, at the end of the link:

- prevent any election, when they are *Head*;
- allow themselves or nodes of lower id to be elected, when they are *Undecided*;
- block the election of any higher ID, when they are *Undecided*.

Now, when the intersection of all of these sets is calculated, by the semantics of parallel composition, the result is the singleton contain the lowest ID of the peer group. Thus each *Undecided* node is left with a single possibility : if its ID is the one in the singleton, then it becomes *Head*; but if its ID is higher than the chosen one, then it becomes a *Member*.

Exposing State for Property Checking. Finally, the connection between this step of the method and the last step is to expose the state of nodes at the global level. This enables the specifications, described in section 5.3, to be coded and model-checked against. For this we need the channel:

channel report : *NodeId.NodeState*

In each node the *stay* event is renamed to the *report* event. Thus in node A, *stay.x* is renamed to *report.A.x*.

With our model of CBRP (or whatever self-configuring system we happen to be studying) complete, we need the last step of our methodology: a formalisation of the properties it must satisfy.

5.3 Specifying and Checking Properties

FDR is a *refinement checker*, it checks whether one CSP_M process, the specification, or *SPEC* is *refined* by another, the implementation, or *IMP*. Refinement is with respect to one of the (three most common) denotational semantics of CSP, *viz.* traces, failures and failures-divergence. And to say that *IMP* refines *SPEC* simply means that the denotational value of *IMP* is a subset of the denotational value of *SPEC*.

We want to check that our system will always terminate its self-configuration, resulting in a 'correct' state. In effect, the CSP_M specification must capture the following:

- The self-configuration terminates.
- The resulting distributed state of the system is 'correct'.

But to prevent FDR stopping a check when the system reaches a transient bad state, the specification must also:

- Permit the system to be in an incorrect state prior to the self-configuration terminating.

FDR establishes the refinement relationship by comparing the operational forms of *SPEC* and *IMP* - which are labelled transition systems. Operational states are either *unstable* - in which case they can perform hidden events, or they are *stable* - in which case they only do visible events. To verify a failures-divergence assertion:

1. FDR checks unstable states of *IMP* for cycles of hidden events, namely *divergences* that are disallowed by *SPEC*'s unstable states.
2. FDR checks that the stable states of *IMP* can refuse no more than *SPEC*'s stable states.

Now consider the following CSP process:

$$SPEC = right \rightarrow SPEC \;\Box\; (STOP \sqcap wrong \rightarrow SPEC)$$

This process:

1. is divergence free, or simpy there is no cycle of hidden events.
2. it only refuses *wrong* events.
3. it will permit *wrong* events to occur.

In a node only the *report* events are visible, all self-configuration events are hidden, thus a divergence, in *IMP*, corresponds to a failure to stabilise. Furthermore, *right* and *wrong* events are mutually exclusive subsets of the *report* events. *SPEC* allows *right* and *wrong* events in unstable states and only *right* events in stable states. Checking that the refusals of stable states are no more than all *wrong* events corresponds to requiring that every single *right* event is allowed in the stable states. A stable state is one in which no further self-configuration is possible, so self-configuration must terminate in states where all *reports* are everything *right*. So to establish the failures-divergences assertion:

$$SPEC \sqsubseteq_{FD} IMP$$

IMP must always eventually terminate its self-configuration in the *right* state. In fact, using this style of specification requires additional finessing by making the *SPEC* insensitive to the topology changing events. But with that done a wide range of properties can be verified of a model, for CBRP these include:

- no node is left in the *Undecided* state,
- every connected component has a *Head*.

6 Conclusions

We have dicussed work that we did to model and analyse a tactical internet using CSP_M and FDR. And we have described the methodology for modelling ad-hoc networks and self-configuring systems, that were inspired by the tactical internet work. The methodology allows tractable models of complex mobile behaviour and dynamic interactions to be created quickly and easily. It is our belief that the power of this methodology depends on a combination of the simplicity and flexibility of the fundamental processes (section 5.1) and the powerful programming constructs supplied by CSP_M, primarily the renamings (section 5.2). This is confirmed by our experience with these techniques on other problems.

For instance, to model the use of mobile IP in partitionable networks, the basic concepts clearly apply, with appropriate changes. So the *BASICNODE* process has to be tailored for each of the participants, *viz.*: the mobile agent, the home router, the remote host and the message; but it is very similar to what we have described here. The partitionable connectivity can be captured by having a *BASICLINK*-type process for each partition. The interactions between these fundamental process is mapped onto them by the appropriate renaming relations. Coding a property, such as a message must always reach the mobile agent, requires an eventual settling specification (section 5.3). Model-checking then shows how a partition can make a message bounce between the home router and a formerly occupied remote host.

We also found this approach very useful when modelling the self-configuring key hierarchy of [6] (this could be regarded as an ad-hoc key hierarchy). There a group of nodes maintain a key hierarchy without a central server; the hierarchy re-configures itself as the group partitions and as partitions heal. Once again processes very similar to the *BASICNODE* and *BASICLINK* are very useful. They model the state transitions of groups of nodes and group keys. In the protocol, the groups of nodes and the group key processes must interact as the connectivity varies and the appropriate renaming relations can capture these interactions. The result is an elegant and efficient model that captures the full dynamic behaviour of the protocol.

Part of the interest of this work is that it calls into question the conventional wisdom that mobility process algebras, like the pi-calculus [8], are necessary for the subjects that we have discussed. Even where it is necessary to model new processes being created this *model-checking* approach may not be substantially less expressive than a mobility algebra. To understand why first note that to permit finite state analysis the total number of processes that can be created has to be bounded - whichever formalism is used. CSP_M can then capture process creation by having a CSP_M process for each *potential* process. Potential processes will have two principal substates, namely *UNCREATED* and *CREATED*, linked by a *create* event. All the interesting behaviour is implemented in the *CREATED* substate, the *UNCREATED* substate simply awaits the *create* event. Nevertheless, we do not claim to have proven that CSP_M is "as good as" a mobility algebra. We simply note that quite complex mobility can be captured in CSP_M and that the comparing the expressive power of a mobility formalism over CSP_M, for finite state analysis, is non-trivial.

The limitations of the methodology are more likely to be found when the local state of node is too rich to be captured by a set of simple values. For instance, if a nodes behaviour is determined by a local clock, then this may pose a problem and it will most likely have to be abstracted. More generally, if the nodes maintain significant local information (which influences state changes), then representing this within the *BASICNODE* paradigm may also cause difficulty. However, the methodology represents an approach for expressing complex dynamic interactions, and without examining specific examples it is difficult to say what the limits are for a skillful programmer.

We feel a strength of this methodology is that the models are usually tractable. Space prevents a detailed discussion of performance, but when this work was done, in 1999, an average desktop PC (about 500MHz) could verify a five node model of CBRP , or a four node model of the tactical internet, in a couple of hours, for any of the properties of interest (examples, for CBRP, are in 5.3). At the time increasing the node count by one, on either example, would increase the check time to over a day.

With regards to related work, in this broad area we are only aware of Khurshid and Jackson's work on [9], but that is not closely related to this work. As far as we are aware there is not much work applying model-checking to MANETs. We feel this work is also interesting because model-checking applications of this sort are uncommon.

Acknowledgements

The authors would like to thank Will Simmonds, Nick Moffat, Sadie Creese and the anonymous referees for helpful comments on drafts of this paper.

References

[1] Perlman, R. *Interconnections: Bridges, Switches and Routers.* Addison-Wesley, 1999. 181, 183
[2] `http://www.cs.uiowa.edu/ftp/selfstab/bibliography/` 181
[3] `http://www.ietf.org/html.charters/manet-charter.html` 181
[4] Roscoe, A. W. *The Theory and Practice of Concurrency.* Prentice-Hall, 1998. 182, 183, 195
[5] `http://www.comp.nus.edu.sg/~tayyc/cbrp/` 182, 186
[6] Rodeh, O., K.Birman, D.Dolev. Optimized Group Rekey for Group Communication Systems. Network and Distributed System Security, 2000. 182, 194
[7] Creese, S. *Data Independent Induction : CSP Model-checking of Arbitrary Sized Networks.* DPhil thesis, University of Oxford, Computing Laboratory, 2001. 182
[8] Milner, R. *Communicating and Mobile Systems: The Pi-Calculus.* Cambridge University Press, May 1999. 194
[9] Khurshid, S., D. Jackson. Exploring the Design of an Intentional Naming Scheme with an Automatic Constraint Analyzer. In *Proceedings of 15th IEEE International Conference on Automated Software Engineering*, Grenoble, France, September 2000. 195

A A Short Introduction to CSP_M

CSP_M is a machine readable version of CSP, embedded in a full functional programming language. Some CSP_M has already been introduced, but this appendix is intended to complete the description of the CSP_M necessary to understand the paper. [4] has a full definition of the syntax.

channel chanid : *TypeId* A channel declaration, the channel, *chanid*, is of type, *TypeId*. Furthermore, *TypeId* may itself be a dotted list of any number of types. For instance, we may have $Type1.Type2.Type3$, examples of this are found in section 5. In this case, when $t1$ is an arbitrary value of type $Type1$, then $chanid.t1$ may itself be regarded as a channel of type $Type2.Type3$.

$a \rightarrow P$ This process performs event a, then proceeds according to process P.

$P \ \Box \ Q$ The external choice of P and Q, the environment chooses from the initials of P or of Q.

$event?x$ If $event$ is a channel of type $Type$, then the ? syntax captures inputing values of $Type$ on $event$. The environment chooses the value from $Type$ and this new value is bound to the variable x. We may thus have $event?x \rightarrow P(x)$, where the new argument of the process P is determined by the value input on $event$. If $event$ was of type $Type1.Type2$ and $t1$ is a value from $Type1$, then $event.t1?x$ allows the environment to input x from $Type2$. The input value can also range over a dotted list of types. For further control the input can be restricted to any subset of the declared type. Thus $event?x : SubsetofType$ only allows the environment to input values from $SubsetofType$, where any CSP_M function can define $SubsetofType$; examples are in section 5.

$P \sqcap Q$ The non-determinstic (or internal) choice between P and Q. The environment is offered either the initials of P or of Q.

Promela Planning

Stefan Edelkamp

Fachbereich Informatik, Universität Dortmund
D-44221 Dortmund
stefan.edelkamp@cs.uni-dortmund.de

Abstract. The paper presents a structured translation from a static (bounded) subset of PROMELA/SPIN to the planning description language PDDL2.1. It exploits the representation of protocols as communicating finite state machines.
First, the state-space representation is defined to handle processes, queues, and shared variables. Second, each basic statement (assignment, input, etc.) is translated into a couple of predicates.
The deadlock detection problem is reformulated as an action planning problem and SPIN is compared to two action planners Metric-FF and MIPS on several benchmarks (e.g. leader election, dining philosophers, optical telegraph).
The difference to existing approaches is the direct use of planning tools. As a byproduct this introduces refined estimates for improved error detection in directed protocol validation.

1 Introduction

Communication protocols [24] are concurrent software systems with main purpose to organize information exchange between individual processes. Due to interleavings of process executions and the communication load, the number of global system states is large even for simple and moderate sized protocol specifications. By this combinatorial growth, called the *state explosion* problem [7], many protocol designs contain subtle bugs. Therefore, in the design process, automated model checking procedures are needed to certify that stated assertions or global invariants are valid, and that no deadlock occurs. Validating these kinds of properties corresponds to solving a reachability problem in the state space graph. For Holzman's awarded SPIN model checker, the protocol has to be provided/modeled in PROMELA [24].

In planning, domains and problem instances are specified in a problem domain description language, PDDL for short [30]. PDDL planning problems come in two parts: the problem domain file and the instance specific file. In the first file, predicates and actions are chosen, while in the second file the domain objects, the initial and the goal states are specified. Only the instance specific file refers to grounded predicates, while actions and predicates are specified with object parameters. Usually, the set of objects is partitioned into object types. For example in *Blocks World* there are actions like `stack` and `unstack` with respect to

T. Ball and S. K. Rajamani (Eds.): SPIN 2003, LNCS 2648, pp. 197–213, 2003.

two parameters of type *block* and with predicates like `on`, `on-table`, and `clear` in the preconditions and effect lists, where the instance file specifies the block configurations such as `clear(a)`, `on(a,b)`, `on(b,c)`, `on(c,t)` with respect to a set of objects, e.g. `a`, `b`, `c` of type `block` and `t` of type `table`. Recent problem domain description languages developed for action planning, like PDDL2.1 [14] are capable to deal with numerical quantities, action duration and plan metrics.

Action planning and model checking problems are closely related [17]. Both areas include Kripke structures, i.e. transition systems with propositionally labeled states. Algorithmic schemes are exported in both directions. For example, satisfiability planning [26] has been given a semantics for automated validation with the term *bounded model checking* [3]. On the other hand, bit-state hashing and hash compaction have shown considerable success in solving single-agent challenges [25]. Furthermore the succinct representation of BDDs has lead to many successful symbolic planning approaches [6, 5, 11].

Besides SAT solving, there is one other major contribution of action planning for model checking, namely heuristic search. Heuristics and corresponding exploration procedures were added to model checkers, e.g. to Uppaal [2]. Heuristic search [31] exploits information of the goal distance to focus the search. In model checking, the error states serve as goals for the exploration, so that the task in *directed model checking* is to falsify the specification. A* [19] and IDA* [27] incorporate the estimated path length into the evaluation function $f(n) = \lambda g(n) + (1 - \lambda)h(n)$, where $g(n)$ is the path length from the initial state to state n and h is the approximated distance from n to the goal. For $\lambda \geq 1/2$ and lower bound h, obtained solutions are optimal.

The evaluation functions that have been applied in protocol validation so far exploit the Hamming distance of the state-vector [32], the number of active processes, the accumulated shortest path distances of each process state, and the tree expansion of the error formulae [12]. The Hamming distance measures the number of different bits (integers) between the current and the error state(s). The active process heuristic is suited to deadlock detection; the larger the number of non-blocked processes the farer the distance from the current state to the deadlock. The shortest path heuristic counts the minimum distance of each local state to the set of local goal states. The individual results are either maximized or added. The formulae heuristic predicts the number of transitions necessary to establish the truth of failure function f and is recursively defined on the structure of f. The estimate assumes independence or full dependence of the sub-formulae and neglects refined correlations between them.

Another guided search technique are genetic algorithms (GAs) [18]. The population is a set of paths in the state space graph. Through the basic operations of recombination, selection and mutation the paths are tuned towards an error trail. Setting the fitness function to the estimated distance of the end of the path to the goal, relates GAs to heuristic search. The remaining difference is that the GAs improve a set of samples in the solution space, while heuristic search algorithms systematically enumerate it.

In action planning the impact of heuristic search is distinctive. Forward heuristic search planners currently outperform all other approaches including SAT and BDD planners, finding plans in very large domains. The best fully automatic planners in the last international planning system competition Metric-FF [21], MIPS [10], and LPG [16] all include variants of the *relaxed plan* approximation to find sequential plans. With respect to the expressiveness of PDDL2.1, Metric-FF can handle floating point arithmetics and linear preconditions constraints (Level 2), while MIPS and LPG also deal with extended real-time aspects such as action duration (Level 3).

In order to make these and other informed heuristic estimates accessible for the exploration of communication protocols, in this paper we contribute a compiler from PROMELA into PDDL2.1 (Level 2). The parser does not yet feature full language expressiveness of PROMELA, e.g. it requires processes to be active, but for many problem specifications it appears to be a sufficiently large basis.

Since all process types are active, the inferred state description is static. PDDL does not allow dynamic state extensions. This may contrast the aim of general program verification, for which dynamic state changes are essential [23], but many symbolic model checkers like SMV also consider fixed-length state encodings only.

The verification scheme avoids internal access to the SPIN validator, which can turn out to be a burden for the unexperienced programmer. Both process communication forms (channels and shared variables) are supported. The approach utilizes the SPIN parser as a pre-processor to begin with the process automata description file as input.

The opposite approach to compile PDDL2.1 into the input format for the real-time model checker Uppaal was also successful [8]. The model checker could successfully and optimally solve smaller planning instances.

In short, this paper studies feasibility and practicability of using a planner to model-check protocols. Up to now, it has been expected that one would need to add planning technology into a model checking tool. In difference to this line of research, the paper puts forth the question of how far one can get without using a existing validator with its domain-specific optimizations, but with having the heuristics of AI planning available. The new way of using planning for model checking is compared with an existing one, namely the HSF-SPIN model checker.

The paper is structured as follows. First we give a state space characterization of a communication protocol system to exploit the structure of the underlying exploration problem. Then the action planning formalism STRIPS and PDDL2.1 and their state space characterizations are introduced. Afterwards we examine the stages of the compiling process in detail, taking the Leader Election protocol as the running example. Next we introduce the plan relaxation heuristic, which solves a polynomial relaxation of the exploration problem on-the-fly for each encountered state. We close with drawn conclusions and a discussion on appropriate extensions of the approach.

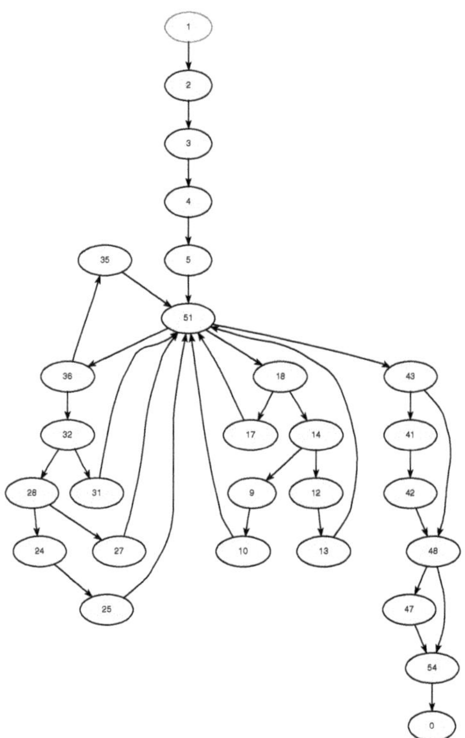

Fig. 1. The process automaton for the Leader Election protocol

2 State Space Representation

To model a protocol communication system, we choose the following representation. For the sake of brevity we neglect advanced aspects such as rendezvous communication and (in-)validity of end-states.

Each process P is a labeled finite state graph $G_P = (S_P, \Sigma_P, i_P, \delta_P)$, with S_P being P's set of states, Σ_P being the set of transitions of P, $i_P \in S_P$ being the initial state of P, and $\delta_P : S_P \times \Sigma_P \rightarrow S_P$ being the transition relation for P. Furthermore, let c_P be the current state in P.

The automata representation for our PROMELA model of the Leader Election protocol is visualized in Figure 1. The graph has been extracted from SPIN's user interface XSPIN. The edge labels correspond to lines in the PROMELA code. Figure 2 depicts some transition labels as inferred in SPIN.

To deal with different process parameters, we highlight that in SPIN each process can be accessed by the process identifier `_pid`. This allows to organize the access to queues, when specifying arrays of active processes. For the ease of

```
state  1 -> state  2 line 38 => Active[_pid] = 1
state  2 -> state  3 line 39 => know_winner[_pid] = 0
state  3 -> state  4 line 40 => maximum[_pid] = 0
state  4 -> state  5 line 41 => mynumber[_pid] = 0
state  5 -> state 51 line 43 => q[((_pid+1)%2)]!one,mynumber[_pid]
...
state 48 -> state 54 line 85 => ((know_winner[_pid]>0))
state 48 -> state 47 line 85 => else
state 54 -> state  0 line 91 => -end-
state 47 -> state 54 line 87 => q[((_pid+1)%2)]!winner,nr[_pid]
state 41 -> state 42 line 82 => nr_leaders[0] = (nr_leaders[0]+1)
state 42 -> state 48 line 83 => assert((nr_leaders[0]==1))
```

Fig. 2. Transition labels for one process in the Leader Election protocol

presentation, we have transformed all local variables into shared variable arrays, once more to be addressed by the identifier _pid.

Similar to each process, every communication channel is modeled as a queue Q, which in turn can be represented as a finite state graph $G_Q = (S_Q, \delta_Q, mess_Q, cont_Q)$, with S_Q being the set of queue states, $mess_Q \in M^{|S_Q|}$ being the vector of messages in Q (M is the set of all messages), $cont_Q \in \mathbb{R}^{|S_Q|}$ being the vector of variable values in Q and $\delta_Q : S_Q \to S_Q$ being the successor relation for Q; if $S_Q = \{s_1, \ldots, s_k\}$ then $\delta(s_i) = s_{(i+1) \bmod k}$. Explicitly modeling head and tail positions of Q as $head_Q$ and $tail_Q$, respectively, trades space for time, since queue updates reduce to constant time operations.

Shared and local variables are modeled by real numbers. The only difference of local variables compared to shared ones is the restricted visibility scope.

A state S in the global state space $\mathcal{S}$ is fully described by its processes, its queue contents, and the current assignments to shared and local variables. Given a fixed number of processes and queues, a constant number of local and shared variables the global system state space $\mathcal{S}$ can be expressed as $\mathcal{S} \subset \mathbb{R}^l$, for some fixed value $l \in \mathbb{N}$.

Having fixed the set of states, we still need to explain the set of transitions we allow. Transitions are specified with respect to the set of processes they are declared in. Therefore, we consider the following fundamental set of operations:

$Q!m, v$ The transition writes compound (m and v) into Q at the tail pointer. The returned value is true if successful, false otherwise.

$Q?m, v$ If m matches the one at the head in Q, the transition reads the according contents into v. The returned value is true if successful, false otherwise.

$v = e$ The evaluated expression e is assigned to the according (local/shared) variable, where e itself is an expression with different variables and constants.

(c) Continue execution, if condition c is true; else branches are equivalents to $(\neg c)$

Since sequential composition, selection and assignments are already sufficient to model Turing machine computation, the reachability problem in this context is in fact undecidable. Explicit model checkers like SPIN bypass this fact by restricting the range of the variables to a finite domain, resulting into a large but finite state space graph.

3 Propositional and Numerical Planning

All transition can be specified in form of operators with preconditions and effects. E.g. for transition $Q!m, v$ from state s_1 to s_2 in process P, we have preconditions $c_P = s_1$ and effects $tail_Q = (tail(Q) + 1)\ mod\ |S_Q|$, $mess_Q[tail_Q] = m$, $cont_Q[head_Q] = v$, and $c_P = s_2$. This has lead to the idea that transitions in protocol verification may be interpreted as planning operators.

A grounded STRIPS [13] planning task considers a set of actions of type $a = (pre(a), eff(a)^+, eff(a)^-)$. States in Strips are sets of propositional *facts* or *atoms*. The result of applying a in state S is a state $S \cup eff(a)^+ \setminus eff(a)^-$ if $pre(a) \subseteq S$. The state space $\mathcal{S}$ is the power set of the propositions, so that each $S \in \mathcal{S}$ can also be characterized as a vector in $\mathbb{B}^l$, for a fixed value $l \in \mathbb{N}$.

In the extended formalism PDDL2.1 [14], numerical conditions are of the form $e \oplus e'$ with $\oplus \in \{=, \leq, <, \geq, >\}$, where e, e' are arithmetic and boolean expressions over the set of variables, and assignments are of the form $v \otimes e$ with $\otimes \in \{\texttt{:=}, \texttt{+=}, \texttt{-=}\}$, where v is a variable.

In order to cast a protocol validation problem as a planning problem with propositional and numerical state information, predicates and numbers are to be indexed by process identifiers, by local and shared variables as well as by queue identifiers. The predicates we use are $at(P, s)$ for $c_P = s$, $head(Q, s)$ for $head_Q = s$, and $tail(Q, s)$ for $tail_Q = s$. For the numerical part we choose $mess(Q, s)$ for $mess_Q[s]$, and $cont(Q, s)$ for $cont_Q[s]$. Unfortunately, accesses like $mess_Q[(head_Q + 1)\ mod\ |S_Q|]$ are no longer available. Therefore, we take the current queue position q_1 and q_2 as additional parameters, where we know that $q_2 = \delta_Q(q_1)$. E.g, for $Q?m(v)$ this results to the formula: If $head(Q, q_1)$, $mess(Q, q_1) = m$, and $curr(P, s_1)$ then $\neg curr(P, s_1)$, $\neg head(P, q_1)$, $curr(P, s_2)$, $head(P, q_2)$, and v is set to $cont(Q, q_1)$.

The binary encoding of process and communication queue states and the upgrade of variables and messages to $\mathbb{R}$ are not as critical as the first glance may indicate. It can be compensated by static analyzer tools as available in Stan [29] and Discoplan [15]. The planners efficiently detect and eliminate constant predicates and can partition atoms into groups of mutually exclusive facts.

As an example of possible gains of the compilation process we next explain the probably most influencing heuristic in action planning, *relaxed plan*. This estimate is computed in each state to approximate the hardness of the remaining planning problem.

The relaxation a^+ of action $a = (pre(a), eff(a)^+, eff(a)^-)$ is defined as $a^+ = (pre(a), eff(a)^+, \emptyset)$. The relaxation of a planning problem is the one in which all actions are substituted by their relaxed counterparts. It is used to compute heuristic values for the explored nodes. The following properties are satisfied by *relaxed plan* [22]:

- P1: Any solution that solves the original plan also solves the relaxed one.
- P2: All preconditions and goals can be achieved if and only if they can in the relaxed task.
- P3: The relaxed plan can be solved in polynomial time.

Solving relaxed plans can efficiently be done by building a relaxed problem graph, followed by a greedy plan generation process. Table 1 depicts the implementation of the plan construction and the solution extraction phase.

The first phase constructs the layered plan graph identical to the first phase of *Graphplan* [4]. In Layer i all facts are given that are reachable by applying an operator with satisfied precondition facts in any Layer j with $1 \leq j < i$. In Layer 0 we have all facts present in the initial state. Since we have a finite number of grounded propositions the process eventually reaches a fix-point. The next loop marks the goal facts. In the implementation, the fact layer and goal lists are given as bit-vectors with the latter one constructed on-the-fly.

The second phase is the greedy plan extraction phase. It performs a backward search to match facts to enabling operators. The goal facts build the first set of unmarked facts. As long as there are unmarked facts in Level i, select an operator that makes this fact true and mark all add effects, and queue all preconditions as unmarked new goals. If there is no unmarked fact left in Level i continue with Level $i-1$ until the only unmarked facts are the initial ones in Layer 0. The heuristic is constructive, i.e. it not only returns the estimated distance but also a corresponding sequence of actions.

Extending the above estimate to numbers has been achieved as follows [21]. Conditions are of the form $(v \oplus c)$, where $\oplus \in \{\geq, >\}$ and $c \in \mathbb{R}$ and assignments are of the form $(v \otimes c)$, where $\otimes \in \{\texttt{+=}, \texttt{-=}\}$ and $c \in \mathbb{R}^+ \setminus \{0\}$. The *restricted numerical task* is obtained by dropping the delete and the decrease effects and by neglecting numerical preconditions. For restricted expressions, conditions P1-P3 can be satisfied, but through the lack of numerical preconditions the restricted language is too limited for our proposes. Therefore, *strongly monotonic actions* are introduced. The conditions are of the form $(e \oplus e')$, with e, e' being expressions, $\oplus \in \{=, \leq, <, \geq, >\}$, so that the conditions prefer larger variable values, and there exists at least one variable assignment that makes the condition true. The assignments $(v \otimes e')$ with $\otimes \in \{\texttt{:=}, \texttt{+=}, \texttt{-=}\}$ require that the value which the effect adds to the affected variable, increases with the variable (ensuring that repeated application diverges the value), and that the expressions diverge in all numerical values.

For monotone expressions P1-P3 are satisfied, yielding the following set of numerical operations $(e \oplus 0)$, $\oplus \in \{\geq, >\}$ and $(v \otimes e)$, where $\otimes \in \{\texttt{:=}, \texttt{+=}\}$ and e is a linear expression. General linear expressions can be dealt with, since conditions of the form $(e \oplus e')$, with e, e' being linear expressions on the set of numerical variables with $\oplus \in \{=, \leq, <, \geq, >\}$, and assignments of the form $(v \otimes e)$, where $\otimes \in \{\texttt{:=}, \texttt{+=}, \texttt{-=}\}$ can be automatically transformed into the ones above.

Table 1. Relaxed propositional heuristic

procedure Relax(S, *goal*)
  $P_0 \leftarrow S$; $t \leftarrow 0$
  while ($goal \not\subseteq P_t$) **do**
    $P_{t+1} \leftarrow P_t \cup \bigcup_{pre(a) \subseteq P_t} eff(a)^+$
    if ($P_{t+1} = P_t$) **return** ∞
    $t \leftarrow t + 1$
  for $i \leftarrow t$ **downto** 1
    $G_i \leftarrow \{g \in goal \mid level(g) = i\}$
  for $i \leftarrow t$ **downto** 1
    for $g \in G_i$
      if $\exists a.\ g \in eff(a)^+$ **and** $level(a) = i - 1$
      $A \leftarrow A \cup \{a\}$
      for $p \in pre(a)$
        $G_{level(p)} = G_{level(p)} \cup \{p\}$
  bf return $|A|$

For the proper implementation of the heuristic estimate, that is: constructing the relaxed planning graph for the monotone set of linear expressions and extracting the relaxed plan, the reader is referred to [21]. The author also observes topological properties of the existing planning benchmarks with respect to the above heuristic, and started to theoretically prove that these observations hold true.

4 Compilation Process

As main input for our parser, instead of the PROMELA file itself, we start with the automata representation that is produced by SPIN, i.e. we take the PROMELA input file, generate the corresponding c-file, and run the executable with option `-d` to obtain the finite state representations of all processes. We avoid state merging by setting parameter `-o3` as a option to SPIN.

As said, we assume all processes to be active. This imposes some restrictions to the PROMELA model. However, in our set of benchmark problems, all PROMELA processes (`proctypes`) are invoked by a single init process, such that it is not difficult to provide the entire benchmark set in this format. The corresponding PROMELA simplifications are more or less textual substitutions, which presumably can be provided by automated procedures. So far these simplifications have been performed manually. Even for involved examples this step is not a burden even for an untrained SPIN user.

The array dimensions of process types, variables, and queues as well as queue capacity are read from the PROMELA input file. This is the only additional information, that is not present in the finite state representation file. To avoid

```
(:action activate-trans
   :parameters (?p - process ?t - transition ?s1 ?s2 - state)
   :precondition (and (trans ?t ?s1 ?s2) (at ?p ?s1))
   :effect (and (activate ?p ?t)))

(:action perform-trans
   :parameters (?p - process ?t - transition ?s1 ?s2 - state)
   :precondition (and (trans ?t ?s1 ?s2) (ok ?p ?t) (at ?p ?s1))
   :effect (and (at ?p ?s2) (not (at ?p ?s1)) (not (ok ?p ?t))))
```

Fig. 3. Preparing and executing a process state transition

conflicts with precompiler directives, we substitute all `defines` beforehand with the c-compiler command line option `-E`, which runs the precompiler only.

4.1 State Transitions

For protocol modeling, we identify processes, their proctype, and a propositional description of the finite state system with states and state transitions as objects. If we have variables in the PROMELA specification, these are also to be found and declared as possible objects. Communication queues are defined by their channel type and content configuration. All these objects are inferred in the parser by instantiating the process identifier `_pid` with respect to the established array bounds in the automata process description file.

As an example the set of objects for the Leader Election problem with automata description of Figure 2, we have `node-0` and `node-1` as `process` objects, `node` as `proctype` object, `q[0]` and `q[1]` as `queue` objects, `queue-4` as `queuetype` object, `Active[pid]`, ...as `variable` objects, `state-1`, ..., `state-54` as process `state` objects and, last but not least, `Active[pid]=1` and others as state `transition` objects.

4.2 Operators

In pure message passing domains, no inference of domain file ingredients is necessary. But in the presence of local/shared variables (as in our example) the parser additionally generates action schemas for variable conditioning and change.

In the first step, we describe fixed actions applicable to all protocol domains. Note that one objective in a good model of a planning problem is to keep the number of parameters small. Grounding actions and predicates with more than five object parameters causes problems for almost any planner that we know. The reduction of parameters can best be achieved by some additional flags that are set by one action and queried by another one.

Figure 3 shows how we prepare and execute state transitions. Action `activate-trans` activates transition t in process P if in the current local state we have an option to perform t starting from s_1. Action `process-trans` triggers the transition t in process P to move from s_1 to s_2. It queries the flag `ok` which is deleted afterwards. Hence, for each transition t there is an appropriate action that performs all necessary changes according to t and that that sets the flag(s) `ok`. These operations are purely propositional.

4.3 Queue Organization

Queue organization with head and tail pointer has already been mentioned in the formal characterization of the problem structure. Figure 4 gives an action specification for reading a variable v from the queue q in transition t querying message m, i.e. $Q?m(v)$. The PDDL representation of $Q!m(v)$ is analogous.

We can see that the state transition enabling flag `ok` is set. The according queue update `increase-head` is shown in Figure 5. As the name indicates it actualizes the head position and eliminates the *settled* flag, which is preconditioned in any queue access action. To disallow actions to be activated twice, before an action is performed we additionally precondition `active-trans` and `perform-trans` with the settlement of all queues. The required `(forall (q - queue) (settled ?q))` construct can be avoided by removing the queue parameter in the predicate `settled`.

4.4 Variable Handling

As said, variable conditioning and updating is more difficult than other operations, since they require both changes to the instance and problem domain file.

To tame the number of actions, for each condition or assignment the parser generates a pattern structure. For example, setting variable `Active[0]` to 1 corresponds to a `V0=1` pattern. The assignment of any variable to the content of another corresponds to a `V0=V1` pattern.

```
(:action queue-read
   :parameters (?p - process ?t - transition
                ?q - queue ?v - variable)
   :precondition
      (and
        (activate ?p ?t) (settled ?q)
        (reads ?p ?q ?t) (reads-val ?p ?t ?v)
        (>= (size ?q) 1) (= (head-msg ?q) (mess ?t)))
    :effect
      (and
        (advance-head ?q) (ok ?p ?t)
        (not (activate ?p ?t)) (not (settled ?q)))
        (assign (value ?v) (head-value ?q)))
```

Fig. 4. Reading variables from a queue

```
(:action increase-head
   :parameters (?q - queue ?qt - queuetype
                ?qs1 ?qs2 - queue-state)
   :precondition
     (and
        (next ?qt ?qs1 ?qs2) (is-a-queue ?q ?qt) (head ?q ?qs1)
        (>= (size ?q) 1) (advance-head ?q))
   :effect
     (and
        (settled ?q)  (head ?q ?qs2)
        (not (head ?q ?qs1)) (not (advance-head ?q))
        (assign (head-value ?q) (queue-value ?q ?qs2))
        (assign (head-msg ?q) (queue-msg ?q ?qs2))
        (decrease (size ?q) 1)))
```

Fig. 5. Increasing the head pointer to settle the queue

Conditions on `else` branches are made explicit by the negation of the condition at the corresponding `if` branch.

Inferred patterns generate actions and initial state patterns. E.g. `V0=V1` generates a `is-V0=V1` predicate, to be grounded in the initial state for each variable-to-variable assignment according to the given transition and process for the initial state. The inferred action declaration for the domain file is shown in Figure 6.

The `inside` predicate avoids a fourth parameter in the `is-V0=V1` predicate[1].

5 Experiments

In the experiments, we include the results of the parser as inputs for recent domain-independent planners. The experiments we performed were run on a Linux PC with with 800 MHz and 128 MByte main memory. We selected *Metric-FF* and *MIPS* as two action planners and *SPIN* and *HSF-SPIN* as two PROMELA model checkers. *Metric-FF* is suited to mixed propositional and numerical problems and restricts to linear precondition constraints. *MIPS* is the more general system and can handle problems with arbitrary precondition trees, actions with durations, while producing plans that are in fact schedules.

SPIN is selected to use a DFS with partial order reduction (and default depth bound 10,000) and HSF-SPIN is selected to use Weighted A* with weight 2 and the formula-based heuristic [12]. Since SPIN does not provide the number of expanded nodes, we took the number of stored nodes instead. Both planners apply heuristic search with variants of the relaxed planning heuristic described above. Similar to HSF-SPIN for *MIPS* we choose A* with weight 2, while *Metric-FF* applies *Enforced Hill-Climbing.* As in usual Hill-Climbing this exploration algorithm commits a change to a global system state that can never be withdrawn.

[1] Actually, this modeling turned out to be crucial for the planner to parse the code

```
(:action V0=V1
  :parameters (?p - process ?t - transition ?v0 ?v1 - variable)
  :precondition
    (and
      (activate ?p ?t) (inside ?p ?t ?v0) (inside ?p ?t ?v1)
      (is-V0=V1 ?t ?v0 ?v1))
  :effect
    (and
      (ok ?p ?t)  (not (activate ?p ?t))
      (assign (value ?v0) (value ?v1))))
```

Fig. 6. Reading variables from a queue

Different to Hill-Climbing the neighborhood of the current state is traversed with a breadth-first search until a node is found that has a smaller h-value than the current one. Even though the algorithm is incomplete for directed graphs it turns out to be efficient in practice.

The planner *MIPS* solves the Leader Election example problem with 107 node expansions in 1.5 seconds [2]. The according plan length is 58. SPIN finds the bug with only 30 nodes stored, while HSF-SPIN solves the same problem with 95 node expansions. Both model checker run about a 0.01 second to come up with the according error trail.

Tables 2 and 3 show that the planners are also capable to efficiently solve deadlock problems in pure message passing systems like the Dining Philosopher and the Optical Telegraph protocol. The comparison for this case is not fair, since exact deadlock state descriptions were used for the planners and not for the model checkers. Through the differences in the interpretation of an executed transition, the trail length also do not match. But that's not the point. At the current level of implementation we do not want to challenge refined model checker implementations, but trademark that efficient action planners can indeed model check communication protocols.

In the philosophers example we see that directed search pays off, since *SPIN* searches to large depths until it finds an error. Its DFS exploration order misses shallow errors. On the other hand, by its refined implementation, *SPIN*'s node exploration time is very small. In the optical telegraph example it runs fastest (less than 1/100 second), while expanding the largest number of nodes. HSF-SPIN takes some more time to expand a node, but performs well in both domains, and its efficiency is better than or equal to the fastest planner.

[2] As a current drawback, *Metric-FF* cannot compete with its refined numerical relaxed planning heuristic, since it cannot properly parse the code provided in the Leader's Election protocol, our running example. The problem is that it detects cyclic assign conditions to be problematic. We are currently in contact to the author of the planner to circumvent this difficulty. The process goal states have further been simplified to 13.

Table 2. Results in the deadlock solution for the Dining Philosopher protocol (t is execution time in seconds, l is the counter-example length, e is the number of expanded, and s the number of stored nodes; o.m denotes a run exhausting memory resources and the numbers in brackets [] denote parallel plan lengths)

	Metric-FF			MIPS			SPIN			HSF-SPIN		
p	t	l	e	t	l	e	t	l	s	t	l	e
3	0.02	6	7	0.19	6[2]	7	0.00	18	10	0.01	14	17
4	0.02	8	13	0.27	8[2]	9	0.00	54	45	0.01	18	22
5	0.04	10	21	0.31	10[2]	11	0.00	66	51	0.01	22	27
6	0.05	12	31	0.38	12[2]	13	0.01	302	287	0.01	26	32
7	0.06	14	43	0.47	14[2]	15	0.01	330	309	0.01	30	37
8	0.10	16	57	0.56	16[2]	17	0.02	1.362	1,341	0.02	34	42
9	0.12	18	73	0.69	18[2]	19	0.02	1,466	1,440	0.01	38	47
10	0.15	20	91	0.85	20[2]	21	0.12	9,422	9,396	0.01	42	52
11	0.20	22	111	1.01	22[2]	23	0.15	9,382	9,349	0.01	46	46
12	0.27	24	133	1.23	24[2]	25	1.35	9,998	43,699	0.02	50	62
13	0.32	26	157	1.44	26[2]	27	43.06	9,998	722,014	0.01	54	67
14	0.40	28	183	1.75	28[2]	29	o.m	o.m.	o.m	0.03	58	72
15	0.48	30	211	2.05	30[2]	31	o.m	o.m	o.m	0.03	62	58

MIPS exploration engine turns out to be the slow. However, the number of expanded nodes in both example protocols is at most 1 from the optimal possible. The suboptimal numbers of expansions in the model checkers are due to graph contraction features, especially due to state merging. The planner *Metric-FF* has a node expansion routine about as fast as HSF-SPIN, which is very good, considering that the planner uses propositional information, computes an involved estimate and does not have any information on the application domain.

6 Conclusions

We have seen a parser that transforms active processes from PROMELA into PDDL2.1. The parsing process exploits the automata representation produced by SPIN for its visualizer XSPIN. The intermediate result is comprehensible by an end user and can serve as an independent alternative to PROMELA for modeling communication protocols.

The work targets the transfer between the state space exploration areas AI planning and model checking by making protocols accessible for action planners. It provides a practical study of the expressiveness of different input specifications, and compares search, pruning and acceleration methods.

The experimental results are preliminary but encouraging. In some sample protocols, planners perform close to state-of-the-art model checkers. However, the parser is experimental and cannot interpret full PROMELA specification. Moreover, experimental results were given for simpler-structured protocols only. We currently work on larger protocols starting with the elevator simulator of

Table 3. Results for the Optical Telegraph protocol

	Metric-FF			MIPS			SPIN			HSF-SPIN		
n	t	l	e	t	l	e	t	l	e	t	l	e
3	0.14	18	57	0.55	18[5]	12	0.00	23	11	0.09	21	23
4	0.20	24	80	0.73	24[5]	24	0.00	30	14	0.10	28	30
5	0.31	30	122	1.30	30[5]	30	0.00	37	17	0.20	35	37
6	0.41	36	173	1.46	36[5]	36	0.00	44	20	0.36	42	44
7	0.65	42	233	1.80	42[5]	42	0.00	51	23	0.45	49	51
8	0.90	48	302	2.12	48[5]	48	0.00	58	26	0.61	56	58
9	1.12	54	271	2.46	54[5]	54	0.00	65	29	1.07	63	65
10	1.60	60	331	2.85	60[5]	60	0.00	72	32	1.24	70	72
11	2.20	66	397	3.31	66[5]	66	0.00	79	35	1.86	77	79
12	2.85	72	469	3.74	72[5]	72	0.00	86	38	2.32	84	84
13	3.95	78	547	4.22	78[5]	78	0.00	93	41	4.01	91	93
14	5.05	84	631	4.92	84[5]	84	0.00	100	44	4.83	98	100

A. Biere. The domain does not use any queue communication and parses fine except of indirectly referenced variables.

Through the inferred intermediate planner input format, we provide the basis for a new algorithmic aspects to the exploration process, bridging the gap between the two disciplines model checking and action planning. For example, new, apparently more informed heuristics can be applied to the validation of protocols.

The paper is ambitious in the sense that it proposes to bypass the model checker with a domain-independent action planner. A fairer comparison would be to devise domain-dependent pruning rules very similar to LTL specifications, concurrently checked during the planning process. Examples of these kinds of planners rules are TL-Plan [1] and Tal-Plan [28].

The work initiates experiments with concurrency problems in AI planners. The current research focus is the exploitation of similarities and differences of model checkers and planners on comparable benchmark inputs to improve both areas with algorithmic contributions of the other. Our choice to implement the parser was influenced by the fact, that it could be slightly harder to implement the heuristics into an existing model checker than to export the description to PDDL. In the long term we expect some of these estimates to become an integral part of directed model checkers like HSF-SPIN [12]. The other motivation is to use communication protocols as benchmarks for the next international planning competition.

The plan relaxation heuristic is not the only effective guidance. We highlight the pattern database heuristic [9], which is to be computed as a large lookup-table prior to the search. This heuristic can be included in BDD exploration engines as shown in the planner *MIPS*. Since the estimates were adapted from efficient domain-independent action planners, the design patterns are more general and likely to transfer to the validation of security protocols or other model checking exploration tasks.

In future research we plan to look at probabilistic model checking and planning also, taking factored Markov Decision Processes (FMDPs) as a welcome theoretical fundament. By means of the contributed work, we think of using a FMDP solver like SPUDD [20] and to transfer annotated PROMELA into an intermediate probabilistic action planning description language. SPUDD takes algebraic decision diagrams (ADDs) for internal state representation structure and performs the Bellman update for real-time dynamic programming symbolically. We will also look at symbolic heuristic search for FMDP by joining And/Or-tree search with the SPUDD approach.

Acknowledgments

The author would like to thank DFG for support in the projects *Heuristic Search and its Application to Protocol Verification*, *Directed Model Checking (with AI exploration algorithms)* and *Heuristic Search*. Thanks to Alberto Lluch-Lafuente for providing appropriate PROMELA benchmark models.

References

[1] F. Bacchus and F. Kabanza. Using temporal logics to express search control knowledge for planning. *Artificial Intelligence*, 116:123–191, 2000. 210

[2] G. Behrmann, A. Fehnker, T. Hune, K.G. Larsen, P. Petterson, J. Romijn, and F.W. Vaandrager. Efficient guiding towards cost-optimality in uppaal. In *Tools and Algorithms for the Construction and Analysis of Systems (TACAS)*, 2001. 198

[3] A. Biere, A. Cimatti, E. Clarke, and Y. Zhu. Symbolic model checking without BDDs. In *Tools and Algorithms for the Construction and Analysis of Systems*, Lecture Notes in Computer Science. Springer, 1999. 198

[4] A. Blum and M.L. Furst. Fast planning through planning graph analysis. In *International Joint Conferences on Artificial Intelligence (IJCAI)*, pages 1636–1642, 1995. 203

[5] A. Cimatti and M. Roveri. Conformant planning via model checking. In *European Conference on Planning (ECP)*, pages 21–33, 1999. 198

[6] A. Cimatti, M. Roveri, and P. Traverso. Automatic OBDD-based generation of universal plans in non-deterministic domains. In *National Conference on Artificial Intelligence (AAAI)*, pages 875–881, 1998. 198

[7] E.M. Clarke, O. Grumberg, and D.A. Peled. *Model Checking*. MIT Press, 1999. 197

[8] H. Dierks, G. Behrmann, and K.G. Larsen. Solving planning problems using real-time model checking (translating pddl3 into timed automata). In *Artificial Intelligence Planning and Scheduling (AIPS)-Workshop on Temporal Planning*, pages 30–39, 2002. 199

[9] S. Edelkamp. Planning with pattern databases. In *European Conference on Planning (ECP)*, 2001. 13-24. 210

[10] S. Edelkamp. Taming numbers and durations in the model checking integrated planning system. *Journal of Artificial Research (JAIR)*, 2003. Submitted, A draft is available at PUK-Workshop 2002. 199

[11] S. Edelkamp and M. Helmert. The model checking integrated planning system MIPS. *AI-Magazine*, pages 67–71, 2001. 198

[12] S. Edelkamp, S. Leue, and A. Lluch-Lafuente. Directed explicit-state model checking in the validation of communication protocols. *International Journal on Software Tools for Technology (STTT)*, 2003. 198, 207, 210

[13] R. Fikes and N. Nilsson. Strips: A new approach to the application of theorem proving to problem solving. *Artificial Intelligence*, 2:189–208, 1971. 202

[14] M. Fox and D. Long. PDDL2.1: An extension to PDDL for expressing temporal planning domains. Technical report, University of Durham, UK, 2001. 198, 202

[15] A. Gerevini and L. Schubert. Discovering state constraints in DISCOPLAN: Some new results. In *National Conference on Artificial Intelligence (AAAI)*, pages 761–767, 2000. 202

[16] A. Gerevini and I. Serina. LPG: a planner based on local search for planning graphs with action costs. In *Artificial Intelligence Planning and Scheduling (AIPS)*, pages 13–22, 2002. 199

[17] F. Giunchiglia and P. Traverso. Planning as model checking. In *European Conference on Planning (ECP)*, pages 1–19, 1999. 198

[18] Patrice Godefroid and Sarfraz Khurshid. Exploring very large state spaces using genetic algorithms. In *Tools and Algorithms for the Construction and Analysis of Systems (TACAS)*, 2002. 198

[19] P. E. Hart, N. J. Nilsson, and B. Raphael. A formal basis for heuristic determination of minimum path cost. *IEEE Transactions on on Systems Science and Cybernetics*, 4:100–107, 1968. 198

[20] J. Hoey, R. Aubin, A. Hu, and C. Boutilier. Spudd: Stochastic planning using decision diagrams. In *Conference on Uncertainty in Artificial Intelligence (UAI)*, 1999. 211

[21] J. Hoffmann. Extending FF to numerical state variables. In *European Conference on Artificial Intelligence*, 2002. 199, 203, 204

[22] J. Hoffmann and B. Nebel. Fast plan generation through heuristic search. *Artificial Intelligence Research*, 14:253–302, 2001. 203

[23] G. J. Holzmann and M. H. Smith. Software model checking: Extracting verification models from source code. In *Formal Description Techniques for Distributed Systems and Communication Protocols, Protocol Specification, Testing and Verification (FORTE/PSTV)*, pages 481–497, 1999. 199

[24] Gerard J. Holzmann. *Design and Validation of Computer Protocols.* Prentice Hall, 1990. 197

[25] Falk Hüffner, S. Edelkamp, H. Fernau, and R. Niedermeier. Finding optimal solutions to Atomix. In *German Conference on Artificial Intelligence (KI)*, pages 229–243, 2001. 198

[26] H. Kautz and B. Selman. Pushing the envelope: Planning propositional logic, and stochastic search. In *National Conference on Artificial Intelligence (AAAI)*, pages 1194–1201, 1996. 198

[27] R. E. Korf. Depth-first iterative-deepening: An optimal admissible tree search. *Artificial Intelligence*, 27(1):97–109, 1985. 198

[28] J. Kvarnström, P. Doherty, and P. Haslum. Extending TALplanner with concurrency and ressources. In *European Conference on Artificial Intelligence (ECAI)*, pages 501–505, 2000. 210

[29] D. Long and M. Fox. Efficient implementation of the plan graph in STAN. *Artificial Intelligence Research*, 10:87–115, 1998. 202

[30] D. McDermott. The 1998 AI Planning Competition. *AI Magazine*, 21(2), 2000. 197

[31] J. Pearl. *Heuristics.* Addison-Wesley, 1985. 198

[32] C. H. Yang and D. L. Dill. Validation with guided search of the state space. In *Conference on Design Automation (DAC)*, pages 599–604, 1998. 198

Thread-Modular Model Checking

Cormac Flanagan[1] and Shaz Qadeer[2]

[1] Systems Research Center, HP Labs,
1501 Page Mill Road, Palo Alto, CA 94304
[2] Microsoft Research,
One Microsoft Way, Redmond, WA 98052

Abstract. We present thread-modular model checking, a novel technique for verifying correctness properties of *loosely-coupled* multithreaded software systems. Thread-modular model checking verifies each thread separately using an automatically inferred environment assumption that abstracts the possible steps of other threads. Separate verification of each thread yields significant space and time savings. Suppose there are n threads, each with a local store of size L, where the threads communicate via a shared global store of size G. If each thread is finite-state (without a stack), the naive model checking algorithm requires $O(G.L^n)$ space, whereas thread-modular model checking requires only $O(n.G.(G + L))$ space. If each thread has a stack, the general model checking problem is undecidable, but thread-modular model checking terminates in polynomial time.

1 Introduction

Designing correct multithreaded software is difficult due to subtle interactions among threads operating concurrently on shared data. Errors in such systems are easy to introduce but difficult to diagnose and fix. Model checking [2, 10] is a promising technique for verifying correctness properties of multithreaded software systems. However, due to the large state spaces of such systems, they are difficult to model check. In this paper, we present a novel technique called thread-modular model checking to alleviate the problem of exploring large state spaces of multithreaded software.

We consider multithreaded software systems with a finite number of threads where the shared global store and the local store of each thread are finite. However, each thread also has an unbounded stack which allows us to model procedure calls and recursion. We focus on the verification of safety properties such as assertions and global invariants. Verification of such safety properties can be reduced to the problem of checking whether an error state is reachable from the system's initial state. This problem is undecidable [7, 11] in general. Thread-modular model checking is a conservative (sound and incomplete) algorithm for this problem that is powerful enough to verify a variety of multithreaded software systems occurring in practice.

T. Ball and S. K. Rajamani (Eds.): SPIN 2003, LNCS 2648, pp. 213–224, 2003.

Thread-modular reasoning for shared-memory programs was first introduced by Jones [9]. The basic idea behind this technique is to verify each thread separately using an environment assumption to model interleaved steps of the other threads. The environment assumption of each thread is a binary relation over the set of global stores, and includes all global store updates that may be performed by other threads.

In earlier work, we extended the proof rule of Jones and implemented it in the Calvin checker [4, 5] for multithreaded Java programs. Our experience using Calvin indicates that the threads in most software systems are *loosely-coupled*, *i.e.*, there is little correlation among the local states of the various threads, and thread-modular reasoning is sufficiently powerful to verify these systems. However, a significant cost of using Calvin is that the programmer is required to provide the appropriate environment assumption. The thread-modular model checking technique in this paper avoids this cost by automatically inferring these environment assumptions.

Thread-modular model checking infers the environment assumption for each thread by first inferring a *guarantee* for each thread, which models all global store updates performed by that thread. The environment assumption of a thread is then the disjunction of the guarantees of all the other threads. The guarantee of each thread is initially the empty relation, and is iteratively extended during the model checking process. Each thread is verified using the standard algorithm for model checking a sequential pushdown system except that at each control point of the thread, the global state is allowed to mutate according to the guarantees of the other threads. In addition, whenever a thread modifies the global store, that transition on the global states is added to that thread's guarantee. The iteration continues until the reachable state space and guarantee of each thread converges. The space complexity of this procedure is $O(n.G^2.L^2.F)$, where n is the number of threads, F is the number of stack symbols, G is the size of the global store, and L is the size of local store per thread.

Even if the threads do not have a stack and are consequently finite-state, thread-modular model checking offers significant savings over standard model checking. The naive model checking algorithm explicitly models the program counters of all threads. Therefore, it explores all interleavings of the various threads and its complexity is exponential in the number of threads. However, thread-modular model checking verifies each thread separately and its space complexity $O(n.G.(G + L))$ is significantly better than that of the naive algorithm.

1.1 Example

To illustrate the benefits of thread-modular model checking, we consider its application to a simple multithreaded program. The multithreaded program *Simple*(n) has n threads which are concurrently executing the procedure `p`. Each thread is identified by unique integer value from the set $Tid = \{1, \ldots, n\}$. These threads manipulate a shared integer variable `x` initialized to 1. The variable `x` is protected by a mutex `m`, which is either the (non-zero) identifier of the thread holding the lock, or else 0, if the lock is not held by any thread. Thus, the type $\mathtt{Mutex} = \{0\} \cup \mathit{Tid}$. The mutex `m` is manipulated by two operations, **`acquire`** and **`release`**. The operation `acquire` blocks until $\mathtt{m} = 0$ and then atomically sets `m` to *tid*, the identifier of the current thread. The operation **`release`** sets `m` back to 0. For each thread, there is an implicit local variable called `pc`, which is the program counter of the thread. The variable `pc` takes values from the set $\mathtt{Loc} = \{1, \ldots, 6\}$ of control locations. We denote the program counter of thread *tid* by $\mathtt{pc}[\mathit{tid}]$.

A simple multithreaded program

```
int x := 1;
Mutex m := 0;

     void p() {
1:     acquire;
2:     x := 0;
3:     x := 1;
4:     assert x > 0;
5:     release;
6:   }
```

$$\mathit{Simple}(n) = \underbrace{\mathtt{p()} \mid \cdots \mid \mathtt{p()}}_{n \text{ times}}$$

We would like to verify three correctness properties for the program *Simple*(n). A correctness property is given by a set of error states; the program satisfies the correctness property if no error state is reachable.

1. There are no races on the data variable `x`. The error set is
$$\exists i, j \in \mathit{Tid}.\ i \neq j \wedge \mathtt{pc}[i] \in \{2,3,4\} \wedge \mathtt{pc}[j] \in \{2,3,4\}\ .$$
2. The assertion at control location 4 does not fail for any thread. The error set is
$$\exists i \in \mathit{Tid}.\ \mathtt{pc}[i] = 4 \wedge \mathtt{x} \leq 0\ .$$
3. Every reachable state satisfies the invariant $\mathtt{m} = 0 \Rightarrow \mathtt{x} = 1$. The error set is
$$\mathtt{m} = 0 \wedge \mathtt{x} \neq 1\ .$$

Thread-modular model checking can verify these correctness properties. Our algorithm computes the guarantee

$$\mathcal{G} \subseteq \mathit{Tid} \times (\mathtt{Mutex} \times \mathtt{int}) \times (\mathtt{Mutex} \times \mathtt{int})$$

where $\mathtt{Mutex} \times \mathtt{int}$ is the set of all global stores, and the thread-local reachable set

$$\mathcal{R} \subseteq \mathit{Tid} \times (\mathtt{Mutex} \times \mathtt{int}) \times \mathtt{Loc}.$$

The set $\mathcal{G}$ has the property that if the thread with identifier *tid* ever takes a step in which the pair $(\mathtt{m}, \mathtt{x})$ of global variables is modified from (m_1, x_1) to (m_2, x_2), then $(tid, (m_1, x_1), (m_2, x_2)) \in \mathcal{G}$. The set $\mathcal{R}$ has the property that if there is a reachable state in which the pair $(\mathtt{m}, \mathtt{x})$ has the value (m, v) and the program counter of thread with identifier *tid* has the value *pc*, then $(tid, (m, x), pc) \in \mathcal{R}$.

These sets are given by the following predicates:

$$
\begin{aligned}
\mathcal{G} \stackrel{\text{def}}{=} & \vee \mathtt{m} = 0 \wedge \mathtt{m}' = tid \wedge \mathtt{x} = \mathtt{x}' = 1 \\
& \vee \mathtt{m} = tid \wedge \mathtt{m}' = 0 \wedge \mathtt{x} = \mathtt{x}' = 1 \\
& \vee \mathtt{m} = \mathtt{m}' = tid \wedge \mathtt{x} = 0 \wedge \mathtt{x}' = 1 \\
& \vee \mathtt{m} = \mathtt{m}' = tid \wedge \mathtt{x} = 1 \wedge \mathtt{x}' \in \{0, 1\}
\end{aligned}
$$

$$
\begin{aligned}
\mathcal{R} \stackrel{\text{def}}{=} & \vee \mathtt{pc}[tid] \in \{1, 6\} \wedge \mathtt{m} = 0 \wedge \mathtt{x} = 1 \\
& \vee \mathtt{pc}[tid] \in \{1, 6\} \wedge \mathtt{m} \in Tid \setminus \{tid\} \wedge \mathtt{x} \in \{0, 1\} \\
& \vee \mathtt{pc}[tid] \in \{2, 4, 5\} \wedge \mathtt{m} = tid \wedge \mathtt{x} = 1 \\
& \vee \mathtt{pc}[tid] = 3 \wedge \mathtt{m} = tid \wedge \mathtt{x} = 0
\end{aligned}
$$

The environment assumption of the thread *tid* can be computed from the guarantee as follows:

$$
\mathcal{E}(tid) \stackrel{\text{def}}{=} \exists t \in Tid : t \neq tid \wedge \mathcal{G}[tid := t]
$$

An examination of $\mathcal{R}$ proves that *Simple*(n) satisfies its three correctness properties:

1. The thread with identifier *tid* accesses $\mathtt{x}$ only when $\mathtt{pc}[tid] \in \{2, 3, 4\}$. Every member of $\mathcal{R}$ satisfies the property that if $\mathtt{pc}[tid] \in \{2, 3, 4\}$ then $\mathtt{m} = tid$. Therefore, it is impossible for two different threads to be at a control location in $\{2, 3, 4\}$ simultaneously. Consequently, there is no race on the variable $\mathtt{x}$.
2. Every member of $\mathcal{R}$ satisfies the property that $\mathtt{x} = 1$ when $\mathtt{pc} = 4$. Therefore, the assertion at control location 4 holds.
3. Every member of $\mathcal{R}$ satisfies the condition $\mathtt{m} = 0 \Rightarrow \mathtt{x} = 1$, which is therefore an invariant of *Simple*(n).

To verify the program *Simple*(n), the thread-modular model checking algorithm analyzes each thread separately. When analyzing thread *tid*, each global state stored by the algorithm contains values for $\mathtt{m}$, $\mathtt{x}$, and the program counter of thread *tid*. The algorithm explores $O(n)$ states and transitions for each thread. Since there are n threads, the number of explored states and transitions is $O(n^2)$.

On the other hand, each state stored by a naive model checking algorithm will provide values for $\mathtt{m}$, $\mathtt{x}$, and the program counters of all the threads. Consequently, the number of states and transitions explored are $O(2^n)$. Thus, for this example, the thread-modular model checking algorithm provides exponential savings in the time and space required for state-space enumeration.

1.2 Limitations

Thread-modular model checking avoids the overhead of correlating the local stores of the various threads by checking each thread separately using an environment assumption to abstract the effect of other threads on the global store.

This approach works provided the global store contains sufficient information about the overall system state. For example, in the program *Simple*(n), our model of the mutex `m` encodes in the global state which thread, if any, is in its critical section.

Conversely, if the global store does not contain sufficient information about the overall system state, thread-modular model checking may yield false alarms. To illustrate this idea, suppose we instead model the mutex `m` as a boolean, such that `m` is *true* when locked and *false* when unlocked. The mutex `m` is initialized to *false*. The operation `acquire` blocks until $\mathtt{m} = \mathit{false}$ and then atomically sets `m` to *true*. The operation `release` sets `m` back to *false*. Then, thread-modular model checking computes the following sets for $\mathcal{G}$ and $\mathcal{R}$:

$$\begin{aligned}
\mathcal{G} \stackrel{\text{def}}{=} & \vee\, \mathtt{m} = \mathit{false} \wedge \mathtt{m}' = \mathit{true} \wedge \mathtt{x} = \mathtt{x}' \in \{0,1\} \\
& \vee\, \mathtt{m} = \{\mathit{false}, \mathit{true}\} \wedge \mathtt{m}' = \mathit{false} \wedge \mathtt{x} = \mathtt{x}' \in \{0,1\} \\
& \vee\, \mathtt{m} = \mathtt{m}' \wedge \mathtt{x} \in \{0,1\} \wedge \mathtt{x}' \in \{0,1\} \\
\mathcal{R} \stackrel{\text{def}}{=} & \ \mathtt{x} \in \{0,1\}
\end{aligned}$$

These sets are too coarse to verify the correctness properties from Section 1.1.

Despite the incompleteness of thread-modular reasoning, we can still use it to verify any correctness property simply by explicating additional information as part of the global store. In *Simple*(n), we provided this information by storing in the mutex `m` the identifier of the current holder of the mutex. A more general approach for providing this information is to include in the global store a suitable abstraction of the local store of each thread.

1.3 Related Work

We refer the reader to our earlier papers [4, 5] for a discussion of the related work on verification of multithreaded software by compositional reasoning and model checking.

Giannakopoulou et al. [6] present a method for automatically generating the weakest environment assumption under which a component of a concurrent software system satisfies a given safety property. Although the environment assumption generated by our approach may not be the weakest, it may be more concise. They also leave open the question of verifying the environment once the assumption has been generated. In our paper, we show how to use the generated assumptions to verify all threads in a multithreaded program.

Cobleigh et al. [3] share our motivation of reducing the annotation cost of compositional reasoning. They use a counterexample-guided learning algorithm to infer environment assumptions, an approach that is very different from ours. Our algorithm is based entirely on model checking; the correctness properties of the program are verified and appropriate environment assumptions are inferred solely by state-space enumeration.

Bouajjani et al. [1] present a generic approach to the static analysis of concurrent programs. Unlike our work on shared-memory programs, they focus on synchronous message-passing programs. They present several abstractions for such programs, including a commutative abstraction that ignores message order. Our thread-modular model checking algorithm focuses on concurrent updates to the shared heap, but has a similar flavor to this commutative abstraction, in that it ignores the order of heap updates performed by a thread.

2 Concurrent Finite-State Systems

A *concurrent finite-state system* consists of a number of concurrently executing threads. The threads communicate through a global store, which is shared by all threads. In addition, each thread has its own local store containing data not manipulated by other threads, such as the program counter of the thread. Each thread also has an associated thread identifier. A state of the system consists of a global store g and a mapping ls from thread identifiers to local stores. We use the notation $ls[t := l]$ to denote a mapping that is identical to ls except that it maps thread identifier t to local store l.

Domains

$$
\begin{array}{rl}
t, e \in & Tid = \{1, \ldots, n\} \\
g \in & GlobalStore \\
l \in & LocalStore \\
ls \in & LocalStores = Tid \rightarrow LocalStore \\
\Sigma \in & State = GlobalStore \times LocalStores
\end{array}
$$

We model the behavior of the individual threads as the transition relation T:

$$T \subseteq Tid \times (GlobalStore \times LocalStore) \times (GlobalStore \times LocalStore)$$

The relation $T(t, g, l, g', l')$ holds if the thread t can take a step from a state with global store g and where thread t has local store l, yielding a new state with global and local stores g' and l', respectively.

We assume that program execution starts in an initial state $\Sigma_0 = (g_0, ls_0)$ consisting of an initial global store g_0 and a mapping ls_0 that provides the initial local store for each thread. The correctness condition for the program in our system is provided by an *error set* $E \subseteq GlobalStore \times LocalStores$. A state (g, ls) is *erroneous* if $E(g, ls)$ is true. Our goal is to determine if, when started from the initial state Σ_0, the system can reach an erroneous state.

2.1 Standard Model Checking

Since the set of possible states is finite, we can use standard model checking to determine if any erroneous state is reachable from the initial state. In particular, the least solution $R \subseteq State$ to the following inference rules describes the set of reachable states.

Standard model checking

(BASIC INIT)
$$\frac{}{R(g_0, ls_0)}$$

(BASIC STEP)
$$\frac{R(g, ls) \qquad T(t, g, ls(t), g', l')}{R(g', ls[t := l'])}$$

Although we provide a declarative definition of R here, it is easily computed using a worklist-based algorithm. Having computed R, it is straightforward to determine if any erroneous state is reachable, *i.e.*, if there exist g, and ls such that $R(g, ls) \wedge E(g, ls)$.

Unfortunately, the computational cost of this algorithm becomes excessive in the presence of multiple threads. Let $n = |Tid|$ be the number of threads and let $G = |GlobalStore|$ and $L = |LocalStore|$ be the sizes of the global and local stores, respectively. Then the size of R and the space complexity of this algorithm is $O(G.L^n)$. Furthermore, for each entry in R there may be $n.G.L$ applications of (BASIC STEP). Hence the time complexity of this algorithm is $O(n.G^2.L^{n+1})$. A more accurate time complexity can be obtained by accounting for the bounded nondeterminism of the transition relation of each thread. Let d be the bound on the number of (g', l') pairs for any thread t, global store g, and local store l such that $T(t, g, l, g', l')$ holds. Then, for each entry in R, there are at most $n.d$ applications of (BASIC STEP) and the time complexity is $O(n.d.G.L^n)$.

2.2 Thread-Modular Model Checking

The complexity of standard model checking is exponential in the number of threads, since it explicitly correlates the local states (and program counters) of all the various threads. However, since the threads in most software systems are predominantly loosely-coupled, this correlation is largely redundant. Thread-modular model checking provides a means to avoid this redundancy.

Under thread-modular model checking, each thread is checked separately, using the guarantees that abstract the behavior of interleaved steps of other threads. The algorithm works by computing two relations: $\mathcal{R}$, which specifies the reachable states of each thread, and $\mathcal{G}$, which is the guarantee of each thread. Thus, the guarantee is inferred automatically during the model checking process.

$$\mathcal{R} \subseteq Tid \times GlobalStore \times LocalStore$$
$$\mathcal{G} \subseteq Tid \times GlobalStore \times GlobalStore$$

The relation $\mathcal{R}(t, g, l)$ holds if the system can reach a state with global store g and where the thread t has local store l. Similarly, $\mathcal{G}(t, g, g')$ holds if a step by thread t can go from a reachable state with global store g to a state with global store g'. While model checking a thread with identifier different from t, we know that whenever the global store is g and $\mathcal{G}(t, g, g')$ holds, an interleaved step of thread t can change the global store to g'. The relations $\mathcal{R}$ and $\mathcal{G}$ are defined as the least solution to the following rules.

Thread-modular model checking

(AG INIT)	(AG ENV)	(AG STEP)
$\dfrac{}{\mathcal{R}(t, g_0, ls(t))}$	$\dfrac{\mathcal{R}(t,g,l) \quad \mathcal{G}(e,g,g') \quad t \neq e}{\mathcal{R}(t,g',l)}$	$\dfrac{\mathcal{R}(t,g,l) \quad T(t,g,l,g',l')}{\mathcal{R}(t,g',l') \quad \mathcal{G}(t,g,g')}$

The set of reachable states determined using thread-modular reasoning is a conservative approximation of the set of actual reachable states, as illustrated by the following lemma.

Lemma 1. *For all global stores g and local store maps ls, if $R(g, ls)$ then for all thread identifiers t, $\mathcal{R}(t, g, ls(t)))$.*

Our algorithm reports an error if there is an erroneous state (g, ls) such that $\mathcal{R}(t, g, ls(t))$ for all $t \in Tid$. If a software error causes an erroneous state to be reachable, *i.e.*,

$$\exists g, ls.\ (E(g, ls) \wedge R(g, ls)) ,$$

then the thread-modular algorithm will catch that error, *i.e.*,

$$\exists g, ls.\ E(g, ls) \wedge \forall t.\ \mathcal{R}(t, g, ls(t)) .$$

Thread-modular model checking can be performed using a worklist-based algorithm, whose complexity is much less than that of standard model checking. The space complexity is $O(n.G.(G + L))$. There may be $n^2.G^2.L$ applications of (AG ENV) and $n.G^2.L^2$ applications of (AG STEP). Hence the time complexity of this algorithm is $O(n.G^2.L.(n + L))$. Again, we improve the bound to $O(n.G.L.(n.G + d))$ using the bound d on the nondeterminism of the transition relation.

3 Concurrent Pushdown Systems

The thread-modular approach described so far works well for checking multi-threaded finite state software systems. However, its applicability to realistic systems is somewhat limited, because such systems are typically constructed using procedures and procedure calls, and hence rely on the presence of an unbounded stack for each thread. In this section, we extend our thread-modular approach to handle such systems.

We assume that, in addition to a local store, each thread now also has its own private stack, which is sequence of frames. We leave the exact structure of each frame unspecified, but it might contain, for example, the return address for a procedure call. A state of the concurrent pushdown system consists of a global store, a collection of local stores, one for each thread, and a collection of stacks, one for each thread.

Domains

$$\begin{aligned} f &\in \mathit{Frame} \\ s &\in \mathit{Stack} = \mathit{Frame}^* \\ ss &\in \mathit{Stacks} = \mathit{Tid} \to \mathit{Stack} \\ \Sigma &\in \mathit{State} = \mathit{GlobalStore} \times \mathit{LocalStores} \times \mathit{Stacks} \end{aligned}$$

We model the behavior of the individual threads using three relations:

$$\begin{aligned} T &\subseteq \mathit{Tid} \times (\mathit{GlobalStore} \times \mathit{LocalStore}) \times (\mathit{GlobalStore} \times \mathit{LocalStore}) \\ T^+ &\subseteq \mathit{Tid} \times (\mathit{GlobalStore} \times \mathit{LocalStore}) \times (\mathit{LocalStore} \times \mathit{Frame}) \\ T^- &\subseteq \mathit{Tid} \times (\mathit{GlobalStore} \times \mathit{LocalStore} \times \mathit{Frame}) \times \mathit{LocalStore} \end{aligned}$$

The relation T models thread steps that do not manipulate the stack. The relation $T(t, g, l, g', l')$ holds if the thread t can take a step from a state with global and local stores g and l, respectively, yielding (possibly modified) stores g' and l', and where the stack is not accessed or updated during this step. The relation $T^+(t, g, l, l', f)$ models steps of thread t that push a frame onto the stack. The global and local stores are initially g and l, the global store is unmodified during this step, the local store is updated to l', and the frame f is pushed onto the stack. Similarly, the relation $T^-(t, g, l, f, l')$ models steps of thread t that pop a frame from the stack. The global and local stores are initially g and l and the frame f is initially on top of the stack. After the step, the global store is unmodified, the local store is updated to l', and the frame f has been popped from the stack.

The correctness condition is still specified by an error set $E \subseteq \mathit{GlobalStore} \times \mathit{LocalStores}$. Note that although the error set depends on the local stores of the threads, it does not depend on their stacks. A state (g, ls, ss) is erroneous if $(g, ls) \in E$.

We assume that all stacks are empty in the initial state, and let ss_0 map each thread identifier to the empty stack. The set of reachable states is then defined by the least relation $R \subseteq \mathit{State}$ satisfying the following rules.

Basic PDA model checking

(BASIC PDA INIT)

$$\frac{}{R(g_0, ls_0, ss_0)}$$

(BASIC PDA STEP)

$$\frac{R(g, ls, ss) \quad T(t, g, ls(t), g', l')}{R(g', ls[t := l'], ss)}$$

(BASIC PDA PUSH)

$$\frac{R(g, ls, ss) \quad T^+(t, g, ls(t), l', f)}{R(g', ls[t := l'], ss[t := ss(t).f])}$$

(BASIC PDA POP)

$$\frac{R(g, ls, ss) \quad ss(t) = s.f \quad T^-(t, g, ls(t), f, l')}{R(g, ls[t := l'], ss[t := s])}$$

Since the stack sizes are unbounded, the set of reachable states may also be unbounded. Consequently, any algorithm to compute R may diverge. In fact, the model checking problem for concurrent pushdown systems is undecidable, a result that can be proved by reduction from the undecidable problem of determining if the intersection of two context-free languages is empty [11].

3.1 Thread-Modular Model Checking

Although sound and complete model checking of concurrent pushdown systems is undecidable, thread-modular reasoning allows us to model check such systems an a conservative yet useful manner. Again, we model check each thread separately, using the guarantees to reason about the effect of interleaved steps of other threads. The algorithm works by computing the guarantee relation $\mathcal{G}$ and the reachability relations $\mathcal{P}$ and $\mathcal{Q}$.

$$\begin{aligned}
\mathcal{G} &\subseteq \mathit{Tid} \times \mathit{GlobalStore} \times \mathit{GlobalStore} \\
\mathcal{P} &\subseteq \mathit{Tid} \times \mathit{GlobalStore} \times \mathit{LocalStore} \times \mathit{GlobalStore} \times \mathit{LocalStore} \\
\mathcal{Q} &\subseteq \mathit{Tid} \times \mathit{GlobalStore} \times \mathit{LocalStore} \times \mathit{Frame} \times \mathit{GlobalStore} \times \mathit{LocalStore}
\end{aligned}$$

The guarantee $\mathcal{G}(t, g, g')$ holds if a step by thread t can go from a reachable state with global store g to a state with global store g'. The reachability relation $\mathcal{P}(t, g, l, g', l')$ holds if (1) the system can reach a state with global store g and where thread t has local store l, and (2) from any such state, the system can later reach a state with global store g' and where thread t has local store l', and where the stack is identical to that in the first state. Similarly, the reachability relation $\mathcal{Q}(t, g, l, f, g', l')$ holds if (1) the system can reach a state with global store g and where thread t has local store l, and (2) from any such state, the system can later reach a state with global store g' and where thread t has local store l', and where the stack is identical to that in the first state except that the frame f has been added to it. These relations are defined as the least solution to the following rules.

Thread-modular PDA model checking

(AG PDA INIT)

$$\frac{}{\mathcal{P}(t, g_0, ls_0(t), g_0, ls_0(t))}$$

(AG PDA ENV1)

$$\frac{\mathcal{P}(t, g_1, l_1, g_2, l_2) \quad \mathcal{G}(e, g_2, g_3) \quad e \neq t}{\mathcal{P}(t, g_1, l_1, g_3, l_2)}$$

(AG PDA ENV2)

$$\frac{\mathcal{Q}(t, g_1, l_1, f, g_2, l_2) \quad \mathcal{G}(e, g_2, g_3) \quad e \neq t}{\mathcal{Q}(t, g_1, l_1, f, g_3, l_2)}$$

(AG PDA STEP1)

$$\frac{\mathcal{P}(t, g_1, l_1, g_2, l_2) \quad T(t, g_2, l_2, g_3, l_3)}{\mathcal{P}(t, g_1, l_1, g_3, l_3) \quad \mathcal{G}(t, g_2, g_3)}$$

(AG PDA PUSH)

$$\frac{\mathcal{P}(t, g_1, l_1, g_2, l_2) \quad T^+(t, g_2, l_2, l_3, f)}{\mathcal{Q}(t, g_1, l_1, f, g_2, l_3) \quad \mathcal{P}(t, g_2, l_3, g_2, l_3)}$$

(AG PDA STEP2)

$$\frac{\mathcal{Q}(t, g_1, l_1, f, g_2, l_2) \quad \mathcal{P}(t, g_2, l_2, g_3, l_3)}{\mathcal{Q}(t, g_1, l_1, f, g_3, l_3)}$$

(AG PDA POP)

$$\frac{\mathcal{Q}(t, g_1, l_1, f, g_2, l_2) \quad T^-(t, g_2, l_2, f, l_3)}{\mathcal{P}(t, g_1, l_1, g_2, l_3)}$$

The set of reachable states determined using thread-modular reasoning is a conservative approximation of the set of actual reachable states, as illustrated by the following lemma.

Lemma 2. *For all global stores g and local store maps ls and stack maps ss, if $R(g, ls, ss)$ then for all thread identifiers t, there exists some g', l' such that $\mathcal{P}(t, g', l', g, ls(t))$.*

Our algorithm reports an error if there is $(g, ls) \in E$ such that for all $t \in Tid$, there is a global store g' and a local store l' with $\mathcal{P}(t, g', l', g, ls(t))$. If a software error causes an erroneous state to be reachable, *i.e.*,

$$\exists g, ls, ss.\ (E(g, ls) \wedge R(g, ls, ss))$$

then the thread-modular algorithm will catch that error, *i.e.*,

$$\exists g, ls.\ E(g, ls) \wedge \forall t.\ \exists g', l'.\ \mathcal{P}(t, g', l', g, ls(t))\ .$$

Let F=$|Frame|$. Then, the space complexity of this algorithm is $O(n.G^2.L^2.F)$. The time complexity of this algorithm is $O(n^2.G^3.L^3.F)$ since each inference rule can be applied at most $n^2.G^3.L^3.F$ times.

4 Discussion

We have presented a new technique called thread-modular model checking for verifying multithreaded software systems. Although incomplete for general systems, this technique is particularly effective for loosely-coupled multithreaded software where the the various threads synchronize using primitives such as mutexes, readers-writer locks, etc. If the synchronization primitives are modeled with appropriate auxiliary information, these systems can be verified one thread at a time.

Realistic software systems often have dynamic thread creation that may lead to unbounded number of threads. This aspect of multithreaded software is currently not handled by our algorithm. However, the set of thread identifiers, even if infinite, is a scalarset type [8]. Consequently, these systems are amenable to symmetry reduction which we plan to exploit in future work.

The thread-modular model checking algorithm constructs a particular abstraction of multithreaded software using environment assumptions. However, the abstraction might be too coarse to verify the relevant correctness property. If the algorithm reports an error, we would like an efficient procedure to check whether the violation is real or introduced due to the abstraction process. In the second case, we would like to automatically refine the environment assumptions by possibly explicating some aspect of the program counters of the other threads in the environment. After the refinement, the model checking algorithm can be repeated. Thus, the thread-modular model checking algorithm may be converted to a semi-algorithm that is sound and also complete on termination.

References

[1] A. Bouajjani, J. Esparza, and T. Touili. A generic approach to the static analysis of concurrent programs with procedures. In *POPL 03: Principles of Programming Languages*, pages 62–73. ACM Press, 2003. 217

[2] E. M. Clarke and E. A. Emerson. Design and synthesis of synchronization skeletons using branching-time temporal logic. In *Workshop on Logic of Programs*, Lecture Notes in Computer Science 131, pages 52–71. Springer-Verlag, 1981. 213

[3] J. M. Cobleigh, D. Giannakopoulou, and C. S. Păsăreanu. Learning assumptions for compositional verification. In *TACAS 03: Tools and Algorithms for the Construction and Analysis of Systems*, 2003. To appear. 217

[4] C. Flanagan, S. N. Freund, and S. Qadeer. Thread-modular verification for shared-memory programs. In *ESOP 02: European Symposium on Programming*, Lecture Notes in Computer Science 2305, pages 262–277. Springer-Verlag, 2002. 214, 217

[5] C. Flanagan, S. Qadeer, and S. A. Seshia. A modular checker for multithreaded programs. In *CAV 02: Computer Aided Verification*, Lecture Notes in Computer Science 2404, pages 180–194. Springer-Verlag, 2002. 214, 217

[6] D. Giannakopoulou, C. S. Păsăreanu, and H. Barringer. Assumption generation for software component verification. In *ASE 02: Automated Software Engineering*, pages 3–12. IEEE Computer Society, 2002. 217

[7] J. E. Hopcroft and J. D. Ullman. *Introduction to Automata Theory, Languages, and Computation.* Addison-Wesley Publishing Company, 1979. 213

[8] C. N. Ip and D. L. Dill. Better verification through symmetry. *Formal Methods in System Design*, 9(1–2):41–75, 1996. 223

[9] C. B. Jones. Tentative steps toward a development method for interfering programs. *ACM Transactions on Programming Languages and Systems*, 5(4):596–619, 1983. 214

[10] J. Queille and J. Sifakis. Specification and verification of concurrent systems in CESAR. In *Fifth International Symposium on Programming*, Lecture Notes in Computer Science 137, pages 337–351. Springer-Verlag, 1981. 213

[11] G. Ramalingam. Context-sensitive synchronization-sensitive analysis is undecidable. *ACM Transactions on Programming Languages and Systems*, 22(2):416–430, 2000. 213, 221

Unification & Sharing in Timed Automata Verification

Alexandre David[1], Gerd Behrmann[2], Kim G. Larsen[2], and Wang Yi[1]

[1] Department of Information Technology, Uppsala University, Sweden
[2] Department of Computer Science, Aalborg University, Denmark

Abstract. We present work on unifying the two main data structures involved during reachability analysis of timed automata. We also present result on sharing common elements between states. The experimental evaluations show speedups of up to 60% and memory savings of up to 80% compared to previous implementations.

1 Introduction

Timed automata (TA) is a popular formalism for modelling real-time aspects. The distinctive feature of TA is the use of clocks. Clocks are non-negative real valued variables, that can be compared and reset, and which increase at identical rates during delay transitions. A number of verification tools for TA exist. Like all verification tools, they suffer from the state explosion problem. In addition, they must deal with the infinite state-space of TA (due to the real valued clocks). Most tools use a pseudo-explicit state-space exploration algorithm based on *zones*. Zones describe infinite sets of clock valuations, and the state-space is represented by pairs (l, Z) called *symbolic states* containing the current *location* and the zone (more generally, the state-space of a network of TA extended with bounded integer variables might be represented by triples $(\boldsymbol{l}, \boldsymbol{\nu}, Z)$ containing a location vector $\boldsymbol{l}$, a variable vector $\boldsymbol{\nu}$ and a zone Z).

During state-space exploration, it is for reasons of termination and efficiency necessary to keep track of both which symbolic states have been explored as well as which still need to be explored. In this paper we present results on unifying these two data structures into a common structure. We also present orthogonal results on sharing common location vectors, variable vectors and zones between symbolic states. We will motivate these decisions and evaluate them through experiments in a prototype implementation based on the real-time verification tool UPPAAL.

Related work The sharing approach presented in this paper is similar to the one in [1] for hierarhical coloured Petri nets. Both approaches share similarities with BDDs in that common substructures are shared, but avoid the overhead of the fine grained data representation of BDDs. The unification has been applied to Petri Nets [2] for the purpose of distributed model-checking. Our approach aims at reducing look-ups in the hash table and eliminating waiting states earlier. To our knowledge, there has been no work on these issues in the context of TA.

T. Ball and S. K. Rajamani (Eds.): SPIN 2003, LNCS 2648, pp. 225–229, 2003.

2 Unification and Sharing

During state-space exploration, there is a fundamental need to maintain two sets of symbolic states: States that need to be explored (the waiting list) and states that have been explored (the passed list). States are taken from the waiting list, compared to the states in the passed list, and if unexplored added to the passed list while successors are added to the waiting list.

Since symbolic states are sets of concrete states, it makes sence to define inclusion between states having the same location and variable vector, *i.e.*, $(\boldsymbol{l}, \boldsymbol{\nu}, Z) \subseteq (\boldsymbol{l}, \boldsymbol{\nu}, Z')$ iff $Z \subseteq Z'$. We say that $(\boldsymbol{l}, \boldsymbol{\nu}, Z)$ is covered by $(\boldsymbol{l}, \boldsymbol{\nu}, Z')$. Three observations are essential for good performance:

- When determining whether a state s has already been explored by comparing it to the passed list, rather than searching for states identical to s, we might as well look for states covering s.
- When adding a state s to the waiting list, there is no need to add s if it is covered by an existing state.
- When adding a state s to the passed list or the waiting list, all states covered by s can be removed.

The traditional approach to implementing these operations is to use a hash table and define the hash function on the location vector and variable vector, but not on the zone. Thus, it is easy to find states with the same location vector and variable vector. This approach has a major drawback: It is often the case that many states in the waiting list are covered by states in the passed list, but this is not realized until the states are moved from the waiting list to the passed list. This enlarges the waiting list, wasting memory and increasing the cost of adding new states. One solution would be to move the passed list lookup s.t. states are added to the passed list and the waiting list at the same time, see Fig. 1. Then the waiting list is guaranteed to only contain unexplored states. However, this solution is undesirable: First, states in the waiting list are duplicated. Second,

```
WL = PL = {s0}
while WL ≠ ∅ do
  s = select and remove state from WL
  if s ⊨ φ then return true
  ∀s' : s ⇒ s' do
    if ∀s'' ∈ PL : s' ⊈ s'' then
      PL = PL ∪ {s}
      WL = WL ∪ {s}
    endif
  done
done
return false
```

Fig. 1. Explicit state reachability algorithm. States are inserted into both the passed list and the waiting list

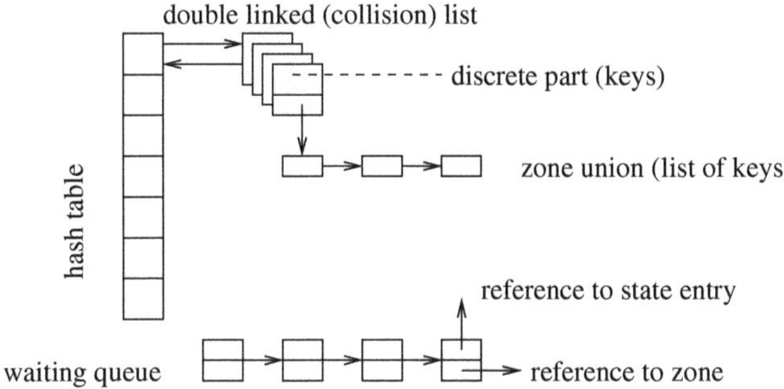

Fig. 2. Implementation of a unified passed and waiting list

Table 1. The number of unique location vector, variable vectors and zones, measured in percent for four different examples. The lower the number, the more copies of the same data there are

Model	Unique locations	Unique variables	Unique zones
Audio	52.7%	25.2%	17.2%
Dacapo	4.3%	26.4%	12.7%
Fischer4	9.9%	0.6%	64.4%
Bus coupler	7.2%	8.7%	1.3%

although it is not apparent from Fig. 1, adding a state s to the passed and waiting lists still requires a partial traversal of those data structures in order to eliminate states covered by s.

Instead we propose to unify the two data structures into a single data structure – for lack of a better name we call it the *unified list*. When adding a state s to the unified list, it is compared to existing states: If s is covered by any of the existing states, then s is not added. Otherwise, all states covered by s are removed and s is added. Internally, it is still necessary to keep track of which states have been explored and when retrieving a state from the list, it is marked as explored, but not actually removed. Figure 2 shows one possible implementation of the unified list data structure. A hash table provides fast access to a linked list of zones sharing the same location vector and variable vector. At the same time, a list (ordered either in FIFO or LIFO depending on the desired exploration order) of references to unexplored states is maintained.

Unifying the passed and waiting lists reduces the number of needless states, *i.e.* states covered by previously explored states, stored on the waiting list. It does not reduce the amount of memory needed to store each symbolic state. Our second proposal is to share common location vectors, variable vectors, and zones among states. This is motivated by the results shown in Tab. 1. This can be implemented by storing location vectors, variable vectors, and zones in different hash tables. The unified list then only maintains references (keys) to the elements in those hash tables.

Table 2. Experimental results for 8 examples without unification, with unification, and with unification and sharing

Model	Before		Unification		Unication & Sharing	
Audio	$\leq 0.5s$	2M	$\leq 0.5s$	2M	$\leq 0.5s$	2M
Engine	$\leq 0.5s$	3M	$\leq 0.5s$	4M	$\leq 0.5s$	5M
Dacapo	3s	7M	3s	5M	3s	5M
Cups	43s	116M	37s	107M	36s	26M
BC	428s	681M	359s	641M	345s	165M
Master	306s	616M	277s	558M	267s	153M
Slave	440s	735M	377s	645M	359s	151M
Plant	19688s	$> 4G$	9207s	2771M	8513s	1084M

3 Experiments

We conduct our experiments on development version 3.3.24 of UPPAAL on an Ultra Sparc II 400MHz with 4GB of memory. This version incorporates a new architecture and is already twice as fast as the official 3.2 version. Here we compare results without and with the unified list structure for an audio protocol (Audio), a TDMA protocol (Dacapo), an engine gear controller (Engine), a combinatorial problem (Cups), a field bus communication protocol (different parts BC, Master, and Slave), and a production plant with three batches. We refer to the UPPAAL web-site for references to these examples.

Table 2 shows time and space requirements to generate the whole state-space, except for cups where a reachability property is used because the whole state space is too large. The result $> 4G$ means the verifier crashed because it ran out of memory. In all examples, zones were represented using the DBM data structure, and active clock reduction was enabled. In the four last examples, the hash table size of the passed list and waiting list was enlarged to 273819 (using the default size doubles the verification time). The unified list implementation automatically resizes the hash table and does not suffer from this problem.

Focusing on the experiments with unification and without sharing, we see an increase in speed and a slight reduction in memory usage. This is due to not wasting space on storing states in the waiting list, that are not going to be explored anyway and due to keeping a list of zones having the same location and variable vector. The latter is also responsible for the speedup. This is in particular the case in the plant example, which has 9 clocks and 28 integer variables. Focusing on the experiments with sharing, we see a significant reduction in memory usage of up to 80%. We also observe a slight speedup, which we expect is due to the smaller memory footprint - this seems to compensate for the computational overhead caused by maintaining extra hash tables. For small examples, the results are identical for all versions. The results scale with the size of the models, in particular the sharing property of the data holds. In total, we observe a speedup of up to 60%.

Acknowledgments

Go to Ahiable Antoinette and Johan Bengtsson.

References

[1] S. Christensen and L. M. Kristensen. State space analysis of hierarchical coloured petri nets. In B. Farwer, D.Moldt, and M-O. Stehr, editors, *Proceedings of PNSE'97*, number 205, pages 32–43, Hamburg, Germany, 1997. 225

[2] Gianfranco F. Ciardo and David M. Nicol. Automated parallelization of discrete state-space generation. In *Journal of Parallel and Distributed Computing*, volume 47, pages 153–167. ACM, 1997. 225

The Maude LTL Model Checker and Its Implementation*

Steven Eker[1], José Meseguer[2], and Ambarish Sridharanarayanan[2]

[1] Computer Science Laboratory, SRI International
Menlo Park, CA 94025
eker@csl.sri.com

[2] CS Department, University of Illinois at Urbana-Champaign
Urbana, IL 61801
{meseguer,srdhrnry}@cs.uiuc.edu

1 Introduction

A model checker typically supports two different levels of specification: (1) a *system specification* level, in which the concurrent system to be analyzed is formalized; and (2) a *property specification* level, in which the properties to be model checked—for example, temporal logic formulae—are specified. The Maude LTL model checker has been designed with the goal of combining a very expressive and general system specification language (Maude [1]) with an advanced on-the-fly explicit-state LTL model checking engine.

Maude specifications are *executable logical theories* in rewriting logic [9], a logic that is a flexible logical framework for expressing a very wide range of concurrency models and distributed systems [9]. A rewrite theory is a triple $\mathcal{R} = (\Sigma, E, R)$, with (Σ, E) an equational theory specifying a system's *distributed state structure* and with R a collection of rewrite rules specifying the *concurrent transitions* of the system. Since no domain-specific model of concurrency is built into the logic, the range of applications that can be naturally specified is indeed very wide. For example, besides conventional distributed system specifications, properties of signalling pathways in mammalian cells have been model checked [3]. Another advantage of Maude as the system specification language is that integration of model checking with theorem proving techniques becomes quite seamless. The same rewrite theory $\mathcal{R} = (\Sigma, E, R)$ can be the input to the LTL model checker and to several other proving tools in the Maude environment [2]. For a lengthier discussion of the Maude LTL model checker and its LTL satisfiability and tautology procedures, see the companion paper [4].

* The first two authors' work has been partially supported by DARPA through Air Force Research Laboratory Contract F30602-97-C-0312, NSF grants CCR-9900326 and CCR-9900334, ONR Contract N00012-99-C-0198, and DARPA through Air Force Research Laboratory Contract F30602-02-C-0130. The last two authors' work is also supported in part by the ONR Grant N00014-02-1-0715.

T. Ball and S. K. Rajamani (Eds.): SPIN 2003, LNCS 2648, pp. 230–234, 2003.

2 LTL Model Checking of Maude Specifications

A Maude module is a rewrite theory $\mathcal{R} = (\Sigma, E, R)$. Fixing a distinguished sort *State*, the initial model $\mathcal{T}_{\mathcal{R}}$ of the rewrite theory $\mathcal{R} = (\Sigma, E, R)$ has an underlying Kripke structure $\mathcal{K}(\mathcal{R}, \mathit{State})$ given by the total binary relation extending its one-step sequential rewrites. To the initial algebra of states $T_{\Sigma/E}$ we can likewise associate equationally-defined *computable state predicates* as atomic predicates for such a Kripke structure. In this way we obtain a language of LTL *properties* of the rewrite theory $\mathcal{R}$. Maude 2.0 supports on-the-fly LTL model checking for initial states $[t]$, say of sort *State*, of a rewrite theory $\mathcal{R} = (\Sigma, E, R)$ such that the set $\{[u] \in T_{\Sigma/E} \mid \mathcal{R} \vdash [t] \rightarrow [u]\}$, of all states *reachable* from $[t]$ is *finite*. The rewrite theory $\mathcal{R}$ should satisfy reasonable executability requirements, such as the confluence and termination of the equations E and coherence of the rules R relative to E [1]. In Maude the rewrite theory $\mathcal{R}$ is specified as a module, say `M`. Then, given an initial state, say `init` of sort $\texttt{State}_{\texttt{M}}$, we can *model check* different LTL properties beginning at this initial state by doing the following:

- defining a new module, say `CHECK-M`, that includes the modules `M` and the predefined module `MODEL-CHECKER` as submodules;
- giving a *subsort declaration*, `subsort` $\texttt{State}_{\texttt{M}}$ `< State .`, where `State` is one of the key sorts in the module `MODEL-CHECKER`;
- defining the *syntax* of the *state predicates* we wish to use (which can be parametric) by means of constants and operators of sort `Prop`, a subsort of the sort `Formula` (i.e., LTL formulas) in the module `MODEL-CHECKER`;
- defining the *semantics* of the state predicates by means of equations.

Once the semantics of each of the state predicates has been defined, we are then ready, given an initial state `init`, to model check any LTL formula, say `form`, involving such predicates. We do so by evaluating in Maude, the expression `modelCheck(init,form) .` Two things can then happen: if the property `form` holds, then we get the result `true`; if it doesn't, we get a counterexample expressed as a finite path followed by a cycle.

3 Model Checking Algorithms and Implementation

On-the-fly LTL model checking is performed by constructing a Büchi automaton from the negation of the property formula and lazily searching the synchronous product of the Büchi automaton and the system state transition diagram for a reachable accepting cycle.

Büchi Automaton Construction. The negated LTL formula is converted to negative normal form and heuristically simplified by a set of Maude equations, mostly derived from the simplification rules in [5, 10]. Rather than the classical tableaux construction [7], we use a newer technique proposed in [6] based on very weak alternating automata, comprising three basic steps: (1) construct a very weak alternating automaton from the formula, (2) convert the very weak

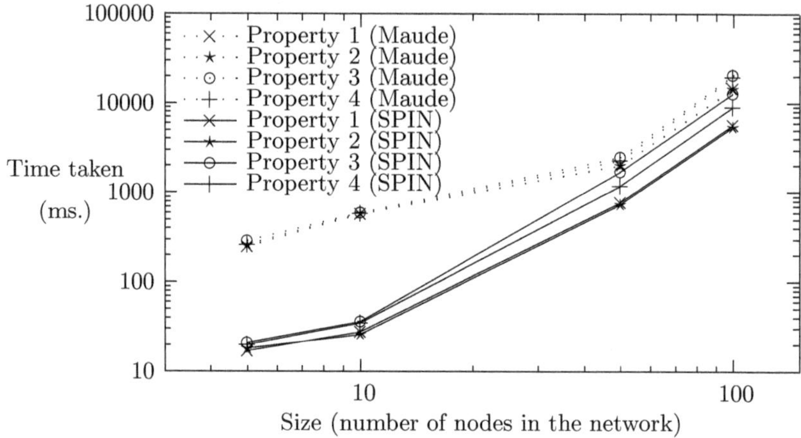

Fig. 1. Execution time for the leader-election problem - Maude vs. SPIN

alternating automaton into a generalized Büchi automaton (with multiple fairness conditions on arcs) and (3) convert the generalized Büchi automaton into a regular Büchi automaton. Optimizations and simplifications are performed after each step and we add some strongly connected component optimizations adapted from those in [10]. Throughout the computation, the pure propositional subformulae labelling the arcs of the various automata are stored as BDDs to allow computation of conjunctions, elimination of contradictions, and combination of parallel arcs by disjunction.

Searching the Synchronous Product. We use the double depth first method of [8] to lazily generate and search the synchronous product. For each system state generated we keep five bit vectors to record: (1) which propositions have been tested in the state; (2) which propositions were true in the state; (3) which product pairs (with automaton states) have been seen by the first depth first search; (4) which product pairs are currently on the first depth first search stack; and (5) which product pairs have been seen by the second (nested) depth first search. The full term graph representation of each system state is maintained (in order to test propositions) in a separate hash table which also keeps track of rewrites between system states.

Performance Evaluation. We compared the performance of the Maude LTL model checker vis-a-vis the SPIN LTL model checker as follows. Given a system specified in PROMELA, we specify it in Maude, and then compare the running times and the memory consumptions of the two model checkers on the respective specifications. The PROMELA specifications used — a solution to the mutual exclusion problem, a solution to the leader election problem for a unidirectional

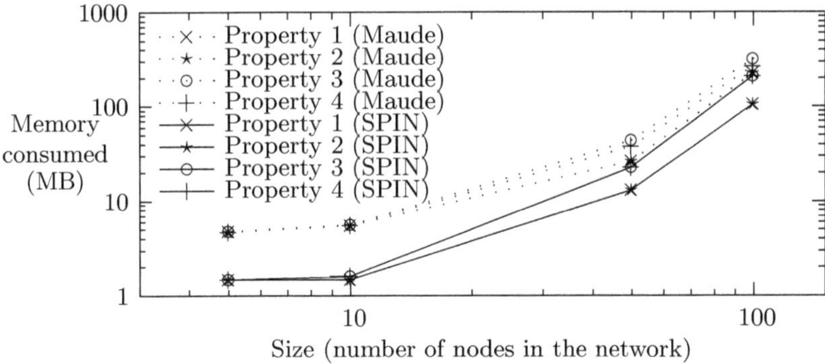

Fig. 2. Total memory consumption for the leader-election problem - Maude vs. SPIN

ring network, and a translation of the π-calculus description of a mobile handoff scenario — are all available on the SPIN web-page.

In all the above situations, only properties satisfied by the corresponding systems were model checked; no generation of counterexamples was attempted. Except in one instance, the default settings for SPIN were used everywhere. The analyses were carried out on a 1.13 GHz Pentium III machine with 384 MB RAM running Red Hat Linux. In most of the cases, both model checkers finished fairly quickly whenever memory was available; lack of memory proved to be the main bottleneck for scalability. The benchmarks showed a comparable performance of SPIN and the Maude LTL model checker, in terms of both speed and memory consumption. The results for the leader election problem are given in Figures 1 and 2. A fuller description of the algorithms and the properties (including properties 1–4 mentioned above), as well as of their respective comparisons, is available in [4].

References

[1] M. Clavel and et al. Maude: specification and programming in rewriting logic. *Theoretical Computer Science*, 285:187–243, August 2002. 230, 231

[2] Manuel Clavel and et al. Building equational proving tools by reflection in rewriting logic. In *CAFE: An Industrial-Strength Algebraic Formal Method.* Elsevier, 2000. 230

[3] Steven Eker and et al. Pathway logic: Executable models of biological networks. In *Proc. WRLA'02*, volume 71 of *ENTCS*. Elsevier, 2002. 230

[4] Steven Eker, José Meseguer, and Ambarish Sridharanarayanan. The Maude LTL model checker. In *Proc. WRLA '02*, volume 71 of *ENTCS*. Elsevier, 2002. 230, 233

[5] Kousha Etessami and Gerard J. Holzmann. Optimizing Büchi automata. In *CONCUR 2000*, number 1877 in LNCS, pages 153–167. Springer-Verlag, 2000. 231

[6] Paul Gastin and Denis Oddoux. Fast LTL to Büchi automata translation. In *CAV '01*, number 2102 in LNCS, pages 53–65. Springer-Verlag, 2001. 231

[7] Rob Gerth and et al. Simple on-the-fly automatic verification of linear temporal logic. In *Protocol Specification Testing and Verification*, pages 3–18. Chapman & Hall, 1995. 231

[8] G. J. Holzmann, D. Peled, and M. Yannakakis. On nested depth first search. *Design: An International Journal*, 13(3):289–307, nov 1998. 232

[9] José Meseguer. Conditional rewriting logic as a unified model of concurrency. *Theoretical Computer Science*, 96(1):73–155, 1992. 230

[10] F. Somenzi and R. Bloem. Efficient Büchi automata from LTL formulae. In *CAV '00*, number 1633 in LNCS, pages 247–263. Springer-Verlag, 2000. 231, 232

Software Verification with BLAST*

Thomas A. Henzinger[1], Ranjit Jhala[1], Rupak Majumdar[1], and Grégoire Sutre[2]

[1] EECS Department, University of California, Berkeley
{tah,jhala,rupak}@eecs.berkeley.edu
[2] LaBRI, Université de Bordeaux, France
sutre@labri.u-bordeaux.fr

1 Introduction

BLAST (the Berkeley Lazy Abstraction Software verification Tool) is a verification system for checking safety properties of C programs using automatic property-driven construction and model checking of software abstractions. BLAST implements an abstract-model check-refine loop to check for reachability of a specified label in the program. The abstract model is built on the fly using predicate abstraction. This model is then checked for reachability. If there is no (abstract) path to the specified error label, BLAST reports that the system is safe and produces a succinct proof. Otherwise, it checks if the path is feasible using symbolic execution of the program. If the path is feasible, BLAST outputs the path as an error trace, otherwise, it uses the infeasibility of the path to refine the abstract model. BLAST short-circuits the loop from abstraction to verification to refinement, integrating the three steps tightly through "lazy abstraction" [5]. This integration can offer significant advantages in performance by avoiding the repetition of work from one iteration of the loop to the next.

We now describe the algorithm in more detail. Internally, C programs are represented as control flow automata (CFA), which are control flow graphs with operators on edges. The lazy abstraction algorithm is composed of two phases. In the forward-search phase, we build a reachability tree, which represents a portion of the reachable, abstract state space of the program. Each node of the tree is labeled by a vertex of the CFA and a formula, called the reachable region, constructed as a boolean combination of a finite set of abstraction predicates. Initially the set of abstraction predicates is empty. The edges of the tree correspond to edges of the CFA and are labeled by basic program blocks or assume predicates. The reachable region of a node describes the reachable states of the program in terms of the abstraction predicates, assuming execution follows the sequence of instructions labeling the edges from the root of the tree to the node. If we find that an error node is reachable in the tree, then we go to the second phase, which checks if the error is real or results from our abstraction being too coarse (i.e., if we lost too much information by restricting ourselves to a particular set of abstraction predicates). In the latter case, we ask a theorem prover

* This work was supported in part by the NSF grants CCR-0085949 and CCR-9988172, the DARPA PCES grant F33615-00-C-1693, the MARCO GSRC grant 98-DT-660, and a Microsoft Research Fellowship.

T. Ball and S.K. Rajamani (Eds.): SPIN 2003, LNCS 2648, pp. 235–239, 2003.

to suggest new abstraction predicates which rule out that particular spurious counterexample. The program is then refined locally by adding the new abstraction predicates only in the smallest subtree containing the spurious error; the search continues from the point that is refined, without touching the part of the reachability tree outside that subtree.

Thus the benefits are three-fold. First, we only abstract the reachable part of the state space, which is typically much smaller than the entire abstract state space. Second, we are able to have different precisions at different parts of the state space, which effectively means having to process fewer predicates at every point. Third, we avoid redoing the model checking over parts of the state space that we know are free of error from some coarser abstraction. Moreover, from the reachable set constructed by BLAST, invariants that are sufficient to prove the safety property can be mined, and a short, formal, easily checkable proof of correctness can be constructed [4]. BLAST has successfully verified and found violations of safety properties of large device driver programs up to 60,000 lines of code. A beta version of BLAST has been released and is available from `http://www.eecs.berkeley.edu/~tah/blast`.

2 Implementation

The input to BLAST is a C program and a safety monitor written in C. The program and the monitor are compiled into a single program with a special error location that is reachable iff the program does not satisfy the safety property. The lazy-abstraction algorithm runs on this program and returns either a genuine error trace or a proof of correctness (or fails to terminate). The proof is encoded in binary ELF format as in proof-carrying code [6]. Our tool is written in Objective Caml, and uses the CIL compiler infrastructure [7] as a front end to parse C programs. Our handling of C features follows that of [1]. We handle all syntactic constructs of C, including pointers, structures, and procedures (leaving the constructs not in the predicate language uninterpreted). However, we model integer arithmetic as infinite-precision arithmetic (no wrap-around), and we assume a logical model of the memory. In particular, we disallow casting that changes the "layout pattern" of the memory, disallow partially overlapped objects, and assume that pointer arithmetic in arrays respects the array bound. Currently we handle procedure calls using an explicit stack and do not handle recursive functions.

Our implementation works on a generic *symbolic abstraction structure* which is an internal representation that provides a symbolic interface suitable for model checking, namely a representation of sets of states ("regions"), and functions to compute the concrete and abstract predecessor and successor regions, analyze counterexamples, and refine abstractions.

A C program is represented internally as a CFA. A region is a tuple of CFA state (location), data state, and stack state. We represent the CFA state explicitly, but represent the data state symbolically as boolean formulas over the abstraction predicates. The stack state is a sequence of CFA states. The boolean formulas are stored in canonical form as BDDs.

Given a region and an edge of the CFA, the concrete successor and predecessor operators are implemented using syntactic strongest postcondition and weakest precondition operators, respectively. Given a region, a set of abstraction predicates, and an edge of the CFA (an operation in the program), the symbolic abstract predecessor and successor operators compute an overapproximation of the concrete predecessor and successor sets representable using the abstraction predicates, by making queries to the decision procedures Simplify [3] or CVC [8].

Counterexample analysis is implemented by iterating the concrete predecessor or successor operators and checking for unsatisfiability. Finally, the refinement operator takes an infeasible counterexample trace (whose weakest precondition w.r.t. *true* is, by definition, unsatisfiable), and generates new abstraction predicates by querying a proof generating theorem prover (like Vampyre or CVC in proof generation mode) for a proof of unsatisfiability, and taking the atomic formulas appearing in the proof.

The lazy abstraction algorithm is implemented on top of the interface provided by the symbolic abstraction structure. It does not depend on internal data structures of the symbolic abstraction structure. The advantage of separating the model checking algorithms from the particular internal representation of the system is that we can reuse much of the code to build a model checker for different front ends (for example, for Java programs), or for different region representations. A clean symbolic abstraction structure interface also allows us to experiment with different model checking algorithms and heuristics.

3 Optimizations

In order to be practical, the tool uses several optimizations. The cost is dominated by the cost of theorem proving, so we extensively optimize calls to the theorem prover. First, we compute a fast (linear in the number of predicates) abstract successor operation which is less precise than [2] but usually strong enough to prove the desired properties [5]. Moreover, when computing the abstract successor operator w.r.t. a statement s, we check if the predicate p is affected by the statement s (by checking if $p \neq wp(p, s)$, where wp is the weakest precondition operator), and invoke theorem prover calls only on the subset of predicates which are affected. Second, while constructing the weakest precondition, we only keep satisfiable disjuncts (disjuncts appear in the weakest precondition because of aliasing). Third, we remove predicates that relate variables not in the current program scope. To do this without losing information, we use the theorem prover data structures to add additional useful predicates. Apart from reducing the theorem proving burden, this optimization enables us to reach the fixpoint quicker. Fourth, the check for region inclusion is performed (without sacrificing precision) entirely at the boolean level by keeping the predicates uninterpreted.

We apply a set of program analysis optimizations up front: these include interprocedural conditional constant propagation, dead code elimination, and redundant variable elimination. We have also implemented simple program slicing based on the cone of influence on variables appearing in conditionals.

All the heuristics can be independently turned on or off through command line options; this allows us to experiment with several combinations. With these optimizations, BLAST routinely runs on several thousand lines of C code in a few minutes.

4 Experiences

Frequently, reachability analysis requires only models of certain functions, and not their actual implementation. For example, in checking for locking behavior in the Linux kernel, one simply requires a model of the `spin_unlock` and `spin_lock` functions that sets a particular state variable of the specification, and not the actual assembly code that implements locking in the kernel. We model such kernel calls manually using stub functions that implement the required behavior. We found nondeterministic choice to be a useful modeling tool (for example, to model that a function can return either 0 or 1 nondeterministically), so we added explicit support for nondeterministic choice. By default, if the body of a called function whose return value is dropped is not available, BLAST makes the optimistic assumption that the function is of no relevance to the particular property being checked, and so no predicate values are updated (but a warning message is printed).

Sometimes the predicate discovery is not strong enough to find all predicates of interest and we take (as optional input) a file with programmer specified predicates; the syntax of predicates follows the C syntax for expressions. We find in our experiments that efficient discovery of good predicates is still an important issue. We have implemented various heuristics to find more predicates, including a scan of a counterexample trace to find multiple causes of unsatisfiability.

BLAST has been used to verify several large C programs [4]. Most of these programs are device driver examples from the Microsoft Windows DDK or from the Linux distribution. The properties we checked ranged from simple locking mechanisms to checking that a driver conforms to Windows NT rules for handling I/O requests. We have found bugs in several drivers, we have proved that other drivers correctly implement the specification.

Acknowledgments

We thank George Necula and Westley Weimer for various discussions and for providing support with CIL.

References

[1] T. Ball, R. Majumdar, T. Millstein, and S. K. Rajamani. Automatic predicate abstraction of C programs. In *PLDI 01: Programming Language Design and Implementation*, pages 203–213. ACM, 2001. 236

[2] S. Das, D. L. Dill, and S. Park. Experience with predicate abstraction. In *CAV 99: Computer-Aided Verification*, LNCS 1633, pages 160–171. Springer-Verlag, 1999. 237

[3] D. Detlefs, G. Nelson, and J. Saxe. Simplify theorem prover. 237

[4] T. A. Henzinger, R. Jhala, R. Majumdar, G. C. Necula, G. Sutre, and W. Weimer. Temporal-safety proofs for systems code. In *CAV 02: Computer-Aided Verification*, LNCS 2404, pages 526–538. Springer-Verlag, 2002. 236, 238

[5] T. A. Henzinger, R. Jhala, R. Majumdar, and G. Sutre. Lazy abstraction. In *POPL 02: Principles of Programming Languages*, pages 58–70. ACM, 2002. 235, 237

[6] G. C. Necula. Proof-carrying code. In *POPL 97: Principles of Programming Languages*, pages 106–119. ACM, 1997. 236

[7] G. C. Necula, S. McPeak, S. P. Rahul, and W. Weimer. CIL: Intermediate language and tools for analysis and transformation of C programs. In *CC 02: Compiler Construction*, LNCS 2304, pages 213–228. Springer-Verlag, 2002. 236

[8] A. Stump, C. Barrett, and D. L. Dill. CVC: A cooperating validity checker. In *CAV 02: Computer-Aided Verification*, LNCS 2404, pages 500–504. Springer-Verlag, 2002. 237

Author Index

GPSR Compliance
The European Union's (EU) General Product Safety Regulation (GPSR) is a set of rules that requires consumer products to be safe and our obligations to ensure this.

If you have any concerns about our products, you can contact us on

ProductSafety@springernature.com

In case Publisher is established outside the EU, the EU authorized representative is:

Springer Nature Customer Service Center GmbH
Europaplatz 3
69115 Heidelberg, Germany

www.ingramcontent.com/pod-product-compliance
Ingram Content Group UK Ltd.
Pitfield, Milton Keynes, MK11 3LW, UK
UKHW021828190726
13853UKWH00003B/1258

* 9 7 8 3 6 6 2 1 9 4 8 2 9 *